THE GLOSSARY OF
PRODUCT
MANAGEMENT

Compiled & Edited By:
Dr. Padmaja Saha
Manasi Pathak

Rhythm

Independent
Publication

THE GLOSSARY OF PRODUCT MANAGEMENT

Compiled & Edited By:
Dr. Padmaja Saha
Manasi Pathak

ISBN:9798862571615

9798862571615

Published by:

Rhythm Independent Publication,

Jinkethimmanahalli, Varanasi, Bengaluru, Karnataka, India - 560036

For all types of correspondence, send your mails to the provided address above.

The information presented herein has been collated from a diverse range of sources, comprehensive perspective on the subject matter.

A/B Testing Integration

A/B testing integration is a process employed in product management to optimize and evaluate the success of new features or changes to a product. It involves the systematic comparison of two or more variations, known as variants, of a product to determine which variant performs better in terms of user behavior and desired metrics. This method is typically used when introducing a new feature or making modifications to an existing product. By randomly dividing users into different groups, each exposed to a different variant, product managers are able to gather valuable data on user behavior and preferences. This data-driven approach allows them to make informed decisions based on statistical significance and objective results.

A/B Testing Tools

A/B testing tools are software platforms that enable product managers to conduct controlled experiments to compare the performance of different versions of a product or feature. Product managers use A/B testing tools to gather quantitative data on how small variations in a product or feature impact user behavior and key metrics. These tools allow product managers to create and administer experiments in which users are randomly assigned to different versions of a product, and their interactions with each version are measured and analyzed.

A/B Testing

A/B testing is a method used in product management to evaluate the effectiveness of two or more variants of a web page or feature by randomly dividing users into groups and presenting each group with a different variant. It is a quantitative research technique that provides valuable insights into user behavior and preferences, helping product managers make data-driven decisions and optimize the user experience. In A/B testing, the control group is typically shown the original version of the web page or feature, while the treatment group is shown a modified version. The groups are randomly selected to ensure a representative sample and minimize bias. By comparing the performance of the two variants, product managers can determine which version performs better in terms of predefined metrics such as click-through rates, conversion rates, or user engagement. One of the key advantages of A/B testing is that it allows product managers to test hypotheses and validate design changes without making permanent modifications to the product. It provides an opportunity to experiment with different elements, such as layout, colors, call-to-action buttons, or content to understand how these variations impact user behavior. By measuring the impact on key metrics, product managers can identify the most effective design choices and optimize the product accordingly. A/B testing also enables product managers to understand how different segments of users respond to variations in the product. By segmenting the user base, product managers can analyze the performance of different variants among specific user groups. This helps in identifying whether certain changes work better for certain types of users, allowing for personalized user experiences. However, it is important to carefully plan and execute A/B tests to ensure accurate and reliable results. Factors such as sample size, test duration, statistical significance, and potential confounding variables need to be considered to avoid false conclusions. Additionally, A/B testing should be an iterative process, with product managers continuously using the learnings from previous tests to make informed decisions and further improve the product.

Advertising Campaigns

An advertising campaign is a strategic and coordinated set of activities aimed at promoting a product or service to a specific target audience. It is one of the essential components of product management, as it helps in creating awareness, generating interest, and driving sales for the product. The primary goal of an advertising campaign is to deliver a compelling message about a product or service to capture the attention of the target audience and persuade them to take the desired action, such as making a purchase or requesting more information. Product managers play a crucial role in designing and implementing advertising campaigns. They work closely with marketing teams, creative agencies, and other stakeholders to develop a comprehensive plan that aligns with the product's positioning, target market, and overall marketing strategy. Prior to launching an advertising campaign, product managers conduct market research and analysis to identify the target audience and understand their preferences, needs, and media consumption habits. This information helps them determine the most effective communication channels and messaging techniques to reach and engage the target customers. Once the target audience is defined, product managers collaborate with creative teams to develop compelling and memorable advertising messages. They focus on highlighting the product's unique features, benefits, and value proposition to differentiate it from competitors and attract customer attention. Product managers also oversee the selection of appropriate advertising mediums, such as television, radio, print, online platforms, or a combination of these, based on the target audience's media preferences and consumption habits. They allocate the budget and closely monitor the campaign's performance to ensure that it achieves the desired objectives. In addition to creating brand awareness and driving sales, advertising campaigns also help product managers gather valuable feedback and insights from customers. They can analyze the campaign's response, track customer engagement, and measure the impact on sales and brand perception. This data informs future marketing and product decisions, enabling product managers to refine their strategies and improve the product's overall performance in the market.

Affiliate Marketing

Affiliate marketing refers to a form of online marketing where a product or service owner partners with individuals or businesses (affiliates) who promote their products or services in exchange for a commission. It is a performance-based marketing strategy that allows companies to expand their reach and generate sales leads without incurring significant upfront costs. In the context of Product Management, affiliate marketing plays a crucial role in driving product awareness, increasing customer base, and boosting sales. By leveraging the power of affiliate networks and partnerships, product managers can tap into a vast pool of potential customers and establish a strong presence in the market.

Agile Boards

Agile boards are a crucial tool in product management, allowing teams to visualize and track the progress of their projects in an iterative and flexible manner. These boards provide a visual representation of the work that needs to be done, enabling the team to prioritize tasks, collaborate, and adapt to changes effectively. Agile boards are typically divided into columns that represent different stages of the project, such as "To Do," "In Progress," and "Done." Each column contains individual cards or tickets that represent specific tasks or user stories. These cards can be easily moved between columns to indicate their current status or progress.

Agile Coach Resources

Agile Coach Resources in the context of Product Management refer to the tools, materials, and support systems available for Agile Coaches to effectively guide and facilitate Agile methodologies within a product development team. Agile Coaches play a crucial role in helping product development teams adopt and implement Agile practices to enhance productivity, collaboration, and continuous improvement. Agile Coach Resources provide them with the necessary materials and support to fulfill their responsibilities.

Agile Coach Responsibilities Descriptions

An Agile Coach is responsible for guiding and coaching product management teams in implementing Agile methodologies and practices. They work closely with the Product Manager and other stakeholders to facilitate collaboration, improve processes, and drive continuous improvement. The Agile Coach plays a critical role in helping the product management team embrace Agile principles and values. They provide guidance and support in understanding and implementing Agile frameworks, such as Scrum or Kanban. The coach ensures that the team is aligned with Agile best practices and helps them tailor these practices to suit their specific needs. One of the key responsibilities of an Agile Coach is to foster a culture of collaboration and continuous learning within the product management team. They facilitate communication and cooperation between team members, encouraging them to work together to achieve their goals. The coach helps establish effective feedback loops and retrospectives, which enable the team to learn from each iteration and make iterative improvements. Another important aspect of the Agile Coach's role is to help the product management team remove any impediments or roadblocks that may hinder their progress. They identify areas for improvement and recommend strategies for overcoming challenges. The coach also assists in setting realistic goals and objectives, ensuring that the team is focused on delivering value to the customers. The Agile Coach acts as a mentor and coach for the product management team, providing guidance and support in their Agile journey. They help team members develop skills and competencies in Agile practices, such as user story writing, backlog refinement, and sprint planning. The coach also promotes a culture of experimentation and innovation, encouraging the team to continuously improve and adapt their processes.

Agile Coach Responsibilities

An Agile Coach in the context of Product Management is responsible for guiding and facilitating the adoption of Agile principles and practices within a product development team. They aim to maximize efficiency and effectiveness by promoting collaboration, continuous improvement, and iterative development. The primary responsibility of an Agile Coach is to act as a catalyst for change. They help the team understand Agile principles and values and how to apply them in their day-to-day work. This involves teaching and coaching the team on Agile frameworks such as Scrum or Kanban, as well as related tools and techniques. Another key responsibility of the Agile Coach is to ensure that the team follows Agile practices and ceremonies. They facilitate the planning, daily stand-ups, reviews, and retrospectives to help the team stay focused and aligned with the product goals. The coach also encourages open communication and collaboration within the team and with stakeholders. Additionally, an Agile Coach supports the team in removing any impediments or obstacles that may be hindering their progress. They work closely with the Product Manager to ensure that the product backlog is well-groomed and prioritized, and that the team has a clear understanding of the product vision and goals. An Agile Coach also plays a crucial role in fostering a culture of continuous improvement. They encourage the team to reflect on their processes, identify areas for improvement, and experiment with different approaches. They facilitate regular retrospectives and help the team implement the necessary changes to optimize their productivity and delivery. Overall, an Agile Coach acts as a servant leader, empowering the team to take ownership and responsibility for their work. They provide guidance, support, and mentorship, helping the team to continuously learn and grow.

Agile Coaching Resources

Agile Coaching is a set of practices and methodologies aimed at helping product managers and teams adopt and implement Agile principles and practices in their product development processes. It involves the guidance and support provided by an experienced Agile coach who acts as a mentor, facilitator, and advisor to the product management team. The main goal of Agile coaching in the context of product management is to enable product managers to effectively manage the development and delivery of products in an Agile environment. This includes helping them understand and apply Agile frameworks such as Scrum or Kanban, as well as facilitating their adoption of Agile practices such as iterative development, continuous improvement, and collaboration. An Agile coach works closely with the product management team to assess their current practices, identify areas for improvement, and develop strategies to overcome any challenges or obstacles they may face. The coach provides guidance and training on Agile principles and techniques, helps the team establish Agile rituals and ceremonies, and facilitates their implementation. They also act as a mediator and communicator between the product management team and other stakeholders, ensuring that the Agile mindset and values are effectively communicated and understood by all parties involved. Through Agile coaching, product managers can develop a deep understanding of Agile principles and practices, which allows them to better prioritize and plan product development efforts, increase productivity and efficiency, and deliver higher quality products to market. The coaching process fosters a culture of continuous learning and improvement, empowering product managers and teams to adapt and respond to changing customer needs and market dynamics. In summary, Agile coaching in

3

product management is an essential resource for teams looking to adopt and thrive in an Agile environment. It provides the necessary guidance, support, and expertise to help product managers successfully implement Agile principles and practices, enabling them to deliver value to customers faster and more effectively.

Agile Coaching Workshops

Agile Coaching Workshops in the context of Product Management refer to formal instructional sessions aimed at providing guidance and support for individuals or teams involved in managing and delivering products using Agile methodologies. These workshops are specifically designed to enhance the knowledge and skills of Agile practitioners, while also fostering a collaborative and iterative approach to product development. The primary objective of Agile Coaching Workshops is to equip participants with the necessary tools, techniques, and mindset to effectively implement Agile practices in their product management processes. The workshops typically cover a wide range of topics, including Agile principles and values, Scrum framework, Kanban methodology, user-centric design, backlog grooming, sprint planning, and continuous improvement. Through a combination of theory, practical exercises, and real-world case studies, participants are encouraged to actively engage in the learning process and apply Agile principles to their own product management context. During the Agile Coaching Workshops, participants are guided by experienced Agile coaches who provide expert knowledge and guidance. These coaches leverage their industry experience and deep understanding of Agile methodologies to facilitate interactive discussions, address specific challenges faced by participants, and offer practical solutions. By sharing real-world examples and best practices, the coaches aim to inspire and empower individuals to embrace Agile principles and adapt them to their unique product management needs. Agile Coaching Workshops also emphasize the importance of collaboration, teamwork, and effective communication within product management teams. The workshops encourage participants to adopt a transparent and feedback-oriented approach, allowing for continuous learning and adaptation throughout the product lifecycle. By promoting cross-functional collaboration and self-organizing teams, Agile Coaching Workshops aim to foster a culture of accountability, innovation, and customer-centricity in product management.

Agile Development Support

Agile development support refers to the assistance and resources provided to facilitate the implementation of the agile development methodology within the realm of product management. Agile development is a collaborative and iterative approach to software development, which emphasizes flexibility, adaptability, and customer satisfaction. It involves breaking down the development process into short, time-boxed iterations called sprints, during which cross-functional teams work on delivering small increments of functionality. The role of agile development support in product management is to ensure the successful adoption and execution of agile practices throughout the product development lifecycle. This support encompasses various aspects, including providing training and education to product teams on agile principles and methodologies, facilitating the use of agile tools and techniques, and offering guidance and coaching on agile practices. In the context of product management, agile development support plays a crucial role in enabling the product team to effectively collaborate, prioritize tasks, and respond to changing customer needs. It helps the team to embrace an iterative approach, where they continually gather feedback, refine requirements, and make adjustments to the product backlog. By doing so, they can quickly adapt to evolving market conditions and deliver value to customers in a more timely and efficient manner. Furthermore, agile development support also involves fostering a culture of transparency, trust, and continuous improvement within the product team. It encourages open communication, regular retrospectives, and the sharing of best practices, which leads to enhanced collaboration, innovation, and learning. This support facilitates the empowerment of the team members, enabling them to make decisions and take ownership of their work. Overall, agile development support in product management is essential for organizations aiming to embrace an agile mindset and achieve success in delivering high-quality products. It provides the necessary resources, guidance, and coaching to enable teams to adopt and maximize the benefits of agile development methodologies, ultimately driving customer satisfaction and business growth.

Agile Methodology Support

Agile Methodology is a flexible and iterative approach to product development that emphasizes collaboration, adaptation, and customer feedback. It is widely used in Product Management to efficiently and effectively deliver high-quality products that meet customer needs and expectations. At its core, Agile Methodology focuses on breaking down complex projects into smaller, manageable tasks that can be completed in short iterations called sprints. Each sprint typically lasts between one to four weeks, during which a cross-functional team collaboratively works on prioritized tasks, communicates regularly, and adapts to changes as they arise. One of the key principles of Agile Methodology in Product Management is the emphasis on customer collaboration and feedback. Throughout the development process, the product team engages with customers and stakeholders to gather feedback, validate assumptions, and ensure that the product meets their needs. This feedback is incorporated into future sprints, allowing for continuous improvement and the ability to deliver a product that truly adds value. Another important aspect of Agile Methodology is its focus on adaptability. As sprints progress, the team regularly evaluates and reprioritizes tasks based on the evolving needs of the project. This adaptive approach allows for quick response to changes in customer requirements, market conditions, or technological advancements, ensuring that the product remains relevant and competitive. Agile Methodology also promotes collaboration and close communication within the product team. Cross-functional teams, including product managers, developers, designers, and testers, work closely together, sharing knowledge and expertise to deliver a high-quality product. Regular meetings, such as daily stand-ups and sprint reviews, facilitate transparency and alignment, enabling efficient decision-making and progress tracking. In summary, Agile Methodology is a flexible and iterative approach to product development that emphasizes collaboration, adaptation, and customer feedback. By breaking down complex projects into smaller tasks, incorporating regular feedback, and promoting collaboration, Agile Methodology enables Product Managers to efficiently deliver products that meet customer needs and succeed in a competitive market.

Agile Methodology

Agile Methodology is an iterative and incremental approach to project management and product development that emphasizes flexibility, collaboration, and adaptability. It is commonly used in the field of Product Management to deliver value to customers in a faster and more efficient manner. Agile Methodology is based on the Agile Manifesto, a set of principles that prioritize individuals and interactions over processes and tools, working software over comprehensive documentation, customer collaboration over contract negotiation, and responding to change over following a plan. The core principles of Agile Methodology include: 1. Iterative Development: Agile projects are divided into small, manageable iterations or sprints, typically lasting 1-4 weeks. Each iteration results in a potentially shippable increment of the product, allowing for frequent feedback and course correction. 2. Collaboration: Agile teams work closely together, with constant communication and collaboration among team members, stakeholders, and customers. This promotes transparency, shared understanding, and shared accountability. 3. Empowered Teams: Agile encourages self-organizing and cross-functional teams who have the autonomy to make decisions and deliver value. This fosters creativity, ownership, and a sense of collective responsibility. 4. Customer Focus: Agile places a strong emphasis on customer collaboration and prioritizes delivering value to the customer early and continuously. Regular feedback loops and customer involvement throughout the development process ensure that the final product meets customer needs and expectations. 5. Adaptive Planning: Agile embraces change and recognizes that requirements and priorities may evolve over time. Rather than sticking to a rigid plan, Agile teams adapt and adjust their approach based on feedback and new insights, enabling them to deliver a better end product. In summary, Agile Methodology in the realm of Product Management is a customer-centric and flexible approach to product development that empowers cross-functional teams to deliver incremental value through iterative development, collaboration, and adaptive planning.

Agile Product Owner Role

An Agile Product Owner is a key role in the field of Product Management. A Product Owner serves as the primary point of contact between the development team, stakeholders, and customers. They are responsible for defining and prioritizing the product backlog, ensuring that the development team has a clear understanding of the product vision and goals. The Agile Product Owner works closely with stakeholders to gather requirements and define user stories that align with the product vision. They prioritize the product backlog based on the value delivered to customers and the business, taking into account input from stakeholders and the development team. This prioritization helps ensure that the most valuable and important features are delivered first. The Agile Product Owner collaborates with the development team throughout the development process, answering questions, providing clarifications, and making decisions on behalf of the stakeholders. They work closely with the Scrum Master to ensure that the development team has a clear understanding of the requirements and that any obstacles or impediments are addressed in a timely manner. In addition to managing the product backlog, an Agile Product Owner plays a vital role in sprint planning, sprint review, and sprint retrospective meetings. They work with the development team to determine the scope of each sprint and ensure that the team remains focused on delivering the highest value features. The Agile Product Owner is responsible for continuously refining and updating the product backlog based on changing customer needs, market conditions, and business priorities. They interact with stakeholders and customers to gather feedback, validate assumptions, and ensure that the product remains aligned with the needs of the target market and the business goals. Overall, the Agile Product Owner is a key player in product development, responsible for defining, prioritizing, and managing the product backlog. They act as the primary liaison between stakeholders, customers, and the development team, ensuring that the product meets the needs of the target market and delivers value to the business.

Agile Project Management

Agile Project Management, in the context of Product Management, is a framework and approach that emphasizes flexibility, collaboration, and rapid iteration to deliver high-quality products. It involves breaking down the project into small, manageable tasks, often referred to as user stories or features, and continuously adapting and refining these tasks based on customer feedback and changing requirements. The key principles of Agile Project Management include active customer involvement, self-organizing cross-functional teams, and a focus on delivering working software or products at regular intervals, typically in short time periods known as sprints. Each sprint is a time-boxed iteration that lasts for a fixed duration, usually ranging from one to four weeks, during which the team collaboratively works on completing a set of prioritized tasks. Agile Project Management promotes close collaboration between the development team and stakeholders, including customers, end-users, and product managers. Through frequent communication and feedback loops, the team continuously gathers and incorporates input to ensure that the product meets the desired goals and delivers value to the customers. One of the core practices in Agile Project Management is the daily stand-up, also known as a daily scrum, where team members briefly share their progress, obstacles, and plans. This facilitates transparency, shared understanding, and identification of potential roadblocks or issues that require immediate attention. Another important aspect of Agile Project Management is the use of visual management tools, such as Kanban boards or Scrum boards, to visualize the workflow and track the progress of tasks. These tools provide a clear overview of the project status, help identify bottlenecks, and enable the team to make informed decisions to optimize their work processes. In summary, Agile Project Management in Product Management is a flexible and iterative approach that prioritizes customer collaboration, adaptability, and incremental delivery. By breaking down projects into smaller tasks and regularly incorporating feedback, Agile Project Management enables teams to deliver high-quality products that meet customer needs and expectations.

Agile Release Planning Meetings

Agile release planning meetings are an essential part of product management in an Agile development framework. These meetings serve as a means for the product management team to collaborate with the development team to plan and prioritize the features, enhancements, and bug fixes that will be included in a specific release of the product. During an Agile release planning meeting, the product management team works closely with key stakeholders to identify and prioritize the various items that will be included in the release. This may include features that have been requested by customers, bug fixes that are critical for the product's stability, and enhancements that have been identified as necessary to meet business goals. The goal of the Agile release planning meeting is to create a comprehensive and realistic plan for the upcoming release. This involves estimating the effort required for each item on the release backlog and determining the order in which they will be implemented. The product management team and development team work together to assign priority levels to each item, taking into consideration factors such as customer needs, business goals, and technical feasibility. During the meeting, the product management team provides the development team with all the necessary information they need to understand the requirements for each item. This may include user stories, wireframes, design mockups, and any other documentation that will help the development team implement the feature or fix the bug effectively. After the Agile release planning meeting, the development team will have a clear understanding of what needs to be accomplished in the upcoming release. They can then start breaking down the items into smaller tasks and estimating the effort required for each task. In conclusion, Agile release planning meetings are a crucial part of product management in an Agile development framework. They allow the product management team and development team to collaborate and create a realistic and comprehensive plan for the upcoming release, ensuring that customer needs are met, business goals are achieved, and the development team has a clear understanding of what needs to be done.

Agile Release Planning Tools

Agile release planning tools are software applications or platforms used by product managers to efficiently plan and manage the release of new features, enhancements, or updates to a product or software application using agile principles and methodologies. These tools help product managers effectively collaborate with cross-functional teams, prioritize and track the progress of work, and maintain transparency and visibility throughout the release planning process. Agile release planning tools provide a centralized platform where product managers can create and manage a backlog of user stories or tasks that need to be completed for each release. They enable product managers to prioritize these tasks based on factors such as business value, customer impact, and technical feasibility. These tools also allow product managers to assign tasks to specific team members or resources, set deadlines and milestones, and track the progress of work in real-time. These tools often include features such as visualization boards, such as Kanban boards or scrum boards, which provide a visual representation of the workflow and enable product managers to easily monitor the status of each task or user story. They also offer collaboration features, such as commenting and tagging, which facilitate communication and feedback among team members. Additionally, agile release planning tools often provide reporting and analytics capabilities, allowing product managers to track key metrics and generate reports to assess the performance and progress of each release. Overall, agile release planning tools play a crucial role in product management by helping product managers streamline the release planning process, improve team collaboration and communication, and ensure that releases are delivered on time, within budget, and meet the needs and expectations of customers. By providing a centralized platform and integrating various agile principles and methodologies, these tools enable product managers to effectively plan, execute, and evaluate the release of new features or updates, ultimately driving the success and growth of the product or software application.

Agile Reporting

Agile reporting is a method of gathering and delivering information related to the progress, performance, and outcomes of a product development project using agile methodologies. It focuses on providing timely and relevant updates to stakeholders, facilitating transparency, and supporting the decision-making process in product management. In agile product management, where iterative development and continuous improvement are key, agile reporting plays a crucial role in monitoring the project's progress, identifying potential issues or blockers, and making data-driven decisions throughout the product lifecycle.

Agile Sprint Retropectives

An Agile Sprint Retrospective is a formal meeting held at the end of each sprint in Agile Product Management, where the team reflects on their performance and collaboratively identifies areas for improvement. It is a core component of the Agile methodology, promoting continuous learning and adaptation. The objective of the Agile Sprint Retrospective is to provide a structured opportunity for the team to assess their effectiveness and identify potential adjustments to their processes, tools, and collaboration strategies. The focus is on what went well, what did not go well, and what should be done differently in the future.

Agile Sprint Retrospective Templates

An Agile Sprint Retrospective is a formal meeting that takes place at the end of each sprint in Agile Product Management. It serves as an opportunity for the product team to reflect on their recent work and identify areas for improvement. During the retrospective, the team gathers to discuss what went well during the sprint and what challenges they faced. They use various templates to structure their discussions and capture their findings. These templates provide a framework for the team to systematically analyze their performance and come up with actionable steps to enhance their future sprints.

Agile Sprint Review

An Agile Sprint Review is a formal meeting that occurs at the end of each sprint in the Agile product development process. The purpose of this review is to evaluate and demonstrate the work that has been completed during the sprint to all relevant stakeholders, including the product owner, development team, and other key decision-makers. During the Agile Sprint Review, the development team presents the features and user stories that have been implemented during the sprint. This may include live demos, prototypes, or other visual representations of the product. The goal is to provide a comprehensive overview of the completed work and gather feedback from stakeholders.

Agile Workflow Automation

Agile Workflow Automation refers to the use of an iterative and flexible approach to manage and streamline product development processes in the field of Product Management. It involves the integration of automation tools and techniques to enhance collaboration, efficiency, and visibility across all stages of the product development lifecycle. In an Agile Workflow Automation, the product development process is divided into small, manageable increments called sprints or iterations. Each sprint typically lasts for a fixed duration, usually two to four weeks, during which cross-functional teams work collaboratively to complete a set of prioritized tasks. One of the key principles of Agile Workflow Automation is continuous integration and delivery. This means that product updates and new features are frequently tested, reviewed, and released to end-users. Automation tools, such as continuous integration servers, version control systems, and automated testing frameworks, play a pivotal role in streamlining these processes. Agile Workflow Automation also emphasizes the importance of feedback and learning. Cross-functional teams regularly engage with stakeholders, including customers, to gather user feedback and incorporate it into the product development process. This iterative feedback loop enables teams to quickly adapt and respond to changing market demands. Another crucial aspect of Agile Workflow Automation is the use of visual boards, such as Kanban boards or scrum boards. These boards provide a visual representation of the project's progress and help teams track tasks, identify bottlenecks, and optimize workflow. Overall, Agile Workflow Automation in Product Management focuses on empowering teams to deliver high-quality products efficiently and effectively. By using automation tools and following an iterative approach, organizations can minimize time-to-market, increase customer satisfaction, and continuously improve their products based on real-time feedback.

Analytics Dashboard Creation

An analytics dashboard is a comprehensive tool used in product management to provide a visual representation of data and insights gathered from various sources. It allows product managers to quickly assess the performance and impact of their products by displaying key metrics and trends in a user-friendly interface. The main purpose of an analytics dashboard is to enable product managers to make informed decisions based on the data they collect. By consolidating data from different sources, such as user feedback, sales figures, and market research, the dashboard helps product managers understand how their products are being used and how they can be improved. One of the key features of an analytics dashboard is its ability to display real-time data. This means that product managers can view the latest information and trends without having to manually gather and analyze data from various sources. By presenting up-to-date information, the dashboard enables product managers to stay informed about the current status of their products and make timely decisions. Another important function of an analytics dashboard is to highlight key performance indicators (KPIs). KPIs are specific measurements that reflect the success or failure of a product or feature. By displaying KPIs on the dashboard, product managers can quickly identify areas that need attention and prioritize their efforts accordingly. The design of an analytics dashboard is crucial in order to make it easy to understand and navigate. The layout should be intuitive, with clear labels and visual cues to guide the user. Additionally, the dashboard should be customizable, allowing product managers to choose the metrics and information they want to display. In conclusion, an analytics dashboard is a vital tool for product managers as it provides a comprehensive overview of the performance and impact of their products. It enables informed decision-making based on real-time data and highlights key performance indicators. With its user-friendly interface and customizable design, the dashboard helps product managers stay informed and prioritize their efforts effectively.

Backlog Management

Backlog management in the context of Product Management refers to the practice of prioritizing and organizing a list of tasks, features, and enhancements, known as the backlog, that need to be completed in order to deliver a successful product. The backlog is a dynamic document that acts as a roadmap for the development and improvement of a product over time. The primary goal of backlog management is to ensure that the most valuable and important items are delivered in a timely manner. It involves regularly reviewing and refining the backlog, as well as effectively communicating with stakeholders to understand their needs and expectations. By managing the backlog, Product Managers can align the development team's efforts with the overall product vision and strategy.

Backlog Prioritization

Backlog prioritization, in the context of Product Management, refers to the process of arranging and ordering product backlog items based on their importance, value, and impact on the overall product strategy and goals. It involves evaluating and categorizing user stories, features, and tasks in a backlog to determine their relative priority for implementation. The primary purpose of backlog prioritization is to ensure that the most valuable and high-priority items are worked on first, in order to deliver maximum value to the users and stakeholders. By prioritizing the backlog effectively, Product Managers can optimize the allocation of resources and focus the development efforts on delivering the most impactful features and improvements.

Beta Test Management Platforms

Beta Test Management Platforms are software tools or systems used by product managers to simplify and streamline the process of beta testing a product before its official release. These platforms provide a centralized and efficient way to manage all aspects of a beta testing program, from recruiting and selecting beta testers to collecting feedback and analyzing results. The primary function of a Beta Test Management Platform is to facilitate communication and collaboration between the product team and the beta testers. It allows product managers to easily invite and onboard testers, provide them with necessary documentation and resources, and keep them updated on the progress and objectives of the beta test. This helps ensure that testers have a clear understanding of their role and responsibilities, which in turn results in more valuable and relevant feedback. Additionally, Beta Test Management Platforms typically include features for monitoring and tracking the performance and usage of the product during the beta test. This allows product managers to gather quantitative data on factors such as user engagement, number of bugs reported, and overall product stability. Analyzing this data can help identify areas for improvement and inform decision-making regarding the product's readiness for launch. Furthermore, these platforms often offer tools for organizing and categorizing feedback received from beta testers. Product managers can centralize all feedback in one place, making it easier to prioritize and address issues raised by the testers. Some platforms may also provide analytics and reporting capabilities to help the product team gain insights and patterns from the feedback, enabling them to make data-driven decisions and iterate on the product accordingly. In summary, Beta Test Management Platforms are essential tools for product managers, enabling them to effectively manage and coordinate beta testing programs. By streamlining the process, facilitating communication, and providing tools for monitoring and analyzing feedback, these platforms help ensure that beta tests are successful in collecting meaningful insights and driving product improvements.

Beta Test Management Tools

Beta test management tools are software applications or platforms designed to facilitate and streamline the process of managing and conducting beta tests for new products or features. Product managers use beta test management tools to ensure that their beta tests are organized, efficient, and effective in gathering feedback and insights from real users before the product or feature is launched to the wider market. These tools typically offer a range of features and functionalities that help product managers manage all aspects of the beta testing process, from recruiting and selecting beta testers to collecting feedback and analyzing results.

Beta Testing Groups

Beta testing groups in the context of Product Management refer to a selected group of individuals or organizations who are invited to test a product before its official release in order to provide feedback, identify issues, and contribute to its refinement. These groups typically consist of target users or customers who have expressed interest in the product or have been specifically chosen based on their fit with the product's intended market. The purpose of beta testing groups is to gather real-world insights and validate the product's functionality, usability, and overall user experience. By involving these groups in the testing phase, product managers can gain valuable feedback that can help identify and address any issues or shortcomings in the product, as well as gather suggestions for improvement. When selecting individuals or organizations for beta testing groups, product managers aim to include a diverse range of perspectives and experiences to ensure that the product meets the needs and expectations of different user segments. This can involve targeting specific demographics, industries, or user behaviors that are relevant to the product's intended market. Beta testing groups are typically formed after an initial round of internal testing by the product development team. This is to ensure that the product is at a stage where it is functional enough for external testing, while still allowing room for improvements based on the feedback received. Throughout the beta testing phase, product managers work closely with the selected individuals or organizations to provide guidance, collect feedback, and address any questions or concerns that arise. This can involve hosting regular meetings or online forums to facilitate communication and encourage open dialogue. The insights gathered from beta testing groups are then used by product managers to make informed decisions on how to refine and improve the product before its official release. This can involve making changes to the product's features, user interface, performance, or any other aspect based on the feedback received. In summary, beta testing groups play a crucial role in the product development process by providing valuable feedback and insights that help product managers refine and improve a product before its official release. By involving target users or customers in the testing phase, product managers can ensure that the product meets the needs and expectations of its intended market.

Beta Testing Management Tools

Beta testing management tools are software applications or platforms that help product managers organize, coordinate, and monitor the beta testing phase of a product's development and release. These tools typically provide a range of features and functionalities that enable product managers to efficiently manage the entire beta testing process, from recruiting and selecting beta testers to collecting feedback and analyzing results.

Brand Ambassador Engagement

A brand ambassador engagement in the context of product management involves the strategic utilization of individuals who are representative of a brand to promote and advocate for the brand's products or services. These brand ambassadors are typically passionate and knowledgeable about the brand, and their role is to create positive associations with the brand and drive engagement and sales. A brand ambassador engagement program is designed to leverage the influence and reach of these individuals to enhance brand awareness, generate excitement and interest around new products or campaigns, and build relationships with customers. This can be done through various activities, such as social media posts, content creation, event appearances, and product reviews. The key objective of brand ambassador engagement is to create a strong connection between the brand and its target audience. By leveraging the credibility and influence of these individuals, companies can tap into their networks and reach a wider audience that may be more receptive to the brand's message. Brand ambassadors can actively engage with customers, answer their questions, and provide valuable insights and feedback, thus fostering a sense of trust and loyalty. Furthermore, brand ambassador engagement provides an opportunity for companies to gather valuable data and insights about their customers. By analyzing the impact and effectiveness of brand ambassador activities, companies can better understand customer preferences and behavior, identify opportunities for improvement, and refine their product marketing strategies. In summary, brand ambassador engagement is a strategic approach used by product management teams to leverage the influence and credibility of individuals who are passionate about a brand. By engaging these brand ambassadors, companies can enhance brand awareness, build relationships with customers, and gather valuable insights for product marketing and development.

Brand Ambassadors

Brand Ambassadors in the context of Product Management refers to individuals or influencers who are appointed by a company to represent and promote their products or brand. They act as the face of the brand, helping to build awareness, generate excitement, and drive sales for the products they are assigned to. These individuals are usually selected based on their alignment with the brand's values, target audience, and overall image. They are often experts in their respective fields and possess a strong following or influence on social media platforms. Their role is to create a positive association between the brand and its products, ultimately influencing the purchasing decisions of consumers.

Brand Awareness Campaigns

Brand awareness campaigns refer to strategic marketing initiatives that aim to enhance the recognition and familiarity of a specific brand's products or services among target customers. These campaigns are designed to create brand recall and ensure that potential customers are aware of the brand's presence in the market. In the context of product management, brand awareness campaigns play a crucial role in creating a strong brand identity and positioning a product or service effectively. These campaigns are typically implemented through various marketing channels, such as advertising, social media, influencer partnerships, public relations, and content marketing.

Brand Awareness Metrics

Brand awareness metrics are quantitative indicators used by product managers to measure the level of recognition and familiarity that consumers have with a particular brand. These metrics help product managers evaluate the effectiveness of their branding and marketing strategies in creating awareness and generating brand recall among target audiences. One commonly used brand awareness metric is brand recall, which measures the ability of consumers to remember a particular brand when asked about a specific product category or industry. It assesses the extent to which a brand has become synonymous with a specific product or service in the minds of consumers. Another important metric is brand recognition, which gauges the level of familiarity that consumers have with a brand by assessing their ability to identify it among a set of other competing brands. This metric determines the extent to which consumers can recognize and differentiate a brand from its competitors. Furthermore, aided and unaided brand awareness metrics also play a vital role in evaluating the effectiveness of a brand's marketing efforts. Aided brand awareness measures the level of recognition a brand receives when prompted or provided with some form of assistance, such as showing consumers a logo or tagline. On the other hand, unaided brand awareness measures the level of brand recognition without any prompts or assistance, reflecting the level of spontaneous awareness among consumers. Product managers also use metrics like brand reach, which assesses the total number of unique individuals exposed to a brand's marketing efforts across various channels. This metric helps in understanding the overall visibility and exposure of a brand among potential consumers. Furthermore, social media metrics, such as the number of followers, likes, comments, and shares, are also significant in measuring brand awareness. These metrics provide insights into the level of engagement and interaction that consumers have with a brand's online presence, indicating the level of brand awareness and interest among online audiences. In summary, brand awareness metrics provide product managers with quantifiable measures to evaluate the effectiveness of their branding and marketing strategies. By measuring brand recall, recognition, reach, and online engagement, they can gauge the level of awareness and familiarity consumers have with a brand, enabling them to make informed decisions about their marketing efforts and improve brand positioning.

Brand Consistency Audits

A brand consistency audit is a systematic evaluation of a company's products, messaging, and visual elements to ensure they are aligning with the brand's core values, positioning, and guidelines. It involves analyzing various aspects of the brand, such as logo usage, color palette, typography, packaging design, website layout, and overall communication across different touchpoints. The purpose of a brand consistency audit in the context of Product Management is to assess whether the products and associated marketing materials are consistent with the brand's identity and promise. It helps ensure that the brand is being presented cohesively and accurately to the target audience, regardless of the platform or medium used. During a brand consistency audit, Product Managers typically review and compare the following elements: 1. Visual Identity: This includes examining the consistent usage of the logo, color scheme, typography, and graphic elements. It ensures that the visual identity remains consistent across different product lines and marketing materials. 2. Packaging Design: This involves analyzing the packaging materials, labels, and graphics used for the products. The audit assesses whether they align with the brand's style and convey the desired message to customers. 3. Messaging and Communication: This aspect focuses on analyzing the language, tone, and style used in various customer-facing communication channels, such as websites, social media, advertisements, and product descriptions. It ensures that the brand's voice is consistent and resonates with the target audience. 4. User Experience (UX): The audit assesses the consistency of the user experience provided by the products, including the interface design, navigation, and overall user journey. It ensures that the products meet the brand's usability and design standards. By conducting regular brand consistency audits, Product Managers can identify any inconsistencies or deviations from the brand guidelines. This allows them to take corrective actions to ensure a consistent brand experience for customers, which in turn strengthens brand equity and fosters brand loyalty.

Brand Consistency Checks

A brand consistency check, in the context of product management, refers to the process of evaluating and ensuring that a company's brand is consistently represented across all touchpoints and marketing efforts. It involves regular assessment and analysis of various aspects, such as design elements, messaging, tone of voice, and overall brand identity, to identify any deviations or inconsistencies. The purpose of conducting brand consistency checks is to maintain a strong and unified brand image, which is essential for building trust, loyalty, and recognition among customers. By ensuring that all brand elements align with the established brand guidelines, businesses can communicate a clear and cohesive message to their target audience, regardless of the channels or platforms through which they interact with the brand.

Brand Crisis Communication

Brand crisis communication refers to the strategic approach taken by a product management team to effectively manage and mitigate a crisis situation that may damage the reputation or perception of a brand or its products. In the context of product management, brand crisis communication involves developing and implementing a comprehensive plan to address and respond to any crisis that may arise, such as product recalls, safety concerns, negative publicity, or other incidents that could negatively impact the brand's image or consumer trust.

Brand Licensing Agreements

A brand licensing agreement is a legal contract between two parties, where the owner of a brand grants another party the right to use their brand name, trademark, or other intellectual property in exchange for specified royalties, fees, or other benefits. In the context of product management, a brand licensing agreement enables a company to expand its product offerings by leveraging the reputation, goodwill, and recognition associated with an established brand. Product managers can enter into brand licensing agreements to gain access to well-known brands and utilize their brand equity for their own products or services.

Brand Licensing

Brand licensing in the context of product management refers to the legal agreement between a brand owner and a third party, allowing the third party to use the brand's intellectual property, such as trademarks, logos, and brand name, to market and sell a product or service. Through brand licensing, a brand owner can extend and leverage their brand's equity and goodwill to enter new markets or product categories without having to directly invest in manufacturing, distribution, or marketing. This allows the brand owner to generate additional revenue streams and increase brand exposure, while the licensee benefits from the association with a well-known and established brand.

Brand Reputation Management

Brand Reputation Management is the practice of actively monitoring and influencing the public perception and reputation of a brand in order to maintain a positive and favorable image. It involves the strategic and systematic management of a brand's reputation to ensure that it aligns with the values, goals, and objectives of the brand and effectively communicates its identity and offerings to its target audience. In the context of Product Management, Brand Reputation Management plays a crucial role in ensuring the success and longevity of a product in the market. It involves cultivating and maintaining a positive reputation for the brand and its products, addressing and managing any potential negative feedback or issues that may arise, and continuously monitoring and improving brand perception to drive customer loyalty and increase market share.

Brand Reputation Tracking

Brand Revamp Strategies

A brand revamp strategy refers to the process of revitalizing and repositioning a brand in order to better meet the needs and preferences of the target market. It involves a comprehensive analysis of the brand's current position, strengths, weaknesses, and opportunities, as well as a thorough understanding of the market trends and consumer behavior. Product management plays a crucial role in developing and implementing brand revamp strategies. The product manager is responsible for understanding the target audience, defining the brand's unique value proposition, and aligning the brand's attributes with customer expectations.

Brand Revitalization Plans

Brand revitalization plans in the context of product management refer to strategic initiatives undertaken by companies to reinvigorate and refresh their brand image, positioning, and relevance in the market. These plans are typically implemented when a brand starts to lose its appeal, faces declining sales, or fails to resonate with its target audience. The purpose of brand revitalization plans is to breathe new life into the brand, reignite consumer interest, and regain competitive advantage. This involves a holistic evaluation of the brand's current position, market dynamics, consumer preferences, and emerging trends to identify the areas that need improvement and create a roadmap for revitalization. Typically, the first step in a brand revitalization plan is conducting a comprehensive brand audit. This entails assessing the brand's strengths, weaknesses, opportunities, and threats. It involves evaluating the brand's current equity, perception, and performance in the market, as well as analyzing customer feedback, market research, and competitor analysis. Based on the findings of the brand audit, the next step is to redefine the brand vision, mission, and values. This may involve refining the brand's positioning, target audience, and value proposition to better align with the changing market dynamics and consumer preferences. Once the brand's strategic direction is defined, the revitalization plan focuses on developing and implementing marketing strategies to communicate the brand's new positioning and drive consumer engagement. This may include a combination of advertising, public relations, digital marketing, and social media campaigns, as well as product enhancements and innovation. Brand revitalization plans also often involve revitalizing the brand's physical presence, such as updating packaging, logos, and store design, to create a fresh and modern image that resonates with consumers. The success of a brand revitalization plan depends on effective execution, monitoring, and adaptation. It requires continuous evaluation of the marketing strategies, consumer response, and market trends to make necessary adjustments along the way.

Brand Sponsorship Negotiation

Brand sponsorship negotiation is the process of establishing mutually beneficial agreements between a brand and a sponsor regarding the promotion and support of a product or event. In the context of product management, brand sponsorship negotiation involves the product manager working with potential sponsors to secure financial or other resources to help promote and market the product. During the brand sponsorship negotiation process, the product manager and the potential sponsor discuss and strategize the terms and conditions of the sponsorship agreement. This includes determining the financial investment or resources the sponsor will provide, such as funding for advertising campaigns, product placement, or event sponsorship. The negotiations may also involve discussions on the duration of the sponsorship, exclusivity rights, and the specific promotional activities the sponsor will undertake. One of the key objectives of brand sponsorship negotiation is to ensure that both the brand and the sponsor benefit from the partnership. The product manager must carefully consider the brand's target market and the sponsor's target audience to evaluate the compatibility of the partnership. Additionally, the negotiations aim to achieve a fair exchange of value, where the sponsor's investment aligns with the expected return on investment in terms of brand exposure and increased sales. Successful brand sponsorship negotiation requires effective communication, negotiation skills, and a deep understanding of both the product and the potential sponsor's objectives and interests. Product managers must emphasize the unique value proposition and the potential benefits the sponsorship can bring to the sponsor's brand. Additionally, they should be open to compromising and find mutually agreeable terms that satisfy both parties. In conclusion, brand sponsorship negotiation in the field of product management involves the process of establishing agreements between a brand and a sponsor to secure resources for the promotion and support of a product. It aims to create mutually beneficial partnerships that align with both the brand's and the sponsor's objectives. Effective negotiation skills and a thorough understanding of both parties' interests are essential for successful brand sponsorship negotiation.

Brand Sponsorships

Brand Sponsorships in the context of Product Management refers to the collaboration between a brand and a sponsoring entity to promote or endorse a product or service. It involves a mutual agreement between the brand and the sponsor, wherein the sponsor provides financial support or resources to the brand in exchange for exposure and association with the brand's product or service. This type of partnership is a common marketing strategy used by brands to leverage the sponsor's reputation, customer base, or resources to enhance their own brand image, increase product visibility, and drive sales. Brand sponsorships often involve various forms of promotional activities, such as event sponsorship, sports team sponsorship, celebrity endorsements, and product placement in popular media.

Branding Guidelines

A branding guideline refers to a set of rules and standards established by a company or organization to ensure consistent and coherent representation of its brand across various touchpoints. It provides instructions and recommendations on how to use the brand elements such as logo, colors, fonts, taglines, and imagery in a way that reflects the brand's personality, values, and positioning. The primary objective of branding guidelines in the context of product management is to maintain brand consistency and integrity throughout the product's lifecycle. This involves aligning the product's visual identity, messaging, and overall brand experience with the larger brand strategy. By adhering to these guidelines, product managers can reinforce the brand's positioning, enhance brand recognition, and support brand equity.

Branding Style Guides

A branding style guide is a formal document that provides guidelines and standards for the visual and verbal representation of a brand. It serves as a comprehensive resource for product managers to ensure consistency and coherence in the way their brand is presented across various touchpoints.The branding style guide outlines specific rules and recommendations for the use of elements such as logos, colors, typography, imagery, and messaging. These guidelines help product managers and other stakeholders understand how to accurately represent the brand in different contexts, whether it's on packaging, advertisements, websites, social media, or other marketing materials.

Bug Reporting Channels

Bug reporting channels are the designated channels through which users, customers, or internal stakeholders can report issues, problems, or defects encountered while using a product. These channels serve as a direct communication pathway between users and the product management team responsible for resolving and addressing these reported bugs. The purpose of bug reporting channels is to streamline the process of bug identification, collection, and resolution. By providing users with specific channels to report bugs, product management teams can efficiently gather information about the issues and prioritize them based on their impact and severity. Effective bug reporting channels typically include a combination of the following methods: 1. Online bug tracking systems: These systems are web-based platforms where users can submit bug reports, detailing the steps to reproduce the issue, providing screenshots or error messages, and assigning relevant tags or categories. The bug tracking system allows the product management team to track the progress of bug resolution, assign tasks to the development team, and communicate with users regarding bug status updates. 2. Customer support email or ticketing system: This channel enables users to directly contact the product management team through email or a dedicated customer support platform. Users can describe the encountered bug and provide relevant information for investigation, such as the software version, operating system, or device used. The product management team can then categorize, prioritize, and respond to these bug reports accordingly. 3. Feedback or contact forms on the product's website: Including a feedback or contact form on the product's website allows users to report bugs or issues they encounter while using the product. Users can describe the problem, provide contact information, and submit their bug reports. The product management team can then review, analyze, and address these reported bugs. Bug reporting channels play a vital role in ensuring product quality and user satisfaction. They enable a structured and systematic approach to bug resolution, allowing the product management team to understand and address users' concerns promptly. By leveraging these channels, product management teams can improve the overall user experience by actively resolving bugs and continually enhancing the product's performance and functionality.

Bug Tracking

Bug Tracking is a systematic process in Product Management that involves the identification, recording, and management of software bugs or defects throughout the software development life cycle. It is aimed at providing an organized and structured approach to keep track of bugs from the moment they are reported until they are resolved. This process helps ensure that bugs are effectively prioritized, assigned to the appropriate teams or individuals, and ultimately resolved in a timely manner.

Bug Triage

Bug Triage is a formal process in Product Management that involves the evaluation and prioritization of reported software bugs or issues. It aims to classify and prioritize bugs based on their severity, impact on the product, and the resources available for resolution. During the Bug Triage process, the product management team, along with relevant stakeholders such as developers, testers, and support representatives, come together to review and assess the reported bugs. The primary objectives of Bug Triage are to: 1. Classify bugs: Bugs are evaluated and categorized based on their impact on the product and the severity of the issues they cause. This classification helps in prioritizing bug resolution efforts and allocating resources effectively. Bugs may be classified as Critical, High, Medium, or Low, depending on their impact on the product functionality and user experience. 2. Prioritize bugs: Once bugs are classified, they are prioritized based on factors such as severity, impact, frequency, and customer feedback. Critical or High priority bugs that significantly affect the product functionality or user experience are given top priority for resolution. Medium and Low priority bugs may be addressed in subsequent releases or based on available resources. 3. Assign ownership: Bugs are assigned to the appropriate team members or developers responsible for resolving them. Clear ownership ensures that bugs are not overlooked or left unaddressed, and accountability is established for timely resolution. 4. Determine resolution timeline: The Bug Triage process also helps in setting realistic timelines for bug resolution. By considering the severity and complexity of bugs, as well as resource availability, the product management team can estimate the time required for resolving each bug and plan accordingly. Overall, Bug Triage is a crucial process in Product Management as it helps in effectively managing and prioritizing bug fixes, ensuring that critical issues are addressed promptly, and maintaining the overall quality and stability of the product.

Buyer Personas

A buyer persona is a fictional representation of the ideal customer for a particular product or service. It is a way for product managers to understand and empathize with their target audience, allowing them to develop and deliver products that precisely meet the needs and preferences of their customers. A buyer persona is created using market research, customer data, and insights gathered from various sources. It helps product managers and marketing teams gain a deep understanding of their target customers by combining demographic information, psychographic details, and behavioral patterns of their ideal customers.

Campaign ROI Assessment

Campaign ROI Assessment is a formal process conducted in Product Management to measure the return on investment (ROI) of a marketing campaign. It involves analyzing the success and effectiveness of a campaign in generating revenue and achieving its desired goals. The assessment begins with defining the goals and objectives of the campaign, such as increasing brand awareness, driving customer acquisition, or boosting sales. These goals provide a basis for measuring the campaign's impact on the overall business. Key performance indicators (KPIs) are then established to track the campaign's progress and determine its success. The main components of Campaign ROI Assessment include data collection, analysis, and evaluation. Data is collected from various sources, such as sales reports, website analytics, and customer feedback. This data provides insights into the performance of the campaign and helps in understanding the customer's response to marketing efforts. The collected data is then analyzed to determine the campaign's ROI. Financial metrics, such as revenue generated, cost per acquisition, and customer lifetime value, are used to calculate the return on investment. By comparing the campaign's costs to its revenues, product managers can assess the financial effectiveness of the campaign and its impact on the company's bottom line. In addition to financial metrics, non-financial metrics are also considered to assess the qualitative impact of the campaign. These include brand awareness, customer satisfaction, and engagement metrics. By evaluating these factors, product managers can gain insights into the campaign's effectiveness in building customer loyalty and generating long-term value. The final step of Campaign ROI Assessment involves evaluating the results and making data-driven decisions. Product managers analyze the campaign's performance against the established goals and KPIs to identify areas of improvement and make recommendations for future campaigns. This iterative process helps in optimizing marketing strategies and allocating resources effectively. Ultimately, Campaign ROI Assessment provides product managers with valuable insights into the success and effectiveness of their marketing campaigns. By measuring the financial and non-financial impact of a campaign, product managers can make informed decisions, allocate resources wisely, and drive the overall growth and success of the company.

Case Study Development

Case Study Development in the context of Product Management refers to the process of conducting comprehensive research and analysis to understand and document real-life scenarios and experiences related to a specific product or product-related issue. It involves collecting qualitative and quantitative data, identifying trends and patterns, and drawing meaningful conclusions. During case study development, a product management team investigates various aspects of the product, such as its features, performance, user feedback, competition, and market dynamics. This research helps them gain insights into the product's strengths, weaknesses, opportunities, and threats, which are vital for making informed decisions and driving product improvement.

Churn Prediction Model Tools

A churn prediction model is a tool used in product management to identify and predict customer churn. Churn refers to the situation when customers stop using a product or service and switch to a competitor or cancel their subscription altogether. It is an important metric for businesses as the loss of customers can have a significant negative impact on revenue and market share. In order to minimize customer churn, product managers employ churn prediction models to forecast which customers are most likely to churn. These models use advanced statistical and machine learning techniques to analyze customer data and identify patterns or signals that indicate a higher risk of churn. The process of building a churn prediction model involves several steps. Firstly, product managers gather relevant data such as customer demographics, transaction history, customer behavior, and feedback. This data is then preprocessed and transformed to remove any noise or inconsistencies. In the next step, product managers select appropriate statistical and machine learning algorithms to train the model. These algorithms learn from historical data to establish patterns and relationships between customer attributes and churn. Among the commonly used algorithms are logistic regression, decision trees, random forests, and neural networks. Once the model is trained, product managers evaluate its performance using various metrics such as accuracy, precision, recall, and F1 score. This evaluation helps to assess the model's effectiveness in predicting churn accurately. Finally, product managers use the churn prediction model to generate a list of customers with a high probability of churn. They then develop targeted retention strategies to proactively engage and retain these customers. These strategies may include personalized offers, special discounts, improved customer support, or product enhancements.

Churn Prediction Models

A churn prediction model is a statistical tool used in product management to predict and anticipate customer churn, which refers to the occurrence of customers discontinuing their relationship with a company's product or service. The model analyzes customer data and behavior to identify patterns and factors that are indicative of potential churn, allowing the company to take proactive measures to retain the customer. Churn prediction models typically use historical customer data, such as purchase history, usage data, and demographic information, as well as external data sources, such as market trends and competitor analysis. By analyzing this data, the model identifies key variables and patterns that are associated with customer churn. The churn prediction model applies various statistical techniques, such as logistic regression, decision trees, and machine learning algorithms, to create a predictive model. These models are typically built using a training dataset, which contains instances of both churned and non-churned customers. The model is then tested and validated using a separate dataset to measure its accuracy and performance. Once the churn prediction model is developed and validated, it can be used to forecast the likelihood of churn for individual customers. This allows product managers to prioritize and target specific customers who are at a higher risk of churn with tailored retention strategies. By identifying potential churners in advance, companies can implement targeted interventions, such as personalized offers, discounts, or loyalty programs, to mitigate churn and retain valuable customers. In addition to predicting churn on an individual customer level, churn prediction models can also provide insights at a larger scale. These models can help identify patterns and trends in customer behavior that may contribute to churn, allowing product managers to make data-driven decisions to improve customer satisfaction and reduce churn rates as a whole.

Churn Rate

Churn rate is a key metric used in product management to measure the rate at which customers or users stop using a product over a given period of time. It serves as an important indicator of customer satisfaction and loyalty, as well as a measure of product success and stickiness. Churn rate is typically expressed as a percentage and can be calculated by dividing the number of customers who churned during a specific period by the total number of customers at the beginning of that period. The result is then multiplied by 100 to obtain the churn rate percentage.

Competitive Analysis Frameworks

A competitive analysis framework is a structured approach used in product management to

17

evaluate and compare the market position of a company's product or service against its competitors. It involves gathering and analyzing relevant information about competitors, such as their strengths, weaknesses, strategies, and market share, in order to identify opportunities and threats in the market. There are several popular frameworks used in competitive analysis, each with its own unique focus and purpose. Two commonly used frameworks are the SWOT analysis and the Porter's Five Forces analysis. The SWOT analysis, which stands for strengths, weaknesses, opportunities, and threats, is a simple yet effective framework for understanding a company's competitive position. It involves identifying internal factors (strengths and weaknesses) that are within the company's control, as well as external factors (opportunities and threats) that are influenced by the market and competition. By examining these factors, product managers can gain insights into what sets their product apart from competitors and identify areas for improvement or potential risks. Porter's Five Forces analysis, on the other hand, focuses on the external forces that shape an industry, including competition, supplier power, buyer power, threat of new entrants, and threat of substitutes. This framework helps product managers understand the overall attractiveness of an industry and identify the drivers of competitive intensity. By analyzing these forces, product managers can determine the potential risks and opportunities associated with entering or competing in a particular market.

Competitive Analysis Integration

Competitive Analysis Integration in the context of Product Management refers to the process of gathering and analyzing information about the competition to inform strategic decision-making and improve product performance and market positioning. It involves systematically evaluating the strengths and weaknesses of competitors, understanding their product offerings, pricing strategies, target markets, distribution channels, and marketing tactics. The goal is to gain insights into how the competition is addressing customer needs, identifying any gaps or opportunities in the market, and determining the best course of action for the product to gain a competitive advantage.

Competitive Analysis Tools

A competitive analysis tool in the context of product management refers to a software or platform that provides insights and data on a company's competitors and their products. It is used by product managers to gain a comprehensive understanding of the competitive landscape and make informed decisions regarding their own products. These tools help product managers gather and analyze data about their competitors' offerings, including features, pricing, customer reviews, and market share. They often provide data in real-time, allowing product managers to stay up-to-date with industry trends and changes in the competitive landscape.

Competitive Analysis

A competitive analysis is a systematic process of evaluating and understanding the strengths and weaknesses of businesses or products that compete directly with a particular product or service. It involves gathering and analyzing information about the competitors' strategies, offerings, market share, customer base, pricing, distribution channels, and other key factors that can affect the success of the product. The purpose of conducting a competitive analysis in the context of product management is to gain insights that can inform decision-making and help develop effective strategies for positioning and marketing the product. By understanding the competitive landscape, product managers can identify opportunities for differentiation, assess potential threats, and make informed decisions about pricing, features, and marketing tactics.

Competitive Intelligence Platforms

Competitive Intelligence Platforms refer to the software tools and platforms that gather, analyze, and present data and information related to a company's competitors and the overall market. These platforms are used by Product Managers to gain insights into their competitors' strategies, offerings, and performance, in order to inform their own product development and decision-making processes. These platforms serve as a central hub for collecting and organizing various types of competitive intelligence, such as market share data, product features and functionalities, pricing information, customer reviews, and industry trends. They employ data mining and analysis techniques to identify patterns and key insights from this vast amount of information, enabling Product Managers to effectively monitor and understand the competitive landscape.

Competitive Intelligence Tools

Competitive intelligence tools are software or services that provide product managers with valuable insights and information about their competitors in order to make informed decisions about their product strategy. These tools gather and analyze data from various sources, such as competitor websites, social media platforms, market research reports, and customer feedback, and present it in a structured and organized manner. By using competitive intelligence tools, product managers can track their competitors' product offerings, pricing strategies, marketing campaigns, and customer engagement activities. They can also gain visibility into market trends, industry news, and customer sentiments, which can help them identify potential threats and opportunities. With this information, product managers can make data-driven decisions about product positioning, feature prioritization, and marketing strategies.

Competitive Intelligence

Competitive Intelligence in the context of Product Management refers to the systematic collection, analysis, and interpretation of data and information about competitors and their products or services. It involves gathering information from various sources and using it to gain insights into the competitive landscape, thereby enabling product managers to make informed decisions and develop effective strategies. The primary goal of Competitive Intelligence in Product Management is to understand the strengths, weaknesses, opportunities, and threats posed by competitors. By carefully studying competitors' products, pricing strategies, marketing tactics, and customer feedback, product managers can identify areas where their own products can gain a competitive advantage.

Competitor Benchmarking

Competitor Benchmarking refers to the process of evaluating and analyzing the strengths and weaknesses of competing products or services in order to gain insights and strategize for product management. It involves collecting data and information on competitors' offerings and comparing them to one's own product to identify areas for improvement and potential opportunities. The primary goal of competitor benchmarking is to gain a competitive edge by understanding how a product stacks up against its competitors in terms of features, quality, pricing, marketing, and overall value proposition. By conducting a thorough analysis, product managers can identify gaps in the market, evaluate market trends, and make informed decisions to better position their product in the marketplace.

Content Marketing Strategy

Content marketing strategy in the context of product management refers to the planned approach and process of creating, distributing, and promoting valuable and relevant content to attract, engage, and retain a specific target audience. It aims to provide informative and useful content that aligns with the target audience's interests and needs, thereby establishing credibility, trust, and loyalty towards the product or brand. A successful content marketing strategy for product management involves several key elements. Firstly, it requires a deep understanding of the target audience and their preferences, challenges, and pain points. This knowledge is crucial in creating content that resonates with the audience and provides them with solutions or insights they are seeking. Secondly, a product management content marketing strategy requires a clear objective or goal. This could be increasing brand visibility, generating leads, driving sales, enhancing customer loyalty, or positioning the product as a thought leader in the industry. Defining a specific goal helps in shaping the content creation process and measuring its success. Thirdly, a comprehensive content marketing strategy entails choosing the appropriate content types and formats. This can include blog posts, articles, videos, infographics, podcasts, webinars, and social media content. The chosen content types should align with the target audience's preferences and the product management goals. Fourthly, the strategy involves identifying the most effective distribution channels for reaching the target audience. This could involve leveraging social media platforms, email marketing, search engine optimization (SEO), guest blogging, influencer collaborations, and other relevant channels. The distribution channels should be selected based on their reach, relevance, and potential to engage the target audience. Lastly, a product management content marketing strategy requires consistent and regular content production and promotion. This involves creating a content calendar, brainstorming and generating ideas, producing high-quality content, and promoting it through the chosen distribution channels. Consistency and regularity in content creation and promotion help in building brand awareness and maintaining audience engagement.

Content Marketing Tools

Content marketing tools refer to various software and platforms that assist product managers in creating, managing, and distributing content to support their product marketing strategies. These tools automate and streamline the content production process, helping product managers create engaging and relevant content to attract and retain customers. Product managers utilize content marketing tools to develop and execute content strategy, create and edit content, optimize content for search engines, and distribute content across various channels. These tools provide a range of features and functionalities that enable product managers to effectively plan and execute their content marketing efforts.

Content Marketing

Content Marketing is a strategic approach that involves creating and distributing valuable, relevant, and consistent content in order to attract and engage a specific target audience. It is an integral part of Product Management as it plays a crucial role in promoting and driving the success of a product. The primary goal of content marketing in the context of Product Management is to educate and inform potential customers about the product, its features, and its benefits. Through well-crafted content, such as blog articles, videos, social media posts, and email campaigns, product managers aim to create awareness, generate interest, and build trust among their target audience. Content Marketing in Product Management goes beyond simply advertising or promoting the product. It aims to establish the product as a reliable source of information and a solution to the target customers' pain points. By providing valuable and insightful content, product managers position themselves as trusted advisors, guiding potential customers through their decision-making process. Furthermore, content marketing allows product managers to demonstrate the unique value proposition of the product. They can showcase its features, functionalities, and use cases through informative content that resonates with the target audience. By highlighting the product's strengths and addressing potential concerns or objections, content marketing helps to build confidence and drive conversions. Content marketing also plays a pivotal role in creating brand awareness and loyalty. Through consistent content creation and distribution, product managers can establish a strong brand identity and foster a community around the product. They can engage with customers, address their feedback and questions, and build long-lasting relationships that go beyond the initial purchase. In conclusion, Content Marketing in the context of Product Management involves the strategic creation and distribution of valuable and relevant content to attract, engage, and inform target customers. It aims to educate potential customers about the product, build trust, and establish the product as a solution to their pain points. Content marketing also contributes to brand awareness and loyalty, fostering a community around the product.

Continuous Deployment (CD)

Continuous Deployment (CD) is a product management strategy that focuses on automating the software release process to enable frequent and fast deployment of new features and enhancements to customers. It is a key component of the broader concept of Continuous Integration/Continuous Delivery (CI/CD). In CD, software changes are deployed to production as soon as they are ready, without the need for manual intervention or the accumulation of a large number of changes. This allows product teams to deliver value to customers more quickly and respond promptly to their feedback and evolving needs. The CD process begins with developers committing their code to a version control system (VCS), which triggers an automated build and test process. This ensures that any changes made to the codebase do not introduce bugs or break existing functionality. If the build and tests pass, the code is then automatically deployed to a staging environment, where it undergoes further testing and validation. Once the code is deemed ready for release, it is automatically deployed to production, making the new features and enhancements available to customers. This deployment process is typically seamless and transparent to end-users, as it does not require any downtime or disruption to the service. Monitoring and alerting systems are in place to catch any issues or anomalies that may arise after deployment. CD relies heavily on practices such as automated testing, continuous integration, and infrastructure as code. These practices ensure that the software is always in a releasable state and that any changes to infrastructure or dependencies are version-controlled and reproducible. Continuous Deployment brings several benefits to product management. It allows for rapid iteration and experimentation, as new features and improvements can be quickly deployed and tested. This enables faster learning and the ability to make data-driven decisions based on real customer usage. Additionally, CD reduces the risk associated with large, infrequent releases, as changes are deployed in small, incremental steps. It promotes a culture of collaboration and accountability among development, QA, and operations teams, as everyone is responsible for continuously delivering high-quality software.

Continuous Integration (CI)

Continuous Integration (CI) is a product management practice that involves the automated and frequent integration of code changes into a shared repository, allowing for the early detection of defects and faster delivery of new features. It is a vital component of agile development methodologies, enabling teams to collaborate effectively and ensure the stability and quality of the software throughout the development process. In CI, developers integrate their code changes into a shared version control system multiple times a day. This practice helps identify problems early on, as the integration process triggers automated tests and builds the entire codebase. The aim is to identify any conflicts, errors, or defects as soon as possible to prevent them from accumulating and causing delays or impacting the overall quality of the product.

Conversion Rate Optimization (CRO)

Conversion Rate Optimization (CRO) is a strategic process used in Product Management to improve the effectiveness of conversion metrics on a digital platform or website. It involves analyzing user behavior, identifying areas of improvement, and implementing targeted changes to optimize the conversion rate and maximize the desired actions taken by users. The main objective of CRO is to enhance the overall user experience and increase the conversion rate, which refers to the percentage of visitors who perform the desired action, such as making a purchase, filling out a form, or subscribing to a service. By optimizing the conversion rate, Product Managers aim to maximize the value generated from their digital assets and ultimately achieve the desired business objectives.

Conversion Rate Testing

Conversion Rate Testing, also known as Conversion Rate Optimization (CRO), is a crucial technique used in Product Management to analyze and improve the effectiveness of a website or digital product in converting visitors into customers or achieving a desired action. It involves conducting controlled experiments and using statistical analysis to evaluate and optimize various elements of the product that affect user behavior and conversion. The primary objective of Conversion Rate Testing is to increase the conversion rate, which is the percentage of users who complete a desired action, such as making a purchase, signing up for a newsletter, or filling out a form. By identifying areas of improvement and making data-driven changes, product managers can enhance the overall user experience and maximize the number of users who take the desired action.

Crisis Communication Plans

A crisis communication plan in the context of product management is a strategic plan that outlines how a company will effectively and efficiently communicate with its stakeholders during times of crisis. As a product manager, it is essential to have a crisis communication plan in place to address any unforeseen issues that may arise in the product lifecycle, such as product defects, safety concerns, security breaches, or regulatory violations. The primary goal of a crisis communication plan is to minimize the negative impact of a crisis on the company's reputation, customer trust, and overall business operations. It provides a structured approach to managing and responding to crises, ensuring that all key stakeholders are informed, engaged, and reassured. A crisis communication plan typically includes the following components: 1. Crisis

Team: A designated team responsible for managing and coordinating all communication efforts during a crisis. This team comprises representatives from various departments, including product management, public relations, legal, customer support, and executive leadership. The crisis team should be well-trained and prepared to respond promptly and effectively to any crisis situation. 2. Communication Channels: A list of communication channels that will be used to disseminate information to different stakeholders, including customers, employees, investors, media outlets, and regulatory authorities. These channels may include press releases, social media, website updates, email notifications, and direct customer outreach. The crisis communication plan should define the primary and backup channels for each stakeholder group. 3. Messaging Templates: Pre-drafted messaging templates that can be customized and deployed quickly during a crisis. These templates should provide clear, concise, and consistent messaging that addresses the issue at hand, demonstrates empathy, and outlines the steps being taken to resolve the crisis. The messaging should also align with the company's brand values and reputation. 4. Spokesperson Guidelines: Guidelines for designated spokespersons who will represent the company during a crisis. These guidelines should include media training, key talking points, message consistency, and transparency expectations. The spokespersons should be well-versed in the crisis communication plan and prepared to address various stakeholders' concerns both internally and externally. 5. Monitoring and Evaluation: A plan for monitoring and evaluating the effectiveness of the crisis communication efforts. This includes tracking media coverage, social media sentiment, customer feedback, and overall stakeholder perception. Regular evaluation allows for adjustments to the crisis communication plan as needed and ensures continuous improvement in crisis response capabilities.

Cross-Functional Collaboration Software

Cross-functional collaboration software in the context of Product Management refers to a digital tool or platform that enables individuals from different departments or functional areas within an organization to work together efficiently and effectively to achieve common goals and objectives related to the development and management of products or services. This type of software is designed to break down the silos that often exist between departments, such as product development, marketing, sales, and customer support, and facilitate seamless communication and collaboration across teams. It provides a centralized space or workspace where team members can share information, documents, and resources, and collaborate on various activities and tasks.

Cross-Functional Collaboration Solutions

Cross-functional collaboration solutions refer to the strategies, tools, and processes implemented in product management to facilitate effective communication and coordination among teams from different functional areas within an organization. In product management, cross-functional collaboration plays a vital role in ensuring the successful development and delivery of products that meet customer needs and align with business goals. Product management involves various functions such as marketing, design, engineering, sales, and customer support. Each function has unique expertise and responsibilities related to the product lifecycle, and effective collaboration among these functions is essential to ensure a product's success. Cross-functional collaboration solutions aim to overcome the challenges of siloed working environments and foster a culture of collaboration. These solutions typically involve the use of technology platforms, communication tools, and structured processes to enable teams to work together seamlessly and efficiently. One common example of a cross-functional collaboration solution in product management is the use of collaborative project management tools. These tools allow teams to create and track tasks, set deadlines, and share documents in a centralized platform, improving communication and visibility across functions. Another example is the implementation of cross-functional meetings or workshops, where representatives from different functions come together to discuss the product's strategy, roadmap, and key decisions. This fosters alignment, encourages diverse perspectives, and facilitates decision-making based on the input and expertise of all stakeholders. Effective cross-functional collaboration solutions also focus on creating a shared understanding of the product vision, goals, and priorities. This can be achieved through the use of documentation, such as product requirements documents or user stories, that provide a clear explanation of the product's features and objectives. Ultimately, cross-functional collaboration solutions in product management help create an environment where teams from different functions work together

22

towards a common goal, leveraging their expertise and insights to create products that delight customers and drive business success.

Cross-Functional Team Collaboration

A cross-functional team collaboration in the context of Product Management refers to the process of bringing together individuals with diverse skills, backgrounds, and expertise from different departments or functions within an organization to work towards a common goal of creating and delivering high-quality products. This collaboration is essential in Product Management as it allows for the integration of various perspectives and specializations, resulting in the development of well-rounded and innovative products. By leveraging the unique strengths and knowledge of each team member, cross-functional collaboration fosters a holistic approach to product development, ensuring that all aspects, from design to marketing to manufacturing, are considered early on in the process.

Cross-Functional Team

A cross-functional team in the context of Product Management refers to a group of individuals with diverse skill sets and expertise who come together to work collaboratively towards achieving a common goal or objective. This type of team is typically composed of members from different functional areas or departments within an organization and is specifically formed to address complex problems or projects that require a broad range of knowledge and capabilities. The primary purpose of a cross-functional team in Product Management is to promote cross-departmental collaboration and ensure that all perspectives and viewpoints are considered when making important decisions related to the development and management of a product. By bringing together members from various functional areas, such as marketing, design, engineering, and sales, the team can leverage the collective expertise of its members to generate innovative ideas, solve complex problems, and deliver high-quality products that meet the needs and expectations of customers.

Customer Acquisition Cost (CAC)

Customer Acquisition Cost (CAC) refers to the cost incurred by a company to acquire a new customer. It is a key metric in Product Management that helps in assessing the effectiveness and efficiency of a company's marketing and sales strategies. CAC provides insights into the resources and investment required to attract and convert potential customers into paying customers. CAC is calculated by dividing the total costs expended on acquiring customers by the number of customers acquired during a specific time period. These costs include marketing and advertising expenses, sales commissions, salaries of sales and marketing personnel, and any other direct costs related to customer acquisition. The time period can vary depending on the company's preferences, but it is typically measured on a monthly or yearly basis.

Customer Acquisition

Customer Acquisition is the process of attracting and converting new customers to a product or service. It is a critical component of Product Management, as it directly impacts the growth and success of a company. The goal of Customer Acquisition is to find new customers who are likely to have a need or desire for the product or service and convince them to make a purchase. This involves a careful targeting and segmentation strategy to identify the right customer segments to focus on. Customer Acquisition can be achieved through various marketing and sales tactics, including advertising, content marketing, direct mail, email marketing, social media marketing, search engine optimization (SEO), and more. These tactics are aimed at creating awareness and interest in the product or service among the target audience. Once potential customers are aware of the product or service, the next step is to convert them into actual customers. This typically involves a combination of persuasive messaging, effective pricing strategies, and a seamless and user-friendly purchasing process. Product Managers play a key role in understanding customer needs and preferences and aligning the product offering accordingly. Customer Acquisition is not a one-time event but an ongoing process. It requires continuous monitoring and optimization to ensure that the company is attracting and converting the right customers. This involves analyzing customer data, measuring the effectiveness of different acquisition channels, and refining the marketing and sales strategies as needed. Overall,

23

Customer Acquisition is a crucial aspect of Product Management as it directly contributes to the growth and success of a product or service. By attracting and converting new customers, Product Managers can help the company expand its customer base, increase revenue, and achieve its business goals.

Customer Advocacy Programs

A customer advocacy program in the context of product management can be defined as a strategic initiative implemented by a company to engage, support, and empower customers in order to build strong and loyal relationships. It focuses on providing customers with a platform to voice their opinions, provide feedback, and contribute to the improvement and development of the company's products. Customer advocacy programs aim to create a two-way communication channel between the company and its customers, fostering a sense of partnership and collaboration. By actively involving customers in the product development process, companies can gain valuable insights, identify pain points, and address specific needs more effectively.

Customer Advocacy Tools

Customer Advocacy Tools refer to the suite of software or services designed to help product management teams effectively understand, manage, and address customer feedback, concerns, and needs. These tools provide a platform for companies to engage with their customers, gather insights, and build strong relationships based on trust and mutual understanding. Customer advocacy tools typically offer a range of features and functionalities that enable product managers to collect and analyze customer feedback from various channels such as surveys, social media, and support tickets. They help consolidate and categorize customer feedback to identify trends, patterns, and common issues. This data can then be used to inform product decision-making, prioritize feature development, and address any pain points or gaps in the product's overall offering. These tools often provide mechanisms for customers to provide feedback directly and easily, such as through feedback forms or online communities. They also offer features for tracking customer satisfaction metrics, including Net Promoter Score (NPS), customer retention rates, and customer sentiment analysis. By monitoring these metrics, product managers can gauge customer satisfaction levels and identify opportunities for improvement. Customer advocacy tools also facilitate efficient communication and collaboration between product management teams, customer support teams, and customers themselves. They often provide a centralized platform for managing customer interactions, allowing product managers to track and respond to customer inquiries or issues in a timely manner. This helps foster a proactive and customer-focused approach to product management, ensuring that customer needs are addressed and prioritized throughout the product lifecycle.

Customer Engagement Platforms

A customer engagement platform refers to a software solution or tool that enables companies to effectively interact and connect with their customers throughout their entire journey. It is a key component of product management as it helps companies understand and address the needs of their customers, while also fostering loyalty and satisfaction. At its core, a customer engagement platform facilitates communication, collaboration, and interaction between a company and its customers. It provides a centralized hub where customer data and information can be collected, analyzed, and utilized to personalize and optimize the customer experience.

Customer Feedback Analysis

Customer feedback analysis refers to the process of systematically collecting, organizing, analyzing, and interpreting customer feedback with the objective of identifying insights and trends that can guide product management decisions. This analysis provides product managers with valuable information about customer preferences, needs, and expectations, enabling them to make informed decisions about product development, improvements, and marketing strategies.

Customer Feedback Collection

Customer Feedback Collection refers to the process of gathering, analyzing, and leveraging feedback from customers in order to understand their needs, preferences, and satisfaction levels with a specific product or service. This crucial aspect of Product Management allows companies to make data-driven decisions and improve their offerings based on real customer insights. The collection of customer feedback involves various methods such as surveys, interviews, focus groups, reviews, and social media monitoring. These channels enable companies to obtain a wide range of feedback, including both qualitative and quantitative data. Qualitative feedback provides in-depth insights into customer experiences, perceptions, and expectations, while quantitative feedback quantifies customer opinions through metrics and ratings. Once collected, customer feedback is carefully analyzed to identify patterns, trends, and key themes. This analysis helps product managers understand the strengths, weaknesses, and areas for improvement in their products. Additionally, it allows managers to assess customer satisfaction and product-market fit, as well as identify opportunities for innovation or new features. The insights gained from customer feedback collection are not limited to product improvements only. They also play a pivotal role in shaping the overall customer experience and driving customer loyalty. By listening to their customers, companies can personalize their offerings, tailor communication strategies, and address pain points effectively, resulting in increased customer satisfaction and retention. In the realm of Product Management, customer feedback collection serves as a continuous feedback loop. It involves not only collecting feedback before and during the development phase but also capturing post-launch feedback to evaluate the success of new features or enhancements. By consistently collecting feedback, product managers can iterate and evolve their products to meet changing customer needs and stay ahead of the market competition.

Customer Feedback Integration

Customer Feedback Integration in the context of Product Management refers to the process of systematically collecting, analyzing, and incorporating feedback from customers into the development and improvement of a product or service. Product managers play a crucial role in ensuring that customer feedback is effectively integrated into the product development lifecycle. This involves gathering feedback from various sources, including customer surveys, customer support interactions, social media comments, and online reviews. The feedback is then categorized, analyzed, and prioritized based on its relevance and potential impact on the product. Once the feedback has been thoroughly analyzed, product managers work closely with cross-functional teams, such as engineering, design, and marketing, to implement the necessary changes and enhancements to the product. This may involve refining existing features, adding new features, or addressing any usability or performance issues identified by customers. Customer Feedback Integration is an ongoing process that requires continuous monitoring of customer feedback and the ability to adapt and iterate on product features and functionalities. It allows product managers to align the product roadmap and strategy with the needs and expectations of customers, ultimately resulting in a product that better meets customer requirements and drives customer satisfaction and loyalty. By incorporating customer feedback into the product development process, organizations can gain valuable insights into customer preferences, pain points, and emerging trends. This enables them to make data-driven decisions and develop products that are more likely to succeed in the market.

Customer Feedback Surveys

Customer feedback surveys in the context of product management refer to the systematic process of collecting and analyzing feedback from customers regarding a particular product or service. These surveys serve as a valuable tool for product managers to gather insights, understand customer needs and preferences, and make data-driven decisions to improve the overall product experience. Customer feedback surveys typically involve the creation and distribution of questionnaires or surveys to customers who have interacted with the product. These surveys can be conducted through various channels, such as email, online forms, mobile apps, or even in-person interviews. The questions in the survey are designed to capture feedback on different aspects of the product, including its functionality, usability, design, pricing, and overall satisfaction. The primary objective of customer feedback surveys is to listen to the voice of the customer and gain a deep understanding of their experiences, opinions, and perceptions. By collecting and analyzing this feedback, product managers can identify potential pain points, uncover areas for improvement, and prioritize product enhancements or feature requests based on customer needs and preferences. Feedback surveys also play a critical role in measuring customer satisfaction and loyalty. By regularly measuring customer satisfaction levels, product managers can track changes over time and identify trends or patterns that reflect the impact of product updates or changes in customer expectations. Moreover, customer feedback surveys enable product managers to assess the product-market fit and validate their assumptions. By gathering feedback from a representative sample of customers, product managers can validate whether their product aligns with target market needs and make informed decisions regarding future product development or market positioning strategies. Overall, customer feedback surveys are a vital component of the product management process. They provide product managers with valuable insights, help them make data-driven decisions, and ensure that the product is continuously improved to meet customer expectations and drive business success.

Customer Feedback

Customer feedback in the context of Product Management refers to the information and opinions provided by customers regarding a specific product or service. It encompasses the thoughts, feelings, and experiences that customers have during their interaction with the product, including its features, usability, quality, and overall satisfaction. Customer feedback serves as a crucial tool for product managers to gather insights and understand the needs and preferences of their target audience. It helps in evaluating the product's performance, identifying areas of improvement, and making informed decisions to enhance the product's value and user experience.

Customer Journey Analysis

A customer journey analysis is a methodical examination of the entire process a customer goes through when interacting with a product or service, from the initial awareness stage to the final purchase decision and beyond. It is an essential tool for Product Managers to gain a deep understanding of how customers perceive and experience a product, as well as identify pain points, opportunities, and potential improvements. The journey analysis starts by mapping out each step or touchpoint of the customer's interaction with the product. This includes all the different channels and mediums through which customers become aware of the product, research it, make the purchase, and engage with it post-purchase. For instance, it might involve analyzing how customers discover the product through marketing campaigns, how they research it online, or how they interact with customer support after the purchase. Once the touchpoints are identified, Product Managers analyze customers' emotions, behavior, motivations, and expectations at each stage. This helps to gain insights into customers' pain points and moments of delight throughout the journey. They might conduct user surveys, interviews, or use analytics tools to gather data and understand customers' needs and desires, as well as any obstacles they encounter. Next, the findings from the analysis are used to create customer journey maps. These visual representations illustrate the customer's experience, emotions, and interactions at each touchpoint. The maps enable Product Managers to identify critical moments, identify pain points, and opportunities for improvement. They can help uncover gaps in the customer experience, areas where the product can be optimized, or where new features can be added to enhance customer satisfaction. By conducting a customer journey analysis, Product Managers gain valuable insights into customers' experiences and are better equipped to make data-driven decisions that lead to customer-centric improvements. They can identify areas where the product can be enhanced, refine marketing strategies, and improve customer support processes. Ultimately, a customer journey analysis empowers Product Managers to create products and experiences that align with customers' preferences and expectations, driving customer loyalty, retention, and business growth.

Customer Journey Map

A Customer Journey Map is a visual representation of the entire customer experience with a product or service, from the initial contact to post-purchase interactions. It provides product managers with a comprehensive view of the customer's interactions, emotions, and motivations throughout their journey. The customer journey typically consists of multiple touchpoints, or interactions, between the customer and the product or service. These touchpoints can be both online and offline, and can include actions such as researching, ordering, using, and seeking support for the product or service. The purpose of creating a customer journey map is to better understand the customer's perspective and identify areas for improvement in the product or service. By visualizing the customer's journey, product managers can uncover pain points, gaps in communication, and opportunities for enhancing the overall customer experience. A customer journey map typically includes several key components. First, it outlines the different stages of the customer's journey, such as awareness, consideration, purchase, and advocacy. Second, it identifies the various touchpoints and channels that the customer interacts with during each stage. These touchpoints can include websites, social media, physical stores, customer support, and more. Third, it highlights the customer's emotions and motivations at each touchpoint, which can help product managers understand the customer's needs and expectations. Product managers can use customer journey maps to inform their decision-making process and guide product development efforts. By identifying pain points and areas for improvement, they can prioritize enhancements and allocate resources accordingly. Additionally, customer journey maps can help product managers align cross-functional teams and stakeholders around a shared understanding of the customer's experience, fostering a customer-centric mindset within the organization.

Customer Journey Mapping Tools

A customer journey mapping tool is a software or platform that helps product managers visualize and understand the entire customer journey, from the initial discovery of a product or service to post-purchase experiences. It allows product managers to create visual representations of the various touchpoints, interactions, and emotions that customers experience throughout their journey. These tools typically provide a user-friendly interface where product managers can input data and create comprehensive customer journey maps. These maps help product managers gain insights into the needs, pain points, and motivations of their customers at each stage of the journey.

Customer Journey Mapping

A customer journey map is a visual representation of the journey a customer takes when interacting with a product or service. It captures the complete end-to-end experience of the customer, from the initial awareness and discovery stage, through the various touchpoints and interactions, to the final purchase decision and post-purchase support. The purpose of creating a customer journey map is to gain a deep understanding of the customer's experience and identify opportunities for improvement. It allows product managers to uncover pain points, bottlenecks, and areas of friction that may hinder the customer's progress or satisfaction. By highlighting these key moments in the customer journey, product managers can focus their efforts on enhancing the overall experience and delivering greater value to the customer.

Customer Journey Maps Repository

A customer journey maps repository is a central location where Product Managers store and manage customer journey maps. Customer journey maps are visual representations of the end-to-end experience that customers have while interacting with a product or service. They capture the various touchpoints, emotions, and pain points that customers may encounter throughout their journey. By creating a repository dedicated to customer journey maps, Product Managers can effectively organize and maintain these valuable insights. The repository serves as a secure and easily accessible platform where teams can collaborate, update, and reference the customer journey maps.

Customer Knowledge Base Software

A customer knowledge base software is a tool specifically designed for product management teams to store, organize, and share knowledge about their customers. It serves as a centralized repository of information that enables product managers to better understand their customers' needs, preferences, and behaviors. The primary purpose of a customer knowledge base software is to collect and document relevant customer data, such as contact information, demographics, purchase history, and support interactions. It also allows product managers to capture qualitative insights through notes, feedback, and comments provided by customers and customer-facing teams. With a customer knowledge base software, product managers can easily access and analyze the collected information to gain a comprehensive understanding of their target customers. This knowledge can help them identify customer pain points, prioritize product features and enhancements, and make data-driven decisions during the product development process. Furthermore, customer knowledge base software facilitates collaboration among product managers, allowing them to securely share and discuss insights with other team members. This promotes cross-functional communication and alignment, ensuring that everyone is working towards a common goal of delivering a product that meets customers' expectations. Additionally, some customer knowledge base software may provide advanced analytical features, such as segmentation and data visualization, enabling product managers to derive deeper insights from the collected customer data. These insights can help them identify trends, patterns, and opportunities that can inform product strategies and roadmaps. In summary, a customer knowledge base software is a vital tool for product management teams, providing them with a centralized repository of customer information and insights. It enables product managers to better understand their customers, collaborate effectively, and make informed decisions to deliver products that meet customer needs.

Customer Knowledge Base Systems

A Customer Knowledge Base System, in the context of Product Management, refers to a centralized repository of information that captures, organizes, and shares knowledge and data about customers. It is a tool used by product managers to collect and store valuable insights about customers, their preferences, behavior, and interactions with the product or service. Customer Knowledge Base Systems are designed to facilitate the acquisition and management of customer information, enabling product managers to better understand and serve their target audience. These systems typically include features such as data storage, search functionality, analytics, and collaboration tools, which assist product managers in leveraging customer insights for decision-making.

Customer Knowledge Base

A Customer Knowledge Base is a centralized repository of information about customers, their preferences, behaviors, and interactions with a product or service. It is a valuable tool for Product Management as it provides a deep understanding of customers, allowing for better decision-making, targeted product development, and effective communication. The Customer Knowledge Base is composed of various types of data collected from multiple sources, such as customer surveys, feedback, support tickets, user analytics, and sales data. This data is then organized, analyzed, and stored in the knowledge base to enable easy access and retrieval for Product Managers and other relevant stakeholders. With a Customer Knowledge Base, Product Managers can gain insights into customer needs, pain points, and expectations. By studying customer interactions and behavior patterns, they can identify trends, discover new opportunities, and make data-driven decisions. This knowledge helps prioritize product features, enhancements, and bug fixes based on customer demands and market trends. Furthermore, the Customer Knowledge Base enables Product Managers to create targeted marketing campaigns and effectively communicate product updates or launch new features. By understanding customer segments, personas, and user journeys, they can tailor messaging and positioning to resonate with the intended audience, leading to higher customer satisfaction and adoption rates. In addition, the Customer Knowledge Base fosters collaboration among different teams within an organization. It serves as a central hub of customer insights, accessible to product development teams, marketing teams, sales teams, and customer support teams. This shared understanding of customers enhances cross-functional collaboration, leading to a more cohesive approach to product planning, development, and customer engagement. In summary, a Customer Knowledge Base is a powerful tool for Product Management, providing a comprehensive view of customers and their interactions with a product or service. It empowers Product Managers to prioritize features, drive targeted marketing efforts, and foster collaboration across teams. By leveraging the knowledge base, Product Managers can make informed decisions, deliver customer-centric solutions, and ultimately achieve greater success in the market.

Customer Lifetime Value (CLV)

The Customer Lifetime Value (CLV) is a metric used in Product Management to determine the total revenue a business can expect to generate from a single customer over the course of their relationship with the company. CLV helps product managers understand and quantify the long-term value a customer brings to the business. CLV is calculated by multiplying the average value of a customer's purchase by the average number of purchases they make in a given time period, and then multiplying that by the average retention time of a customer. This calculation provides product managers with an estimate of how much revenue a customer will generate over their lifetime. In order to accurately calculate CLV, product managers need to consider several key factors. First, they need to understand the customer's average purchase value, which is the average amount of money a customer spends on each transaction. This can be determined by analyzing past sales data and customer behavior. Second, product managers need to determine the average number of purchases a customer makes in a given time period. This can be influenced by factors such as the product's lifecycle, the customer's needs, and the business's marketing efforts. Finally, product managers need to estimate the average retention time of a customer, which is the amount of time a customer continues to make purchases from the company. This can be influenced by factors such as customer satisfaction, product quality, and competition. Understanding CLV is crucial for product managers as it helps them make informed decisions about customer acquisition and retention strategies. By knowing the estimated value of a customer over their lifetime, product managers can allocate resources effectively and prioritize activities that will maximize customer value. For example, product managers can invest in initiatives to improve customer satisfaction and increase customer loyalty, knowing that these efforts will result in higher CLV. Additionally, product managers can use CLV to evaluate the success of different marketing campaigns and assess which ones are bringing in customers with higher long-term value.

Customer Onboarding Strategy

A customer onboarding strategy in the context of product management refers to the process and approach used by a company or organization to guide new customers through the initial stages of using their product or service. The goal of this strategy is to provide a smooth and positive experience for customers as they transition from being prospects to becoming active users or subscribers. The customer onboarding strategy typically involves a series of steps and activities aimed at welcoming new customers and helping them understand and effectively utilize the product. This may include providing access to documentation, tutorials, or onboarding materials that explain the product's features and functionalities. It may also involve personalized communication or support from the company to address any questions, concerns, or issues that new customers may have.

Customer Onboarding Tools

Customer onboarding tools are software applications or platforms that enable product managers to streamline and automate the process of integrating new customers into their products or services. These tools provide a structured and efficient way to manage the various stages of customer onboarding, from initial contact to successful adoption. Product managers use customer onboarding tools to simplify and standardize the onboarding process, ensuring that each new customer receives a consistent and positive experience. These tools typically offer a range of features and functionalities designed to enhance the onboarding process, such as: 1. User-friendly onboarding portals: Customer onboarding tools often include self-service portals that new customers can use to register, complete profile information, and access necessary resources or documentation. These portals streamline the initial steps of onboarding, minimizing the need for manual data entry and reducing the likelihood of errors or delays. 2. Workflow automation: Customer onboarding tools enable product managers to create customizable workflows that guide new customers through the necessary steps and tasks. These workflows can automate the assignment of tasks, send automated notifications to customers, and track progress to ensure nothing falls through the cracks. 3. Integration capabilities: To ensure a smooth onboarding process, customer onboarding tools often integrate with other essential systems and applications, such as customer relationship management (CRM) software or payment gateways. This integration enables seamless data transfer and synchronization, minimizing the need for manual data entry or duplication. 4. Analytics and reporting: Customer onboarding tools provide product managers with valuable insights and metrics to measure the effectiveness of the onboarding process. These tools often include dashboards and reporting features that offer visibility into key performance indicators, such as onboarding completion rates or customer satisfaction scores. In conclusion, customer onboarding tools are valuable resources for product managers to manage and optimize the onboarding process. These tools streamline and automate various tasks, ensuring a smooth and consistent onboarding experience for new customers.

Customer Onboarding

Customer onboarding in the context of Product Management refers to the process of guiding and assisting new customers as they begin their journey with a product or service. It involves providing them with the necessary information, resources, and support to ensure a smooth and successful transition into becoming active and engaged users. The primary goal of customer onboarding is to facilitate a positive user experience from the very beginning, ultimately leading to customer satisfaction, retention, and advocacy. It is a critical step in the overall customer lifecycle management, as it sets the foundation for building a long-term relationship with the customer.

Customer Persona Development

A customer persona is a fictional representation of the ideal customer for a particular product or service. It is a tool used in product management to understand and empathize with the target audience, their needs, and their behaviors. By creating customer personas, product managers can gain insights into the preferences, motivations, and pain points of their customers, which helps them make informed decisions about product development and marketing strategies. A customer persona typically includes demographic information such as age, gender, location, and occupation, as well as psychographic details such as interests, values, and attitudes. It may also include information about the customer's goals, challenges, and buying habits. The creation of a customer persona involves conducting research through surveys, interviews, and data analysis to collect relevant information about the target market.

Customer Persona Profiles

A customer persona profile is a tool used by product managers to represent and understand their target customers. It is a fictional character that encompasses the various characteristics and behaviors of the ideal customer, providing insights into their needs, preferences, and motivations. Customer persona profiles are created through a combination of research, data analysis, and market understanding. The purpose of developing customer persona profiles is to ensure that the product being developed meets the specific needs and expectations of the target customers. By creating these profiles, product managers can gain a clearer understanding of who their customers are, what they want, and how they make purchasing decisions. This knowledge allows them to tailor their product strategy and design efforts to better address these customer needs.

Customer Personas

Customer Personas in the context of Product Management refer to fictional representations of the different types of customers that a product or service is targeted towards. These personas are created based on research, data, and observations of the target audience's behaviors, demographics, and preferences. They help product managers and teams better understand the needs, motivations, and goals of their target customers, enabling them to make informed product decisions and develop more effective marketing strategies. Customer personas typically include information such as the target customer's age, gender, occupation, income level, geographic location, and other demographic details. Additionally, they also capture their interests, preferences, and pain points related to the product or service. Customer personas go beyond mere statistical data and aim to create a relatable and multidimensional representation of the target audience.

Customer Portal Integration

A Customer Portal Integration in the context of Product Management refers to the process of connecting a customer portal with other systems or platforms, such as a CRM (Customer Relationship Management) system or an eCommerce platform. This integration enables seamless information transfer and enhances the overall customer experience by providing a centralized platform for customers to access relevant information and perform various self-service tasks. By integrating a customer portal with external systems, product managers can streamline customer interactions and enhance their ability to gather valuable insights. The integration enables real-time synchronization of data, such as customer profiles, purchase history, support tickets, and feedback, between the customer portal and other systems. This integration allows for a holistic view of the customer, improving the accuracy and effectiveness of personalized marketing efforts, product recommendations, and support services.

Customer Portal

A customer portal is a secure and interactive online platform that allows customers to access and manage their accounts, interact with support teams, and engage with the products and services offered by a company. It serves as a centralized hub where customers can conveniently perform various activities related to their relationship with the business. With a customer portal, customers can view and update their personal information, such as contact details, billing preferences, and shipping addresses. They can also access their purchase history, track order status, and make payments or manage subscriptions. This self-service feature empowers customers to take control of their account management and reduces the dependency on customer support for routine tasks. Furthermore, a customer portal acts as a communication channel between customers and a company's support teams. Customers can submit inquiries, raise support tickets, and seek assistance from customer service representatives directly through the portal. This ensures a streamlined and efficient support process, as all customer communications are consolidated in one place, enabling faster response times and reducing the risk of miscommunication. Besides managing account information and seeking support, a customer portal also facilitates product interactions. Customers can access product documentation, user guides, and FAQs, which help them understand and make the most out of the products or services they have purchased. In addition, some portals provide a community or forum feature where customers can collaborate with each other, share insights, and exchange best practices. This fosters a sense of belonging and enables customers to contribute to the overall improvement of the products and services. In summary, a customer portal is a secure online platform that enables customers to manage their accounts, interact with support teams, and engage with the products and services offered by a company. It facilitates self-service account management, streamlines support interactions, and provides access to relevant product resources. By offering a centralized and interactive space for customer engagement, a customer portal enhances the overall customer experience and empowers customers to effectively interact with the company.

Customer Relationship Management (CRM)

Customer Relationship Management (CRM) is a strategic approach that involves managing and nurturing the relationships between a company and its customers in order to maximize customer satisfaction and loyalty. It is a crucial aspect of product management, as it helps to identify and understand customer needs, preferences, and behaviors, and enables product managers to tailor their offerings to meet those requirements effectively. CRM in product management involves the use of various tools and techniques to collect and analyze customer data, such as purchase history, feedback, and interactions. This data is then used to establish and maintain a comprehensive database of customer information, which can be used to segment customers into different groups based on their characteristics and behaviors. This segmentation allows product managers to target specific customer groups with customized product offerings and marketing messages, increasing the likelihood of customer satisfaction and repeat purchases. In addition to segmentation, CRM also enables product managers to track and measure customer interactions and engagement across multiple touchpoints, such as websites, social media platforms, and customer service channels. This helps product managers to gain insights into customer behavior and preferences, as well as identify any gaps or areas for improvement in the customer experience. By understanding the customer journey and the pain points along the way, product managers can develop strategies and initiatives to enhance the overall customer experience and drive customer loyalty. Furthermore, CRM allows product managers to proactively manage customer relationships by providing personalized support and tailored solutions. By leveraging customer data and insights, product managers can anticipate customer needs and provide proactive assistance, whether it's through targeted recommendations, personalized offers, or timely and relevant communications. This level of personalized attention helps to build strong and long-lasting customer relationships, fostering brand loyalty and advocacy. In summary, CRM in product management is about effectively managing customer relationships through the collection, analysis, and application of customer data. It involves using customer insights to develop targeted and customized product offerings, tracking and measuring customer interactions, and providing personalized support and solutions. By focusing on CRM, product managers can better understand and meet customer needs, enhance the customer experience, and ultimately drive business growth and success.

Customer Relationship

Customer Relationship in the context of Product Management refers to the establishment, development, and maintenance of a strong and mutually beneficial relationship between a company and its customers. It involves understanding, anticipating, and fulfilling the needs and expectations of customers in order to enhance customer satisfaction and loyalty. A strong customer relationship is essential for the success of any product or business. It helps in building a loyal customer base, increasing customer retention, and driving repeat purchases. Additionally, it provides valuable insights into customer preferences, market trends, and competition, which can be used to improve the product and create better customer experiences.

Customer Retention Rate

Customer Retention Rate refers to a metric used in product management to measure the ability of a company or organization to retain its existing customers over a specific period of time. It represents the percentage of customers that continue to use or purchase a product or service from a company, compared to the total number of customers at the beginning of the period. The customer retention rate provides valuable insights into the effectiveness of a company's customer retention strategies and the overall satisfaction and loyalty of its customer base. A high customer retention rate indicates that the company is successful in retaining its customers, which is crucial for sustaining business growth and profitability.

Customer Retention

Customer retention, in the context of product management, refers to the ability of a company to retain its existing customers and encourage repeat purchases or continued use of its products or services. It is a critical metric for businesses as it directly impacts their revenue and growth. Customer retention can be achieved through different strategies and tactics that focus on building strong customer relationships, delivering exceptional customer experiences, and providing value that keeps customers coming back. These strategies may include personalized communication, loyalty programs, customer support, and continuous product improvements.

Customer Satisfaction Feedback

Customer Satisfaction Feedback is a method used in Product Management to gather information from customers regarding their level of satisfaction with a particular product or service. It is an essential tool for product managers to assess the success of their product and identify areas for improvement. The feedback process typically involves soliciting input from customers through surveys, interviews, or online platforms. By collecting and analyzing this feedback, product managers can gain valuable insights into customers' opinions, needs, and preferences.

Customer Satisfaction Metrics

Customer satisfaction metrics in the context of product management refer to the parameters and measurements used to assess the level of satisfaction customers have with a particular product or service. These metrics provide valuable insights into how well a product meets the needs and expectations of its users, and assist in identifying areas for improvement to enhance overall customer satisfaction. There are several key customer satisfaction metrics that product managers utilize to gauge and quantify customer satisfaction. One common metric is the Net Promoter Score (NPS), which measures the likelihood of customers recommending a product or service to others. The NPS is determined through a survey where customers rate their likelihood of recommending on a scale of 0 to 10. The responses are then classified into three categories: promoters (rating 9-10), passives (rating 7-8), and detractors (rating 0-6). The NPS is calculated by subtracting the percentage of detractors from the percentage of promoters, resulting in a score that represents the product's overall customer satisfaction level. Another important customer satisfaction metric is the Customer Satisfaction Score (CSAT), which measures the satisfaction of customers after using a product or service. It typically involves asking customers to rate their satisfaction on a numerical scale or by choosing from a range of predefined categories. The CSAT score is then calculated by averaging the ratings or categorizations provided by the customers. A higher CSAT score indicates higher customer satisfaction with the product or service. Other commonly used customer satisfaction metrics include Customer Effort Score (CES), which measures the ease of using a product or service, and Customer Churn Rate, which quantifies the number of customers who stop using a product over a specific period of time. These metrics, along with others like customer retention rate, customer lifetime value, and customer loyalty, provide product managers with valuable data to track and analyze customer satisfaction levels, identify pain points, and prioritize improvements to enhance the overall customer experience.

Customer Satisfaction Surveys

A customer satisfaction survey is a formal evaluation tool used by product managers to gather feedback directly from customers regarding their satisfaction with a product or service. The purpose of a customer satisfaction survey is to measure and assess customers' overall experience with a product, identify areas of improvement, and gather insights to enhance the product's performance and meet customer expectations. These surveys typically consist of a series of structured questions that customers are asked to answer based on their experiences.

Customer Segmentation Models

Customer segmentation models are analytical tools used in product management to divide a company's customer base into distinct groups or segments based on common characteristics, behaviors, or needs. These models enable organizations to better understand their customers, effectively tailor their products, services, and marketing strategies for each segment, and efficiently allocate resources to maximize growth and profitability. Segmentation models are built upon the recognition that not all customers are the same and that targeting all customers with a one-size-fits-all approach is not the most efficient or effective way to drive business success. By segmenting customers into meaningful groups, product managers can gain insights into the unique needs, preferences, and behaviors of each segment, allowing them to develop and offer products and services that better meet those specific customer requirements.

Customer Segmentation Tools

Customer segmentation tools are software or applications used by product managers to divide a target market into distinct groups, or segments, based on various criteria. These tools help product managers understand the different needs, preferences, and behaviors of a diverse customer base, allowing them to tailor their marketing and product development strategies effectively. Customer segmentation is crucial for product managers to identify and prioritize the most valuable segments within a market. By using customer segmentation tools, product managers can analyze data and identify patterns that reveal common characteristics among customers. These tools can incorporate demographic, psychographic, geographic, and behavioral criteria to create segments with similar needs and preferences. One key benefit of customer segmentation tools is their ability to provide insights into the distinct motivators and pain points of different customer segments. This information can be used to develop targeted marketing messages, positioning strategies, and even personalized product offerings. By understanding the unique needs and desires of each segment, product managers can optimize their product features, pricing, and distribution to better meet customer demands. Customer segmentation tools also enable product managers to uncover new market opportunities and niches. By understanding the characteristics of existing customer segments, product managers can identify potential gaps or unaddressed needs in the market. This knowledge can guide the development of new products or the modification of existing ones to effectively target these opportunities. Furthermore, customer segmentation tools allow product managers to measure the success of their marketing and product strategies. By tracking and analyzing customer data within each segment, they can evaluate the impact of their actions on customer behavior and identify areas for improvement. These tools provide valuable insights into the effectiveness of marketing campaigns, product features, pricing strategies, and customer engagement initiatives. In summary, customer segmentation tools are essential for product managers in understanding and targeting different customer groups. These tools enable them to analyze customer data, identify common characteristics, and tailor marketing and product strategies to meet the unique needs of each segment. By leveraging customer segmentation tools effectively, product managers can optimize their market positioning, uncover new opportunities, and measure the success of their initiatives.

Customer Segmentation

Customer segmentation is the process of dividing a customer base into distinct groups or segments based on specific characteristics or behaviors. It is a crucial component of product management as it allows businesses to tailor their products, services, and marketing strategies to target each segment effectively and cater to their unique needs and preferences. The goal of customer segmentation is to identify and understand different customer groups within a larger market and create distinct profiles for each segment. This involves analyzing various factors such as demographics, geographic location, psychographics, purchasing behavior, and customer preferences. By grouping customers with similar characteristics together, businesses can gain valuable insights into their target audience, enabling them to develop and enhance products that meet and exceed their expectations.

Customer Support Documentation

Customer Support Documentation refers to the collection of information, guidelines, and resources that are created and provided by a company to assist customers in resolving their issues or queries related to a product or service. It serves as a reference for both customers and support agents to effectively and efficiently handle customer inquiries and concerns. The purpose of customer support documentation is to provide comprehensive, concise, and structured information that addresses the common questions, problems, and troubleshooting steps associated with a product or service. It plays a vital role in enhancing customer satisfaction, reducing support costs, and improving overall customer experience.

Customer Support Integration Solutions

Customer Support Integration Solutions refer to the processes and tools used by Product Managers to effectively manage and streamline customer support within an organization. These solutions typically involve integrating customer support systems and platforms with the product management workflow, enabling seamless communication and collaboration between customer support teams and product development teams. By implementing Customer Support Integration Solutions, product managers can ensure that they have a holistic view of customer issues and feedback, allowing them to make informed decisions and prioritize product enhancements and bug fixes. These solutions enable product managers to gather and analyze support requests, bug reports, and feature requests from customers, and seamlessly transfer this information to the product development team for action.

Customer Support Integration

Customer Support Integration refers to the process of incorporating customer support services into a product management strategy. This entails aligning customer support goals, processes, and resources with the overall product vision and roadmap. The objective is to provide seamless support to customers throughout their journey, from pre-sales inquiries to post-sales assistance, and ultimately enhancing the overall customer experience. By integrating customer support into product management, organizations can streamline their operations, improve customer satisfaction, and drive product success. It involves various key elements: 1. Aligning Goals: Customer support integration requires aligning the goals and metrics of the customer support team with the product management team. This ensures that both teams are working towards common objectives, such as reducing customer churn, improving product adoption, and enhancing customer loyalty. 2. Feedback Loop: Establishing a feedback loop between customer support and product management is vital. Customer support agents can provide valuable insights into customer pain points, common issues, and feature requests. This feedback can help prioritize product enhancements and guide the product roadmap. 3. Knowledge Base: Integrating customer support into product management involves developing a comprehensive knowledge base. This central repository of information includes product documentation, troubleshooting guides, frequently asked questions, and best practices. It equips customer support agents with the resources needed to efficiently assist customers and reduces the need for repetitive support requests. 4. Cross-functional Collaboration: Collaboration between customer support, product management, engineering, and other relevant teams is essential for a successful integration. Regular meetings, shared communication channels, and collaborative problem-solving facilitate a holistic approach to addressing customer needs and concerns. Overall, customer support integration in product management is crucial for creating a customer-centric organization. It enables companies to deliver exceptional support experiences, gather valuable insights, and continuously improve their products to meet customer expectations.

Customer Support Ticket Integration

A customer support ticket integration in the context of product management refers to the process of integrating a ticketing system or software into a product or service to efficiently manage and address customer inquiries or issues. Customer support ticket integrations are designed to streamline and improve the customer support experience by providing a centralized platform for managing and tracking customer issues. This integration allows for the seamless creation, assignment, tracking, and resolution of customer support tickets within a product management system.

Customer Support Ticketing Systems

A customer support ticketing system is a software application or platform used by businesses to manage and track customer support requests or tickets. It provides a centralized location for customer inquiries, allowing support teams to efficiently handle and resolve customer issues or concerns. The primary purpose of a ticketing system is to streamline customer support processes by organizing and prioritizing incoming tickets, assigning them to the appropriate support agents, and tracking their progress until resolution. When a customer initiates a support request, the ticketing system assigns a unique identifier or ticket number to it, which helps in tracking and referencing the ticket throughout its lifecycle.

Customer Support

Customer Support in the context of Product Management refers to the set of activities and services provided by a company to assist customers throughout their experience with a product. It encompasses various forms of assistance, such as answering inquiries, resolving issues, and providing guidance to ensure customer satisfaction and product adoption. Customer Support plays a crucial role in Product Management as it directly impacts customer loyalty, retention, and the overall success of a product. It involves proactive and reactive measures to address customer needs, concerns, and feedback. By offering effective support, companies can foster positive relationships with their customers, enhance their brand reputation, and drive business growth.

Design Handoff Collaboration Tools

Design handoff collaboration tools are software platforms or applications that facilitate the seamless transfer and communication of design assets and specifications between designers and developers during the product development process. These tools serve as a central hub for all design-related information, ensuring that designers and developers are on the same page and work together efficiently. They enable effective collaboration and eliminate any misunderstandings or discrepancies in design implementation.

Design Handoff Tools

A design handoff tool is a software or platform that facilitates the transfer of design files, assets, and specifications from designers to developers, allowing for a seamless handover of design work in the product development process. It serves as a communication bridge between the design and development teams, ensuring that both sides have access to the necessary information and resources to successfully implement the design. These tools typically offer features that enable designers to organize and package their design files, including design mockups, style guides, and asset libraries. This ensures that developers can easily access and retrieve the required design elements without any confusion or miscommunication. The design handoff tool may also provide functionalities for annotation and collaboration, allowing designers to provide detailed explanations or instructions for specific design elements or interactions. One

35

of the main benefits of using a design handoff tool is that it streamlines the design-to-development workflow, reducing the time and effort required for communication and clarification between designers and developers. It eliminates the need for lengthy email chains or in-person meetings to discuss design specifications, as all the relevant design assets and information are centralized in one place. In addition, design handoff tools often support integration with other project management or development tools, such as project management software, prototyping tools, or version control systems. This ensures a smooth handoff process and allows for better alignment and coordination between the design and development teams. Overall, a design handoff tool is a crucial component of the product management process as it facilitates effective collaboration and communication between designers and developers. It helps ensure that the design vision is accurately implemented in the final product, resulting in a higher quality user experience.

Design System Creation Tools

A design system creation tool is a software tool used by product managers to create and manage design systems. Design systems are a set of guidelines and components that help maintain consistency and improve efficiency in the design and development process of a product or service. These tools provide a platform for product managers to define and document the visual and interaction design elements, including typography, colors, iconography, and layouts, that form the foundation of a design system. They also enable the creation and management of reusable components and patterns that can be easily implemented across different projects and platforms.

Design System Implementation

A design system implementation refers to the process of integrating and incorporating a design system into a product management strategy. A design system is a set of guidelines, components, and patterns that aim to create a consistent and cohesive user experience across different products and platforms. Implementing a design system involves several key steps. First, product managers need to assess the current state of their products and identify areas for improvement. This involves conducting a thorough audit of existing design elements, user interface patterns, and user experiences. By understanding the strengths and weaknesses of the current design, product managers can determine what aspects of the design system need to be prioritized during implementation. Next, product managers collaborate with designers, developers, and other stakeholders to define a clear vision and roadmap for the design system implementation. This includes establishing clear goals, objectives, and milestones for the project. By involving all relevant parties in the planning process, product managers can ensure that the design system aligns with the overall product strategy and meets the needs of all stakeholders. Once the vision and roadmap are established, product managers work with designers to create a set of design guidelines, components, and patterns. These guidelines define the visual elements, typographic styles, color palettes, and interactions that will be used throughout the product. By providing designers with a clear set of standards, the design system enables them to create consistent and on-brand user experiences. After the design guidelines are established, developers come into play by translating these guidelines into code. They build reusable components and templates that can be easily integrated into the product's codebase. This allows developers to work more efficiently and consistently, as they can leverage pre-built components rather than starting from scratch for every new feature or page. Throughout the process, product managers should continuously iterate and improve the design system implementation. They should gather feedback from users, designers, and developers to identify any issues or areas for enhancement. By maintaining an iterative approach, product managers can maximize the value and impact of the design system, ensuring its long-term success in creating a cohesive and delightful user experience.

Design System Libraries

Design System Libraries, in the context of Product Management, refer to a collection of pre-designed and reusable components, styles, patterns, and guidelines that are used to build consistent and cohesive user interfaces and experiences. These libraries are created and maintained by product teams to ensure design consistency, efficiency, and scalability across different products, platforms, and devices. They serve as a single source of truth for design

36

assets, allowing multiple teams to work collaboratively and leverage the same design principles and elements.

Design Thinking Workshop Resources

Design thinking is a methodology employed by product managers to solve complex problems and develop innovative solutions for various products and services. It is an iterative process that focuses on understanding the users' needs, generating creative ideas, and testing and refining those ideas to create user-centric solutions. The design thinking approach consists of five key stages: empathize, define, ideate, prototype, and test. In the empathize stage, product managers immerse themselves in the users' world to gain a deep understanding of their needs, behaviors, and pain points. This involves conducting interviews, observations, and user research to gather insights and develop user personas. In the define stage, product managers synthesize the information gathered in the empathize stage to identify the core problem statement or opportunity. This stage involves reframing the problem statement to ensure that it focuses on user needs rather than assumptions or preconceptions. In the ideate stage, product managers generate a wide range of creative ideas to address the problem statement. This involves brainstorming sessions, mind mapping, and other ideation techniques to encourage diverse and out-of-the-box thinking. The goal is to generate as many ideas as possible without any judgment or evaluation. The prototype stage involves building low-fidelity representations of the proposed solutions. These prototypes can be in the form of sketches, wireframes, or even physical models. The purpose is to quickly test and gather feedback on the ideas generated in the ideate stage. The final stage is testing, where product managers gather feedback on the prototypes from the users and other stakeholders. This feedback is used to refine and iterate the solutions until they meet the users' needs effectively. The iterative nature of design thinking allows product managers to continuously learn, adapt, and improve their solutions based on user feedback.

Design Thinking Workshops

Design Thinking Workshops are collaborative problem-solving sessions that utilize the principles of design thinking to generate innovative product management solutions. By bringing together cross-functional teams, these workshops aim to understand user needs and pain points, define problem statements, and ideate possible solutions. The workshops typically follow a structured process that consists of several key stages. The first stage is empathy, where the team conducts research and interviews to gain a deep understanding of the target users and their context. This stage helps the team uncover hidden insights and identify unmet user needs. Following the empathy stage, the workshops move to define the problem statement. The team consolidates their findings from the research and distills them into a clear problem statement that encapsulates the user's pain points and the goals to be achieved. This stage helps align the team's understanding of the problem and sets the foundation for the ideation stage. The ideation stage is the heart of the workshop, where the team generates a wide range of possible solutions to the defined problem. The team employs various brainstorming techniques, such as mind mapping and divergent thinking, to encourage creativity and explore alternative perspectives. The goal is to generate a large quantity of ideas without judgment or evaluation. Once the team has generated a pool of ideas, they move on to the prototyping stage. Here, the team selects the most promising ideas and creates low-fidelity prototypes to quickly test and validate their assumptions. Prototypes can take various forms, such as sketches, wireframes, or even physical mockups, depending on the nature of the solution. The final stage of the workshop is testing, where the team collects feedback from potential users on the prototypes. This feedback helps refine and iterate on the solutions, ensuring that they effectively address the user's needs. The design thinking workshop concludes with a presentation of the refined solutions and a plan for implementation.

Design Version Control

Version control, in the context of Product Management, refers to the systematic process of managing changes and revisions made to a product or project. It allows teams to track, organize, and collaborate on different versions of the product, ensuring that all members are working on the most up-to-date version and are aware of any changes made. By implementing version control, Product Managers can maintain a clear and structured development workflow, ensuring that changes are made in an organized and controlled manner. This process not only facilitates collaboration but also minimizes the risk of errors and conflicts caused by multiple team members working on different versions simultaneously.

Direct Sales

Direct Sales refers to the process of selling products or services directly to consumers, without involving any middlemen or intermediaries. In the context of Product Management, direct sales involve a direct interaction between the product manager or sales representative and the end consumer. This sales approach allows for a more personalized and hands-on experience as the product manager can directly communicate with the customer, understand their needs, and address any concerns or questions they may have. By eliminating the need for intermediaries, direct sales can also result in cost savings for both the company and the consumer.

Distribution Channels

Distribution channels refer to the pathways through which a product or service is brought from the producer or manufacturer to the end consumer. These channels can be physical or digital, and they involve a series of intermediaries or intermediaries that facilitate the movement of the product along the supply chain. The main goal of distribution channels is to ensure that the product reaches the right target customers in a timely and cost-effective manner. There are several types of distribution channels, including direct channels, indirect channels, and dual distribution. In direct channels, the product is sold directly from the manufacturer to the end consumer without the involvement of intermediaries. This can be done through company-owned stores, e-commerce platforms, or direct sales representatives. Direct channels provide the manufacturer with more control over the sales process and customer experience, but they also require significant investments in infrastructure and marketing. In indirect channels, the product goes through one or more intermediaries before reaching the end consumer. These intermediaries can include wholesalers, distributors, retailers, agents, or brokers. Indirect channels are often used when the manufacturer wants to reach a wider customer base or lacks the resources to establish a direct sales network. However, they can also introduce additional costs and complexities, as each intermediary adds their margin to the product's price. Dual distribution combines both direct and indirect channels, allowing manufacturers to reach different customer segments or markets. For example, a company may sell their products through their own e-commerce website while also partnering with retailers to distribute their products in physical stores. Dual distribution can be an effective strategy for maximizing market coverage and generating higher sales volumes. When managing distribution channels, product managers need to consider various factors, such as the target market, customer preferences, competitive landscape, and cost-efficiency. They need to select the most appropriate channels based on these factors and develop a distribution strategy that aligns with the overall product strategy. Product managers also need to continuously evaluate and optimize their distribution channels to ensure they are delivering value to the end customers and maximizing sales opportunities.

E-Commerce Channels

E-commerce channels refer to the various online platforms or channels through which businesses sell their products or services to customers. These channels serve as the interface between the business and the customers, allowing for the online purchase and delivery of goods. The primary purpose of e-commerce channels is to provide a convenient and efficient way for customers to browse, select, and purchase products or services from the comfort of their own homes or wherever they may be. These channels leverage the power of the internet and technology to enable seamless transactions between businesses and customers.

Email Marketing Campaigns

Email Marketing Campaigns are strategic efforts undertaken by product management teams to promote and market their products or services through email communication. These campaigns involve the creation and distribution of targeted emails to a specific audience in order to increase brand awareness, drive sales, and engage customers. The primary goal of Email Marketing Campaigns is to effectively reach and engage with potential or existing customers through their email inbox. This is achieved by carefully crafting compelling and personalized email content that resonates with the target audience. Product management teams use various tactics and strategies such as segmentation, personalization, and automation to optimize the impact and success of these campaigns.

Email Marketing Tools

Email marketing tools are software applications or platforms that enable product managers to create, automate, and manage email campaigns. These tools provide a user-friendly interface that allows product managers to design visually appealing emails, automate email delivery, and analyze the performance of their campaigns. Product managers use email marketing tools to target specific customer segments, deliver personalized content, and build relationships with their audience. These tools often offer a range of features such as email templates, drag-and-drop editors, A/B testing, segmentation, and analytics. With email marketing tools, product managers can streamline their email marketing efforts, maximize deliverability, and optimize campaign performance. They can create and schedule emails in advance, ensuring timely delivery and consistent messaging. The drag-and-drop editors allow product managers to easily design eye-catching emails without the need for coding or design skills. Segmentation features enable product managers to divide their subscriber base into various groups based on demographics, behavior, or past interactions. This allows for targeted and relevant communication, increasing the effectiveness of the email campaigns. A/B testing capabilities within email marketing tools enable product managers to experiment with different versions of their emails and determine which variations generate the highest engagement and conversion rates. This data-driven approach helps optimize future campaigns. The analytics provided by email marketing tools allow product managers to track key metrics such as open rates, click-through rates, and conversions. These insights provide valuable feedback on campaign performance and help identify areas for improvement. Overall, email marketing tools are essential for product managers to effectively engage with their audience, drive customer actions, and generate business results. These tools simplify the process of creating and managing email campaigns, while offering powerful features that optimize performance and deliver tangible results.

Email Marketing

Email marketing is a form of direct marketing that uses email to communicate messages and promotions to existing and potential customers. It is a strategic marketing approach that allows organizations to connect with their target audience directly, with the aim of building customer loyalty, increasing product awareness, and generating sales. Product Management teams play a critical role in email marketing by leveraging their understanding of the product, market, and customer needs to develop and execute effective email marketing campaigns. They work closely with marketing and sales teams to define the objectives, target audience, and messaging for each campaign. Product Managers oversee the entire email marketing process, starting with identifying the target audience and segmenting it based on various criteria such as demographics, preferences, or past purchase behavior. They collaborate with the marketing team to design and write compelling email content that aligns with the brand voice and reflects the value proposition of the product. Product Managers also work with the development team to ensure that the email marketing platform and tools are set up to capture data and insights on subscriber behavior. This data is analyzed to measure the effectiveness of email campaigns, track key metrics such as open rates and click-through rates, and make data-driven decisions to improve future campaigns. Additionally, Product Managers continuously monitor and optimize email marketing campaigns based on performance indicators and customer feedback. They conduct A/B testing to experiment with different subject lines, content variations, or call-to-action buttons to determine what resonates best with the target audience. In conclusion, email marketing is a powerful tool for Product Management teams to engage with customers, promote products, and drive sales. Through careful audience segmentation, compelling content creation, and data-driven optimization, Product Managers can leverage email marketing to effectively communicate and build relationships with both existing and potential customers.

Feature Dependency Analysis Platforms

Feature Dependency Analysis Platforms are tools or software that are used in Product Management to analyze and understand the interrelationships between different features of a product or service. These platforms help product managers identify the dependencies between

39

various features and assess the impact of changes or additions to one feature on the others. Product managers use Feature Dependency Analysis Platforms to visualize and map out the relationships between different features of a product. This allows them to gain a holistic understanding of how changes in one feature can potentially affect the overall functionality and performance of the product. By analyzing these dependencies, product managers can make informed decisions about prioritizing feature development, managing resources, and planning roadmaps.

Feature Dependency Analysis

Feature Dependency Analysis is a crucial method in product management to identify and understand the relationships and dependencies between different features within a product. It helps product managers prioritize and plan feature development, make informed decisions, and avoid potential conflicts or issues. At its core, Feature Dependency Analysis involves examining the dependencies that exist between various features of a product. A feature is defined as a distinct functionality or capability that provides value to users. A dependency, on the other hand, refers to the relationship between two or more features where the implementation or availability of one feature is dependent on the existence or functionality of another. By conducting Feature Dependency Analysis, product managers can gain insights into how each feature interacts with others and determine which features are essential for the proper functioning of the product. This analysis allows them to establish the order in which features should be developed or released, identify potential roadblocks or bottlenecks, and ensure that the development process is well-structured and efficient. During the analysis, product managers typically create a dependency map or matrix that visually represents the dependencies between features. This map serves as a reference point to understand the relationships and visualize any interdependencies among features. It helps identify critical features that must be implemented first, as well as features that can be developed in parallel or independently. Furthermore, the analysis helps mitigate risks and prevent unnecessary delays. By identifying feature dependencies upfront, product managers can proactively address potential conflicts or issues that may arise during the development process. They can allocate resources appropriately, plan for any necessary adjustments or workarounds, and ensure a smooth and seamless progression of feature development. In conclusion, Feature Dependency Analysis is a valuable tool in product management for understanding and managing the relationships and dependencies between various features of a product. It enables product managers to prioritize feature development, make informed decisions, and ensure the successful delivery of a high-quality product to the market.

Feature Dependency Mapping Tools

A feature dependency mapping tool is a solution that helps product managers understand and visualize the complex relationships between different features of a product or software. It enables them to identify and manage dependencies among various features to ensure a smooth and successful product development process. These tools provide a comprehensive overview of the interdependencies between different features, allowing product managers to analyze the impact of adding, modifying, or removing a specific feature on other features of the product. By mapping out these dependencies, product managers can make informed decisions, prioritize feature development, and plan product roadmaps more effectively.

Feature Dependency Mapping

Feature Dependency Mapping refers to the process of identifying and understanding the relationships and dependencies between different features or components of a product during the product management process. Product Managers often have to make decisions about which features should be prioritized for development, and understanding the dependencies between features is crucial in making these decisions. By mapping out the dependencies, Product Managers can gain insights into the impact that changes or additions to one feature may have on other features.

Feature Prioritization

Feature prioritization is a fundamental aspect of product management that involves determining the order in which product features should be developed, based on their importance, value, and alignment with business goals. It serves as a framework to guide the product team in making informed decisions about which features to focus on, given limited resources and time constraints. There are various methodologies and techniques that can be used for feature prioritization, such as the MoSCoW method, Kano model, and the Eisenhower matrix. These approaches help identify and evaluate features based on different criteria, such as user needs, market demand, technical feasibility, and potential impact on the business.

Feature Request Management

Feature request management is a crucial aspect of product management that involves effectively handling and prioritizing the suggestions, ideas, and requirements for new features from various stakeholders. It is the process of collecting, reviewing, organizing, and tracking feature requests to ensure that they align with the product vision, goals, and roadmap. During the feature request management process, product managers gather input from different sources such as customers, sales teams, support teams, and internal stakeholders. These requests can come in various forms, including direct communication, customer feedback channels, or even market research. Once the feature requests are received, product managers evaluate and categorize them based on various criteria such as impact, feasibility, alignment with business objectives, and customer needs. This evaluation ensures that the most valuable and feasible requests rise to the top and receive the necessary attention. Following the evaluation, the prioritization of feature requests becomes crucial. This involves assessing the potential benefits, impact, urgency, and strategic alignment of the requested features. Product managers need to consider the overall product strategy and roadmap, development resources, and market demand to determine which requests should be addressed first. After prioritization, the feature requests are then documented, tracked, and communicated to the necessary teams, including engineering, design, and QA. Clear communication ensures that everyone is aware of the requested features and their priority. It also enables cross-functional collaboration and facilitates alignment between different teams. Throughout the feature request management process, product managers engage in ongoing communication with stakeholders to provide updates on the status of feature requests. This transparency helps manage expectations and ensures that stakeholders are aware of the progress being made. In addition to prioritizing and managing incoming feature requests, product managers should also maintain a repository or backlog of requests that were not actively pursued. This allows for future reference and keeps track of valuable insights that could influence future product decisions. Overall, effective feature request management is crucial for product managers to balance the needs and expectations of various stakeholders while ensuring the long-term success and value of the product.

Feature Request Tracking

A feature request tracking is a process used in Product Management to gather, record, and manage customer requests for new features or enhancements to a product or service. It involves collecting, evaluating, prioritizing, and tracking these requests throughout their lifecycle. At the core of feature request tracking is the idea of bridging the gap between customers/users and the product development team. By capturing and organizing customer feedback and feature ideas, it ensures that product managers have a comprehensive view of customer needs and demands. Typically, the feature request tracking process starts with the collection of customer feedback. This can be done through various channels such as surveys, support tickets, user forums, or direct interactions. The feedback is then compiled and analyzed to identify recurring themes or patterns. Once the feedback is collected, the next step is to evaluate and prioritize the feature requests. This involves assessing factors like the impact on the user experience, market demand, business goals, technological feasibility, and resource constraints. Product managers collaborate with stakeholders, such as developers, designers, and executives, to determine which requests will be pursued and in what order. Once the feature requests are prioritized, they are tracked to ensure visibility and accountability. This can be done using a variety of tools, such as project management software or dedicated feature request tracking systems. These tools enable product managers to monitor the progress of each request, assign it to the appropriate teams, set deadlines, and communicate updates to stakeholders. Feature request tracking also involves communication with customers. Product managers may need to provide updates on the status of the requested features, seek clarifications or additional input, or notify customers about the implementation and release of requested features. Effective communication helps manage

41

customer expectations and fosters a sense of transparency and trust. In summary, feature request tracking is a vital component of Product Management, enabling product managers to capture and prioritize customer feedback and translate it into actionable features or enhancements. It facilitates collaboration, ensures transparency, and contributes to the overall success of the product or service.

Freemium Feature Management

Freemium feature management refers to the strategic management of features in a product that utilizes a freemium business model. Freemium, a combination of the words "free" and "premium," refers to a pricing model where the basic features of a product are offered for free, while advanced or premium features are available for a price. In the context of product management, freemium feature management involves a systematic approach to understanding, developing, and implementing features that drive user acquisition, engagement, and conversion in a freemium product. The first step in freemium feature management is identifying the core features that are offered for free. These features should provide enough value to attract and retain a significant number of users without requiring them to pay. It is important to strike a balance between the functionality of the free features and the value proposition of the premium features. Next, product managers need to define the premium features that will be offered for a price. These features should provide additional value or enhanced functionality that goes beyond the basic free features. Product managers may conduct market research, analyze user feedback, and consider industry best practices to identify the most compelling premium features. Once the core and premium features are defined, product managers need to prioritize the development and release of these features. They should consider factors such as user demand, technical feasibility, and potential revenue impact. Product managers may use techniques like feature prioritization frameworks, user surveys, and data analysis to inform their decisions. In addition to developing and releasing features, freemium feature management also involves ongoing monitoring and optimization. Product managers need to track user engagement, conversion rates, and customer feedback to assess the effectiveness of the features. They should regularly analyze data and iterate on the feature set to maximize user satisfaction and monetization. Overall, freemium feature management plays a crucial role in the success of freemium products. By carefully designing, developing, and optimizing the features, product managers can drive user adoption, engagement, and revenue growth in a sustainable manner.

Freemium Monetization Models

Freemium monetization models refer to a strategy in product management where a company offers both free and premium versions of a product or service. The concept behind freemium is to attract a large user base by providing a basic version of the product for free, while offering additional features or functionalities at a cost through a premium version or subscription plan. The free version of the product serves as a marketing tool, allowing users to experience the core value or benefits of the product without any financial commitment. This helps build brand awareness, generates interest, and drives user adoption. By eliminating the upfront cost barrier, companies can acquire a large number of users and create a network effect, where the value and usefulness of the product increases as more people use it. Once users are engaged and find value in the free version, the freemium model allows companies to convert a portion of these users into paying customers. This is achieved by offering additional features, enhanced functionality, or premium content that caters to the needs of more advanced users or those seeking a higher level of service. The premium version is typically priced at a level that provides an attractive value proposition compared to the free version. In order to successfully implement a freemium monetization model, product managers need to carefully balance the features and functionalities offered in the free version and determine which ones should be exclusive to the premium version. It is important to strike a balance where the free version provides enough value to attract and retain users, while the premium version offers compelling benefits that justify the cost. Frequent updates and enhancements to the product are crucial to maintain user engagement and drive conversion. It is important to continuously evaluate user feedback, monitor usage patterns, and gather data to optimize the pricing strategy and the feature set of both the free and premium versions.

Freemium Product Features

A freemium product is a type of product that offers both free and premium versions to users. In product management, freemium product features refer to the specific functionalities and capabilities that are included in the free version of the product, as well as any additional features that are unlocked when users upgrade to the paid or premium version. The purpose of offering freemium product features is to attract users to the product and provide them with a basic set of functionalities at no cost. This allows users to test out the product, get familiar with its capabilities, and evaluate its value before committing to a paid version. Freemium product features are typically designed to provide enough value to users to encourage them to continue using the product, while also enticing them to upgrade to the premium version for additional benefits. Freemium product features are carefully curated and strategically chosen to strike a balance between providing enough value to users in the free version and incentivizing them to upgrade. Product managers need to understand their target audience and their needs in order to determine which features should be included in the free version and which should be reserved for the premium version. The selection of freemium product features can be influenced by various factors, such as the competitive landscape, the target market's willingness to pay, and the overall product strategy. Product managers need to consider the perceived value of the features, the cost of implementing and maintaining them, and the impact on user acquisition and conversion to paid users when making decisions about which features to include in the free version.

Funnel Optimization Strategies

Funnel optimization strategies refer to the techniques and approaches implemented by product managers to improve the effectiveness and efficiency of the sales funnel. The sales funnel represents the journey that a customer takes from initial awareness of a product or service to the final purchase. It is a visual representation of the customer's decision-making process, divided into various stages or steps. The main goal of funnel optimization strategies is to identify and address any barriers or obstacles that may prevent potential customers from moving smoothly through the funnel. By optimizing each stage of the funnel, product managers aim to increase the conversion rates and ultimately generate more sales.

Go-To-Market Strategy

A Go-To-Market strategy, in the context of Product Management, refers to a plan of action formulated by a company to successfully introduce and promote a new product or service in the market. It encompasses a comprehensive set of activities and tactics designed to maximize the product's potential for success, such as identifying target customers, positioning the product, setting effective pricing and distribution strategies, and creating an impactful marketing campaign. The first crucial step in developing a Go-To-Market strategy is to understand the target market and the specific needs and preferences of the customers within that market. This involves conducting thorough market research, analyzing competitor offerings, and gathering customer insights. By gaining a deep understanding of the market dynamics and customer demands, companies can make informed decisions about how to position their product to stand out from competitors and resonate with the target audience. Once the target market is defined, the pricing and distribution strategies can be determined. This involves setting an optimal price that aligns with the perceived value of the product, while also considering factors such as production costs, competitor pricing, and target customer affordability. Additionally, deciding on the most effective distribution channels, such as direct sales or partnerships with retailers, is crucial for ensuring the product reaches the intended customers efficiently. An integral part of the Go-To-Market strategy is the development of a compelling marketing campaign. This includes creating a strong brand identity, crafting key messages and value propositions that resonate with customers, and selecting appropriate marketing channels to reach the target audience effectively. Social media, content marketing, advertising, and public relations activities are often employed to create awareness, generate interest, and drive demand for the product. Throughout the execution of the Go-To-Market strategy, constant monitoring and evaluation are essential to gauge the effectiveness of the implemented tactics and make necessary adjustments. By measuring key performance indicators, such as sales revenue, market share, and customer feedback, companies can identify areas of improvement and refine their strategy accordingly.

Idea Management

Idea management in the context of product management refers to the structured process of collecting, evaluating, and implementing new ideas and suggestions for product improvements or innovations. It involves the systematic handling of ideas from various sources, such as customers, employees, and external stakeholders, with the goal of driving product innovation and enhancing overall business growth. The process of idea management typically begins with idea generation, where ideas are collected from diverse sources. This can be done through brainstorming sessions, suggestion boxes, open innovation platforms, or other means of soliciting ideas. The collected ideas are then reviewed and evaluated based on predefined criteria such as feasibility, market potential, alignment with strategic objectives, and resource availability. Once the ideas have been evaluated, the selected ideas are further developed into concrete concepts or prototypes. This stage involves shaping the initial ideas into more tangible forms that can be tested and validated. Iterative feedback loops may be incorporated at this stage to refine and improve the concepts before moving forward. After concept development, the next step in idea management is prioritization. This involves assessing and ranking the concepts based on their potential impact, strategic fit, technical feasibility, cost implications, and other relevant factors. Prioritizing ideas helps allocate resources effectively and focus on the most promising concepts that align with the company's objectives. Once the ideas have been prioritized, they are further refined into actionable projects or initiatives. This includes defining specific objectives, goals, and deliverables for each idea, as well as allocating necessary resources and forming cross-functional teams to drive implementation. Idea management is an ongoing process that requires effective communication, collaboration, and engagement across different stakeholders. It is not solely about generating ideas, but also about nurturing and developing those ideas into successful products or innovations. By actively managing ideas, organizations can tap into the collective creativity of their employees and customers, and leverage external insights to continuously drive product improvements and stay ahead of the competition.

Idea Prioritization Voting

Idea Prioritization Voting is a process commonly used in Product Management to determine the most valuable ideas or features to develop and incorporate into a product or service. This process involves gathering input and feedback from various stakeholders, such as customers, internal teams, and executives, and conducting a structured voting system to rank and prioritize the ideas based on their importance and potential impact. The goal of Idea Prioritization Voting is to ensure that the limited resources of a company are allocated to the most valuable and impactful ideas. By involving multiple stakeholders in the decision-making process, it helps to avoid biases and create a more objective and data-driven approach to prioritize ideas.

Idea Scoring

Idea scoring, in the context of Product Management, refers to the systematic process of evaluating and ranking ideas based on their potential for success and alignment with the overall product strategy. It helps product managers prioritize ideas and determine which ones are worth pursuing further. The goal of idea scoring is to objectively assess the feasibility, market potential, and strategic fit of each idea, taking into consideration factors such as customer needs, competitive landscape, resource availability, and business goals. It allows product managers to make data-driven decisions and allocate resources effectively to the most promising ideas.

Idea Submission Forms

An Idea Submission Form in the context of Product Management is a structured document used to collect, organize, and evaluate ideas from various stakeholders within an organization. It serves as a standard format for individuals or teams to submit their ideas, suggestions, or proposals related to product improvements, new features, or entirely new product concepts. The purpose of an Idea Submission Form is to provide a systematic and efficient way to capture and evaluate ideas in order to make informed decisions about which ideas have the most potential and align with the product strategy and goals. The form typically includes a set of predefined fields that ask for specific information about the idea, such as: 1. Title: A concise and descriptive title that reflects the essence of the idea. 2. Description: A detailed explanation of the idea, including its intended impact, target audience, and potential benefits. 3. Justification: The rationale behind the idea, including any market research, customer feedback, or business insights that support it. 4. Resources Required: An estimation of the resources (e.g., time, budget, personnel) needed to implement the idea. 5. Risks and Mitigations: Any potential risks or challenges associated with executing the idea and proposed solutions to mitigate them. 6. Expected Outcomes: The anticipated results or outcomes if the idea is implemented successfully. 7. Stakeholder Analysis: A consideration of the key stakeholders who will be affected by or involved in the idea's implementation. 8. Submission Date: The date when the idea was submitted. By using an Idea Submission Form, product managers can streamline the evaluation process and ensure that all ideas are evaluated based on consistent criteria. It also promotes transparency and inclusivity, as anyone within the organization can submit their ideas and have them considered for implementation. Once the forms are collected, product managers can review and prioritize the ideas based on factors such as alignment with the product vision, strategic objectives, feasibility, potential impact, and available resources. The most promising ideas can then be further developed, refined, and potentially integrated into the product roadmap. Overall, Idea Submission Forms provide a structured framework to gather and evaluate ideas, facilitating effective decision-making and empowering teams to contribute to the continuous improvement and innovation of products and services.

Idea Validation Experiment Platforms

Idea validation experiment platforms refer to software or online tools specifically designed for product management professionals to quickly and effectively validate their ideas before investing time and resources into developing a new product or feature. These platforms typically provide a range of features and functionalities that can help product managers collect valuable feedback, analyze market demand, and assess the viability of their ideas. By using such platforms, product managers can minimize the risks associated with launching a new product or feature that may not resonate with the target market or fail to meet their expectations.

Idea Validation Experiments

Idea validation experiments are a set of structured tests and research activities conducted by product managers to assess the viability and potential success of a new product or feature concept. These experiments aim to gather feedback and data from target users, stakeholders, and other relevant sources in order to make informed decisions about whether to pursue or modify the idea. The purpose of conducting idea validation experiments is to reduce the risk associated with investing time, resources, and effort into developing a product that may not meet user needs or bring desired outcomes. These experiments help product managers to understand the market demand, potential customer base, competitive landscape, and overall feasibility of the idea. By systematically testing hypotheses and gathering data, product managers can make data-driven decisions about the future of the product concept. Idea validation experiments typically involve various research methods, such as user interviews, surveys, prototype testing, and market analysis. Through user interviews, product managers can gain insights into user preferences, pain points, and desired features. Surveys can be used to collect quantitative data and measure interest and willingness to pay for the product. Prototype testing allows product managers to gather user feedback on the functionality, usability, and desirability of the product. Market analysis helps assess the competitive landscape, target market size, and potential barriers to entry. By conducting these experiments, product managers can gather feedback and data that will help them answer critical questions, such as whether there is a market need for the product, whether the target audience is willing to pay for it, and whether the product idea aligns with the company's strategic goals. The insights gained from idea validation experiments provide a solid foundation for making informed decisions about the next steps in product development, such as refining the concept, adjusting the features, or even pivoting to a different direction.

Idea Validation

Idea validation, in the context of product management, refers to the process of testing and evaluating a potential product or feature concept to determine its viability and potential success in the market. It involves gathering data and feedback from target users, customers, and stakeholders to assess the demand, feasibility, and potential impact of the idea. During idea validation, product managers aim to validate several aspects of the concept, including its problem-solution fit, market demand, customer needs, and potential value proposition. The goal is to gather evidence and insights to determine whether the idea is worth pursuing further, refining, or discarding.

Idea Voting

Idea voting is a process in product management where stakeholders and team members are given the opportunity to express their preferences and opinions about different ideas or options for a product. It is a tool used to gather feedback and insights to prioritize and make informed decisions. The purpose of idea voting is to involve the relevant parties in the decision-making process, ensuring that the final choices reflect the input and consensus of the group. By allowing individuals to express their preferences, idea voting encourages participation, collaboration, and a sense of ownership among team members. During idea voting, stakeholders and team members are typically presented with a set of options or ideas and are asked to evaluate and rank them based on criteria such as feasibility, strategic alignment, customer desirability, and business impact. This evaluation can be done through various methods, including online surveys, in-person meetings, or specialized software tools. Idea voting provides several benefits to the product management process. Firstly, it helps surface valuable insights and perspectives from different stakeholders, ensuring that product decisions are well-rounded and consider various viewpoints. Additionally, idea voting helps identify the most promising ideas or options, enabling teams to focus their efforts and resources on the most impactful initiatives. Furthermore, idea voting fosters transparency and trust within the organization by providing a structured and fair evaluation process. It allows everyone to have a voice and contributes to a culture of collaboration and collective decision-making. This inclusiveness also boosts team morale and engagement, as individuals feel valued and heard. Overall, idea voting is a valuable tool in product management as it enables teams to harness the collective intelligence of stakeholders and team members, prioritize effectively, and make informed decisions that align with business goals and customer needs.

In-App Feedback Collection Widgets

In-App Feedback Collection Widgets refer to the user interface components within a mobile application that prompt and facilitate the collection of feedback from users. These widgets are typically embedded within the application's interface and allow users to provide their thoughts, suggestions, and comments directly to the product management team. The main purpose of In-App Feedback Collection Widgets is to actively engage users and capture their feedback in real-time while they are using the application. By integrating these widgets seamlessly into the user experience, product managers can gather valuable insights and enhance their understanding of user needs, preferences, and pain points.

In-App Feedback Collection

In-App Feedback Collection refers to the process of gathering feedback directly from users within a mobile application. It involves soliciting and capturing users' opinions, suggestions, and concerns about the app's features, usability, performance, and overall user experience. Product Managers utilize In-App Feedback Collection as a valuable tool to understand and address user needs, enhance app functionality, and guide decision-making in their product development lifecycle. By integrating feedback mechanisms into the app, Product Managers empower users to share their insights and provide valuable input that can drive product improvements.

In-App Feedback Widgets

In-App Feedback Widgets are user interface components implemented within a software product to gather feedback directly from users while they are actively engaging with the application. These widgets provide a convenient and accessible way for users to express their thoughts, opinions, and suggestions about the product, allowing the product management team to collect valuable insights and make data-driven decisions. From a product management perspective, In-App Feedback Widgets serve as an essential tool for understanding user needs, preferences, and pain points. By placing these widgets directly within the application, users can easily provide feedback without having to navigate to external platforms or resort to alternative communication channels. This convenience facilitates a higher response rate and ensures that the feedback received is more relevant and timely.

Indirect Sales

Indirect sales, in the context of product management, refers to the distribution and selling of products through intermediaries or third-party channels rather than directly to the end users or customers. It involves using a network of resellers, dealers, distributors, or other intermediaries who act as the bridge between the manufacturer or producer and the end consumer. With indirect sales, the manufacturer or producer relies on these intermediaries to market, promote, sell, and distribute their products to the target market. This enables the manufacturer to reach a larger customer base, expand into new markets, and increase sales without the need for direct involvement in every sale. Indirect sales can be advantageous for product managers and manufacturers in several ways. First, it allows them to tap into the existing networks, expertise, and resources of the intermediaries, which can help in reaching customers more efficiently and effectively. The intermediaries have established relationships with the target market and possess valuable knowledge about customer preferences, needs, and behaviors. Second, indirect sales can help reduce costs and risks associated with direct selling. Instead of investing in setting up and managing a direct sales force, product managers can leverage the established distribution channels and sales networks of intermediaries. This can result in significant cost savings in terms of recruitment, training, salaries, and other overhead expenses. Third, indirect sales can enable product managers to focus more on their core competencies, such as product development, innovation, and customer insights, rather than getting involved in the intricacies of sales and distribution. By relying on intermediaries, they can offload the responsibilities of sales and focus on driving product strategy, differentiation, and competitive advantage. In conclusion, indirect sales in product management refers to the use of intermediaries or third-party channels to distribute and sell products on behalf of the manufacturer or producer. It offers benefits such as leveraging existing networks, reducing costs, and allowing product managers to focus on core competencies. Overall, indirect sales is an important strategy for expanding market reach and driving sales growth in the competitive business landscape.

Influencer Identification

Influencer identification in the context of Product Management refers to the process of identifying individuals or organizations that have significant impact and influence over a target market or specific customer segment. These influencers possess the ability to shape the opinions, preferences, and purchasing decisions of their followers or audience. The identification of influencers is a crucial task for product managers as it allows them to understand the key players within a particular market and strategically engage with them to promote their products or services. By collaborating with influencers, product managers can leverage their credibility, reach, and expertise to build brand awareness, create positive associations, and ultimately drive customer adoption and loyalty. Effective influencer identification involves a systematic approach that combines various methods and techniques such as social media analysis, market research, customer insights, and industry knowledge. Product managers typically employ the following steps to identify influencers: 1. Define the target audience: Product managers first need to define the specific target market or customer segment they wish to focus on. This includes identifying demographics, interests, behaviors, and relevant industry or niche communities. 2. Conduct research: Product managers then gather data and insights about the target audience to understand their preferences, influencers they follow, and the platforms they engage with. This may involve analyzing social media profiles, monitoring conversations, and employing tools and technology to track online activities. 3. Analyze influence metrics: Product managers utilize various influence metrics to assess the impact and relevance of potential influencers. These metrics may include follower count, engagement rate, reach, credibility, and resonance within the target market. 4. Evaluate alignment: Product managers evaluate the alignment between the influencer's values, audience interests, and the product or brand they represent. This ensures that the influencer is a suitable fit for promoting the product and can effectively communicate its value to their audience. 5. Engage and build relationships: Once influencers are identified, product managers establish relationships with them through collaborations, partnerships, and targeted marketing campaigns. This involves negotiating terms, defining objectives, and providing necessary support to maximize the impact of influencer-led promotions. By effectively identifying influencers, product managers can capitalize on their ability to influence customer behavior and drive product success. It allows them to tap into existing communities, build trust, and generate authentic recommendations that resonate with their target audience.

Influencer Marketing Platforms

In the context of product management, influencer marketing platforms can be defined as online platforms that connect product managers with influencers or social media influencers for the purpose of promoting their products or services. These platforms facilitate the collaboration between product managers and influencers by providing a centralized space for them to connect, negotiate, and track the progress of influencer marketing campaigns. Influencer marketing platforms typically offer a range of features and functionalities that help product managers streamline their influencer marketing efforts. These may include: 1. Search and Discovery: Influencer marketing platforms allow product managers to search and discover influencers based on various criteria such as niche, audience demographics, location, and social media platforms. This helps product managers find influencers who align with their target market and brand values. 2. Influencer Outreach: These platforms provide a messaging system or direct contact information to reach out to influencers and initiate collaborations. Product managers can send personalized messages or collaboration proposals to influencers and negotiate terms such as compensation, content requirements, and campaign timelines. 3. Campaign Management: Influencer marketing platforms offer tools to manage and track influencer marketing campaigns. Product managers can set campaign goals, define key performance indicators (KPIs), and monitor the progress of campaigns in real-time. They can also track the performance of individual influencers and measure the return on investment (ROI) of their influencer marketing efforts. 4. Content Management: These platforms often include content creation and management tools. Product managers can provide influencers with guidelines, brand assets, and content templates to ensure consistency and quality in the content produced. They can also review and approve the content before it is published. Overall, influencer marketing platforms enable product managers to leverage the reach, credibility, and influence of social media influencers to promote their products or services. By providing a platform for seamless collaboration and campaign management, these platforms empower product managers to effectively execute and track influencer marketing campaigns, ultimately driving brand awareness, engagement, and sales.

Influencer Marketing

Influencer Marketing is a strategic approach in Product Management that involves collaborating with individuals who have a significant online presence and a large following in a specific niche. These individuals, known as influencers, have the ability to sway the purchasing decisions of their followers through their expertise, credibility, and online influence. The main objective of influencer marketing in Product Management is to leverage the influencers' reach and impact to promote and endorse a product or brand. This is done through various strategies such as sponsored content, product reviews, brand mentions, and social media collaborations.

KPI Monitoring

KPI Monitoring, also known as Key Performance Indicator Monitoring, is a crucial aspect of Product Management that involves tracking and analyzing predefined performance metrics to measure the success and effectiveness of a product or service. Product Managers use KPI Monitoring to gain insights into how well a product or service is performing, identify areas for improvement, and make data-driven decisions to drive the product's growth and success. By regularly monitoring and analyzing KPIs, Product Managers can assess the impact of their strategies, initiatives, and changes made to the product, and gauge whether they are achieving the desired outcomes.

Kanban Board Visualization

Kanban Board Visualization is a visual method used in Product Management to visually represent and track the progress and status of tasks within a project or workflow. It provides a clear and concise view of the work that needs to be done, work in progress, and work that has been completed. A Kanban Board typically consists of columns that represent different stages or statuses of the tasks or items being tracked. The columns are typically labeled with headers such as "To-Do," "In Progress," and "Done." Each task or item is represented by a card or sticky note that is placed in the appropriate column based on its current status.

Kanban Board

A Kanban board is a visual tool used in Product Management to manage and track tasks within a project or workflow. It is designed to provide a clear and easy-to-understand representation of work progress, enabling teams to work more efficiently and prioritize tasks effectively. The Kanban board consists of columns and cards, where each column represents a stage in the workflow, and each card represents an individual task or work item. The columns typically include stages such as "To Do," "In Progress," "Review," and "Done," but can be customized to fit the specific needs of the project or team. Team members use the Kanban board to move cards across the columns as they progress through the workflow. For example, when a task is started, the corresponding card is moved from the "To Do" column to the "In Progress" column. This visual representation allows everyone involved to quickly understand the status of each task and identify any bottlenecks or blockers that may be impeding progress. The Kanban board also helps with task prioritization. By having a clear overview of all tasks and their respective stages, teams can easily identify which tasks need immediate attention and which ones can be deprioritized until later. This ensures that resources are allocated to the most critical tasks and that work is completed in a timely manner. In addition to its visual representation, the Kanban board can also include additional information on the cards themselves. This can include details such as task descriptions, due dates, assignees, and any dependencies or related tasks. By having all relevant information readily available, team members can quickly grasp the context of each task and make informed decisions on how to proceed. Overall, the Kanban board is a powerful tool for Product Management as it provides a clear visual representation of work progress, facilitates task prioritization, and enhances communication and collaboration within the team. By utilizing a Kanban board, teams can improve productivity, reduce waste, and deliver value to customers more efficiently.

Kanban Boards

A Kanban board is a visual tool that is used in product management to track work items and provide a clear and transparent overview of the progress of tasks in a project or workflow. It is a representation of a work pipeline or project plan, divided into different stages or columns, with work items or tasks represented as cards that move across the board as they are completed or progress through different stages. The main purpose of a Kanban board is to provide a visual representation of the work that needs to be done, the work that is currently in progress, and the work that has been completed. This allows product managers and teams to easily track and monitor the progress of tasks and identify any bottlenecks or areas where work might be getting stuck. The visual nature of the board provides a clear and concise overview of the project status, making it easier for the team to plan and prioritize their work.

Kanban Method

The Kanban Method is a visual project management system that enables product teams to manage and optimize their workflow effectively. It provides a visual representation of tasks, known as cards, moving through various stages of development, allowing teams to easily track progress and identify bottlenecks. The primary goal of the Kanban Method in the context of Product Management is to maximize efficiency and deliver value to customers by streamlining the flow of work. It achieves this by imposing limits on the number of tasks that can be in progress at any given time, fostering a focus on completing work before accepting new tasks.

Kanban

Kanban is a visual project management tool that helps product managers and their teams efficiently manage and track work in progress. Derived from the Japanese word for "signboard" or "billboard," Kanban provides a clear and transparent way to visualize the flow of tasks and improve workflow efficiency. At its core, Kanban consists of a board divided into columns representing different stages of the project or task lifecycle. Each task, represented by a card, moves through these columns from left to right as it progresses towards completion. This visual representation enables product managers to identify bottlenecks, prioritize work, and ensure a smooth and steady workflow.

Label Design Optimization

Label design optimization in the context of Product Management refers to the process of improving the design of a product label to enhance its effectiveness in communicating key information and attracting the target audience. The goal of label design optimization is to create a visually appealing, informative, and persuasive label that effectively communicates the product's attributes, benefits, and usage instructions. It involves understanding the needs and preferences of the target market, as well as complying with legal and regulatory requirements.

Landing Page Optimization

Landing Page Optimization refers to the process of improving the performance and effectiveness of a landing page with the goal of increasing conversions or desired actions from visitors. This optimization focuses on enhancing the layout, content, design, and overall user experience of the landing page to maximize its impact and achieve the desired business objectives. A landing page is a specific web page that is created with the purpose of capturing leads or driving a specific action from visitors, such as making a purchase, signing up for a newsletter, or filling out a form. It is typically designed to be highly focused, with a clear call to action and minimal distractions, in order to encourage visitors to take the desired action. Landing Page Optimization involves analyzing and understanding user behavior, preferences, and expectations to identify areas for improvement and implement changes that can lead to better results. This optimization process can include conducting A/B testing, user testing, and data analysis to gather insights and make informed decisions on changes to be made. The optimization efforts can involve various aspects of the landing page, such as the headline, subheadings, body text, images, forms, buttons, and navigation. It aims to create a seamless and engaging user experience that addresses the visitor's needs and motivations, while aligning with the overall brand message and marketing objectives. Effective Landing Page Optimization can help increase conversion rates, improve lead generation, and ultimately drive business growth. It enables product managers and marketers to make data-driven decisions and continuously iterate on the landing page to achieve better results.

Lead Generation Tactics

Lead generation tactics in the context of product management refer to the strategies and actions implemented to identify and attract potential customers or leads for a particular product or service. These tactics are essential for product managers to generate interest and capture qualified leads, ultimately driving revenue and business growth. The primary goal of lead generation tactics is to increase the number of targeted individuals or organizations who are interested in a specific product. Product managers utilize various methods to achieve this objective, such as: 1. Content Marketing: Creating and distributing valuable and relevant content, such as blog posts, articles, and videos, to attract potential leads. This tactic aims to provide informative and helpful resources that address the pain points or challenges of the target audience, positioning the product as a solution. 2. Social Media Marketing: Leveraging social media platforms to engage with prospects, build brand awareness, and share product information. Product managers can utilize both organic posts and paid advertising to reach a wider audience and generate leads. 3. Email Marketing: Building an email list of interested individuals or organizations and sending targeted email campaigns to nurture leads. This includes sharing product updates, offering exclusive content, or providing discounts and promotions to encourage conversions. 4. Search Engine Optimization (SEO): Optimizing product-related web pages and content to appear higher in search engine results. By improving visibility in search engines like Google, product managers can attract organic traffic and increase the likelihood of capturing leads. 5. Referral Programs: Implementing referral programs that incentivize existing customers or advocates to recommend the product to their network. This tactic taps into the power of word-of-mouth marketing and leverages existing customers' trust and satisfaction to generate new leads. Overall, lead generation tactics in product management play a crucial role in identifying and attracting potential customers. By strategically implementing these tactics, product managers can increase brand exposure, build a pipeline of qualified leads, and drive business growth.

Lead Generation

Lead generation in the context of product management refers to the process of identifying and attracting potential customers or leads for a specific product or service. It involves gathering information about individuals or organizations that have shown interest in the product and converting them into sales opportunities. The ultimate goal of lead generation is to increase the number of qualified leads, which can then be passed on to the sales team for further nurturing and conversion. In order to generate leads, product managers utilize various strategies and tactics. This typically involves creating targeted marketing campaigns, developing compelling content, leveraging social media platforms, and continuously analyzing and optimizing lead generation efforts. By understanding the target audience and their needs, product managers can effectively tailor their messaging and optimize their marketing channels to attract the right leads.

Lead Nurturing Workflows

Lead nurturing workflows in the context of product management refer to the automated processes and strategies implemented to guide potential customers through their journey from initial interest to final purchase. These workflows involve a series of targeted and personalized communications that are designed to nurture and cultivate leads, with the ultimate goal of converting them into paying customers. The lead nurturing process typically starts with capturing leads through various channels such as website forms, landing pages, or lead generation campaigns. Once leads are captured, they are then segmented based on criteria such as demographic information, behavior, or interest, in order to tailor the subsequent communication and content to their specific needs and preferences.

Lead Nurturing

Lead nurturing is a key aspect of Product Management that involves building and maintaining relationships with potential customers throughout their buying journey. It is a strategic process aimed at guiding leads through the sales funnel, from initial awareness to final conversion. The goal of lead nurturing is to educate and engage potential customers, providing them with relevant and valuable information at each stage of the buying process. This helps to build trust, establish credibility, and ultimately, drive conversions. Product Managers play a crucial role in developing and implementing effective lead nurturing strategies.

Lead Scoring Algorithms

Lead scoring algorithms are analytical models used in product management to prioritize and rank potential customers, or leads, based on their likelihood to convert into paying customers. The algorithms assign a numerical score to each lead based on a combination of demographic, behavioral, and firmographic data. The purpose of lead scoring algorithms is to help product managers efficiently allocate their limited resources and focus their efforts on leads that are most likely to result in a sale. By using data-driven models, product managers can objectively evaluate leads and prioritize their follow-up actions to maximize conversions.

Lead Scoring Methodologies

Lead scoring methodologies refer to the systematic approach used by product management teams to rank and prioritize potential customers or leads based on their level of interest and likelihood to make a purchase. It involves assigning numeric values or scores to different lead attributes such as demographic information, behavior, and engagement with the company's marketing and sales activities. The purpose of lead scoring is to help product management teams identify and focus on the most promising leads, allowing them to allocate their resources efficiently and effectively. By implementing lead scoring methodologies, product management teams can prioritize leads that are more likely to generate a positive return on investment and reduce time and effort spent on leads that are less likely to convert.

Lead Scoring

Lead scoring is a widely-used method in Product Management that assigns a numerical value to potential customers based on their actions and behaviors, allowing companies to prioritize and target those leads that are more likely to convert into paying customers. By implementing a lead scoring system, Product Managers can track and analyze various data points, such as website browsing behavior, email engagement, and social media interactions, to assess the quality and potential value of each lead. These data points are typically weighted and combined into a single lead score, which helps Product Managers identify and focus their efforts on the most promising leads.

Lean Canvas Creation Tools

Lean Canvas creation tools are software or platforms designed to facilitate the creation and management of Lean Canvas documents. Lean Canvas is a strategic tool used in product management to visualize and communicate the key components of a business idea or product concept. It is a one-page framework that enables product managers and entrepreneurs to outline and validate their hypotheses and assumptions. The Lean Canvas creation tools allow users to digitally create and update Lean Canvas documents. These tools typically come with pre-built templates and drag-and-drop functionalities, making it easier for users to populate the canvas with relevant information. The tools also provide various features and capabilities to enhance the user experience and facilitate collaboration among team members. In the context of product management, Lean Canvas creation tools offer several benefits. Firstly, they provide a structured and organized format for capturing the key elements of a product concept, such as customer segments, problem statements, value propositions, and revenue streams. This helps product managers distill complex ideas into concise and actionable components. Secondly, Lean Canvas creation tools enable product managers to iterate and refine their business models quickly. By allowing easy modifications and updates to the canvas, these tools support the agile and iterative nature of product development. Product managers can test and validate their hypotheses, make necessary adjustments, and pivot their strategies based on feedback and insights. Thirdly, Lean Canvas creation tools enhance collaboration and enable cross-functional teams to work together effectively. By providing a central platform for sharing and reviewing the Lean Canvas, these tools promote transparency and alignment within the team. Users can invite team members, stakeholders, and subject matter experts to contribute their inputs and perspectives, fostering a collaborative and iterative approach to product management. Overall, Lean Canvas creation tools play a crucial role in streamlining the process of developing, validating, and communicating product concepts. They provide a user-friendly interface for creating and managing Lean Canvas documents, offer flexibility for iterations and refinements, and support collaboration among product teams. By leveraging these tools, product managers can effectively articulate their ideas, align their teams, and make informed decisions to drive product success.

Lean Canvas Templates

Lean Canvas is a strategic management and planning tool that facilitates the development and validation of a product or business idea. It is widely used in the field of product management to organize thoughts, gather feedback, and iterate on a product's value proposition and business model. The Lean Canvas template, introduced by Ash Maurya, is a simplified version of the traditional business plan. It condenses the essential elements needed to build a viable product and achieve product-market fit, making it easier to communicate and collaborate with stakeholders, investors, and team members. The Lean Canvas consists of nine sections, each focusing on a different aspect of the product's development and delivery. These sections are: Problem, Customer Segments, Unique Value Proposition, Solution, Key Metrics, Channels, Cost Structure, Revenue Streams, and Unfair Advantage. By addressing each section, product managers are able to define and refine their product in a structured manner. The Problem section helps identify specific customer challenges or pain points that the product aims to solve. Customer Segments define the target audience and potential customer personas. The Unique Value Proposition describes the product's key advantages over competitors and why customers would choose it. The Solution section presents the product features and solutions in response to the identified problem. The Key Metrics section focuses on the core metrics that will be used to measure the product's success and performance. Channels refer to the different distribution and marketing channels that will be utilized to reach customers. Cost Structure outlines the various costs associated with developing, marketing, and maintaining the product, while Revenue Streams identify the sources of income or monetization strategies. Lastly, the Unfair Advantage section highlights any unique assets, intellectual property, or expertise that give the product a competitive edge. The Lean Canvas is a dynamic tool that encourages continuous learning and iteration throughout the product development process. It allows product managers to quickly evaluate and pivot their strategies based on feedback and market insights, leading to more effective decision-making and product-market fit. By using Lean Canvas, product managers can efficiently validate assumptions, identify risks, and align their product vision with customer needs.

Lean Product Management Workshops

Lean Product Management Workshops are structured sessions designed to help product managers learn and apply the principles and practices of lean product management. This approach emphasizes a customer-centric mindset, iterative development, and continuous improvement in order to create and deliver products that meet customer needs and drive business value. During these workshops, product managers engage in hands-on activities and collaborative exercises to gain a deep understanding of lean product management concepts and techniques. They learn how to define and validate customer problems, prioritize product features, conduct experiments, and gather feedback to make data-driven decisions. The workshops also provide opportunities for participants to practice applying these principles and techniques to real-life product management challenges. By attending Lean Product Management Workshops, product managers can enhance their skills and knowledge in areas such as customer empathy, rapid experimentation, and effective prioritization. They learn how to identify and validate customer problems, refine product ideas, and develop minimum viable products (MVPs) that can be quickly tested and iterated upon. This iterative approach enables product managers to minimize wasted effort and resources, while maximizing the chances of success for their products. The workshops also focus on fostering a culture of continuous learning and improvement within product teams. Participants learn how to gather and analyze user feedback, make data-driven decisions, and adapt their product strategies based on changing market conditions. They also gain insights into effective collaboration and communication techniques that help facilitate cross-functional alignment and drive product success.

Lean Product Management

Lean Product Management is a methodology based on the Lean Startup principles, that aims to maximize value creation by focusing on continuous learning and feedback-driven development. It is a customer-centric approach to product management that emphasizes quick experimentation, iterative improvement, and efficient resource allocation. The key idea behind Lean Product Management is to eliminate waste and minimize risks by identifying and validating assumptions early in the product development process. It encourages product managers to prioritize learning over execution and emphasizes the importance of data-driven decision-making.

Lean Startup Principles

The Lean Startup principles are a set of guidelines that are widely used in the field of product management. They aim to help product managers build successful products by focusing on experimentation, validated learning, and iterative development. At its core, the Lean Startup principles emphasize the importance of learning from customer feedback and using that feedback to make continuous improvements to a product. This approach encourages product managers to test their assumptions and hypotheses early and often, rather than making big bets based on untested assumptions. One key principle of the Lean Startup is the concept of "validated learning." This means that product managers should focus on designing experiments that help them quickly and accurately learn about their customers' needs and preferences. By gathering data and feedback from real customers, product managers can validate or invalidate their assumptions, and make informed decisions about the direction of the product. Another important principle is the idea of "iterative development." Instead of trying to build a perfect product from the start, the Lean Startup encourages product managers to create minimum viable products (MVPs) that can be tested and refined. By releasing MVPs early and often, product managers can gather feedback, learn from their customers, and iterate on the product to meet their needs. The Lean Startup principles also advocate for a process of continuous improvement and adaptation. This means that product managers should be open to change and willing to pivot if they discover that their initial assumptions were incorrect. By embracing a flexible mindset and being open to feedback, product managers can adjust their strategies and make better decisions based on real-world data.

MQL And SQL Definition

53

MQL (Marketing Qualified Lead) is a term used in Product Management to describe a potential customer who has shown interest in a company's product or service, and has been identified as a potential sales opportunity. MQLs are individuals or organizations that have engaged with marketing efforts, such as filling out a form, downloading a whitepaper, or attending a webinar, and have met specific criteria that indicate they could be a good fit for the product or service being offered. MQLs are typically passed from marketing to sales teams for further nurturing and qualification before being converted into a sales opportunity or a customer. SQL (Sales Qualified Lead), on the other hand, refers to a potential customer who has been identified by the sales team as ready and likely to make a purchase. SQLs have completed the marketing qualification process and have been further vetted by the sales team to ensure they match the ideal customer profile and have expressed a strong intent to purchase. SQLs are considered higher-quality leads compared to MQLs as they have shown stronger interest and higher readiness to make a purchase. Sales teams prioritize SQLs for immediate sales engagement, focusing their efforts on closing the deal.

MVP Testing Frameworks

MVP testing frameworks refer to a set of methodologies, tools, and processes used by product management teams to test the minimum viable product (MVP) of a product or service. An MVP is an early version of a product that is developed with minimal features and functionality. The goal of testing an MVP is to gather feedback from users and stakeholders in order to refine and improve the product before a full-scale release. The use of testing frameworks in the context of MVPs is crucial for product management teams to effectively validate assumptions, identify potential issues, and make informed decisions about the product's development and future iterations. These frameworks typically include a combination of qualitative and quantitative research methods, as well as testing techniques specific to the MVP concept.

MVP Testing Platforms

MVP testing platforms refer to software tools or platforms that are used by product managers to test and validate minimum viable products (MVPs). MVPs are the stripped-down versions of a product that are developed with minimal features and functionalities, aiming to collect feedback from users and validate assumptions before investing significant resources in building a fully functional product. The primary purpose of using MVP testing platforms is to gather insights and feedback from real users in order to make data-driven decisions about the product's development. These platforms provide product managers with a range of tools and features to design experiments, define metrics, collect user feedback, and analyze data to make informed decisions.

Management (CRM) Systems

A Customer Relationship Management (CRM) system in the context of Product Management refers to a software tool or platform that allows businesses to effectively manage, organize, and analyze their interactions and relationships with their customers. A CRM system acts as a central repository for all customer-related data and activities, providing product managers with a holistic view of their customers' interactions, preferences, and needs. It helps product managers to streamline their processes, improve customer satisfaction, and ultimately drive business growth. With a CRM system, product managers can store and access important customer information such as contact details, purchase history, support tickets, and feedback. This allows them to have a comprehensive understanding of their customers and personalize their products or services accordingly. One of the key benefits of a CRM system in Product Management is the ability to track customer interactions and engagements throughout the product lifecycle. Product managers can record customer interactions at various touchpoints such as website visits, email communications, social media interactions, and customer support requests. This helps them to identify patterns, capture customer feedback, and make data-driven decisions to optimize their products. CRM systems also facilitate effective communication and collaboration within product management teams. By providing a centralized platform for tracking customer data, tasks, and communications, CRM systems enable product managers to collaborate on customer-related activities, share insights, and ensure consistent and informed decision-making. Furthermore, CRM systems provide valuable analytics and reporting capabilities to product managers. These tools allow product managers to analyze customer data, identify trends, and evaluate the success of product launches or marketing campaigns. By leveraging these insights, product managers can make data-driven decisions, refine their product strategy, and drive customer satisfaction and loyalty. In conclusion, a CRM system in the context of Product Management is a software tool or platform that enables product managers to effectively manage and analyze their interactions with customers. It serves as a central repository for customer-related data, helps track customer interactions and engagements, facilitates team collaboration, and provides analytics and reporting capabilities to drive informed decision-making.

Market Entry Assessments

Market Entry Assessments are strategic evaluations conducted by Product Managers to determine the feasibility and potential success of entering a new market with a product or service. These assessments involve analyzing various factors including market dynamics, customer needs, competition, regulatory environment, and potential risks to make informed decisions about entering a new market. The goal is to assess the market's attractiveness and identify potential barriers to entry. Market Entry Assessments typically begin with defining the target market and conducting thorough market research to understand customer preferences, behavior, and existing competition. This involves gathering data through surveys, interviews, and market analysis to gain comprehensive insights into customer needs and market potential. Product Managers then analyze the competition within the target market to identify key players, their market share, strengths, weaknesses, and potential threats. This analysis helps in determining the unique value proposition and competitive advantage of the product or service being considered for market entry. Regulatory and legal factors are also evaluated during Market Entry Assessments to ensure compliance with local laws, regulations, and industry standards. Product Managers assess the potential impact of these factors on market entry and ensure that all necessary certifications and approvals are obtained before launching the product or service. In addition to analyzing the market and competition, Product Managers also assess potential risks and challenges associated with entering a new market. This includes evaluating economic, political, and social risks, as well as any potential reputational risks that may arise from entering the market. The findings and insights gathered from Market Entry Assessments are then used to develop a comprehensive market entry strategy. Product Managers create a roadmap for entering the new market, which includes pricing strategies, positioning strategies, marketing campaigns, and distribution channels. Market Entry Assessments play a crucial role in minimizing risks, maximizing opportunities, and increasing the likelihood of success when entering a new market. By thoroughly evaluating market dynamics, competition, customer needs, and potential risks, Product Managers can make informed decisions and develop effective strategies for successful market entry.

Market Exit Strategies

Market exit strategies refer to the planned actions and decisions taken by a product management team to withdraw a product from the market effectively. These strategies are implemented when a product is no longer generating the desired revenue or if it is facing significant challenges that cannot be overcome. Market exit strategies aim to minimize losses and maximize the organization's ability to allocate resources to more successful products or ventures.There are several types of market exit strategies that product managers can consider:1. Product Discontinuation: This strategy involves completely ceasing the production and sale of the product. It is typically employed when a product is nearing the end of its lifecycle, becoming obsolete, or failing to meet market demand.2. Product Divestment: In this strategy, the product is sold off to another company or individual. Divestment allows the organization to recover some of its investments and free up resources for other strategic initiatives.3. Market Consolidation: Sometimes, it may be beneficial to merge or consolidate the product with a similar offering from another company. This strategy allows for a stronger market presence and a more competitive position.4. Market Exit with Partnerships: Instead of discontinuing the product outright, product managers can explore partnerships with other companies. This strategy involves licensing the product, joint ventures, or other collaborative arrangements that allow the product to continue generating revenue under a different ownership structure.5. Spin-off or Diversification: This strategy involves spinning off the product into a separate entity or business unit. By doing so, the product can maintain independence and focus on its target market, while the parent company can focus its resources on other strategic areas.When considering a market exit strategy, product managers should carefully assess the impact on customers, employees, and the organization as a whole. It is crucial to communicate the decision effectively and provide support to affected stakeholders. Additionally, developing a contingency plan and considering the potential risks and challenges of the chosen market exit strategy is essential to ensure a smooth transition and minimize negative repercussions on the brand or organization.

Market Expansion Plans

Market Expansion Plans refers to the strategic initiatives undertaken by a company to increase its market share and explore new markets. It involves identifying and capitalizing on untapped opportunities in existing markets, as well as expanding into new geographic regions or customer segments. Product Management plays a crucial role in developing and executing market expansion plans. The product manager is responsible for analyzing market data, identifying potential growth areas, and developing strategies to penetrate those markets. The first step in creating a market expansion plan is conducting a thorough market analysis. This involves assessing the current market conditions, including customer needs, trends, and competition. The product manager gathers data from market research reports, customer surveys, and competitor analysis to identify target markets and potential gaps in the market. Once the target markets are identified, the product manager formulates a market entry strategy. This includes determining the value proposition of the product or service, selecting appropriate marketing channels, and establishing pricing and distribution strategies. The product manager also collaborates with cross-functional teams, such as sales and marketing, to ensure alignment and effective implementation of the plan. Market expansion plans may involve modifying existing products or developing new ones to meet the specific needs of the target markets. The product manager works closely with the product development team to identify product enhancements or new features that will appeal to the target customers. They also consider factors such as local regulations, cultural preferences, and customer expectations when adapting the product for new markets. Once the market expansion plan is implemented, the product manager closely monitors and evaluates its effectiveness. They track key performance indicators, such as sales growth, market share, and customer satisfaction, to measure the success of the plan. If necessary, adjustments and refinements are made to optimize the outcomes and maximize return on investment. In conclusion, market expansion plans are essential for companies seeking to grow and explore new opportunities. Product management plays a pivotal role in developing and executing these plans, leveraging market insights to identify target markets, formulate strategies, and adapt products to meet customer needs.

Market Expansion Strategies

Market expansion strategies refer to the methods and approaches employed by product managers to increase the reach and penetration of their products into new markets. These strategies aim to capture new customers, increase sales, and grow the business by targeting untapped geographic areas or customer segments. There are several market expansion strategies that product managers can consider: 1. Geographic Expansion: This strategy involves entering new geographical markets where the product is not yet present. Product managers analyze market potential, local market dynamics, and customer preferences to determine the feasibility and attractiveness of expanding into new regions or countries. They then adapt the product to suit local tastes, preferences, and cultural nuances. 2. Market Segmentation: This strategy involves identifying and targeting new customer segments that have not yet been catered to by the product. Product managers conduct market research and use segmentation techniques to understand different customer groups and their specific needs. They then develop marketing campaigns and product variants that are tailored to appeal to these new segments. 3. Diversification: Diversification strategies involve expanding the product portfolio to enter new markets. Product managers identify related or complementary markets where the existing product can be extended or modified to cater to the needs of different customer groups. This strategy helps to mitigate risks and capitalize on existing brand equity, while also driving growth through new product offerings. 4. Partnerships and Alliances: Product managers can explore strategic partnerships or alliances with other companies to access new markets. These partnerships can range from distribution agreements and joint ventures to licensing and franchising arrangements. By leveraging the established networks and expertise of their partners, product managers can enter new markets quickly and efficiently. 5. Acquisitions: Acquisitions involve purchasing existing companies with a presence in the desired market. This strategy allows product managers to rapidly expand their market share and gain access to new customers and distribution channels. However, acquisitions require careful due diligence and integration to ensure a successful transition and maximize the value of the acquired business.

Market Opportunity Analysis

Market Opportunity Analysis is a strategic process conducted by Product Managers to identify and evaluate potential market opportunities for a product or service. It involves analyzing market trends, customer needs, competitive landscape, and internal capabilities to assess the feasibility and potential success of entering a new market or expanding an existing one. In this process, Product Managers gather data and insights from various sources such as market research, customer feedback, and industry reports to understand the market dynamics and emerging trends. They evaluate the size and growth potential of the target market, taking into account factors like market segmentation, customer demographics, and buying behavior. Product Managers also assess the competitive landscape to determine the presence of existing competitors and their strengths and weaknesses. They analyze the value proposition offered by competitors, potential barriers to entry, and any unique selling points that the product can leverage. Furthermore, Product Managers evaluate their organization's internal capabilities, including resources, expertise, and technology, to determine if they are well-equipped to meet the demands of the target market. They identify any potential gaps or areas for improvement that need to be addressed before entering or expanding in the market. Based on the findings of the analysis, Product Managers develop strategies and recommendations to capitalize on the identified market opportunities. These strategies may include product positioning, pricing, distribution channels, and marketing campaigns. They also consider potential risks and challenges that may arise and devise contingency plans to mitigate them. Overall, Market Opportunity Analysis enables Product Managers to make informed decisions about whether to pursue a particular market opportunity and how to maximize the chances of success. It helps them align their product roadmap with market demand, optimize resource allocation, and stay ahead of the competition.

Market Research Data Integration

Market research data integration refers to the process of combining and analyzing data from various sources to gain insights into the market trends, consumer preferences, and competitive landscape for the purpose of making informed product management decisions. Product managers rely heavily on market research data integration to understand and address the needs and wants of their target customers. By integrating data from multiple sources such as surveys, focus groups, sales figures, and online analytics, they are able to gather a comprehensive view of the market and make data-driven decisions that will ultimately drive the success of their products.

Market Research Integration

Market Research Integration is the process of incorporating insights gathered from market research activities into the product management cycle. It involves the systematic collection and analysis of data and information related to the market, customers, competitors, and industry trends, which is then utilized to inform product decision-making and strategy formulation. This integration enables product managers to gain a comprehensive understanding of the market and its dynamics, identify customer needs and preferences, evaluate market potential and demand, anticipate competitive threats, and identify opportunities for product innovation and differentiation. By integrating market research into product management, organizations can make informed and data-driven decisions throughout the product lifecycle, from ideation and concept development to launch, growth, and obsolescence. This integration helps to minimize the risks and uncertainties associated with product development and marketing by providing insights and evidence to support decision-making, validate assumptions, and justify investments. Market research integration involves several key activities, including: 1. Defining research objectives and questions: Product managers identify the specific information and insights they need to inform their decision-making. They formulate research objectives and questions aligned with the product strategy and goals. 2. Conducting primary and secondary research: Product managers gather data through a variety of research methods, such as surveys, interviews, focus groups, and data analysis. They also leverage existing market research reports, industry studies, competitor analyses, and other secondary sources of information. 3. Analyzing and interpreting data: The collected data is analyzed to identify patterns, trends, correlations, and insights. Product managers interpret the findings in the context of the product's target market, customer segments, and competitive landscape. 4. Integrating findings into decision-making: The insights derived from market research are used to inform product decisions, such as product positioning, pricing, features, packaging, distribution channels, and marketing campaigns. They help product managers align the product with customer needs, preferences, and market trends. Overall, market research integration is a crucial component of successful product management. It enables product managers to make informed decisions, minimize risks, meet customer needs, and stay ahead of the competition by leveraging market insights throughout the product lifecycle.

Market Research Resources

Market research resources are various tools, methods, and data sources used by product managers to gather and analyze information about target markets, consumers, competitors, and industry trends. These resources provide valuable insights that inform decision-making and help guide the development, positioning, and marketing of products. One important market research resource is primary research, which involves the collection of new data directly from the target market or consumers. This can be done through methods such as surveys, interviews, focus groups, and observation. Primary research allows product managers to obtain firsthand information about customer needs, preferences, and behaviors, as well as to gather feedback on existing or potential products. Another essential market research resource is secondary research, which involves the use of existing data and information that has been collected by others. This can include industry reports, market studies, government publications, and academic research. Secondary research enables product managers to gain a broader understanding of the market landscape, industry trends, competitor strategies, and other relevant factors. Market research resources also include online tools and platforms that provide access to data and analytics. These can include market research databases, social media monitoring tools, web analytics platforms, and online surveys. These resources help product managers track and analyze market trends, customer sentiment, and online conversations about their products and brands. In addition to these primary and secondary research resources, product managers may also use other sources of information such as industry experts, trade associations, trade shows, and customer feedback channels. These resources can provide valuable industry knowledge, insights on market dynamics, and feedback from key stakeholders. Overall, market research resources play a critical role in product management by providing the necessary information and analysis to make informed decisions about the creation, launch, and promotion of products. By leveraging these resources, product managers can better understand their target markets, identify customer needs, mitigate risks, and maximize their products' chances of success.

Market Research Tools

Market research tools are software or applications that help product managers collect and analyze data to gain insights into market trends, customer preferences, and competitive landscapes. These tools provide a systematic and structured approach to gathering information, allowing product managers to make informed decisions about product development, marketing strategies, and overall business growth. One essential feature of market research tools is data collection. These tools offer various methods to collect data, such as online surveys, focus groups, and social media monitoring. By using these methods, product managers can gather information about customer needs, preferences, and behaviors. They can also collect data on market trends, industry benchmarks, and competitive activities. The data collected through these tools are often in the form of quantitative and qualitative data, which allows product managers to understand trends, patterns, and customer sentiment. Another critical aspect of market research tools is data analysis. These tools provide powerful analytics capabilities that help product managers process and interpret the collected data. Through data analysis, product managers can identify market segments, customer personas, and market opportunities. They can also uncover customer pain points and unmet needs, which can guide product development efforts. Furthermore, market research tools enable product managers to monitor and track marketing campaigns, evaluate customer satisfaction, and measure the success of product launches. Market research tools also support competitive analysis. By monitoring and analyzing competitors' activities, product managers can identify their strengths, weaknesses, and market positioning. This analysis helps product managers understand the competitive landscape and differentiate their products from competitors. Additionally, market research tools allow product managers to track market disruptions, emerging technologies, and industry trends, enabling them to identify potential threats and opportunities. In summary, market research tools play a vital role in product management by providing data collection, analysis, and competitive intelligence capabilities. By using these tools, product managers can make data-driven decisions, better understand their target market, and develop products that meet customer needs.

Market Research

Market research, in the context of product management, refers to the systematic gathering and analysis of data related to consumers, competitors, and market trends. It involves collecting and analyzing information that helps product managers understand the market, identify potential opportunities, and make informed decisions. Market research plays a crucial role in product management as it provides valuable insights into customer needs, preferences, and buying behavior. By understanding the target market and its dynamics, product managers can tailor their strategies and offerings to better meet customer demands.

Market Segmentation Analysis Tools

Market segmentation analysis tools refer to the various techniques and methodologies used by product managers to divide the market into distinct and homogeneous segments. These tools enable product managers to identify the specific needs, characteristics, behaviors, and preferences of different customer groups, allowing them to target their products and marketing strategies more effectively. The overall goal of market segmentation analysis is to divide the heterogeneous market into smaller, more manageable segments that share similar attributes, such as demographics, psychographics, behavior, or geographic location. By understanding these segments, product managers can tailor their offerings to meet the unique needs and wants of each segment, ultimately driving customer satisfaction, loyalty, and profitability.

Market Segmentation Analysis

Market segmentation analysis is a strategic tool used in product management that involves dividing the target market into distinct subgroups based on common characteristics, needs, preferences, and behaviors. This process enables product managers to better understand and cater to the diverse needs of different customer groups, allowing for more targeted marketing, product development, and customer acquisition strategies. The goal of market segmentation analysis is to identify market segments that are most likely to respond positively to a product or marketing campaign. By dividing the market into smaller, more homogeneous groups, product managers can gain deeper insights into the specific needs, desires, and behaviors of each segment. This knowledge enables them to create customized marketing messages, differentiate their products, and develop tailored strategies to reach and engage customers effectively.

Market Segmentation

Market segmentation is a strategic approach used in product management to divide a heterogeneous market into distinct and homogeneous groups of customers. The objective is to identify and understand specific customer groups with similar needs, preferences, and behaviors in order to design and deliver products and services that effectively meet their requirements.This process involves dividing the market based on various segmentation variables, such as demographic (age, gender, income), geographic (location, climate), psychographic (lifestyle, values), and behavioral (usage patterns, brand loyalty) factors. These variables provide a framework for categorizing customers into meaningful segments that share common characteristics.By segmenting the market, product managers can tailor their marketing strategies, product offerings, and communication messages to cater to the specific needs of each segment. This enables them to develop focused marketing campaigns, optimize product features and pricing, and establish stronger customer relationships.Market segmentation helps product managers make informed decisions about product positioning, targeting, and differentiation. By understanding the unique needs and preferences of different customer segments, they can create value propositions and product experiences that resonate with each group. This leads to increased customer satisfaction and loyalty, as well as higher sales and profitability.Furthermore, market segmentation allows product managers to identify unmet customer needs and uncover new market opportunities. By analyzing customer data and market trends within each segment, they can uncover potential gaps in the market and develop innovative products or services to address these gaps. This helps to drive product innovation and maintain a competitive advantage in the market.In conclusion, market segmentation is a crucial process in product management that enables product managers to understand and target specific customer groups with tailored products and marketing strategies. By dividing the market into distinct segments, they can better serve the needs of customers, drive innovation, and achieve business success.

Market Trend Analysis

Market trend analysis refers to the process of analyzing and evaluating current market conditions, customer behavior, and industry trends to identify patterns and make informed decisions related to product management. This analysis involves gathering market data and information from various sources such as market research reports, customer surveys, industry publications, and competitor analysis. The data is then analyzed and interpreted to identify emerging trends, opportunities, and threats that may impact the success of a product or business.

Market Trends Analysis

Market trends analysis in the context of product management refers to the evaluation and understanding of the current and future trends in the market that can impact the success and growth of a product. It involves the systematic collection, analysis, and interpretation of data and information related to the market, competition, customer preferences, and industry developments, with the aim of making informed decisions about the product's strategy, positioning, and features. Through market trends analysis, product managers can identify emerging opportunities, potential threats, and gaps in the market that their product can address. It helps them stay ahead of the competition by ensuring that their product caters to the evolving needs and preferences of their target audience. By gathering and analyzing data on customer behavior, market dynamics, technological advancements, and industry trends, product managers can make data-driven decisions to optimize their product's performance and maximize its market potential.

Market Trends Monitoring

Market Trends Monitoring in the context of Product Management refers to the systematic and ongoing process of collecting, analyzing, and interpreting data and information related to the market in which a product operates. It involves monitoring various factors and indicators that impact the market and the target audience in order to identify emerging trends, shifts in consumer behavior, and competitive dynamics. The goal of Market Trends Monitoring is to gain valuable insights that can inform product strategy, development, and marketing decisions. By staying updated on market trends, product managers can anticipate changes in customer needs and preferences, identify new opportunities, and mitigate potential risks.

Marketing Analytics Software

A marketing analytics software is a specialized tool used by Product Managers to measure and analyze various marketing activities and initiatives. It enables them to gather data from different marketing channels, extract insights, and make informed decisions to improve marketing performance and drive business growth. Product Managers use marketing analytics software to track and evaluate key metrics such as website traffic, conversion rates, customer acquisition costs, customer lifetime value, campaign effectiveness, and return on investment. By analyzing these metrics, they can identify trends, patterns, and correlations to understand how marketing efforts impact business goals and objectives. With marketing analytics software, Product Managers can conduct comprehensive analyses to answer important business questions. They can perform customer segmentation to better understand their target audience and create personalized marketing campaigns. They can evaluate the success of different marketing channels and determine the most effective ones for reaching their target market. They can also assess the impact of specific marketing campaigns or promotions and optimize their strategies based on the results. The software typically offers features such as data visualization, dashboards, and reporting functionality, making it easier for Product Managers to interpret and communicate data-driven insights to stakeholders. They can generate reports, charts, and graphs to illustrate marketing performance and present the findings to key decision-makers. In addition, marketing analytics software often integrates with other tools and platforms, such as customer relationship management (CRM) systems and advertising platforms. This integration allows Product Managers to access data from multiple sources and gain a holistic view of their marketing efforts, facilitating more informed decision-making. In summary, marketing analytics software provides Product Managers with the means to measure, analyze, and optimize marketing activities. It empowers them to make data-driven decisions, improve marketing performance, and ultimately drive business growth. By leveraging this tool, Product Managers can gain valuable insights into their marketing initiatives and ensure that their strategies align with overall business objectives.

Marketing Attribution Models

Marketing attribution models refer to the techniques or methods used in product management to determine the effectiveness or impact of various marketing channels or touch points on consumer behavior. These models help companies analyze and allocate credit to different marketing efforts, such as advertising campaigns, social media promotions, search engine optimization, and email marketing, among others. The primary objective of marketing attribution models is to provide insights into the customer journey and identify which marketing initiatives are driving sales or key performance indicators (KPIs). By understanding the impact of different touch points, product managers can optimize their marketing strategies and budget allocation, ensuring maximum return on investment (ROI).

Marketing Attribution

Marketing attribution in the context of product management refers to the process of identifying and assigning credit to the marketing channels or touchpoints that contribute to a customer's decision to purchase a product. It involves tracking and analyzing the customer's journey from the initial exposure to a marketing message to the final conversion. The goal of marketing attribution is to understand the effectiveness and return on investment (ROI) of different marketing activities and channels. By determining which marketing efforts have the most impact on driving sales, product managers can allocate resources and make informed decisions to optimize their marketing strategies.

Marketing Automation Platforms

Marketing Automation Platforms (MAPs) are software tools that enable product managers to automate and streamline their marketing efforts. These platforms integrate various marketing channels, such as email, social media, and website, into a single interface, allowing product managers to plan, execute, and track their marketing campaigns more efficiently. MAPs provide a range of functionalities that help product managers better understand their target audience, personalize and automate marketing content, and measure the effectiveness of their campaigns. Through these platforms, product managers can create customer segments based on demographics, behavior, and interests, allowing them to send targeted messages and offers to different groups of customers. Additionally, MAPs enable product managers to automate repetitive marketing tasks, such as sending welcome emails, nurturing leads, and scheduling social media posts. By automating these tasks, product managers can save time and focus on strategic activities, such as developing new marketing strategies, analyzing data, and optimizing campaigns. Moreover, MAPs provide analytics and reporting features that allow product managers to measure the performance of their marketing campaigns. Through these platforms, product managers can track metrics such as open rates, click-through rates, conversion rates, and revenue generated. This data provides valuable insights into the effectiveness of different marketing channels, messages, and strategies, helping product managers make data-driven decisions and optimize their marketing efforts. In conclusion, Marketing Automation Platforms are essential tools for product managers to streamline their marketing activities and improve campaign effectiveness. These platforms enable product managers to integrate, automate, and measure their marketing efforts across multiple channels, while providing valuable insights and analytics to support data-driven decision-making.

Marketing Automation

Marketing automation in the context of product management refers to the use of technology and software tools to automate various marketing tasks and processes. It is a system designed to streamline and enhance the efficiency of marketing campaigns, allowing product managers to reach and engage with targeted audiences more effectively. The primary goal of marketing automation is to automate repetitive marketing tasks, such as email marketing, social media management, customer segmentation, lead generation, and campaign tracking. By automating these tasks, product managers can save time and resources, enabling them to focus on more strategic aspects of product management.

Marketing Budget Allocation

A marketing budget allocation refers to the process of determining how financial resources will be distributed across different marketing activities and initiatives in order to achieve the company's product management objectives. It involves deciding how much money should be allocated to various marketing channels, campaigns, and strategies in order to maximize the return on investment (ROI) and effectively reach the target market. Product managers play a crucial role in this process as they are responsible for analyzing market trends, consumer behaviors, and competitor activities to develop effective marketing strategies for the company's products. Budget allocation decisions are informed by these insights and are aimed at increasing brand visibility, driving product awareness, and generating sales.

Marketing Budget Management

Marketing budget management in the context of product management refers to the strategic planning, allocation, and control of financial resources dedicated to marketing activities for a specific product or product line. It involves the careful consideration of how marketing funds are distributed across various tactics and channels to achieve the desired marketing objectives and maximize return on investment. The process of marketing budget management begins with the establishment of clear marketing goals and objectives. These goals may include increasing brand awareness, generating leads, driving sales, or expanding market share. Once the goals are defined, the marketing budget is determined based on the available financial resources and the projected costs associated with the planned marketing activities. The marketing budget is typically broken down into different categories or line items, such as advertising, public relations, digital marketing, events, and promotions. Each category is assigned a specific portion of the total budget, taking into consideration factors such as the target audience, competitive landscape, and market trends. Effective marketing budget management involves ongoing monitoring and control of the allocated funds. This includes tracking actual expenditures against the budget, evaluating the performance and results of each marketing initiative, and making necessary adjustments to optimize the allocation of resources. By closely monitoring the budget and its impact on marketing outcomes, product managers can ensure that the marketing activities are aligned with the overall product strategy and delivering the desired business outcomes. In addition to financial management, marketing budget management also encompasses evaluating the effectiveness and efficiency of marketing expenditures. This involves analyzing metrics such as return on investment, cost per acquisition, and customer lifetime value to determine the overall effectiveness of the marketing efforts. By understanding the effectiveness of different marketing tactics and channels, product managers can make data-driven decisions to reallocate budget and resources to the most efficient and impactful activities.

Marketing Budget Planning

A marketing budget planning refers to the process of allocating funds for various marketing activities and initiatives to promote a product or service. It involves determining the amount of money that will be allocated to different marketing efforts, such as advertising, promotions, public relations, and market research, in order to achieve specific objectives and goals. In the context of product management, marketing budget planning plays a crucial role in ensuring the success of a product in the market. It involves analyzing the target market, identifying the key marketing strategies, and estimating the required budget for each strategy.

Marketing Budgeting

Marketing budgeting in the context of product management refers to the strategic allocation of financial resources for various marketing activities related to a specific product or range of products. It involves estimating and setting aside a predetermined amount of money to be used for marketing initiatives, such as advertising, promotions, market research, and other relevant activities to support the successful launch and ongoing promotion of a product. The primary purpose of marketing budgeting is to ensure that sufficient funds are available to effectively market and promote a product, while also maximizing return on investment (ROI). By setting a budget, product managers can plan and allocate resources in a controlled and organized manner, allowing them to make informed decisions regarding the most appropriate marketing strategies and tactics for their product.

Marketing Campaign Evaluation

A marketing campaign evaluation is a formal process conducted by product management teams to assess the effectiveness and success of a marketing campaign. It involves analyzing various metrics and data to determine the impact the campaign had on the target audience and whether it achieved the desired objectives. The evaluation begins by setting clear and measurable goals for the campaign, such as increasing brand awareness, generating leads, or driving sales. These objectives serve as the basis for evaluating the campaign's performance. Key performance indicators (KPIs) are identified to measure the campaign's effectiveness against these goals. Product managers analyze data and metrics collected before, during, and after the campaign to gain insights into its impact. This includes reviewing sales data, website traffic, social media engagements, customer feedback, and other relevant data sources. By comparing these metrics to the campaign goals, product managers can assess whether the campaign successfully achieved its intended outcomes. Additionally, product managers evaluate the campaign's messaging, creative elements, and targeting strategies to determine their impact on the target audience. They analyze customer responses to the campaign, such as online reviews, comments, and surveys, to gauge the overall sentiment and effectiveness of the marketing efforts. A comprehensive marketing campaign evaluation also involves assessing the return on investment (ROI) of the campaign. Product managers calculate the cost of running the campaign and compare it to the revenue generated or other desired outcomes. This helps them determine the campaign's overall success and identify areas for improvement in future marketing initiatives. The insights gained from a marketing campaign evaluation guide product managers in making informed decisions about future marketing strategies. By understanding what worked and what didn't in the previous campaign, product managers can refine their approach and optimize their marketing efforts to achieve better results in future campaigns. Ultimately, the evaluation process helps product management teams drive continuous improvement in their marketing activities and maximize the value delivered to customers and the company.

Marketing Collateral Printing

Marketing collateral printing refers to the process of creating and producing various physical materials that are used for promotional and marketing purposes. These materials are designed to communicate information about a company, its products, and its services to potential customers and target audiences. The purpose of marketing collateral printing is to enhance brand awareness, generate leads, and ultimately drive sales. These printed materials serve as tangible assets that can be distributed to prospects, customers, and stakeholders. Examples of marketing collateral include brochures, flyers, catalogs, business cards, posters, banners, and product packaging.

Marketing Dashboards

Marketing Dashboards, in the context of Product Management, refer to visual representations of marketing data and metrics that provide insights and analysis to support decision-making and optimize marketing strategies for a product or a set of products. These dashboards consolidate data from various sources, such as advertising platforms, social media channels, email campaigns, website analytics, and sales data, into a single interface for easy monitoring and analysis. Marketing dashboards typically include key performance indicators (KPIs) and other relevant metrics related to marketing activities and their impact on product performance. They provide a real-time or near-real-time view of marketing performance, allowing product managers to track and measure the effectiveness of marketing campaigns, identify opportunities for improvement, or spot any potential issues or bottlenecks.

Marketing Funnel Optimization

Marketing funnel optimization, in the context of product management, refers to the process of improving and maximizing the effectiveness of each stage of the marketing funnel. The marketing funnel represents the customer journey from initial awareness of a product to the final conversion or purchase decision. The marketing funnel is typically divided into several stages, which may vary depending on the specific product or industry. These stages often include: awareness, interest, consideration, intent, and conversion. At each stage, prospective customers interact with the product through various marketing channels, such as advertising, content marketing, social media, and email campaigns. Optimizing the marketing funnel involves analyzing and enhancing each stage to increase conversion rates and ultimately drive more sales and revenue. This process requires a deep understanding of the target market, customer behaviors, and the competitive landscape. At the awareness stage, the goal is to attract potential customers and create brand awareness. This can be achieved through targeted advertising, content marketing, and search engine optimization. It is important to ensure that the messaging and visuals used in this stage accurately represent the product and its unique value proposition. In the interest stage, the focus is on capturing the attention and interest of potential customers. This can be done through compelling content, engaging social media campaigns, and personalized communication. The goal is to educate and provide relevant information that highlights the benefits and features of the product. During the consideration stage, prospective customers evaluate the product and its alternatives. It is important to provide clear and detailed product information, customer reviews, and comparison charts to facilitate the decision-making process. This stage may involve nurturing leads through targeted email campaigns or retargeting ads. The intent stage signifies a strong interest and readiness to make a purchase. This is the stage where potential customers may request demos, trials, or contact sales representatives for further information. It is crucial to provide seamless and user-friendly experiences to encourage conversions at this stage. The conversion stage represents the final step in the marketing funnel, where prospects make a purchase or take the desired action. This stage requires clear calls-to-action, easy checkout processes, and effective post-purchase communication to ensure customer satisfaction and encourage repeat purchases.

Marketing KPI Definition

A Key Performance Indicator (KPI) in the context of Product Management refers to a measurable metric that is used to evaluate the success or performance of marketing efforts. In the realm of Product Management, KPIs focus specifically on the marketing aspects of a product. They are used to track and quantify the effectiveness of marketing strategies and campaigns, allowing Product Managers to assess their impact on the overall success and growth of a product or brand.

Marketing KPIs

Marketing KPIs, or Key Performance Indicators, are quantitative measurements used to assess and analyze the effectiveness and success of marketing efforts within the context of Product Management. These metrics are crucial in providing valuable insights and guidance to product managers, enabling them to make data-driven decisions and optimize their marketing strategies. Marketing KPIs vary depending on the specific goals and objectives of the product management team. They can be categorized into different types, including acquisition, conversion, retention, and revenue-based KPIs. Each of these KPIs focuses on a different aspect of the marketing funnel and provides a distinct perspective on the performance of the product and its marketing efforts.

Marketing Performance Metrics

Marketing performance metrics are quantitative measurements used to assess the effectiveness and success of marketing strategies and campaigns. In the context of product management, these metrics provide valuable insights into the performance and impact of marketing efforts on the product's success. These metrics help product managers evaluate the performance of various marketing initiatives and make data-driven decisions to optimize their strategies. By analyzing these metrics, product managers can assess the effectiveness of marketing campaigns in terms of generating leads, driving conversions, and increasing revenue.

Marketing Performance Reporting

Marketing Performance Reporting is the process of analyzing and presenting data related to the effectiveness and efficiency of marketing initiatives in order to make informed decisions and drive organizational growth. In the context of Product Management, this involves tracking and evaluating marketing activities and their impact on the success of a product or service. Marketing Performance Reporting provides valuable insights into the effectiveness of marketing strategies and tactics, allowing product managers to assess the return on investment (ROI) of their marketing efforts. It involves the collection and analysis of various key performance indicators (KPIs) such as sales revenue, customer acquisition costs, conversion rates, market share, and customer satisfaction.

Marketing Qualified Leads (MQL)

Marketing Qualified Leads (MQL) refer to individuals or companies who have shown an interest in a product or service offered by a company but have not yet reached the stage of being highly likely to make a purchase. In the context of Product Management, MQLs are potential customers who have been identified as having a higher chance of converting into paying customers based on their engagement with marketing activities and their fit with the target customer profile. Product Managers play a crucial role in identifying and nurturing MQLs as part of their responsibilities to drive product adoption and revenue growth. They work closely with the marketing team to define the criteria that determine when a lead can be classified as an MQL. These criteria typically include factors such as the lead's level of interest, their engagement with marketing materials, and their alignment with the ideal customer profile.

Marketing ROI Calculation

Marketing ROI (Return on Investment) is a metric used in Product Management to measure the effectiveness of marketing campaigns and activities. It provides insights into the financial performance and profitability of these marketing efforts, helping product managers make data-driven decisions and optimize their marketing strategies. The calculation of Marketing ROI involves comparing the financial gains generated from marketing initiatives with the costs incurred in running those campaigns. It helps product managers determine whether their investments in marketing are yielding positive returns or if adjustments or reallocations need to be made.

Marketing Technology Stack Components

A marketing technology stack refers to the collection of tools and software that a company uses to execute its marketing strategies and activities. It is a combination of various components that work together to support the marketing team in managing and analyzing their campaigns, automating processes, and improving overall efficiency and effectiveness. One of the key components in a marketing technology stack is a customer relationship management (CRM) system. This software allows product managers to store and manage customer information, track interactions, and analyze data to gain insights into customer behavior and preferences. The CRM system enables product managers to segment their target audience, personalize their marketing messages, and track the success of their campaigns. Another important component is a marketing automation platform. This tool automates repetitive marketing tasks, such as email marketing, social media posting, lead nurturing, and campaign tracking. By automating these processes, product managers can save time and resources, ensure consistent messaging, and easily measure the performance of their marketing efforts. Data analytics and reporting tools are also a crucial part of the marketing technology stack. These tools provide product managers with the ability to collect, analyze, and interpret data from various channels and campaigns. By tracking key metrics and generating reports, product managers can measure the success of their marketing initiatives, identify areas for improvement, and make data-driven decisions. Other components that can be included in a marketing technology stack include content management systems (CMS), social media management tools, search engine optimization (SEO) software, advertising platforms, and customer feedback systems. These components work together to enhance a product manager's ability to create, distribute, and optimize their marketing content, reach their target audience, and engage with customers effectively.

Minimum Viable Product (MVP) Testing

A Minimum Viable Product (MVP) testing refers to the process of evaluating the essential features and functionality of a product that is developed with minimum resources, time, and effort. It allows product managers to validate and gather feedback on the core value proposition of a product, ensuring that it meets the needs and expectations of the target audience. The main objective of MVP testing is to determine whether the product can solve the identified problem and provide sufficient value to users. It helps product managers gauge the product-market fit and identify areas that require improvement or modifications before investing more resources in development.

Minimum Viable Product (MVP)

A Minimum Viable Product (MVP) is a product with just enough features to satisfy early customers and provide feedback for future development. It is a strategy used in Product Management to quickly test and validate a product idea or concept, while minimizing time and resources. The main objective of an MVP is to learn from actual user feedback and gather insights to make informed decisions about the product's development and future iterations. By releasing a simplified version of a product, Product Managers can gauge user interest, evaluate market demand, and identify any potential flaws or improvements that need to be addressed.

Monetization

Monetization refers to the process of generating revenue from a product or service. In the context of product management, it involves implementing strategies to turn a product or service into a profitable venture by creating various sources of income. Product managers play a crucial role in the monetization process by identifying and implementing strategies that align with the product's goals, target market, and customer needs. They analyze market trends, conduct competitive research, and collaborate with cross-functional teams to develop monetization strategies that maximize the product's potential for generating revenue.

Multivariate Testing

Multivariate testing, in the context of Product Management, refers to a systematic approach for evaluating and comparing multiple variations of a product or feature in order to determine the most effective combination of elements. Product Managers use multivariate testing as a data-driven method to make informed decisions about the best design, layout, content, or functionality of a product or feature. By testing multiple variations simultaneously, they can identify the specific elements that have the greatest impact on user engagement, satisfaction, and conversion rates.

Net Promoter Score (NPS)

Net Promoter Score (NPS) is a widely used metric in product management that measures customer loyalty and satisfaction. It is used to determine the likelihood of customers to recommend a product or service to others, which can be an indicator of business growth and success. NPS is calculated based on a simple survey question that asks customers how likely they are to recommend a product or service on a scale of 0 to 10. The NPS survey question is typically formatted as follows: "On a scale of 0 to 10, how likely are you to recommend [product or service] to a friend or colleague?" Customers are then categorized into three groups based on their responses: Promoters (score 9-10), Passives (score 7-8), and Detractors (score 0-6). Promoters are highly satisfied customers who are loyal and enthusiastic about the product or service. They are likely to recommend it to others, which can lead to positive word-of-mouth and increased customer acquisition. Passives are generally satisfied but not as enthusiastic as Promoters, while Detractors are unsatisfied customers who may actively discourage others from using the product or service. To calculate the Net Promoter Score, the percentage of Detractors is subtracted from the percentage of Promoters. The resulting score can range from -100 to 100, with higher scores indicating a larger proportion of Promoters and lower scores indicating a larger proportion of Detractors. The Passives contribute to the total percentage but do not have a direct impact on the NPS.

Packaging Redesign

Packaging redesign is a strategic process in product management that involves making changes to the packaging design of a product. It aims to enhance the visual appeal, functionality, and overall effectiveness of the packaging to better meet the needs and preferences of consumers, while also aligning with the brand strategy and objectives. The purpose of packaging redesign is to improve various aspects of the packaging to drive sales, create differentiation, and increase customer satisfaction. This may include rethinking the shape, size, materials, colors, graphics, and messaging on the packaging to better resonate with the target market. The goal is to create a packaging design that not only attracts attention on the shelf but also effectively communicates the product's features, benefits, and value proposition to potential buyers. The decision to initiate a packaging redesign may be prompted by various factors. One common reason is the need to revitalize an established product and maintain its relevance in a rapidly evolving market. Packaging redesign can also be driven by changes in consumer preferences, emerging design trends, or the desire to position the product as more premium, eco-friendly, or technologically advanced. During the packaging redesign process, product managers work closely with the design team to identify areas for improvement and develop a new packaging concept. This involves conducting market research, analyzing consumer behavior, and considering competitive landscape and industry norms. The design team then translates these insights into a visual representation of the new packaging design, taking into account factors such as brand identity, product positioning, and regulatory requirements. Once the new packaging design is finalized, product managers collaborate with various stakeholders, such as production teams, suppliers, and marketing personnel, to ensure a smooth transition to the updated packaging. This may involve addressing technical considerations, such as production feasibility and cost implications, as well as developing a communication plan to inform retailers, distributors, and consumers about the packaging change. In conclusion, packaging redesign is a strategic initiative in product management that involves making deliberate changes to the visual and functional aspects of a product's packaging. By aligning with consumer preferences, market trends, and brand objectives, packaging redesign aims to create a compelling packaging design that enhances product visibility, communicates key messages effectively, and ultimately drives sales and customer satisfaction.

Presentation Software

Presentation Software is a tool that allows Product Managers to create and deliver visually engaging and interactive presentations to various stakeholders within an organization. It enables them to articulate their product vision, strategy, and key findings in a clear and compelling manner. With presentation software, Product Managers can design and structure their presentations using a combination of text, images, charts, graphs, and multimedia elements, such as videos and audio clips. This helps them communicate complex ideas and data effectively, making it easier for stakeholders to understand and engage with the information being presented. Moreover, presentation software provides Product Managers with a range of features and capabilities to enhance the visual appeal and interactivity of their presentations. They can choose from a variety of pre-designed templates and themes, enabling them to create professional and consistent-looking slides without the need for advanced design skills. Additionally, presentation software allows Product Managers to customize the design elements, layout, and formatting of their slides to suit the specific needs of their audience or the nature of the information being presented. This flexibility helps them tailor their presentations to different stakeholders, such as executives, development teams, marketing teams, or clients. Furthermore, presentation software offers features like slide transitions, animations, and interactive elements, such as hyperlinks and navigation buttons. These features enable Product Managers to create dynamic presentations that engage the audience and facilitate a more interactive and immersive experience. Overall, presentation software is an essential tool in the Product Manager's toolkit as it allows them to effectively communicate their product strategies, plans, and insights to various stakeholders. It helps them create visually appealing and engaging presentations that facilitate understanding, collaboration, and decision-making within the organization.

Price Bundling

Price bundling is a strategic marketing technique used in product management, wherein two or more products or services are combined and sold together as a single package at a discounted price. It involves offering customers the option to purchase multiple related or complementary items as a bundle, rather than as individual items at their regular prices. The primary objective of price bundling is to increase sales and maximize revenue by encouraging customers to buy more than they would if the products were sold separately. By offering a bundled package at a lower overall price, businesses aim to incentivize customers to purchase additional items they may not have considered otherwise. This can generate incremental sales, enhance customer satisfaction, and create a competitive advantage in the market.

Price Discounting

Price discounting is a product management strategy that involves reducing the price of a product for a specific period of time to stimulate sales or increase market share. It is a marketing tactic used by companies to attract customers and generate demand for their products. Price discounting can be implemented in various ways, such as offering percentage discounts, promotional pricing, or discount codes. The objective is to incentivize customers to make a purchasing decision by making the product more affordable or providing additional value for the price. By lowering the price, companies aim to increase the product's perceived value and create a sense of urgency to drive sales volume.

Price Elasticity

Price elasticity, in the context of Product Management, refers to the responsiveness of the demand for a product to changes in its price. It is a measure of how sensitive customers are to changes in price and how their purchasing behavior is affected by these changes. Price elasticity is calculated by dividing the percentage change in quantity demanded by the percentage change in price. A high price elasticity indicates that customers are highly responsive to price changes, while a low price elasticity suggests that customers are less sensitive to price fluctuations.

Price Penetration

Price penetration is a pricing strategy in product management where a company sets a low initial price for a product in order to attract customers and gain market share. This strategy involves offering a product at a lower price than competitors in order to capture a larger portion of the market. The goal of price penetration is to quickly gain market share and drive sales volume by attracting price-sensitive customers. By offering a lower price, the company aims to entice customers to try the product and create a customer base. This can be particularly effective in highly competitive markets where customers are sensitive to price fluctuations and are constantly seeking better deals.

Price Skimming

Price skimming is a pricing strategy employed by product managers where they set a high initial price for a product or service and then gradually lower it over time. This strategy is typically used when a company introduces a new product or enters a new market. The main objective of price skimming is to maximize profit in the early stages of a product's life cycle. By initially setting a high price, the company aims to attract the most willing and able customers who are willing to pay a premium for the new product. These customers are often early adopters or individuals who highly value the unique features or benefits offered by the product. Price skimming is especially effective in situations where there is limited competition or when the product offers a significant technological advantage over existing alternatives. In these cases, customers may be willing to pay a higher price to be the first ones to experience the benefits of the product. However, as time passes, competitors may enter the market or alternative products may become available. This increases the pressure on the company to lower the price in order to remain competitive. As a result, the company gradually reduces the price over time to attract a broader customer base and take advantage of economies of scale, lowering the production costs and allowing them to pass on the cost savings to the consumers. While price skimming can be an effective strategy to generate early revenues and capture value from the most enthusiastic customers, it is important for product managers to carefully assess market conditions and customer demand elasticity. Setting the initial price too high can result in limited adoption and slow market penetration, while setting it too low may leave money on the table and make it harder to increase prices in the future. In summary, price skimming is a pricing strategy used by product managers to initially set a high price for a new product or market entry. It aims to capture early adopters and maximize profit in the early stages of a product's life cycle. Over time, the price is gradually lowered to attract a wider customer base and remain competitive.

Price Testing

Price testing is a strategic process in product management that involves experimenting with different price points to identify the optimal pricing strategy for a product or service. It is an essential component of pricing optimization, helping businesses determine the price that maximizes revenue and profitability while also considering customer perceptions and market dynamics. This testing approach typically involves conducting controlled experiments where prices are varied and analyzed to measure the impact on sales, revenue, profit margins, and customer behavior. It provides valuable insights into how customers respond to different price levels, allowing product managers to make data-driven decisions on pricing strategies.

Pricing Model

A pricing model is a strategic tool used in product management to determine the optimal price of a product or service. It helps businesses maximize their profits by considering various factors such as production costs, market demand, competitor prices, and customer value perception. The pricing model typically consists of a set of rules or calculations that guide the pricing decision-making process. It takes into account both internal and external factors to establish a pricing strategy that aligns with the company's objectives and market dynamics.

Pricing Strategy Models

A pricing strategy model is a framework or approach that is used by product managers to determine the optimal price at which to sell their products or services in the market. These models consider various factors such as costs, competition, customer preferences, and market dynamics to devise a pricing strategy that maximizes profitability and customer satisfaction. There are several pricing strategy models that product managers can employ, depending on the specific goals and characteristics of their product. Some common pricing strategy models include: 1. Cost-based pricing: This model involves calculating the production and distribution costs of a product and adding a markup to determine the selling price. Cost-based pricing ensures that the price covers all expenses and allows for a reasonable profit margin. However, it may not take into account factors such as customer value perception or market demand. 2. Value-based pricing: This model focuses on the perceived value of a product to the customer. Product managers analyze the benefits, features, and uniqueness of their product compared to competitors and set a price that reflects the value it provides. Value-based pricing allows for higher profits if the product offers significant value to customers. 3. Competitive pricing: In this model, product managers set their prices based on the prices charged by competitors. The goal is to either match the competition's price or offer a lower price to attract customers. Competitive pricing requires monitoring and analyzing competitor pricing and is suitable when the product is similar to those offered by competitors. 4. Penetration pricing: This model involves setting a low initial price to quickly gain market share and attract customers. The aim is to encourage trial and adoption of the product by offering it at a lower price than competitors. Penetration pricing can lead to higher sales volume but may not be sustainable in the long run as prices may need to be increased later. 5. Skimming pricing: Skimming pricing involves setting a high initial price for a new or unique product to capitalize on early adopters who are willing to pay a premium. The price is gradually lowered over time to attract more price-sensitive customers. Skimming pricing allows for maximized initial profits but may limit market penetration. These are just a few examples of pricing strategy models that product managers can use. Each model has its own advantages and considerations, and product managers must carefully evaluate their product and market dynamics to select the most appropriate pricing strategy.

Pricing Strategy Tools

Pricing strategy tools are essential resources used by product managers to determine the optimal pricing strategies for their products or services. These tools include various techniques, models, and frameworks that help product managers analyze market conditions, customer behavior, and competitive positioning to set prices in a way that maximizes profitability and achieves business objectives. One commonly used pricing strategy tool is competitive pricing analysis, which involves analyzing competitor pricing and positioning to determine the appropriate pricing levels for a product. By understanding the prices set by competitors, product managers can assess how their own product's value proposition compares and make informed decisions on whether to price above, below, or at the same level as competitors. Another pricing strategy tool is demand analysis, which involves evaluating customer demand patterns and elasticity of demand to estimate how price changes will impact sales volume and revenue. By understanding the price sensitivity of customers, product managers can identify opportunities to adjust pricing to optimize demand, whether through price decreases to stimulate sales or price increases to maximize revenue. Price sensitivity analysis is another valuable tool for setting prices. This involves conducting surveys or experiments with potential customers to measure their willingness to pay at different price points. By understanding customer perceptions of value and their preferences regarding pricing, product managers can align prices with customer expectations, ensuring that the product is priced competitively and perceived as offering good value. Value-based pricing is another strategy tool that focuses on pricing products based on the value they deliver to customers. This approach involves understanding the benefits and outcomes that customers expect from a product and setting prices accordingly. Product managers can use customer research, market segmentation, and value proposition analysis to identify the key value drivers for different customer segments and price their products accordingly. Lastly, pricing optimization tools use mathematical models and algorithms to analyze large sets of data and identify the optimal prices for different products or customer segments. These tools take into account factors such as costs, demand, price elasticities, and competitive dynamics to recommend pricing strategies that maximize profitability and market share. In conclusion, pricing strategy tools are critical for product managers to make informed decisions about pricing. By utilizing these tools, product managers can analyze market data, customer preferences, and competitive dynamics to set optimal prices that maximize profitability and achieve business objectives.

Pricing Strategy

Pricing strategy in the context of product management refers to the overall approach and methodology applied to determine the optimal pricing for a product or service. It involves setting the price at which the product will be sold to customers, taking into consideration various factors such as production costs, competitors' prices, target market, and the value proposition of the product. A well-defined pricing strategy is essential for product managers as it directly affects the product's perceived value, profitability, market positioning, and ultimately its success in the market. There are several pricing strategies that can be implemented, depending on the product, market conditions, and business objectives. One common pricing strategy is cost-based pricing, which involves determining the price by adding a certain profit margin to the product's production cost. This approach ensures that the product is priced in a way that covers costs and generates a profit. However, it does not take into account customer demand or the competitive landscape. Another strategy is value-based pricing, which focuses on the perceived value of the product in the eyes of the customer. This approach considers the benefits and features of the product, as well as the willingness of customers to pay for those benefits. Value-based pricing aims to capture the maximum value that customers are willing to pay, often resulting in higher prices for products with unique features or superior performance. Penetration pricing is a strategy commonly used for new products or entering new markets. It involves setting the initial price of the product low to attract customers and gain market share. The goal is to encourage early adoption and create a customer base, with the possibility of increasing prices once the product has gained traction. Price skimming is the opposite of penetration pricing, where the product is initially priced high to capture the willingness of early adopters to pay a premium price. This strategy is often used for innovative or technologically advanced products, allowing businesses to recoup development costs and maximize profits before competitors enter the market. Dynamic pricing, also known as demand-based pricing or surge pricing, is a strategy where prices are adjusted in real-time based on supply and demand. This approach is commonly used in industries such as airlines, ride-sharing, and e-commerce, where prices fluctuate based on factors such as seasonality, time of day, and customer demand. In conclusion, choosing the right pricing strategy is a critical decision for product managers. It requires a deep understanding of the product, market dynamics, and customer behavior. By effectively pricing a product, businesses can optimize revenue, gain a competitive advantage, and ultimately drive the success of the product in the market.

Product 3D Printing

Product 3D printing is an additive manufacturing process that involves creating physical objects by layering materials on top of each other based on a digital design. It is a technology that allows for the production of highly complex and customizable products, using a wide range of materials including plastics, metals, ceramics, and even food. One of the key benefits of product 3D printing is its ability to rapidly prototype products, allowing for quicker and more efficient iterations of design. This enables product managers to quickly test and validate product ideas, reducing the time and cost associated with traditional manufacturing methods. With 3D printing, product managers can easily create multiple versions of a product, making it easier to gather feedback from stakeholders and make necessary improvements before manufacturing at scale. Another advantage of product 3D printing is its ability to support mass customization. Traditional manufacturing methods often require expensive tooling and setup costs, making it difficult and costly to produce customized products. With 3D printing, product managers can easily modify the design of a product to meet individual customer requirements, enabling mass customization without the need for additional tooling. Furthermore, product 3D printing enables the production of complex geometries that are not easily achievable with traditional manufacturing methods. This opens up new possibilities for product innovation, allowing product managers to create products with intricate and optimized designs. By leveraging the design freedom offered by 3D printing, product managers can create products that are more lightweight, ergonomic, and efficient, leading to improved performance and user experience. In conclusion, product 3D printing is a powerful technology that offers numerous benefits to product managers. It enables rapid prototyping, mass customization, and the creation of complex geometries, ultimately leading to faster product development cycles, cost savings, and enhanced product innovation.

Product Adoption Tracking

Product Adoption Tracking refers to the process of monitoring and measuring the rate at which a new product is being accepted and used by its target customers. It is an essential aspect of product management that helps businesses understand how well their product is being adopted in the market. In order to track product adoption, product managers use various metrics and tools to collect and analyze data. This data provides insights into customer behavior and allows product managers to make informed decisions about product development and marketing strategies. The primary goal of product adoption tracking is to determine the success of a new product in terms of customer acceptance and usage. By monitoring adoption rates, product managers can identify any challenges or barriers that may be preventing customers from fully adopting the product. This information can then be used to improve the product and its marketing efforts. One common metric used for tracking product adoption is the adoption rate, which measures the percentage of target customers who have started using the product. This metric helps product managers understand how quickly and effectively their product is being accepted in the market. Another important metric is the churn rate, which measures the percentage of customers who stop using the product over a given period of time. A high churn rate may indicate that customers are not finding value in the product or that there are issues with the product that need to be addressed. Product adoption tracking also involves monitoring user feedback and conducting surveys to gather qualitative data. This information helps product managers understand the reasons behind customer adoption or non-adoption and provides insights for improving the product. Overall, product adoption tracking is a critical process for product managers as it allows them to assess the success of their product in the market and make data-driven decisions to improve its adoption. By monitoring and analyzing adoption rates, product managers can identify areas for improvement and take appropriate actions to increase the product's acceptance and usage among its target customers.

Product Agile Development

71

Product Agile Development is a methodology used in Product Management to efficiently and iteratively develop and deliver high-quality products. It emphasizes collaboration, customer feedback, and continuous improvement throughout the development process. This approach is based on the Agile Manifesto, which values individuals and interactions, working products, customer collaboration, and responding to change. Product Agile Development follows a set of principles and practices that enable cross-functional teams to work together and adapt to evolving requirements. In Product Agile Development, the development process is divided into short, time-boxed iterations called sprints. Each sprint typically lasts one to four weeks and includes activities such as planning, development, testing, and review. During each sprint, the team strives to deliver a potentially shippable product increment, which is a working and tested version of the product that adds value to the customers. The Product Owner, a key role in Product Agile Development, represents the interests of the stakeholders and ensures that the development team focuses on delivering the highest value features. The Product Owner collaborates with the team to define and prioritize the product backlog, a list of features and requirements. The team then selects a set of these items to work on in each sprint, based on their capacity and the estimated effort. The development team works closely together in a highly collaborative and self-organized manner. Communication among team members is frequent and informal, enabling quick decision-making and problem-solving. Regular stand-up meetings are held to provide updates on progress, discuss any impediments, and plan the next steps. It encourages transparency and promotes a shared understanding of the work at hand. Throughout the development process, the team regularly gathers feedback from customers and stakeholders. This feedback is used to validate assumptions, make informed decisions, and incorporate changes to the product. It allows for flexible and adaptive planning, as the team can adjust the product backlog and prioritize work based on the feedback received. Product Agile Development enables a fast-paced, customer-centric, and value-driven approach to product development. It focuses on delivering increments of the product that are usable and valuable, while also allowing for continuous learning and improvement. By embracing flexibility and collaboration, organizations can effectively respond to changing market needs and deliver successful and competitive products.

Product Alpha Testing

Product Alpha Testing is a crucial phase in the product development lifecycle that involves testing a product internally before it is released to external users. This testing phase is usually conducted by a select group of users or testers who closely resemble the target audience for the product. During the Alpha Testing phase, the product is tested for functionality, usability, and performance to identify any potential issues or bugs that need to be addressed before the product is launched to a wider audience. The purpose of this testing is to gather feedback and make necessary improvements to ensure a smooth and successful product launch.

Product Analytics Integration

Product analytics integration refers to the process of incorporating data from various sources and tools to gain insights and make informed decisions in product management. It involves collecting, organizing, and analyzing the data generated by users, products, and business operations to understand user behavior, track product performance, and evaluate the effectiveness of product strategies. The integration of product analytics typically involves the following key steps: Firstly, data collection is essential, and it can be done through various channels such as web tracking, mobile tracking, email tracking, and in-app tracking. These sources capture user interactions, feature usage, click-through rates, conversion rates, and other relevant data points. By collecting data from multiple sources, product managers can gather a comprehensive view of user behavior and product performance. Secondly, data organization and centralization play a crucial role in product analytics integration. Product managers need to ensure that the data collected is consistent, accurate, and easily accessible. This involves structuring the data in a way that makes it easy to compare and analyze across different time periods, user segments, and product features. Thirdly, data analysis and visualization are essential steps in product analytics integration. Product managers need to use appropriate analytical tools and techniques to extract meaningful insights from the integrated data. This involves conducting exploratory analysis, segmentation analysis, cohort analysis, and A/B testing to uncover patterns, trends, and correlations. Visualizing the data through charts, graphs, and dashboards can help in communicating the insights effectively to stakeholders.

Finally, using the insights gained through product analytics integration, product managers can make informed decisions and devise strategies to improve product development, enhance user experience, and drive business growth. This could involve identifying areas for improvement, optimizing product features, prioritizing roadmap decisions, and personalizing user journeys based on data-driven insights. In conclusion, product analytics integration is a fundamental aspect of product management that enables product managers to leverage data from multiple sources to gain insights, make informed decisions, and drive product success. By collecting, organizing, analyzing, and visualizing data, product managers can understand user behavior, evaluate product performance, and optimize product strategies for better user experience and business outcomes.

Product Analytics

Product Analytics is the practice of using data and analysis to understand and improve the performance of a product throughout its lifecycle. It involves collecting and analyzing data related to user behavior, market trends, and product metrics to gain insights and make data-driven decisions. Product Analytics plays a crucial role in Product Management as it enables product managers to understand how users interact with the product, identify areas of improvement, and make informed decisions to enhance the product's value and drive business growth.

Product Assembly Line

A product assembly line, in the context of product management, refers to a systematic and highly organized process for manufacturing products in large quantities. It involves a series of steps and operations, typically performed by specialized workers and automated machinery, to transform raw materials and components into finished products. The main objective of a product assembly line is to optimize production efficiency, minimize costs, and ensure consistent quality. The line is carefully designed to streamline the manufacturing process, eliminate bottlenecks, and maximize the utilization of resources. This results in a high-volume production capability, allowing companies to meet customer demands and achieve economies of scale.

Product Backlog Management

Product Backlog Management is a crucial aspect of Product Management that involves the continuous refinement and prioritization of a product backlog. The product backlog is a dynamic list of features, enhancements, bug fixes, and other requirements that need to be worked on to further develop a product. Effective Product Backlog Management ensures that the highest value and most important items are at the top of the backlog, ready to be picked up by the development team for implementation. It involves constant communication and collaboration between the product owner, stakeholders, and development team to ensure that the backlog reflects the changing needs and priorities of the business and its users.

Product Backlog Prioritization

A product backlog is a prioritized list of user stories or requirements that need to be included in the development of a product. It serves as the central tool for product management to communicate and collaborate with stakeholders, development teams, and other parties involved in the product development process. The prioritization of items in the product backlog is a critical aspect of product management, as it determines the order in which features and functionalities are developed and delivered to the market. Backlog prioritization is the process of arranging the items in the product backlog in order of their importance and value to the users and business. This helps in making informed decisions about what should be worked on next and ensures that the development team is focusing on the most valuable features and requirements at any given time. The prioritization of the product backlog is typically done by the product owner, who is responsible for understanding the needs and priorities of the users, customers, and business stakeholders. The product owner works closely with the development team to evaluate and assess the value, effort, and feasibility of each item in the backlog. In doing so, they consider factors such as market demand, customer feedback, business goals, and technical dependencies. The product owner uses various techniques and frameworks, such as MoSCoW (Must, Should, Could, Won't), Kano model, value vs. effort analysis, and cost of delay, to prioritize the items in the backlog. These techniques help in determining the relative importance and urgency of each item and enable the product owner to make informed decisions about what should be included in each development cycle or sprint. The prioritization of the product backlog is an iterative and ongoing process. As new information, feedback, and market changes arise, the product owner reevaluates and adjusts the priorities of the backlog items to ensure that the product development stays aligned with the evolving needs and goals of the users and business. Through effective backlog prioritization, the product owner maximizes the value delivered by the product and ensures that the development efforts are focused on the most important features and requirements.

Product Backlog

A product backlog is a prioritized list of user stories, bug fixes, technical tasks, and other product requirements that a product manager maintains for the product. It serves as the single authoritative source of requirements for the development team and provides visibility into the work that needs to be done to deliver a valuable product. The product backlog is dynamic and continuously evolving. It is typically created at the start of a project or initiative and is regularly refined and reprioritized based on feedback from stakeholders, market changes, and the evolving needs of the users. The product manager continually collaborates with the development team, stakeholders, and users to ensure that the backlog accurately reflects the current understanding of the product requirements. Each item in the product backlog, known as a user story, represents a specific user need or requirement. User stories are brief, simple statements written from the perspective of the user and typically follow the format: "As a [user], I want [goal] so that [reason]." User stories are accompanied by acceptance criteria, which define the specific conditions that must be met for the user story to be considered complete. The product backlog is prioritized to ensure that the most valuable and highest-priority user stories are implemented first. The prioritization is based on various factors such as user and stakeholder needs, business value, technical dependencies, and strategic objectives. This allows the development team to focus on delivering the most important features and functionalities early on, while still maintaining flexibility to adapt to changing requirements and priorities. The product backlog is a living document that facilitates collaboration and communication between the product manager, development team, and other stakeholders. It provides a transparent view of the product requirements and helps align everyone's understanding of the goals and scope of the product. The product manager regularly reviews and reprioritizes the backlog to ensure that it reflects the most up-to-date understanding of the product and that the development team is working on the most valuable items.

Product Barcode

A product barcode is a unique pattern of parallel lines that is printed on a product label or packaging. It serves as an electronic identification code that can be scanned and interpreted by barcode scanners or mobile devices equipped with barcode scanning capabilities. Product barcodes are widely used in the field of product management as a means of efficiently and accurately tracking and managing inventory. Each product barcode is assigned a unique Universal Product Code (UPC) or European Article Number (EAN) by an authorized authority, such as the International Article Numbering Association (EAN) or the Uniform Code Council (UPC). This assigned code is then encoded in the barcode using a specific symbology, typically the linear barcode symbology. When a product barcode is scanned, the barcode scanner reads the encoded data and converts it into a machine-readable format. This data usually includes information such as the product's manufacturer, the product type, and the specific item number. The scanned data is then sent to a central database or inventory management system for further processing. The use of product barcodes simplifies and accelerates the process of inventory management. By scanning product barcodes, product managers can quickly identify, track, and update product information, such as stock levels, pricing, and location. This data can be used to generate reports, optimize inventory levels, and improve supply chain efficiency. In addition to inventory management, product barcodes also facilitate other key processes in product management, such as order fulfillment, point-of-sale transactions, and product authentication. By scanning barcodes, product managers can accurately record and process customer orders, update stock quantities in real-time, and ensure the authenticity and traceability of products.

Product Benefits

74

Product benefits refer to the advantages and positive outcomes that customers gain from using a particular product. These benefits are the driving factors behind a customer's decision to purchase and continue using a product. As a product manager, it is essential to understand and communicate these benefits effectively in order to create a successful and appealing product. There are various types of product benefits that can be categorized into functional, emotional, and symbolic benefits. Functional benefits are tangible and measurable advantages that directly meet the needs and solve the problems of the customers. These benefits can include features, performance, quality, reliability, convenience, and efficiency. For example, a smartphone with a fast processor, long battery life, high-quality camera, and user-friendly interface offers functional benefits to the customer. Emotional benefits are subjective and focus on the feelings and experiences that a product provides. These benefits can include enjoyment, satisfaction, pleasure, excitement, happiness, and peace of mind. For example, a luxury car may offer the emotional benefits of status, prestige, and self-esteem to the customer. Symbolic benefits are associated with the social and cultural meanings that a product conveys to the customer. These benefits can include identity, belonging, self-expression, and social acceptance. For example, a trendy fashion brand may offer symbolic benefits by allowing customers to express their personal style and fit in with a certain social group. By understanding the different types of product benefits, product managers can tailor their marketing strategies and messaging to effectively communicate these benefits to the target customers. This includes highlighting the unique features and functionalities that differentiate the product from competitors, appealing to the emotional desires and aspirations of the customers, and leveraging the symbolic meanings and associations that resonate with the target market. In conclusion, product benefits are the advantages and positive outcomes that customers gain from using a product. By understanding and communicating these benefits effectively, product managers can create successful products that meet the needs and desires of the target customers.

Product Beta Testing

Product Beta Testing is a crucial phase in the Product Management process that involves the evaluation of a product's performance and usability by real users in a controlled environment before its official release. It allows the product team to gather valuable feedback and insights to assess the product's functionality, user experience, and identify potential bugs or issues that need to be resolved. During Product Beta Testing, a selected group of external users, known as beta testers, are invited to use the product and provide feedback based on their experience. These beta testers can be existing customers, prospects, or members of the target market who have expressed interest in trying out the product before its launch. The purpose is to simulate real-world usage scenarios and uncover any issues or areas of improvement that might have been overlooked during the development process. The product team typically provides the beta testers with a set of specific tasks or scenarios to complete, while also encouraging them to explore the product freely. This allows the team to gather both structured and unstructured feedback, ensuring a comprehensive understanding of the product's strengths and weaknesses. Beta testers may be asked to fill out surveys, provide written or verbal feedback, or record their interactions with the product for further analysis. The feedback collected during Product Beta Testing is then analyzed and used to make informed decisions regarding product enhancements, bug fixes, and overall improvements. This iterative process helps refine the product, enhance its user experience, and address any usability or functionality issues before the official release. In addition to gathering feedback, Product Beta Testing also provides an opportunity for the product team to generate awareness and create buzz around the upcoming release. By involving real users in the testing process, beta testers often become advocates for the product and help build anticipation among their peers and networks.

Product Bill Of Materials (BOM)

A Product Bill of Materials (BOM) is a comprehensive list of all the components, parts, and materials required to manufacture or assemble a product. It serves as a crucial document in product management, providing a detailed breakdown of all the necessary elements needed to bring a product to life. The BOM typically includes information such as part numbers, descriptions, quantities, and unit costs of each component. It acts as a central reference point for product managers, engineers, manufacturers, and procurement teams involved in the product development and production process. By creating a BOM, product managers can ensure that all stakeholders have a clear understanding of the materials and components required, enabling effective planning, cost estimation, and procurement. It helps in identifying potential suppliers, calculating costs, and establishing lead times for each item listed in the BOM. The BOM allows product managers to manage the complexity of the production process by breaking it down into manageable parts. It helps in determining the feasibility of manufacturing a product, as well as evaluating the impact of design changes, substitutions, or upgrades to different components. Furthermore, the BOM acts as a valuable tool for inventory management. It allows product managers to track the availability, usage, and consumption of each component, ensuring that there are no shortages or excess stock. It aids in maintaining optimal inventory levels, preventing supply chain disruptions, and minimizing production delays. In addition, the BOM facilitates collaboration and communication between cross-functional teams involved in the product development process. It serves as a common language that all stakeholders can refer to, ensuring that everyone is aligned and working towards the same goal. In conclusion, a Product Bill of Materials is a comprehensive list that outlines all the components, parts, and materials required for the manufacturing or assembly of a product. It plays a crucial role in product management by providing essential information for planning, cost estimation, procurement, inventory management, and collaboration.

Product Brand Awareness

Product brand awareness refers to the level of familiarity and recognition that consumers have with a particular product brand. It can be measured by the extent to which consumers can identify a brand by its name, logo, or other visual or auditory cues associated with the brand. Brand awareness is an important metric for product managers as it indicates the strength of a brand's presence in the market and its ability to attract and retain customers. There are two main types of brand awareness: unaided and aided. Unaided brand awareness is the ability of consumers to spontaneously recall a brand when prompted with a specific product category or need. This type of brand awareness reflects the brand's top-of-mind awareness and is an indication of its strong market presence. Aided brand awareness, on the other hand, refers to the ability of consumers to recognize a brand when prompted with its name, logo, or other cues. This type of brand awareness is often assessed through surveys or tests that measure recognition or recall of specific brand elements.

Product Brand Consistency

Product brand consistency refers to the uniformity and coherence of a brand across all its products and marketing materials. It involves maintaining a consistent visual and verbal identity, as well as delivering a consistent customer experience, in order to build trust, recognition, and loyalty. Consistency is a crucial aspect of product brand management. It ensures that customers can easily recognize and connect with a brand, no matter which product or marketing medium they encounter. When a brand presents a consistent image and message, it becomes more memorable, credible, and differentiated from competitors.

Product Brand Crisis Management

Product Brand Crisis Management refers to the process of effectively handling and mitigating any potential crises or issues that may arise regarding a product's brand. It involves the strategic planning, communication, and execution of various measures to protect and preserve the brand image, reputation, and value. During the course of a product's lifecycle, unforeseen events, negative feedback from customers, competitive challenges, or issues with product quality or safety may occur. These incidents have the potential to negatively impact the brand's perception and reputation among consumers, stakeholders, and the market as a whole. The goal of product brand crisis management is to effectively navigate through these crises, minimize their impact on the brand, and restore trust and loyalty among key stakeholders. This involves several key steps: 1. Anticipating and identifying potential crises: This involves conducting thorough market research, monitoring social media and online platforms, analyzing customer feedback, and staying informed about industry trends and competitors. By identifying potential issues early on, companies can develop proactive strategies to prevent or mitigate them. 2. Developing a crisis management plan: Once potential crises are identified, a detailed plan should be developed, outlining the necessary steps to address each specific scenario. This includes establishing clear roles and responsibilities, setting up communication channels, and determining the protocols for handling media inquiries and public statements. 3. Rapid response and effective communication:

When a crisis occurs, it is essential to respond quickly and transparently. Open communication with customers, stakeholders, and the media is crucial in managing a crisis effectively. This involves providing accurate information, addressing concerns and grievances, and demonstrating empathy and understanding. 4. Monitoring and adapting: After the initial crisis response, it is important to continuously monitor the situation and adapt strategies as needed. Regularly assessing the effectiveness of crisis management efforts allows for adjustments and improvements, ensuring long-term brand resilience. Overall, product brand crisis management is a critical aspect of product management, as it helps safeguard the brand's reputation and maintain customer loyalty. By anticipating and effectively managing potential crises, companies can minimize damage and even turn challenging situations into opportunities for growth and improvement.

Product Brand Equity

Product brand equity refers to the value and perception that consumers associate with a particular product brand. It represents the overall reputation, recognition, and trust that a brand has attained in the market. Building and maintaining strong brand equity is essential for long-term success in product management. Brand equity is influenced by several factors, including brand awareness, brand associations, brand loyalty, perceived quality, and brand personality. Brand awareness refers to how well consumers recognize and recall a brand. It can be measured by factors such as brand recall and brand recognition. Strong brand awareness is crucial as it helps drive customer consideration and choice. Brand associations encompass the thoughts, feelings, and beliefs that consumers link with a brand. Positive associations can include attributes, benefits, attitudes, or experiences. These associations can be built through marketing efforts such as advertising, public relations, and product placement. Brand loyalty is the degree to which consumers consistently choose a particular brand over others. It is achieved through providing superior value and experiences that meet or exceed customer expectations. Loyal customers are more likely to repurchase, recommend the brand to others, and resist competitor offerings. Perceived quality refers to the customer's subjective evaluation of a brand's superiority and excellence. It can be influenced by objective factors such as product performance, durability, and reliability, as well as subjective factors such as brand reputation and trust. Brand personality relates to the human characteristics, traits, and values that consumers associate with a brand. It helps create emotional connections and fosters identification with the brand. A strong brand personality can differentiate a brand from its competitors and build customer loyalty. In summary, product brand equity is the value and perception that consumers attribute to a brand. It is influenced by brand awareness, brand associations, brand loyalty, perceived quality, and brand personality. Building and maintaining strong brand equity is vital for product managers as it contributes to customer preference, loyalty, and long-term success in the market.

Product Brand Extensions

Product brand extensions refer to the practice of extending an existing brand name to a new product or product category within the same brand family. It involves leveraging the equity and recognition of a well-established brand to introduce new offerings that cater to different consumer needs and preferences. Brand extensions can take various forms, including line extensions, which involve adding new products to an existing product line, and category extensions, which involve entering completely new product categories. In both cases, the goal is to leverage the existing brand's reputation, awareness, and associations to create a competitive advantage in the new market.

Product Brand Guidelines

Product brand guidelines are a set of established rules and guidelines that ensure consistency and coherence in the presentation and communication of a product brand. These guidelines serve as a framework for product managers to follow when designing, marketing, and promoting products to maintain a strong and recognizable brand identity. The purpose of product brand guidelines is to provide a roadmap for creating, maintaining, and evolving a product brand. By adhering to these guidelines, product managers can ensure that the brand is consistently represented in a way that aligns with its values, personality, and target audience. The consistency in brand presentation helps build trust, loyalty, and recognition among consumers.

Product Brand Identity

A product brand identity, in the context of product management, refers to the unique set of characteristics, perceptions, and values associated with a specific product or product line. It encompasses the visual elements, messaging, and overall positioning that distinguish the product and shape how it is perceived by consumers. Product brand identity plays a significant role in the success and marketability of a product. It is what sets the product apart from competitors and helps establish a connection with the target audience. A strong and well-defined brand identity not only helps drive customer loyalty but also enables effective marketing and communication strategies.

Product Brand Loyalty

Product brand loyalty refers to the level of commitment or allegiance that consumers have towards a particular brand or products within that brand. It is a measure of how likely consumers are to continuously choose and purchase products from a specific brand over competing alternatives. Brand loyalty is a result of consumers' positive experiences, feelings, and perceptions associated with a particular brand. It is built over time through consistent product quality, innovation, marketing efforts, and positive interactions with the brand. When consumers develop brand loyalty, they are more likely to stick with the brand despite competitive offerings or price fluctuations.

Product Brand Messaging

Product brand messaging refers to the strategic communication and positioning of a brand's products in the market to effectively convey their unique value proposition and connect with the target audience. It involves crafting a compelling and consistent message that resonates with the consumers and influences their perception and purchasing decisions. As part of product management, brand messaging plays a crucial role in differentiating the brand from its competitors and building a strong brand identity. It encompasses the key attributes, benefits, and values that the product offers, as well as the emotions and aspirations it evokes in its consumers.

Product Brand Positioning

Product brand positioning refers to the strategic approach taken by a product management team to establish a distinct and favorable perception of a product in the minds of target customers. It involves identifying and communicating the unique value proposition of the product, as well as differentiating it from competitors in the marketplace. The process of product brand positioning begins with conducting market research to understand the needs, preferences, and buying behavior of the target audience. This includes analyzing the competitive landscape and identifying the key attributes that customers associate with the product category. Once the target audience and competitive landscape have been identified, product managers determine the key differentiating features and benefits of the product. These might include aspects such as price, quality, functionality, design, or customer service. The goal is to find a unique selling proposition that sets the product apart from competitors and resonates with the target audience. Once the unique value proposition has been established, the product management team creates a positioning statement. This statement succinctly describes the target market, the product category, the product's unique attributes, and the desired perception among target customers. The positioning statement serves as a guide for all marketing and communication efforts related to the product. The next step in product brand positioning is to develop a comprehensive marketing and communication strategy to effectively convey the desired brand image to the target audience. This may include advertising, public relations, social media, content marketing, and other promotional activities. The messaging and tone should be consistent across all channels to reinforce the desired brand perception. Regular monitoring and evaluation of the product brand positioning is crucial to ensure it remains relevant and effective. Changes in the market, competition, or customer preferences may require adjustments to the positioning strategy. By continuously monitoring the marketplace and gathering feedback from customers, product managers can make informed decisions to maintain a strong and favorable brand positioning.

Product Brand Revitalization

Product brand revitalization refers to the strategic process of repositioning and reinvigorating a product brand in the market to regain its relevance, competitiveness, and profitability. It involves making significant changes to various aspects of the product, such as its design, packaging, pricing, communication, and distribution, in order to attract and retain customers, and ultimately increase sales and market share. Brand revitalization is often necessary when a product brand is facing challenges, such as declining sales, loss of market share, changing customer preferences, or increased competition. It is a proactive approach that aims to breathe new life into a brand and make it more appealing, distinctive, and competitive in the eyes of consumers.

Product Branding

Product branding is a key component of product management that involves creating a unique identity and image for a product in the market. It encompasses the various strategies and activities aimed at differentiating a product from its competitors and establishing a strong brand presence. Branding goes beyond simply designing a logo or choosing a catchy name for a product. It is the process of shaping the perceptions and associations that consumers have with a product. A well-executed branding strategy can create a strong emotional connection with consumers, instill trust and loyalty, and ultimately drive sales and revenue.

Product CAD Software

Product CAD software is a computer-aided design tool specifically designed for product management. It enables product managers to create and visualize detailed digital models of physical products, allowing them to efficiently design, modify, and analyze their products during the product development process. Product CAD software offers a range of powerful features and tools that facilitate the creation and manipulation of 2D and 3D models. These models can accurately represent the physical attributes of a product, including its dimensions, shape, geometry, materials, and components. The software allows product managers to easily modify and refine these models, making it easier to experiment with different design alternatives and iterate upon the product concept. The software also offers the ability to simulate the behavior and performance of the product in a virtual environment. This enables product managers to assess the functionality, durability, and safety of the product before it is manufactured, helping to identify and address potential design flaws or issues early on. By utilizing simulation capabilities, product CAD software can save both time and money by reducing the need for physical prototypes and extensive testing. Product CAD software often integrates with other software tools used in the product management process, such as product lifecycle management (PLM) systems and computer-aided manufacturing (CAM) tools. This integration allows for seamless data exchange and collaboration between different teams involved in product development, promoting efficiency and ensuring that all stakeholders have access to the most up-to-date information. In conclusion, product CAD software is a crucial tool for product managers, providing them with the ability to create, modify, and analyze digital models of physical products. It empowers product teams to streamline the design process, reduce costs, and enhance product quality by enabling early validation and iteration.

Product Case Studies

Product Case Studies are detailed examinations of specific products or product lines, conducted by product managers, to gain insights into their performance, customer satisfaction, market acceptance, and overall impact on the business. These studies involve analyzing various aspects of a product, including its features, functionality, pricing, positioning, and customer feedback. The goal of a product case study is to understand the strengths, weaknesses, opportunities, and threats associated with the product in order to make informed decisions and improvements. Product managers use case studies to gather quantitative and qualitative data about their products, enabling them to evaluate their performance against key metrics and benchmarks. This analysis often involves comparing the product's performance to competitors, identifying areas where it outperforms or falls short. Through interviews, surveys, and data analysis techniques, product managers can uncover customer preferences, pain points, and satisfaction levels, which can be used to inform future product development and marketing strategies.

Product Certification

Product Change Management

Product Change Management refers to the process of planning, implementing, and monitoring changes to a product throughout its lifecycle, with the aim of improving its performance, features, or other aspects. It is an integral part of product management, as it involves making modifications to the product based on customer feedback, market trends, technological advancements, or other factors. Product Change Management involves several key steps, including identifying the need for change, assessing the impact of the change, planning the implementation, communicating the change to stakeholders, executing the change, and evaluating its effectiveness. These steps ensure that any changes made to the product are well thought out, properly executed, and aligned with the overall product strategy.

Product Changelog Management

Product changelog management refers to the systematic process of documenting and tracking changes made to a product over time, in order to maintain a clear and comprehensive record of its evolution. It is an essential part of product management, as it enables teams to effectively communicate updates to stakeholders, track the progress of development efforts, and ensure the product remains aligned with the overall product strategy. The primary objective of product changelog management is to provide transparency and visibility into the changes made to the product, helping stakeholders understand what has been modified, added, or removed at each stage of its development. By maintaining a detailed and up-to-date changelog, product managers can track the evolution of the product and easily communicate its progress to the rest of the team and stakeholders. The process of managing a product changelog typically involves several key steps. Firstly, product managers need to document all changes made to the product, including bug fixes, feature enhancements, and any other modifications. This documentation should be concise, clear, and structured in a way that makes it easy to understand and navigate. Next, the changelog should be organized and categorized in a logical manner, allowing stakeholders to quickly find and review specific changes of interest. This can be achieved by using headings, subheadings, or other formatting techniques to divide the changelog into sections based on the type of change or the release version. Furthermore, it is important to provide additional context or explanations for each change, particularly for significant modifications or new features. This can help stakeholders understand the rationale behind the change and its impact on the product. Including relevant links, screenshots, or other visual aids can also enhance the clarity and understanding of the changelog. Lastly, product changelog management requires regular updates to ensure that the documentation remains accurate and comprehensive. As new changes are introduced or updates are made to the product, the changelog should be promptly updated to reflect these modifications. This ensures that stakeholders have access to the most recent information and can stay informed about the product's ongoing development. In conclusion, product changelog management is a vital component of product management, enabling teams to document and track changes made to a product over time. By maintaining a clear and comprehensive changelog, product managers can provide transparency, enhance communication, and ensure alignment with the overall product strategy.

Product Changelog Notification Solutions

A product changelog notification solution is a tool or system that enables product management teams to effectively communicate and inform users or customers about the changes made to a product, including new features, improvements, bug fixes, and other updates. The main purpose of a product changelog notification solution is to keep users well-informed about the latest changes and updates in a product, ensuring transparency and providing clear and concise information. This helps build trust with users and demonstrates a commitment to continuous improvement.

Product Changelog Notifications

Product Changelog Notifications refer to the feature or functionality updates communicated to users or stakeholders in a formal and standardized format. These notifications inform users about the changes, enhancements, or bug fixes made to a product, typically through release notes, emails, or in-app notifications. Product Managers are responsible for creating these changelog notifications and ensuring they are accurate, concise, and effectively communicate the value of the updates to the users. These notifications serve multiple purposes: Firstly, they provide transparency and keep users informed about the ongoing improvements in the product. By clearly outlining the changes, users can understand the reasons behind certain modifications and see the value they bring. This helps in managing users' expectations and reduces the chances of confusion or frustration. Secondly, changelog notifications act as a communication channel between the product team and the users. They allow product managers to establish a feedback loop and gather valuable insights from users. By receiving feedback on the changes, the product team can iterate and prioritize future enhancements accordingly. This two-way communication helps in building a strong relationship with the users and fosters a sense of trust and collaboration. Lastly, these notifications play a crucial role in driving user engagement and adoption. By highlighting new features, functionalities, or bug fixes, product managers can create awareness and generate excitement among users. This can lead to increased usage, improved user satisfaction, and ultimately, higher retention. In summary, Product Changelog Notifications are formal announcements that inform users about the updates made to a product. They serve the purposes of transparency, communication, and user engagement. By effectively communicating the changes, product managers can manage user expectations, gather valuable feedback, and drive adoption.

Product Compatibility Testing

Product Compatibility Testing is a crucial aspect of Product Management that focuses on evaluating the compatibility of a product with various other products, systems, or platforms. It involves performing rigorous tests to ensure that the product can seamlessly integrate and function correctly when used in conjunction with other components or environments. The purpose of Product Compatibility Testing is to identify any potential compatibility issues or limitations that may arise when the product interacts with different systems or products. This testing process helps product managers to gauge the performance, reliability, and overall user experience of the product in diverse scenarios.

Product Compatibility

Product compatibility refers to the ability of a product to work seamlessly and efficiently with other products and systems in a given ecosystem. It encompasses the ability of a product to integrate, communicate, and interoperate with other products, ensuring that the overall experience and functionality of the ecosystem are not compromised. Compatibility is a critical aspect of product management as it directly affects customer satisfaction, market adoption, and the overall success of the product. When a product is compatible with other products and systems, it allows users to easily connect, share data, and leverage the capabilities of multiple products together, enhancing the user experience and providing added value. There are different dimensions of product compatibility that product managers need to consider during the product development and planning phases. These dimensions include: 1. Technical Compatibility: This dimension focuses on the technical aspects of compatibility, such as hardware and software requirements, programming interfaces, protocols, and data formats. Ensuring that a product is compatible at the technical level allows it to seamlessly integrate and communicate with other products, systems, and platforms. 2. Functional Compatibility: This dimension relates to the ability of a product to perform its intended functions and collaborate with other products to deliver a desired outcome. It involves ensuring that the product can interact with other products in a way that aligns with the user's needs and expectations. 3. User Experience Compatibility: This dimension involves considering the user experience when using multiple products together. It focuses on ensuring that the interaction between products is intuitive, seamless, and consistent, providing a cohesive user experience across the entire ecosystem. Product managers need to carefully analyze the compatibility requirements of their target market and assess the potential impact of compatibility decisions on the product's success. They need to collaborate with cross-functional teams, including engineers, designers, and developers, to identify compatibility requirements, establish standards, and implement effective integration mechanisms. By prioritizing product compatibility, product managers can enhance the value proposition of their products, differentiate themselves in the market, and attract and retain more customers. It allows customers to build a comprehensive ecosystem of products that work together harmoniously, providing a more integrated and efficient solution to their needs.

Product Competitive Analysis

A product competitive analysis in the context of product management refers to the process of evaluating and comparing a company's product against its competitors' products. It involves examining various factors such as features, pricing, quality, marketing strategies, and customer satisfaction to understand how the product stacks up against the competition. The objective of a product competitive analysis is to gain insight into the strengths and weaknesses of the company's product in relation to its competitors. By understanding the competitive landscape, product managers can make informed decisions and develop strategies to position their product effectively in the market. During a product competitive analysis, product managers gather information about competing products through various methods, including market research, customer surveys, competitor websites, and reviews. They also analyze the target market and identify the key segments in which the product competes. One important aspect of a competitive analysis is comparing the features and functionalities of the product in question with those of its competitors. This helps assess the product's uniqueness, its value proposition, and how it meets the needs of the target customers. It also helps identify areas where the product falls short and where improvements can be made. Pricing is another critical factor in a product competitive analysis. Product managers need to compare the pricing of their product with that of competitors to determine if it is competitive in the market. They also consider the perceived value of the product and whether customers are willing to pay the given price. Adjustments to pricing may be necessary based on this analysis. Additionally, a thorough analysis of competitors' marketing strategies and messaging enables product managers to find ways to differentiate their product and craft effective marketing campaigns. By understanding how competitors reach and engage with customers, product managers can identify opportunities or gaps in the market to gain a competitive advantage. Customer satisfaction and feedback are crucial indicators of a product's performance in the market. Analyzing customer reviews, ratings, and feedback about both the company's product and its competitors' products can provide insights into the strengths and weaknesses of the products and help identify areas for improvement. In conclusion, a product competitive analysis is a systematic evaluation and comparison of a company's product against its competitors' products. It involves analyzing various factors such as features, pricing, quality, marketing strategies, and customer satisfaction to understand the product's position in the market and identify opportunities for improvement and differentiation.

Product Competitors

Product competitors are companies or products that offer similar products or services to the same target market as a particular product. In the context of Product Management, identifying and understanding product competitors is crucial for developing effective product strategies and making informed business decisions. The first step in identifying product competitors is conducting a competitive analysis, which involves researching and gathering information about other companies' products that are similar to the product in question. This analysis helps in understanding the competitive landscape, market trends, and customer preferences.

Product Compliance

Product compliance refers to the adherence of a product to a set of regulations, standards, and requirements imposed by governing bodies or industry organizations. It involves ensuring that a product meets all legal, safety, quality, and environmental requirements before it can be introduced to the market or used by consumers. In the context of product management, product compliance plays a crucial role in the development, launch, and ongoing management of a product. It encompasses various aspects, including product design, development, sourcing, manufacturing, labeling, packaging, distribution, and end-of-life disposal. At the design and development stage, product managers need to consider compliance requirements to ensure that the product meets all applicable standards and regulations. This may involve conducting thorough research to identify the specific regulations and standards that apply to the product's intended market or industry. Product managers collaborate with designers, engineers, and other stakeholders to incorporate compliance considerations into the product's specifications and features. Once the product design is finalized, product managers work closely with suppliers and manufacturers to ensure that the product is produced in compliance with relevant regulations and standards. They may establish quality control processes, conduct audits, and perform testing to verify compliance. This includes assessing factors such as product safety, performance, reliability, and environmental impact. Product compliance also encompasses labeling and packaging requirements. Product managers are responsible for ensuring that all necessary information, warnings, and instructions are provided on the product's label or packaging. This may involve working with legal and regulatory teams to ensure accurate and compliant labeling. Furthermore, product managers need to consider compliance requirements during distribution and marketing activities. They must ensure that the product is distributed and marketed in accordance with relevant laws and regulations. This may involve obtaining the necessary certifications, permits, or licenses, and adhering to advertising and promotion guidelines. Overall, product compliance is an essential aspect of product management, as it helps to mitigate risks, ensure customer safety and satisfaction, maintain legal and regulatory compliance, and protect the brand's reputation. By incorporating compliance considerations throughout the product's lifecycle, product managers can address potential issues proactively and deliver products that meet the highest standards of quality, safety, and legal compliance.

Product Concept

A product concept is a detailed description of a new product idea that is being developed by a company. It outlines the key features, benefits, and value proposition of the product, as well as any unique selling points or competitive advantages it may have. The product concept is an essential tool in the product management process, as it helps align the team's vision and ensures that everyone is on the same page regarding the product's direction. It serves as a guide for the product development process, providing clarity and direction to the team.

Product Configuration Management

Product Configuration Management is a process in Product Management that involves managing and controlling the configuration of a product throughout its lifecycle. It encompasses the identification, documentation, and control of all product components, their relationships, and the changes made to them. The main goal of Product Configuration Management is to ensure that the product being delivered to customers is accurate, consistent, and meets their requirements. It enables organizations to effectively manage product variations and options, ensuring that each configuration is properly defined, documented, and controlled.

Product Configuration Tools

Product Configuration Tools are software applications that enable product managers to define and manage the various configurations and options of a product. These tools provide a structured way for product managers to specify the different features, components, and options that can be included or excluded from a product. By using product configuration tools, product managers can easily define and document the various configurations and options available for a product. This includes specifying the different versions or models of a product, as well as the various features, options, and components that can be selected or customized by the customer. The main purpose of product configuration tools is to streamline the process of managing and documenting the configurations and options of a product. This helps product managers to ensure that the right configurations are available to the customer, and that they are accurately reflected in the product documentation, pricing, and manufacturing processes. Product configuration tools also enable product managers to create rules and dependencies between different configurations and options. For example, they can specify that certain options are only available if specific features or components are selected. This helps to ensure that the selected configurations are feasible and compatible. In addition, product configuration tools often include visualization features that allow product managers to see how different configurations and options affect the overall appearance or functionality of a product. This can help them to make informed decisions about the design and customization of the product. Overall, product configuration tools play a critical role in product management by providing a structured and efficient way to define, manage, and document the configurations and options of a product. They help product managers to ensure that the right configurations are available to the customer, and that they are accurately reflected in the product documentation, pricing, and manufacturing processes.

Product Continuous Improvement

Product continuous improvement is a fundamental aspect of product management that involves an ongoing effort to enhance and refine a product to meet customer needs and expectations better. It is the practice of iteratively assessing, analyzing, and making adjustments to a product throughout its lifecycle to ensure its continued success in the market. The process of product continuous improvement begins with gathering and analyzing feedback from customers, stakeholders, and market trends. This feedback serves as valuable insights into areas of improvement and opportunities for innovation. By actively seeking feedback, product managers can gain a deeper understanding of customer pain points, identify areas where the product is falling short, and uncover potential new features or enhancements that would resonate with users. Once feedback has been collected, it is important for product managers to prioritize and categorize the suggested improvements. They must evaluate the potential impact of each improvement on the product's overall value proposition and align them with the organization's strategic goals. This prioritization helps ensure that the most critical areas for improvement are addressed first, within the available resources and time constraints. After setting priorities, product managers collaborate with cross-functional teams, including designers, engineers, and marketers, to ideate, design, and implement the proposed improvements. This collaborative effort ensures that different perspectives and expertise are considered in the improvement process, leading to more comprehensive and effective solutions. Product continuous improvement also involves measuring and evaluating the impact of implemented improvements. Product managers must establish key performance indicators (KPIs) to gauge the success of each improvement and track the overall performance of the product. These KPIs can include metrics such as user satisfaction, adoption rate, revenue growth, and customer retention. By regularly reviewing and analyzing the performance data, product managers gain insights into the effectiveness of the implemented improvements and identify areas that may require further adjustments. This iterative process of improvement, measurement, and adjustment allows product managers to continuously refine and enhance the product, staying ahead of competitors and meeting evolving customer needs.

Product Copyright

Product copyright refers to the legal protection granted to the original expression or design of a product. It allows the creator or manufacturer of a product to have exclusive rights to reproduce, distribute, and sell the product for a specified period of time. This protection is granted under the copyright law to encourage innovation and creativity in the field of product development. As a product manager, understanding and managing product copyright is essential to ensuring the company's intellectual property is safeguarded and that the product's unique features and design are protected from unauthorized use or imitation. It involves working closely with legal teams and intellectual property experts to obtain and enforce copyright protection for the product.

Product Cost Analysis

A product cost analysis is a method used in product management to determine the total cost associated with the production and delivery of a product. It involves analyzing all the costs incurred throughout the product lifecycle, from the development and manufacturing processes to the distribution and after-sales support. The purpose of a product cost analysis is to provide insights into the various components of the cost structure and help decision-makers identify areas where costs can be reduced or optimized. By understanding the cost drivers and their impact on the overall product cost, product managers can make informed decisions about pricing, profitability, and resource allocation.

Product Cost Reduction

Product cost reduction refers to the process of identifying and implementing strategies to decrease the expenses associated with producing a product, without compromising its quality or functionality. In the context of product management, product cost reduction plays a crucial role in enhancing profitability and staying competitive in the market. It requires a systematic analysis of all components, processes, and resources involved in the production of a product to identify potential areas for cost reduction. Product managers are responsible for overseeing the entire lifecycle of a product, from ideation to development and launch. They collaborate with cross-functional teams, including engineering, manufacturing, procurement, and finance, to ensure that the product is delivered at the optimal cost without sacrificing its value or performance. There are various approaches to achieve product cost reduction. One common strategy is conducting a thorough cost analysis to identify and prioritize cost-saving opportunities. This analysis involves assessing the cost of raw materials, labor, overhead expenses, and other production-related factors. By understanding the cost drivers and their impact on the overall expenses, product managers can make informed decisions for cost reduction. Once the potential cost-saving opportunities are identified, product managers can explore different strategies to achieve the desired reductions. This may involve finding alternative suppliers or negotiating better pricing terms, optimizing manufacturing processes to increase efficiency, or redesigning the product to simplify its production and assembly. However, it is crucial to ensure that cost reduction efforts do not compromise the product's quality, as this could negatively impact customer satisfaction and brand reputation. Product managers must collaborate closely with the engineering and quality teams to ensure that any changes or optimizations are thoroughly evaluated and validated. In conclusion, product cost reduction is an essential aspect of product management, aimed at decreasing expenses associated with producing a product while maintaining its quality and functionality. Through careful analysis, strategic decision-making, and collaboration with cross-functional teams, product managers can maximize profitability and remain competitive in the market.

Product Costing

Product costing refers to the process of determining the total cost incurred in manufacturing a product or providing a service. It involves identifying and assigning all the direct and indirect costs associated with the production or service delivery, including materials, labor, and overhead expenses, to each unit of the product. The purpose of product costing in product management is to gain a comprehensive understanding of the actual cost of producing a product. This information is vital for pricing decisions, profit analysis, and cost control. By accurately determining and analyzing the costs, product managers can make informed decisions about pricing strategies, profit margins, and cost reduction initiatives.

Product Cross-Functional Teams

A Product Cross-Functional Team, in the context of Product Management, refers to a group of individuals from different functional areas within an organization who come together to collaborate on developing and managing a product from conception to market launch. This team is composed of representatives from various departments such as engineering, design, marketing, sales, customer support, and finance. The main purpose of a Product Cross-Functional Team is to ensure that all aspects of the product development process are taken into consideration and to facilitate effective communication and coordination between different departments. By bringing together experts from different disciplines, the team can leverage their diverse knowledge and perspectives to make more informed decisions and solve complex problems. One of the key benefits of a Product Cross-Functional Team is that it helps streamline the product development process and reduces the time and effort required to bring a product to market. By having representatives from each department involved from the beginning, potential issues or bottlenecks can be identified and addressed early on, minimizing the need for rework or delays later in the process. Additionally, a Product Cross-Functional Team enables better alignment between departments and ensures that everyone is working towards the same goal. This collaboration and shared understanding of the product vision and objectives also helps create a sense of ownership and accountability among team members, leading to increased motivation and productivity. The success of a Product Cross-Functional Team relies heavily on effective communication and collaboration. Regular meetings and interactions between team members are essential to exchange information, provide updates on progress, and address any challenges or roadblocks. Transparency and openness are critical for fostering a culture of trust and cooperation within the team. In conclusion, a Product Cross-Functional Team is an integral part of Product Management, bringing together individuals from various departments to collaboratively develop and manage a product. By leveraging the diverse expertise of its members, this team ensures a holistic approach to product development, streamlines the process, and promotes effective communication and alignment.

Product Customer Support

Product Customer Support, in the context of Product Management, is the dedicated team or function responsible for providing assistance and resolving issues faced by customers throughout the product lifecycle. This includes pre-purchase queries, post-purchase support, troubleshooting, and complaint resolution. The primary objective of Product Customer Support is to ensure customer satisfaction by addressing their concerns and providing prompt and effective solutions. The team works closely with various stakeholders, such as product managers, engineers, and sales representatives, to understand customer needs and deliver optimal support.

Product Data API Integration

A Product Data API Integration refers to the process of incorporating an Application Programming Interface (API) into a product management system in order to retrieve, update, and synchronize product data from external sources. An API acts as a bridge between different software applications, allowing them to exchange information and perform tasks seamlessly. In the context of product management, an API integration enables product managers to gather product data such as descriptions, pricing, availability, and specifications from various sources, including vendors, distributors, or internal databases. By integrating a Product Data API, product managers can enhance their ability to efficiently manage and maintain accurate and up-to-date product information. This integration provides several benefits: Firstly, it simplifies the process of gathering product information by automating the retrieval of data from external sources. Instead of manually collecting data from multiple systems or spreadsheets, product managers can rely on the API to fetch the necessary information in real-time, ensuring that they always have access to the most current and accurate data. Secondly, API integration facilitates the synchronization of product data across different systems. This eliminates the need for duplicate data entry or manual updates, reducing the risk of errors and inconsistencies. Product managers can update product information in a central system, and the API takes care of propagating the changes to all integrated platforms or channels, ensuring data consistency. Furthermore, API integration enables product managers to streamline their workflows by integrating product data seamlessly with other essential systems, such as ecommerce platforms, inventory management systems, or customer relationship management (CRM) tools. This interconnectedness enhances the efficiency of product management processes and allows for better decision making based on accurate and holistic product data. In conclusion, a Product Data API Integration empowers product managers by providing a streamlined and automated approach to gathering, updating, and synchronizing product data from various sources. It ensures data accuracy, consistency, and efficiency, facilitating effective product management and ultimately contributing to improved customer experiences and business success.

Product Data API

A Product Data API is an application programming interface that allows product managers to access and manage product data through software applications. It provides a standardized way for software systems to communicate and exchange information related to products, such as their attributes, prices, availability, and other relevant details. The Product Data API acts as a bridge between different software applications, enabling seamless integration and synchronization of product information across multiple systems. It allows product managers to create, update, and retrieve product data without needing to directly access the underlying databases or systems.

Product Data Access Control Mechanism

A product data access control mechanism refers to a system or method implemented in product management to control and regulate access to product data, ensuring that only authorized individuals or entities can view, modify, or retrieve specific information relating to a product. Product data includes various types of information such as product specifications, pricing details, inventory levels, customer feedback, and sales reports. These data are crucial for making informed decisions, managing product lifecycles, and ensuring accurate information dissemination across relevant teams and stakeholders. The access control mechanism is designed to prevent unauthorized access, disclosure, or modification of product data, which could potentially lead to data breaches, unauthorized use of sensitive information, or manipulation of product-related details. It creates a secure environment where only authorized personnel can access and interact with the product data. There are several components involved in a product data access control mechanism: - User authentication: This component ensures that individuals attempting to access product data are authenticated through a secure process, such as login credentials, biometric authentication, or access tokens. This helps verify their identity and restrict access to authorized users only. - Role-based access control: The mechanism implements a system where different users can be assigned specific roles or permissions, enabling them to access only the data and functions relevant to their responsibilities. This ensures that access to sensitive product data is limited to individuals who require it for their job roles. - Access controls and permissions: The mechanism defines and enforces the specific access controls and permissions for different users or user groups. This includes specifying who can view, edit, or delete certain product data, as well as setting restrictions on certain functionalities or data fields. - Logging and auditing: The access control mechanism may include logging and auditing capabilities to track and monitor access to product data. This helps identify any unauthorized access attempts or suspicious activities, ensuring accountability and enabling quick response to any security incidents. Overall, a product data access control mechanism plays a vital role in maintaining the confidentiality, integrity, and availability of product data, protecting it from unauthorized access and ensuring that it is accessed and used only by authorized individuals or entities.

Product Data Access Control

Product Data Access Control refers to the process of managing and regulating the access to product data within an organization. It involves establishing and enforcing rules and policies to ensure that only authorized individuals or systems are granted access to the product data. In the context of Product Management, product data includes information related to the features, specifications, pricing, availability, and other details of a product. This data is crucial for making informed decisions, meeting customer needs, and driving business success. Therefore, it is essential to control access to this data and protect it from unauthorized access, modification, or misuse. The purpose of Product Data Access Control is twofold. Firstly, it aims to maintain the integrity and accuracy of the product data by preventing unauthorized modifications or tampering. By restricting access to trusted and qualified individuals or systems, organizations can ensure that the product data reflects the most up-to-date and reliable information. Secondly, Product Data Access Control aims to protect sensitive or confidential product information from being viewed or accessed by unauthorized individuals. This is particularly important in industries with strict compliance regulations, where the unauthorized disclosure of product data could lead to legal or financial consequences. Product Data Access Control is typically implemented through a combination of technical measures, such as user authentication, role-based access control, encryption, and auditing. User authentication ensures that only authorized individuals with valid credentials can access the product data. Role-based access control assigns specific permissions and privileges based on the user's role or responsibilities within the organization. Encryption is used to secure the transmission and storage of product data, making it unreadable to unauthorized parties. Auditing allows organizations to monitor and track access to the product data, providing an additional layer of accountability and traceability. Overall, Product Data Access Control is a critical aspect of Product Management, ensuring that the right people have access to the right product data at the right time. By implementing robust access control measures, organizations can safeguard their product information, maintain data integrity, and comply with regulatory requirements.

Product Data Access Management Solution Implementation

Product Data Access Management Solution Implementation refers to the process of implementing a system that allows product managers to efficiently manage and control access to product data within an organization. This solution ensures that only authorized personnel can access and modify product information, while also providing a centralized platform for product teams to collaborate and share data. The implementation of a Product Data Access Management Solution involves several key steps. First, organizations need to define their access control policies and roles, determining who should have access to specific product data and what actions they can perform. This includes setting up permissions for different user groups, such as product managers, designers, engineers, and sales representatives. Next, the implementation process involves configuring the solution and integrating it with existing product management systems. This may involve customizing the solution to align with the organization's

87

specific workflows and data structures. Integration with other software tools, such as customer relationship management (CRM) systems or enterprise resource planning (ERP) systems, ensures a seamless flow of product data across different departments. Once the system is configured, organizations need to migrate existing product data into the solution. This could involve importing data from spreadsheets, databases, or other sources. It is essential to ensure data integrity and accuracy during this process to avoid any discrepancies or errors in the product information. After the data migration, organizations must train their product teams on how to effectively use the Product Data Access Management Solution. This includes providing instruction on accessing and editing product data, as well as utilizing the solution's collaborative features for teamwork and information sharing. Ongoing support and training may be necessary as the organization grows and new team members join. In summary, the implementation of a Product Data Access Management Solution enables organizations to streamline their product management processes, ensuring that product data is secure, accessible to authorized personnel, and easily shared among teams. By centralizing and controlling access to product data, organizations can enhance collaboration, improve data accuracy, and make more informed product decisions.

Product Data Access Management

Product Data Access Management refers to the process of controlling and regulating access to product information within an organization. It involves managing the permissions and restrictions on who can view, edit, and manipulate product data, ensuring that only authorized individuals have the appropriate level of access. Effective product data access management is crucial for product management teams, as it helps maintain data integrity, confidentiality, and security. By implementing robust access management practices, organizations can protect their sensitive product information from unauthorized access, misuse, and potential breaches.

Product Data Analysis

Product Data Analysis is the process of examining and interpreting data related to a product's performance, usage, and customer feedback in order to gain insights and make informed decisions to improve the product and its overall strategy. Product Managers use data analysis techniques to extract meaningful insights from various sources of data, such as customer surveys, user feedback, sales data, and market research. By analyzing this data, they can identify patterns, trends, and correlations, which can be used to inform product development, marketing strategies, and overall business decisions.

Product Data Analytics

Product Data Analytics is a critical component of Product Management that involves collecting, analyzing, and interpreting data related to a product's performance, usage, and customer behavior. It enables product managers to make data-driven decisions and strategically improve the product to meet customer needs and drive business growth. In the context of Product Management, Product Data Analytics encompasses the systematic tracking and analysis of various data points that provide insights into the product's lifecycle. This includes gathering data from different sources such as user interactions, sales figures, customer feedback, and market trends. By leveraging this data, product managers gain a deep understanding of how the product is being used, how it is performing in the market, and the customers' preferences and pain points. Product Data Analytics enables product managers to identify patterns, trends, and correlations in the data that can inform their decision-making process. Through data analysis, they can uncover opportunities for product improvements, identify feature gaps, and prioritize development efforts based on customer needs and market demands. Additionally, this analytical approach allows product managers to measure the impact of their decisions and track the success of product initiatives over time. Furthermore, Product Data Analytics empowers product managers to identify key performance indicators (KPIs) that align with the product's goals and objectives. By establishing relevant metrics, they can track the product's performance against these benchmarks and make informed decisions to optimize its success. This data-driven approach also helps in evaluating the effectiveness of marketing campaigns, pricing strategies, and product launches, enabling product managers to make necessary adjustments and improvements. In summary, Product Data Analytics equips product managers with the insights needed to drive product strategy and development. By analyzing and interpreting data related to the product's performance and customer behavior, they can make informed decisions, prioritize development efforts, and continuously improve the product to meet customer needs and achieve business objectives.

Product Data Anonymization Method

A product data anonymization method refers to the process of transforming and obfuscating the sensitive and personally identifiable information (PII) in product-related data, in order to protect the privacy and confidentiality of individuals while still allowing for meaningful analysis and management of the data. The method involves removing or encrypting data elements that could potentially identify individuals, such as names, addresses, phone numbers, and email addresses. Additionally, it may involve the substitution of sensitive values with random or generalized values, or the aggregation of data at higher levels to ensure anonymity. Product data typically includes a wide range of information, such as sales data, customer information, product specifications, and purchase histories. These datasets can be extremely valuable for product management teams, as they provide insights into customer behavior, market trends, and product performance. However, the use of such data must be done in compliance with privacy regulations and ethical considerations. An effective product data anonymization method should strike a balance between preserving the usefulness of the data for analysis and protecting the privacy of individuals. It should ensure that the process of anonymization does not result in the loss of important patterns or relationships within the data, while still preventing re-identification of individuals. There are various techniques and best practices for product data anonymization, such as: - Generalization: replacing specific values with higher-level categories or ranges. For example, replacing exact ages with age brackets. - Masking: replacing sensitive data with masking characters or tokens. For example, replacing the last four digits of a credit card number with 'X'. - Perturbation: adding random noise or altering values slightly to prevent exact identification. For example, adding a small random offset to geographic coordinates. - Data obfuscation: transforming the data in a way that makes it difficult to interpret. This may involve data shuffling, substituting values with synonyms, or applying encryption. Implementing a robust product data anonymization method is crucial for product management teams to protect customer privacy, comply with regulations, and build trust with customers and stakeholders. By ensuring that the data is anonymized effectively, product managers can confidently use the insights gained from data analysis to make informed decisions and drive product strategy.

Product Data Anonymization

Product data anonymization refers to the process of removing or altering personal or identifying information from a product dataset in order to protect the privacy and confidentiality of individuals. This is done by transforming the data in such a way that it can no longer be attributed to a specific person or entity. The goal of product data anonymization is to enable organizations to use and share product data for analysis, research, and development purposes without violating privacy regulations or compromising the security of sensitive information. By anonymizing the data, organizations can reap the benefits of data-driven decision making and innovation while ensuring that the privacy rights of individuals are protected.

Product Data Asset Management Platform Utilization

A Product Data Asset Management Platform is a centralized system that is utilized by product managers to effectively manage and organize product data throughout its lifecycle. It allows product managers to collect, store, organize, and analyze various types of data related to a product, such as specifications, descriptions, images, pricing information, and customer feedback. This platform serves as a comprehensive repository for all product-related information, enabling product managers to access and update data easily and efficiently. It provides a structured framework for organizing and categorizing product data, ensuring that it is accurate, up-to-date, and easily searchable. By utilizing a Product Data Asset Management Platform, product managers can streamline their workflows and improve collaboration among cross-functional teams involved in product development and marketing. It facilitates effective communication and alignment across departments, ensuring that everyone has access to the latest and most accurate product information. In addition, this platform enables product managers to gain valuable insights through data analysis. They can track and analyze product performance metrics, such as sales, customer satisfaction, and market trends, to make informed decisions and drive product strategy. Furthermore, a Product Data Asset Management Platform plays a crucial role in ensuring data integrity and compliance. It provides controls and security systems to prevent unauthorized access or modification of product data, as well as adhering to regulatory requirements and data privacy standards. In summary, a Product Data Asset Management Platform is a centralized system that allows product managers to efficiently manage, organize, and analyze product data throughout its lifecycle. It streamlines workflows, facilitates collaboration, provides insights through data analysis, and ensures data integrity and compliance. By leveraging this platform, product managers can effectively meet customer needs, drive product innovation, and enhance overall product management processes.

Product Data Asset Management

Product Data Asset Management, in the context of Product Management, refers to the systematic process of organizing, storing, and utilizing product data throughout its lifecycle. Product data, which includes information about a product's attributes, features, specifications, and related documents, is a valuable asset for any organization. Effective management of this data is crucial for ensuring accurate, up-to-date, and accessible information that can support various product-related activities, such as development, marketing, sales, and customer support. The main objectives of Product Data Asset Management are: 1. Centralization: It involves consolidating product data from various sources and storing it in a centralized repository. This allows easy access to the data by different teams and departments involved in product management, enabling them to make informed decisions based on accurate and consistent information. It also facilitates collaboration and eliminates duplicate or outdated data. 2. Organization: Product data needs to be effectively organized to enable efficient retrieval and utilization. This involves categorizing and classifying the data based on relevant attributes, such as product type, category, and variations. By structuring the data in a logical manner, it becomes easier to navigate and locate specific information when needed. 3. Maintenance: Product data is dynamic and requires regular updates to reflect the latest changes and improvements. Product Data Asset Management ensures that the data is kept up-to-date by establishing maintenance processes, such as version control and change management. This helps in avoiding confusion and discrepancies caused by outdated or incorrect product information. 4. Integration: Product data is often used by different systems and applications within an organization. Effective Product Data Asset Management involves integrating the product data repository with other systems, such as Enterprise Resource Planning (ERP) and Customer Relationship Management (CRM) systems. This integration ensures seamless data flow between different processes and enhances overall efficiency. By implementing Product Data Asset Management practices, organizations can enhance their product management capabilities, improve decision-making, streamline processes, and ultimately deliver better products to their customers.

Product Data Backup

Product Data Backup refers to the process of creating copies of important product data and storing them in a secure location, in order to protect against potential data loss or corruption. This is a critical aspect of product management, as it ensures that valuable data related to the product's design, features, specifications, and other relevant information is safeguarded and can be easily restored if needed. The primary purpose of product data backup is to minimize the risk of data loss and ensure business continuity. By creating regular backups, product managers can mitigate the impact of potential data disasters, such as system crashes, accidental deletion, or hardware failures. This allows for quick recovery of data and prevents any disruptions to the product development process, customer support activities, or any other key operations.

Product Data Blending Tool

A product data blending tool is a software or tool used in product management to consolidate, integrate, and analyze data from various sources. It enables product managers to bring together data from different systems, such as sales, marketing, customer relationship management (CRM), inventory, and other relevant sources, into a single unified view. The primary purpose of a product data blending tool is to provide product managers with a comprehensive and holistic understanding of their products and their performance in the market. By blending data from different sources, it helps product managers identify patterns, trends, and insights that can inform their decision-making process and drive strategic initiatives. The tool allows product managers to access and analyze data in real-time, providing them with up-to-date information on key performance indicators (KPIs) such as sales revenue, market share, customer satisfaction, and product profitability. This enables them to quickly identify and respond to market opportunities or address any issues that may arise. In addition to consolidating data, a product data blending tool also helps product managers cleanse and standardize the data, ensuring accuracy and consistency. It provides capabilities to transform and map data from different formats and structures, reconciling inconsistencies and resolving any conflicts or duplications. Furthermore, the tool offers advanced analytics and visualization features to help product managers gain actionable insights from the blended data. It provides dashboards, reports, and visualizations that allow them to track product performance, conduct market analysis, monitor competitive landscape, and make data-driven decisions. Overall, a product data blending tool is a crucial component of the product management toolkit. It allows product managers to effectively manage and leverage vast amounts of data from disparate sources, empowering them with the information they need to drive product success, enhance customer experiences, and achieve their business objectives.

Product Data Blending

Product Data Blending is an essential process in Product Management that involves combining and integrating multiple sources of data to create a comprehensive and accurate view of a product and its performance. It allows product managers to analyze and understand various aspects of a product, such as its market, customers, competitors, and sales, by bringing together data from different systems and sources. Data blending involves collecting data from diverse sources, such as sales systems, customer relationship management (CRM) platforms, marketing analytics tools, social media platforms, and market research sources, and blending or merging them into a single dataset. This consolidated dataset provides product managers with a holistic view of the product's performance and helps them make informed decisions for product strategy, development, and marketing. Data blending enables product managers to gain insights into various dimensions of a product, such as its sales trends, customer behavior, market segmentation, and competitive landscape. By blending data from sales systems, they can track product sales and identify patterns or trends in sales performance. By integrating data from CRM platforms, they can understand customer preferences, behavior, and feedback, and tailor the product accordingly. By merging data from marketing analytics tools and social media platforms, they can evaluate the effectiveness of marketing campaigns, identify customer sentiment, and identify opportunities for improvement. By incorporating market research data, they can assess market trends, customer needs, and competitor strategies to position the product effectively. Data blending also facilitates data visualization, where product managers can create visual representations of the blended data to communicate insights effectively to stakeholders. This visualization helps product managers present complex information in a clear and concise manner, enabling better decision-making by product teams, executives, and other stakeholders. In conclusion, Product Data Blending is a critical process in Product Management that involves combining and integrating data from multiple sources to create a comprehensive view of a product's performance. It allows product managers to analyze various dimensions of a product and make informed decisions for product strategy, development, and marketing.

Product Data Catalog Management Solution Deployment

A Product Data Catalog Management Solution Deployment refers to the process of implementing a software system that enables efficient and effective management of product data catalogs. It involves the installation, configuration, and setup of the solution on the organization's infrastructure. The primary objective of a Product Data Catalog Management Solution is to centralize and streamline the management of product information. It provides a digital platform for gathering, organizing, and distributing product data across various channels such as e-commerce websites, mobile applications, and catalogs. During the deployment process, the solution is customized to align with the organization's specific needs and requirements. This may involve configuring the system to support different product categories, attributes, and workflows. Integration with other enterprise systems, such as ERP or CRM, may also be part of the deployment process. Once deployed, the Product Data Catalog Management Solution enables product managers and administrators to efficiently manage and maintain product information. It provides a centralized repository where product data can be stored, updated, and enriched. This includes information such as product descriptions, specifications, images, pricing, and inventory levels. The solution allows for the creation of product hierarchies and taxonomies, making it easier to organize and categorize products. It also supports the management of product attributes, allowing for the definition and association of various product characteristics. This ensures consistent and accurate product information across all sales channels. With a deployed Product Data Catalog Management Solution, organizations can improve their product management processes and enhance the customer experience. It enables faster time-to-market for new products, reduces errors and inconsistencies in product information, and provides a single source of truth for product data across the organization.

Product Data Catalog Management

Product Data Catalog Management is the process of organizing, updating, and maintaining a comprehensive and accurate database of product information within a company or organization. It involves collecting, categorizing, and enriching product data, ensuring its consistency and quality, and making it easily accessible to various stakeholders. Effective product data catalog management is crucial for successful product management as it provides a centralized repository of information that enables better decision-making, streamlines operations, and enhances customer satisfaction. It involves the following key activities: 1. Data Collection: Product data catalog management starts with gathering relevant data from various sources, including suppliers, manufacturers, and internal departments. This data may include product descriptions, specifications, images, pricing information, and other relevant attributes. 2. Categorization and Classification: Once collected, the product data needs to be organized into meaningful categories and classifications. This ensures that products can be easily found, compared, and grouped together based on common characteristics. Categorization also enables effective navigation and search functionalities within the catalog. 3. Enrichment and Enhancement: Product data may need to be enriched with additional information to provide a more comprehensive view of each product. This could involve adding product features, benefits, compatibility information, or cross-referencing with related products or accessories. Enhancing the data improves customers' understanding of the product, leading to better purchase decisions. 4. Data Quality Management: Maintaining data accuracy, completeness, and consistency is crucial for effective catalog management. This involves performing regular data audits, resolving inconsistencies or errors, updating outdated information, and validating data against predefined standards or guidelines. 5. Integration and Syndication: To ensure the availability and consistency of product information across various channels, the product data catalog needs to be integrated with other systems, such as e-commerce platforms, marketing tools, and sales databases. Syndication ensures that the product data is effectively distributed to external marketplaces, catalogs, or websites. Overall, effective product data catalog management improves operational efficiency, reduces errors, enhances customer experience, and empowers businesses to make informed decisions. By centralizing and organizing product information, companies can streamline their product management processes, drive sales, and stay ahead in today's competitive market.

Product Data Catalog

A Product Data Catalog is a centralized repository that stores and organizes all product-related information in a structured and standardized format. It serves as a single source of truth for product data, enabling product managers to efficiently manage and maintain accurate information about their products throughout their lifecycle.

Product Data Cluster Analysis Tool

A Product Data Cluster Analysis Tool is a software tool designed for Product Managers to analyze and extract insights from product data. It helps Product Managers make data-driven decisions by identifying patterns and grouping similar products together based on various attributes and features. The tool uses advanced algorithms and statistical techniques to cluster products based on their similarities in terms of characteristics such as pricing, features, customer ratings, and usage patterns. By applying cluster analysis, the tool can automatically categorize products into meaningful segments, enabling Product Managers to gain a deeper understanding of their product portfolio.

Product Data Cluster Analysis

Product Data Cluster Analysis is a statistical technique used in the field of Product Management to categorize and group similar products based on their attributes and characteristics. This analysis helps product managers gain insights into their product portfolios and make informed decisions regarding product development, marketing strategies, and customer segmentation. The process of Product Data Cluster Analysis involves collecting and analyzing large amounts of product data, such as product features, specifications, pricing, customer reviews, and sales metrics. This data is then used to identify patterns, similarities, and relationships between different products. By clustering products into meaningful groups, product managers can better understand the market dynamics, customer preferences, and competitive landscape.

Product Data Compliance Framework

A Product Data Compliance Framework refers to a set of guidelines, processes, and controls implemented by product management teams to ensure that their product data practices comply with relevant laws and regulations, industry standards, and internal policies. This framework helps establish a structured approach to handling and managing product data, ensuring data integrity, privacy, and security, while also fostering transparency and accountability. The framework typically encompasses various aspects related to the collection, storage, processing, and sharing of product data. It defines the rules and procedures that product management teams must follow to ensure compliance with legal and regulatory requirements, such as data protection and privacy laws (e.g., GDPR, CCPA), industry-specific regulations, and internal data governance policies. One crucial component of a Product Data Compliance Framework is the identification and classification of different types of product data. This involves determining what data is considered personal information, sensitive information, or business-sensitive information. Classification helps guide the appropriate handling of data, including requirements for informed consent, data anonymization, data retention, and data access controls. Another key element of the framework is the establishment of data protection measures and controls. This includes implementing encryption techniques, access controls, and monitoring mechanisms to safeguard the confidentiality, integrity, and availability of product data. Additionally, the framework may outline procedures for incident response and breach notification, ensuring teams are prepared to address data breaches promptly and effectively. Furthermore, the framework may address data sharing practices, outlining guidelines for data exchange with external parties, such as partners, vendors, and customers. This may involve reviewing and assessing third-party data handling practices, establishing data-sharing agreements, and conducting due diligence to ensure compliance with applicable regulations. In summary, a Product Data Compliance Framework serves as a framework that guides product management teams in adhering to legal, regulatory, and internal requirements concerning the handling and management of product data. It helps establish and maintain trust with customers, protect sensitive information, and mitigate legal and reputational risks associated with non-compliance.

Product Data Compliance

Product Data Compliance refers to the adherence and adherence to regulations, standards, and guidelines related to the collection, processing, storage, and use of product data within a product management context. It involves ensuring that all relevant data, including but not limited to product specifications, pricing information, user data, and transaction details, comply with applicable legal and industry requirements. Product managers are responsible for managing and overseeing the product data compliance processes within an organization. They need to ensure that the product data collected and used by the company aligns with legal and industry standards, considering factors such as data privacy, cybersecurity, intellectual property rights, and consumer protection. Product data compliance also includes the proper handling and protection of sensitive customer information. It requires implementing robust data security measures, such as encryption, access controls, and data anonymization, to minimize the risk of data breaches and unauthorized access. Furthermore, product data compliance involves maintaining accurate and up-to-date data records. It includes regularly auditing and validating product data to identify any inaccuracies or discrepancies, and taking corrective actions to rectify them. Product managers also play a crucial role in ensuring compliance with regulations related to product labeling and packaging. They need to ensure that product information, warnings, and instructions provided on the packaging are accurate, complete, and comply with legal requirements, such as health and safety standards. Overall, product data compliance is essential for maintaining trust and credibility with customers, partners, and regulatory authorities.

It helps organizations avoid legal issues, reputational damage, and financial penalties resulting from non-compliance. By prioritizing and proactively managing product data compliance, product managers contribute to building a strong foundation for successful product management and customer satisfaction.

Product Data Correlation Tool

A Product Data Correlation Tool is a software application or tool used in Product Management to analyze and identify correlations between different data points related to a product. It helps product managers make informed decisions by providing insights into the relationships between various aspects of a product's performance, features, customer feedback, and other key metrics. This tool generally takes input in the form of structured data, such as sales data, customer reviews, product ratings, market research, competitor analysis, and more. By processing and analyzing this data, the tool can uncover hidden patterns, associations, and relationships that may not be immediately evident to product managers. The primary purpose of a Product Data Correlation Tool is to provide product managers with data-driven insights to support decision-making throughout the product lifecycle. For example, it can help identify customer preferences, feature usage patterns, or correlations between specific product attributes and sales performance. Using the tool, product managers can conduct various analyses, such as: - Correlation Analysis: This involves identifying the degree of correlation between different variables related to a product. For instance, it can determine whether there is a positive correlation between customer satisfaction ratings and sales volume. - Feature Impact Analysis: This helps product managers understand the impact of specific features or product attributes on key performance metrics. By analyzing data, the tool can identify which features contribute the most to customer satisfaction or sales. - Market Segmentation Analysis: By analyzing customer data, the tool can help identify different customer segments based on their demographic, behavior, or preferences. This information can be used to tailor marketing strategies or develop targeted product offerings. Overall, a Product Data Correlation Tool plays a crucial role in Product Management by leveraging data to provide valuable insights and support data-driven decision-making. It enables product managers to better understand their products, customers, and markets, ultimately leading to more informed and successful product strategies.

Product Data Correlation

Product Data Correlation refers to the analysis and identification of the relationship between various data points and metrics related to a product. It involves examining the correlation between different product attributes, customer behaviors, market trends, and other factors that can impact the success or performance of a product. Product managers use data correlation to gain insights into how different factors interact with each other and influence the overall performance of a product. By analyzing the correlation between different data points, product managers can make more informed decisions, optimize product features, predict customer preferences, and enhance the overall user experience.

Product Data Dictionary Management Solution

A Product Data Dictionary Management Solution is a software tool or system that is used in the field of Product Management to organize and manage information about products in a standardized and centralized manner. The solution provides a structured framework for documenting and categorizing various attributes, characteristics, and specifications of a product. It serves as a central repository that stores and manages all product-related data, ensuring accuracy, consistency, and integrity of information across the organization.

Product Data Dictionary

A Product Data Dictionary is a structured document that provides a comprehensive description of the data elements used in the context of product management. It serves as a reference guide for product managers and other stakeholders to understand the meaning, purpose, and usage of each data element related to a specific product or product line. The purpose of a Product Data Dictionary is to establish a common understanding and clear communication about the data elements used in product management. It helps ensure consistency, accuracy, and integrity of product data across different systems, teams, and processes. By defining and documenting the data elements, their definitions, and attributes, product managers can make informed decisions regarding data capture, storage, analysis, and reporting. In a Product Data Dictionary, each data element is described individually, including its name, definition, format, range, source, dependencies, and any other relevant information. Additionally, it may include guidelines on data entry, data quality, data validation, and data maintenance for each data element. This ensures that everyone involved in product management can apply consistent standards and practices when utilizing and managing product data. Product Data Dictionaries are particularly useful in complex product management environments where multiple systems, applications, and stakeholders are involved. It helps bridge the gap between different teams, such as marketing, sales, engineering, manufacturing, and finance, by providing a shared understanding of product data. This promotes collaboration, improves decision-making, and reduces errors caused by misinterpretation or inconsistent use of data. In conclusion, a Product Data Dictionary is a vital tool for product managers to ensure the consistency, accuracy, and integrity of product data. By providing a comprehensive description of data elements and their attributes, it facilitates effective communication, collaboration, and decision-making in product management processes.

Product Data ETL Framework

A Product Data ETL (Extract, Transform, Load) Framework is a structured system that enables product managers to efficiently collect, organize, and integrate data from various sources into a centralized database or repository. The framework is designed to streamline the process of extracting raw product data, transforming it into a standardized format, and loading it into a database that can be easily accessed and analyzed by product managers. The ETL framework ensures that the data is accurate, consistent, and up-to-date, providing a solid foundation for informed decision-making and effective product management.

Product Data ETL

Product Data ETL, in the context of Product Management, refers to the process of Extracting, Transforming, and Loading (ETL) product data from various sources into a central repository in order to make it accessible and usable for product-related decision-making. Extract: The ETL process starts with extracting product data from multiple sources such as CRM systems, ERP systems, sales databases, customer feedback platforms, and third-party data providers. This involves identifying relevant data fields and extracting the data in a structured format to ensure data consistency and accuracy. Transform: Once the product data is extracted, it needs to be transformed to align with a standardized format that can be easily analyzed and used for decision-making. This includes cleaning and normalizing data, resolving inconsistencies or errors, removing duplicates, and aggregating data from different sources. Transformation also involves enriching the data by adding additional attributes or variables that provide more context and depth to the product information. Loading: After the data is transformed, it is loaded into a central repository or data warehouse specifically designed for product data management. This allows product managers and other stakeholders to access and query the data using analytics tools or Business Intelligence (BI) platforms. Loading the data into a central repository ensures data integrity, enables reliable reporting, and facilitates data-driven decision-making. Product Data ETL plays a critical role in Product Management by providing a single source of truth for product-related information. It enables product managers to gain a holistic view of their products, track performance metrics, identify trends, and generate insights that drive product strategy and decision-making. It also facilitates cross-functional collaboration by providing a shared platform for stakeholders to access and analyze product data in a consistent and efficient manner. In conclusion, Product Data ETL is an essential process in Product Management that involves the extraction, transformation, and loading of product data from various sources into a centralized repository. It ensures data consistency, integrity, and accessibility, empowering product managers to make informed decisions and drive successful product outcomes.

Product Data Encryption Algorithm

A Product Data Encryption Algorithm, in the context of Product Management, refers to a specific method or process for encrypting the data associated with a product. Encryption is the process of transforming readable data into a coded format to protect it from unauthorized access or use. The algorithm used for product data encryption is designed to ensure that sensitive information related to a product, such as user data, confidential or proprietary information, and financial data, is securely stored and transmitted. The encryption algorithm applies a set of rules and calculations to convert the original data into an encrypted form, making it unreadable without the correct decryption key.

Product Data Encryption

Product Data Encryption is a process in which sensitive data related to a product is converted into a coded or encrypted form to ensure its security and confidentiality. It involves the use of cryptographic algorithms to transform the data into an unreadable format, which can only be accessed or decoded by authorized individuals or systems. Product Management is responsible for managing the development, marketing, and distribution of a product throughout its lifecycle. In this role, Product Managers handle various types of data, including customer information, sales data, and competitive analysis. Protecting this data from unauthorized access or breaches is essential for maintaining customer trust and compliance with data protection regulations. Data encryption is a critical component of product management as it helps safeguard sensitive information from being compromised. By encrypting product data, Product Managers can prevent unauthorized individuals or systems from accessing valuable data such as customer contact details, pricing information, or sales performance figures. There are several benefits of implementing product data encryption within the context of Product Management. Firstly, it provides an additional layer of security to protect sensitive information from unauthorized access, reducing the risk of data breaches. This is particularly important in industries where confidential intellectual property or customer data is involved. Secondly, product data encryption helps to ensure compliance with data protection regulations, such as the General Data Protection Regulation (GDPR) or industry-specific standards. By encrypting data, Product Managers can demonstrate that they have implemented appropriate security measures to protect confidential information, reducing legal and reputational risks for their organization. Lastly, data encryption can enhance customer trust and confidence in the product and brand. When customers know that their personal and financial information is being encrypted and protected, they are more likely to trust the product and engage with the organization. This can lead to increased customer loyalty, positive brand perception, and ultimately, higher sales and profitability for the product.

Product Data Exploration Platform

A product data exploration platform is a tool specifically designed for product managers to analyze and understand various aspects of their products. It provides a centralized space where product managers can access, manipulate, and visualize product data in order to make informed decisions and drive product success. This platform allows product managers to gather, organize, and explore data related to their products, such as sales figures, customer feedback, market trends, and competitor analysis. By having a comprehensive view of these data points, product managers can identify patterns, trends, and insights that can contribute to the development and improvement of their products.

Product Data Exploration

Product data exploration refers to the process of gathering, analyzing, and interpreting data related to a product in order to gain insights and make informed decisions about its development, positioning, and success in the market. As a critical component of product management, data exploration involves examining various types of data, such as customer behavior, market trends, competitor analysis, and user feedback, to identify patterns, trends, and opportunities for improvement. By exploring product data, product managers can gain a deeper understanding of their target market, customer needs, and overall product performance, which helps inform product strategy and drive decision-making.

Product Data Flow Diagram Software

A Product Data Flow Diagram (DFD) software is a tool that enables Product Managers to visually represent and analyze the flow of data within a product or system. It helps in understanding how data moves, is processed, and is transformed within various components and stages of the product lifecycle. By using a DFD software, Product Managers can create diagrams that illustrate the data inputs, outputs, processes, and storage of a product. These diagrams provide a clear and concise representation of the data flow, helping the Product Managers to identify potential bottlenecks, inefficiencies, or vulnerabilities in the system.

Product Data Flow Diagram

A Product Data Flow Diagram is a visual representation of the flow of product information within a product management system. It illustrates how data is transmitted, processed, and stored throughout the product management lifecycle. The diagram consists of various components, including processes, data stores, external entities, and data flows. Processes represent the activities or tasks involved in managing a product, such as product planning, development, and marketing. Data stores are locations where product information is stored, such as databases or file systems. External entities are sources or destinations of product data, such as suppliers or customers. Data flows indicate the movement of information between these components. The main purpose of a Product Data Flow Diagram is to provide a clear visual representation of the product management system. It helps product managers and other stakeholders understand how product information flows through different stages and entities. This understanding is crucial for effectively managing products and ensuring efficient communication and coordination among various functions and entities involved in the process. By analyzing the Product Data Flow Diagram, product managers can identify potential bottlenecks or areas where data may get lost or misinterpreted. It also helps in streamlining the product management process by providing insights into how different elements interact and depend on each other. Product managers can use this information to optimize workflows and improve the overall efficiency of the product management system. In summary, a Product Data Flow Diagram serves as a visual representation of the flow of product information within a product management system. It assists product managers in understanding the movement of data, identifying potential issues, and optimizing the product management process.+

Product Data Governance Committee Formation

A Product Data Governance Committee is a formal group within an organization responsible for overseeing and governing the management of product data throughout its lifecycle. This committee is formed by cross-functional members from various departments, such as product management, engineering, marketing, sales, and data governance. Its primary objective is to ensure data accuracy, consistency, and integrity, which ultimately supports the organization's strategic product management goals. The formation of a Product Data Governance Committee typically involves defining clear roles and responsibilities for committee members, establishing data governance policies and processes, and developing a framework for data quality management. The committee works collaboratively to monitor and review the overall data governance strategy, identify areas for improvement, and make informed decisions on data-related matters. The committee plays a crucial role in providing guidance and direction on data standards, definitions, and classifications. This includes defining the attributes, categories, and metadata required for consistent data management practices. By establishing and maintaining data governance standards, the committee ensures that product data is accurate, complete, and accessible to relevant stakeholders within the organization. In addition to data quality, the committee also addresses data privacy and security concerns. It establishes policies and procedures to protect confidential product data, enforce data access controls, and comply with relevant industry regulations or standards. By mitigating data risks and addressing potential data breaches, the committee helps to instill trust and confidence in the organization's product data management practices. The Product Data Governance Committee acts as a central point of communication and coordination between different departments involved in product management. It facilitates the exchange of information and best practices related to data governance, promotes collaboration and alignment across teams, and resolves any conflicts or discrepancies that arise during the data management process. Overall, the formation of a Product Data Governance Committee is essential in enabling effective and efficient product management. It provides a structured approach to manage product data throughout its lifecycle, ensuring accuracy, consistency, and security. By establishing clear roles, policies, and procedures, the committee helps to improve data quality, enhance decision-making processes, and support the organization's product management objectives.

Product Data Governance Committee

A Product Data Governance Committee is a formal group within an organization that is responsible for overseeing the management and maintenance of product data throughout the product lifecycle. This committee is typically comprised of cross-functional representatives from various departments such as product management, marketing, operations, and IT. The main purpose of the Product Data Governance Committee is to ensure that product data is accurate, complete, and consistent across different systems and channels. By establishing a dedicated committee, the organization can streamline the governance process and enable better decision-making based on reliable and high-quality product data.

Product Data Governance Framework Setup

A Product Data Governance Framework Setup refers to the establishment and implementation of a structured framework to manage and govern product data within an organization's product management processes. This framework encompasses the set of policies, procedures, and guidelines that define how product data is captured, stored, organized, processed, and maintained throughout its lifecycle. Its primary objective is to ensure the accuracy, consistency, completeness, and integrity of product data, enabling businesses to make informed decisions, improve operational efficiency, enhance customer experience, and drive overall product success.

Product Data Governance Framework

Product Data Governance Framework refers to a structured and systematic approach that defines the processes, roles, and responsibilities for managing and ensuring the quality, accuracy, and consistency of product data throughout its lifecycle in the context of product management. This framework is designed to establish guidelines and procedures that govern the creation, capture, storage, and maintenance of product data, as well as the workflows and controls for data access, usage, and modification. It encompasses the policies, standards, and practices that are put in place to ensure that product data is reliable, valid, complete, and up-to-date, and that it meets the requirements of various stakeholders. The Product Data Governance Framework outlines the steps and activities that need to be taken to manage product data effectively. This includes defining data governance objectives, identifying the key data elements and attributes to be managed, establishing data quality rules and metrics, and implementing processes for data validation, cleansing, and enrichment. Within this framework, clear roles and responsibilities are defined for different stakeholders involved in product management, such as product managers, data stewards, IT personnel, and business users. These roles help ensure that there is accountability and ownership for product data, and that there is a clear understanding of who is responsible for maintaining data integrity and resolving data-related issues. Furthermore, the Product Data Governance Framework encompasses the tools, technologies, and systems that support the governance of product data. This may include data management software, data integration platforms, master data management systems, and data governance tools. These tools enable organizations to automate data processes, improve data quality, and provide visibility and control over product data assets. In summary, the Product Data Governance Framework is a comprehensive and structured approach that enables organizations to establish effective data management practices for their product data. By implementing this framework, organizations can ensure that product data is accurate, consistent, and reliable, thereby improving decision-making, increasing operational efficiency, and enhancing customer satisfaction.

Product Data Governance

Product Data Governance refers to the processes, policies, and activities implemented by an organization to ensure the quality, consistency, and accuracy of product data throughout its lifecycle. It involves the management and oversight of product data, including attributes, classifications, relationships, and other relevant information, to support effective product management. In the context of product management, data governance plays a crucial role in ensuring that product data is reliable, relevant, and up-to-date. It provides a framework for establishing standards, rules, and procedures to govern the creation, maintenance, and distribution of product data across the organization. By implementing robust data governance practices, product managers can make informed decisions, enhance the overall product experience, and drive business growth.

Product Data Imputation Algorithm

A Product Data Imputation Algorithm is a computational method used in the field of Product Management to fill missing or incomplete information about products in a database or data set. This algorithm utilizes statistical techniques and patterns in existing data to infer and generate the missing product data, making the dataset more complete and usable. The algorithm operates by analyzing the available product data, identifying patterns, and using these patterns to predict the missing values. It takes into account various attributes and features of products, such as their category, brand, price, description, and specifications, to impute missing information accurately.

Product Data Imputation

Product Data Imputation in the context of Product Management refers to the process of filling in missing or incomplete information in a product dataset. It involves using various techniques and algorithms to estimate or predict the values of missing data points based on the available data. When managing a large catalog of products, it is common to encounter missing or incomplete information about certain attributes or characteristics of the products. This can be due to various reasons such as human error, data entry issues, or incomplete data sources. However, having accurate and complete product data is crucial for effective decision-making, marketing, and customer satisfaction. The process of product data imputation typically involves the following steps: 1. Identification of Missing Data: The first step is to identify which attributes or data points are missing or incomplete in the product dataset. This can be done by analyzing the dataset and comparing it with the expected attributes for each product. 2. Selection of Imputation Method: Once the missing data points are identified, a suitable imputation method needs to be selected. There are various techniques available, including mean imputation, regression imputation, hot-deck imputation, and machine learning-based imputation. The choice of method depends on the nature of the data and the specific requirements of the product management process. 3. Imputation Process: In this step, the selected imputation method is applied to estimate or predict the missing values based on the available data. The imputation algorithm uses statistical or machine learning techniques to generate the best possible estimates for the missing data points. 4. Evaluation and Validation: After the imputation process, it is essential to evaluate the quality and accuracy of the imputed values. This can be done by comparing the imputed values with any available ground truth or by using statistical measures such as mean squared error or correlation coefficients. In conclusion, product data imputation is a critical process in Product Management that involves filling in missing or incomplete information in a product dataset. By ensuring accurate and complete product data, organizations can make informed decisions, improve marketing strategies, and provide better customer experiences.

Product Data Ingestion Framework

A Product Data Ingestion Framework is a system or software that enables the collection, processing, and integration of various types of data related to products within a product management context. It provides a streamlined and automated approach to ingest, transform, and standardize product data from multiple sources into a single, unified format. This framework is designed to enhance the overall product management process by facilitating the aggregation and synchronization of product data across different systems, such as e-commerce platforms, ERP systems, CRMs, and other relevant software applications. The key purpose of a Product Data Ingestion Framework is to ensure the accuracy, consistency, and completeness of product data throughout its lifecycle. It enables product managers to effectively manage and govern vast amounts of product-related information, including attributes, classifications, specifications, images, prices, inventory levels, and more. By leveraging this framework, product managers can efficiently onboard new products, update existing product information, and retire outdated products across various channels and touchpoints. It enables them to overcome data silos and achieve a harmonized view of product data, eliminating discrepancies and duplications that often arise due to manual data entry or reliance on disparate systems. Moreover, a Product Data Ingestion Framework supports data enrichment and enrichment processes, allowing product managers to enhance and enrich the product data with additional attributes, descriptions, translations, or other relevant information. This ensures that the product information presented to customers or used internally is comprehensive, accurate, and tailored to specific market needs. Overall, a Product Data Ingestion Framework plays a crucial role in empowering product managers to make informed decisions, drive efficient business processes, and deliver exceptional customer experiences. It acts as a robust foundation for product information management, empowering organizations to optimize their product management strategies, improve time-to-market, and succeed in the highly competitive marketplace.

Product Data Ingestion

Product Data Ingestion refers to the process of collecting, organizing, and importing product data from various sources into a central repository or database. It involves extracting relevant information from multiple data sources, such as suppliers, manufacturers, and internal systems, and transforming it into a standardized format that can be easily analyzed and leveraged for product management activities. This process is essential for product managers and organizations as it enables them to maintain accurate and up-to-date product information, streamline product development workflows, and optimize the overall product management lifecycle. By ingesting data from diverse sources, product managers can gain a comprehensive view of their product portfolio, make informed decisions, and drive business growth.

Product Data Integration Platform

A Product Data Integration Platform is a centralized tool that enables Product Managers to efficiently manage and standardize product data across various systems and channels within an organization. Product Management involves the management of a product throughout its lifecycle, from product ideation and development to marketing, sales, and post-sales support. A critical aspect of product management is ensuring that accurate and up-to-date product information is available to all stakeholders in a consistent and reliable manner. A Product Data Integration Platform provides a single source of truth for product data, consolidating information from different sources such as ERP systems, CRM systems, marketing platforms, and e-commerce platforms. It eliminates data silos and enables Product Managers to have a comprehensive and holistic view of their products. The platform allows Product Managers to easily import product data from various sources and channels, ensuring that the information is accurately captured and standardized. It provides tools for data cleansing, data enrichment, and data mapping, enabling Product Managers to streamline and optimize their product data across different systems. With a Product Data Integration Platform, Product Managers can efficiently manage product information such as product attributes, specifications, pricing, inventory levels, and images in a centralized manner. They can easily update and publish this information to relevant systems and channels, ensuring that all stakeholders have access to the most accurate and up-to-date product data. In addition to managing product data, a Product Data Integration Platform often includes features such as workflow management, collaboration tools, and analytics. These features enable Product Managers to streamline their product management processes, collaborate effectively with cross-functional teams, and gain valuable insights into product performance and customer behavior. In summary, a Product Data Integration Platform is a critical tool for Product Managers to efficiently manage and standardize product data across various systems and channels. By providing a centralized and standardized view of product information, the platform enables Product Managers to make informed decisions, streamline processes, and drive product success.

Product Data Integration

Product Data Integration refers to the process of consolidating and organizing data from multiple sources within a product management system. It involves the seamless extraction, transformation, and loading of data from various internal and external systems to generate a unified and accurate view of product information. By integrating product data, organizations can effectively manage and maintain a comprehensive database that encompasses product attributes, specifications, pricing, inventory levels, and other relevant information. This synchronized product data becomes the foundation for efficient product management, supporting activities such as catalog management, digital asset management, pricing optimization, and order management.

Product Data Lifecycle Framework

A Product Data Lifecycle Framework in the context of Product Management refers to a systematic approach that outlines the various stages and processes involved in managing and maintaining product data throughout its lifecycle. It provides a structured framework for organizations to effectively handle product data from creation to retirement, ensuring data accuracy, consistency, and relevance. The framework typically consists of the following key stages: 1. Data Collection: This stage involves gathering product data from various sources, such as suppliers, manufacturers, internal databases, and market research. The data collected may include product specifications, pricing information, images, and other relevant details. 2. Data Cleansing: This stage focuses on refining and standardizing the collected data to ensure its quality and consistency. It involves processes like data validation, normalization, and de-duplication to eliminate errors, redundancies, and inconsistencies in the data. 3. Data Integration: Once the data is cleaned, it needs to be integrated into a centralized repository or Product Information Management (PIM) system. This stage involves mapping and merging the data from various sources into a unified format, enabling easy access, retrieval, and management of product information. 4. Data Enrichment: In this stage, additional product information is added to enhance the data's value and usefulness. This includes enriching the data with attributes like descriptions, technical specifications, related products, cross-selling opportunities, and other relevant details to provide comprehensive and accurate product information to customers. 5. Data Publication: Once the product data is enriched, it needs to be published or distributed across various channels, such as e-commerce platforms, websites, catalogs, and marketing materials. This stage involves creating data feeds, generating product catalogs, and ensuring timely and accurate data updates across all sales and marketing channels. 6. Data Maintenance: This stage involves ongoing monitoring, maintenance, and updates of the product data throughout its lifecycle. It includes processes like data validation, error identification, price updates, discontinued product management, and ensuring data integrity to prevent any discrepancies or outdated information from reaching customers. 7. Data Retirement: As products reach the end of their lifecycle or are discontinued, this stage involves retiring and archiving the corresponding product data. It includes removing the data from active systems, ensuring its proper storage, and facilitating smooth transitions and replacements for the retired products. In summary, a Product Data Lifecycle Framework provides a structured approach for managing product data from collection to retirement. It encompasses stages like data collection, cleansing, integration, enrichment, publication, maintenance, and retirement, ensuring the accuracy, consistency, and relevance of product data throughout its lifecycle.

Product Data Lifecycle Framework

A Product Data Lifecycle Framework refers to the systematic process of managing and optimizing product data throughout its entire lifecycle. It involves the collection, storage, validation, transformation, and dissemination of product information to various stakeholders, including manufacturers, suppliers, distributors, and customers. This framework is essential in product management as it ensures the accuracy, consistency, and accessibility of product data, enabling efficient decision-making and improved customer experience. It encompasses several stages, each with its specific activities and objectives: 1. Data Collection and Creation: During this stage, product data is gathered from multiple sources, such as market research, customer feedback, and internal teams. It involves capturing attributes like product descriptions, specifications, pricing, images, and videos. 2. Data Storage and Integration: The collected data is stored and organized in a central repository, commonly known as a product information management (PIM) system. Integration with other systems, such as enterprise resource planning (ERP) and customer relationship management (CRM), allows for seamless exchange of data across various business functions. 3. Data Validation and Cleansing: To ensure data accuracy and consistency, validation and cleansing processes are carried out. This involves removing duplicate records, standardizing formats, and conducting quality checks to eliminate errors or inconsistencies. 4. Data Transformation and Enrichment: In this stage, the product data is transformed and enriched with additional information to improve its quality and make it more valuable for stakeholders. This may include translating data into different languages, adding SEO-friendly keywords, or enriching with customer-centric attributes. 5. Data Distribution and Syndication: Once the product data is properly validated and enriched, it needs to be distributed to various channels and partners. This includes syndicating data to online marketplaces, e-commerce platforms, retail partners, or third-party distributors. 6. Data Maintenance and Governance: As product data evolves over time, it requires ongoing maintenance to keep it up to date. This involves monitoring data quality, resolving issues, and enforcing governance policies to ensure compliance with industry standards and regulations. By implementing a Product Data Lifecycle Framework, organizations can streamline their product management processes, enhance data consistency across channels, and ultimately improve their product offerings and customer satisfaction.

Product Data Lifecycle

The product data lifecycle refers to the stages and processes that a product's data goes through from its initial creation and collection to its eventual retirement or end of life. It encompasses all the activities and decisions involved in managing and maintaining the data associated with a product throughout its lifecycle within the context of product management. The lifecycle of product data typically begins with the creation or acquisition of the data. This can include gathering information about a product's physical attributes, specifications, features, and capabilities, as well as any associated digital assets such as images, videos, or documents. The data collected during this stage serves as the foundation for all subsequent product-related activities and decisions. Once the product data is acquired, it needs to be organized and structured in a way that makes it easy to access, update, and analyze. This involves establishing data schemas, taxonomies, and hierarchies that define how the data should be classified and organized. The goal is to ensure consistency, accuracy, and integrity of the data throughout its lifecycle. After the data is organized, it can be enriched and enhanced by adding additional information or attributes. This can include augmenting the data with market research insights, customer feedback, or other relevant data sources. The enriched data enables product managers to make more informed decisions and develop strategies that maximize the value and competitiveness of the product. As the product evolves and undergoes changes, the associated data also needs to be updated and maintained. This includes keeping track of any modifications or updates made to the product's specifications, features, or digital assets. Product managers need to ensure that the data remains accurate, up-to-date, and consistent across all relevant systems and channels. Eventually, as a product reaches the end of its lifecycle, the associated data may need to be retired or archived. This involves determining the appropriate procedures for disposing of or preserving the data in a way that complies with legal and regulatory requirements. The retirement of product data is an essential step in managing data lifecycle and minimizing any potential risks or liabilities associated with outdated or obsolete data.

Product Data Lineage Tracking

Product Data Lineage Tracking refers to the process of tracking and documenting the journey of data throughout the various stages of a product's lifecycle within the context of Product Management. It involves capturing and tracing the origin, transformation, and usage of data to ensure transparency, accuracy, and integrity in decision-making processes related to product development, marketing, and sales. In Product Management, data plays a vital role in understanding customer needs, market trends, and product performance. It is crucial to have a clear understanding of how data is sourced, collected, processed, and utilized in order to make informed decisions. Product Data Lineage Tracking provides a systematic and comprehensive approach to managing and analyzing data, allowing product managers to gain insights and make data-driven decisions. The process of Product Data Lineage Tracking starts with identifying the sources of data and documenting them accurately. This includes tracking data from customer feedback, surveys, social media, market research, and sales reports, among other sources. Once the data sources are identified, it is important to understand how the data is transformed and manipulated to derive meaningful insights. This involves documenting the data pipelines, workflows, and processes involved in data transformation and analysis. By tracking the lineage of data, product managers can assess the accuracy and reliability of the data, identify any potential issues or biases, and ensure the compliance of data with legal and ethical standards. It also enables them to evaluate the impact of data quality on decision-making outcomes and take necessary actions to improve data accuracy and reliability. Furthermore, Product Data Lineage Tracking allows product managers to understand how data is used in different stages of the product lifecycle. This includes tracking how data is used in product ideation, feature prioritization, roadmap planning, and performance monitoring. It helps product managers identify patterns, trends, and gaps in the data, enabling them to make informed decisions and optimize product strategies. In conclusion, Product Data Lineage Tracking is a critical process in Product Management that ensures transparency, accuracy, and integrity in managing and analyzing data. It allows product managers to understand the complete journey of data, from its origin to its utilization, thereby empowering them to make data-driven decisions and optimize product strategies.

Product Data Lineage Visualization Tool

A Product Data Lineage Visualization Tool is a software application designed to provide Product Managers with visual representations of the lineage or history of data used in the development and management of a product. This tool allows Product Managers to trace the origin and transformation of product data as it moves through various stages of its lifecycle. It offers a clear, graphical representation of the data lineage, making it easier for Product Managers to understand the data flow and dependencies between different data points. The visualization tool typically presents the data lineage in the form of a flowchart or a diagram. The flowchart represents the various data sources, processes, and transformations that occur during the product lifecycle. Each data point or process is represented by a node, and the connections between nodes show the sequence of data transformations. By using the Product Data Lineage Visualization Tool, Product Managers can quickly identify the sources of data for a particular product and understand how it has been processed or transformed. This enables them to: 1. Identify data quality issues: The tool helps Product Managers to trace back to the source of data, allowing them to identify any quality issues or errors that may have occurred during the data transformation process. This helps improve the overall quality of the product data and ensures accurate decision-making. 2. Analyze the impact of changes: The visualization tool enables Product Managers to understand the impact of any changes made to the product data or its sources. They can easily assess how modifications in one part of the product data affect other related data points, enabling them to make informed decisions about updates or modifications. 3. Communicate data dependencies: The visualization tool provides a clear and concise way to communicate data dependencies to other stakeholders. Product Managers can use the flowchart or diagram generated by the tool to illustrate the relationships between different data points, making it easier for stakeholders to understand the complex data ecosystem. In conclusion, a Product Data Lineage Visualization Tool is a valuable asset for Product Managers in understanding and managing the lineage of product data. It provides a visual representation of the data flow, aiding in data analysis, quality assurance, and effective communication with stakeholders.

Product Data Lineage Visualization

Product Data Lineage Visualization refers to the graphical representation of the journey and transformation of data within a product throughout its lifecycle. It allows product managers to easily trace the origins and transformations of data, helping them in making informed decisions and understanding the impact of changes. With Product Data Lineage Visualization, product managers can visually analyze how data is collected, stored, processed, and used within their products. It provides a comprehensive view of the data flow, highlighting the sources of data and how it is manipulated at various stages. This visualization helps in identifying potential bottlenecks, inefficiencies, and dependencies within the product's data ecosystem. By understanding the lineage of data, product managers can ensure data integrity, data quality, and compliance with regulations. They can identify any inconsistencies or anomalies in the data, enabling them to take corrective actions promptly. Additionally, data lineage visualization empowers product managers to track the impact of changes made to the product or its underlying data infrastructure. This knowledge aids in risk assessment and mitigating potential issues before they arise. Moreover, product managers can leverage lineage visualization to improve data governance and documentation. They can establish clear data lineage policies, documenting the sources of data, data transformations, and any data dependencies. This documentation ensures transparency and facilitates collaboration among different teams working on the product. Furthermore, data lineage visualization supports decision-making processes within product management. It provides insights into how data is used to generate key performance indicators (KPIs) and metrics, enabling product managers to evaluate the accuracy and relevance of these measurements. This helps in identifying areas for improvement and aligning product strategies with business goals. In conclusion, Product Data Lineage Visualization is a powerful tool for product managers to understand the journey and transformation of data within their products. It improves decision-making, data governance, and promotes transparency and collaboration among different teams. By visualizing data lineage, product managers can effectively manage and harness the power of data to drive product success.

Product Data Lineage

Product Data Lineage refers to the detailed record or tracking of the origin, transformation, and movement of product data throughout its lifecycle in product management. It involves capturing and documenting information about the sources, processes, and platforms involved in the creation, modification, integration, distribution, and consumption of product data.

Product Data Loss Prevention Strategy

A Product Data Loss Prevention Strategy is a comprehensive plan or approach implemented by Product Managers to prevent the loss or compromise of sensitive data related to a product or its users. This strategy aims to protect valuable information from unauthorized access, theft, accidental deletion, or any other potential risks that may result in data loss. The strategy typically includes a combination of technical measures, policies, procedures, and training to ensure the secure handling and storage of product data throughout its lifecycle. It involves identifying potential vulnerabilities or weaknesses in the product's data architecture, and implementing controls and safeguards to mitigate or eliminate those risks.

Product Data Loss Prevention

Product Data Loss Prevention (DLP) is a crucial aspect of Product Management that focuses on protecting and securing the data associated with a product throughout its lifecycle. It involves implementing strategies, policies, and technologies to prevent the unauthorized disclosure, leakage, or destruction of valuable product data. The primary objective of Product Data Loss Prevention is to safeguard sensitive information about the product, such as intellectual property, trade secrets, customer data, and confidential business information. By preserving the integrity and confidentiality of this data, companies can mitigate the risks of competitive advantage erosion, reputational damage, legal repercussions, and financial losses.

Product Data Management (PDM)

Product Data Management (PDM) is a set of processes and tools used to capture, organize, and manage the data related to a product throughout its lifecycle. It encompasses the management of product information, such as specifications, bills of materials (BOMs), drawings, documentation, and other relevant data. The primary goal of PDM is to ensure that accurate and up-to-date product data is readily available to the various stakeholders involved in the product lifecycle, including product managers, engineers, designers, manufacturers, and suppliers. By establishing a centralized repository for product data, PDM enables efficient collaboration and information sharing, leading to improved product quality, reduced time-to-market, and increased overall productivity. PDM involves several key processes, which include: 1. Product Data Capture: This process involves collecting and documenting relevant product information, such as specifications, features, and performance parameters. This data is typically obtained from various sources, including market research, customer feedback, and input from the development team. 2. Product Data Organization: Once the data is captured, it needs to be organized in a structured manner. This includes creating and maintaining a standardized product hierarchy, categorizing information based on different attributes, and establishing links between related data elements. 3. Product Data Storage and Retrieval: PDM systems provide a centralized database or repository where all product data is stored. This allows for easy and efficient retrieval of information whenever needed. Users can search, filter, and access data based on specific criteria, such as product name, part number, or keyword. 4. Product Data Versioning and Control: PDM ensures that changes made to product data are properly managed and controlled. This includes maintaining a version history of all data modifications, implementing workflow processes for reviewing and approving changes, and enforcing access controls to prevent unauthorized modifications. 5. Product Data Distribution: PDM enables the distribution of product data to various systems and individuals within the organization, as well as external partners and suppliers. This ensures that the right information is available to the right people at the right time, facilitating effective collaboration and decision-making. In conclusion, Product Data Management is a critical component of Product Management that enables the efficient and effective management of product-related information throughout its lifecycle. By leveraging PDM processes and tools, organizations can ensure data integrity, streamline collaboration, and ultimately drive product success.

Product Data Mapping Tool

A Product Data Mapping Tool is a software or tool used in Product Management to organize and manage different types of product data across various systems or platforms. It allows product managers to create a comprehensive and structured view of product information, making it easier to track, analyze, and synchronize data as it flows through different stages of the product lifecycle. The main purpose of a Product Data Mapping Tool is to centralize and standardize product data from different sources, such as suppliers, manufacturers, or internal systems, and map them to a common format or schema. This mapping process ensures that the data is accurately translated and can be integrated seamlessly into the product management system. The tool typically offers a user-friendly interface where product managers can define and configure the data mapping rules, mappings, and transformations. These rules specify how the data from different sources should be interpreted and structured within the tool. For example, the tool may allow the mapping of product attributes, such as price, size, or color, from different sources to a standardized set of attributes used in the product management system. Product Data Mapping Tools also provide features for data validation, cleansing, and enrichment. They enable product managers to validate the consistency, completeness, and accuracy of the mapped data. The tool may identify and flag any errors, duplicates, or missing information, helping to ensure the data integrity and reliability. Additionally, these tools often support data enrichment capabilities, allowing product managers to enhance the existing product data with additional information or attributes. This enrichment can include adding images, descriptions, categorizations, or metadata to improve the product catalog and enhance the overall customer experience. In summary, a Product Data Mapping Tool is a valuable resource for product managers to effectively manage and organize product data from various sources. By centralizing and mapping the data to a standardized format, the tool enables better data analysis, synchronization, and integration, ultimately supporting informed decision-making and enhancing the overall product management process.

Product Data Mapping

Product Data Mapping in the context of Product Management refers to the process of organizing and structuring product information in a way that allows for efficient and effective management, analysis, and use of the data. It involves mapping product attributes, features, and specifications to specific data fields or categories, enabling easy identification, retrieval, and manipulation of product data. The purpose of Product Data Mapping is to streamline various product-related activities, such as product development, inventory management, marketing, and sales. By mapping product data, organizations can create a standardized framework for organizing and categorizing information, ensuring consistent and accurate data across different systems and platforms. With Product Data Mapping, product managers can create a comprehensive overview of their entire product portfolio, including details such as pricing, availability, dimensions, and specifications. This allows for easy comparison and analysis of products, facilitates decision-making processes, and enables effective communication with stakeholders. In addition, Product Data Mapping also plays a crucial role in ensuring data integrity and consistency. By mapping product attributes to specific data fields, organizations can enforce data validation rules, preventing data entry errors and ensuring that information is entered correctly. This helps eliminate duplicate or incomplete data, enhancing the overall quality and reliability of product information. Furthermore, Product Data Mapping enables organizations to connect and integrate product data with other systems and applications, such as e-commerce platforms, customer relationship management (CRM) systems, and supply chain management tools. This integration allows for seamless data flow across different business functions, improving operational efficiencies and facilitating data-driven decision-making. Overall, Product Data Mapping serves as a foundational step in managing and utilizing product data effectively. It provides a structured and standardized approach to organizing product information, enabling organizations to optimize their product management processes, enhance data quality, and drive business growth.

Product Data Masking Technique

Product Data Masking Technique is a process used in Product Management to protect sensitive information of a product by replacing it with fictitious data or obfuscating it in order to maintain data privacy and security. This technique involves implementing various data masking methods such as substitution, scrambling, shuffling, encryption, or tokenization to hide or anonymize sensitive product data. The goal is to protect the confidentiality of sensitive information such as customer details, financial data, intellectual property, or any other classified data associated with a product.

Product Data Masking

Product Data Masking is a process used in Product Management to safeguard sensitive information related to a product. It involves replacing real data with fictitious or scrambled data to protect the confidentiality, integrity, and authenticity of the product's data. Product data often contains sensitive information such as personal details, financial data, intellectual property, and trade secrets. To prevent unauthorized access and potential data breaches, product managers use data masking techniques to obfuscate the original data while still preserving its usability for testing, development, and analysis purposes.

Product Data Migration

Product Data Migration is the process of transferring and transforming product-related information, such as attributes, specifications, pricing, and inventory, from one system or platform to another. It involves collecting, cleansing, and mapping the data to ensure its accuracy and compatibility with the target system. This migration process is crucial in product management as it allows organizations to upgrade or replace their existing systems. It ensures a seamless transition without any loss or corruption of data, enabling businesses to continue their operations smoothly. Product data migration involves several steps, including: 1. Data Extraction: The first step involves extracting the product data from the source system in a structured format. This may involve querying databases, accessing APIs, or exporting data files. 2. Data Cleansing: Once the data is extracted, it needs to be cleansed and standardized. This process includes removing duplicate records, validating data against predefined rules, and correcting any inconsistencies or errors. 3. Data Mapping: In this step, the product attributes and fields in the source system are mapped to their equivalent counterparts in the target system. This ensures that the data is transferred accurately and can be used in the new system without any issues. 4. Data Transformation: During this stage, the data is transformed and formatted according to the requirements of the target system. This may involve converting data types, reformatting values, or applying business rules to ensure data consistency. 5. Data Loading: Once the data is cleansed, mapped, and transformed, it is loaded into the target system. This involves importing the data into the appropriate fields and tables, ensuring its proper integration with the existing product management infrastructure. Overall, product data migration plays a vital role in maintaining the integrity and usability of product information across different systems. It enables businesses to leverage new technologies, consolidate their product data, and streamline their operations, ultimately improving their overall product management processes.

Product Data Ownership Policy

A Product Data Ownership Policy in the context of Product Management defines the framework and guidelines for determining the ownership of product-related data throughout its lifecycle. This policy ensures that responsibility and accountability for the collection, maintenance, and usage of product data are clearly defined and adhered to by the relevant stakeholders. Product data refers to the information and attributes associated with a product, including specifications, features, pricing, images, documentation, and customer data. This data is critical for effective product development, marketing, sales, and support activities. By establishing a data ownership policy, organizations can govern the access, control, and usage of product data, while ensuring data integrity, privacy, and compliance with relevant regulations.

Product Data Ownership

Product data ownership in the context of product management refers to the responsibility and authority of an individual or a team to manage and control the data related to a product throughout its lifecycle. This includes gathering, analyzing, storing, organizing, and maintaining product data to support decision-making, communication, and overall product management activities. The ownership of product data is crucial because it ensures that the right people have access to accurate and up-to-date information about the product. This data includes but is not limited to product specifications, features, pricing, branding, marketing collateral, sales data, customer feedback, and performance metrics.

Product Data Pipeline Orchestration

Product Data Pipeline Orchestration is the systematic coordination and management of the flow of data across various stages and processes in the product management lifecycle. It involves the integration, transformation, and movement of data from different sources to support the planning, development, and distribution of products. The purpose of Product Data Pipeline Orchestration is to ensure that relevant and accurate data is collected, processed, and made available to product managers and other stakeholders at each stage of the product management process. This enables data-driven decision-making, facilitates collaboration, and ultimately improves the overall efficiency and effectiveness of product management activities.

Product Data Pipelining Framework

A product data pipelining framework in the context of Product Management is a structured system that facilitates the collection, transformation, and integration of product data from various sources into a unified and actionable format. It encompasses the tools, processes, and technologies required to efficiently manage large volumes of product information throughout its lifecycle. The framework acts as a conduit for product data, enabling the seamless flow of information between different systems, teams, and departments involved in the product management process. It ensures that accurate and up-to-date product data is readily available to support decision-making, drive strategic initiatives, and enhance overall product performance.

Product Data Pipelining

Product data pipelining refers to the process of capturing, transforming, and organizing various types of data related to a product throughout its lifecycle. It involves the collection, integration, and dissemination of product data from various sources, such as customer feedback, sales data, manufacturing data, and market research. Product data pipelining plays a crucial role in product management by providing relevant and accurate information about a product. It enables product managers to make informed decisions and drive product strategy based on insights derived from data analysis.

Product Data Privacy Policy

A product data privacy policy is a formal statement that outlines how a company collects, uses, stores, and protects the personal information of customers and users of its products. It is a crucial document in the field of product management, as it sets the guidelines and principles for ensuring the privacy and security of customer data. This policy typically includes information about the types of personal data that may be collected, such as names, email addresses, phone numbers, and payment details. It also specifies the purpose of collecting this data, which can range from processing orders to improving the product's functionality or personalization. The product data privacy policy explains how the company handles and processes the collected data to safeguard customer privacy. This may include provisions for encryption, access controls, and data retention periods. It also describes how the company protects against unauthorized access, disclosure, and misuse of personal data. In addition to outlining the company's responsibilities in handling personal data, the policy also informs customers about their rights. This includes their right to access, update, and delete their personal information, as well as their right to know how their data is being used. The product data privacy policy is essential for building trust with customers, as it demonstrates a commitment to protecting their privacy. It helps customers make informed decisions about sharing their personal data and provides them with the necessary transparency and control over their information. As a key document in product management, the product data privacy policy should be reviewed and updated regularly to ensure compliance with evolving privacy laws and regulations. It should be easily accessible to customers and clearly communicated during the onboarding process. By following this policy, companies can maintain customer trust, enhance their reputation, and achieve compliance in an increasingly privacy-conscious digital landscape.

Product Data Privacy Regulation Compliance Adherence

Product Data Privacy Regulation Compliance Adherence refers to the process of ensuring that a product, its features, and its data collection practices comply with applicable data privacy regulations. This includes laws, regulations, standards, and best practices established to protect the privacy and personal information of individuals. In the field of product management, this involves understanding and adhering to data privacy regulations and incorporating privacy-preserving measures throughout the lifecycle of a product. It requires a comprehensive approach that encompasses various aspects of product development, including design, development, testing, deployment, and ongoing maintenance.

Product Data Privacy Regulation Compliance

Product Data Privacy Regulation Compliance refers to the adherence and compliance of a product, specifically in regards to the collection, storage, and usage of customer data, with the relevant data privacy regulations and laws. Data privacy regulations dictate how organizations collect, store, and use customer data in order to protect the privacy and security of individuals. These regulations aim to ensure that organizations handle personal data responsibly, and provide individuals with control and transparency over their data.

Product Data Privacy

Product Data Privacy refers to the protection and management of personal and sensitive information collected and stored by a product during its lifecycle, in order to ensure the privacy and security of users' data. It is a crucial aspect of product management, as it involves implementing measures and strategies to safeguard user data against unauthorized access, misuse, and breaches. Product managers play a key role in ensuring product data privacy by working closely with cross-functional teams, including engineering, legal, and security, to develop and enforce data privacy policies and practices. They are responsible for understanding and complying with relevant regulations and standards, such as the General Data Protection Regulation (GDPR) and the California Consumer Privacy Act (CCPA).

Product Data Profiling Software

Product Data Profiling Software refers to a tool or software application that systematically analyzes and evaluates the data related to a product in order to gain insights and make informed decisions in the field of product management. With the vast amount of data available in today's digital world, product data profiling software becomes crucial for product managers to efficiently handle and process large volumes of product-related information. This software enables product managers to understand and analyze various aspects of their products, such as attributes, characteristics, performance, and customer feedback, in a structured and organized manner.

Product Data Profiling

Product Data Profiling, in the context of Product Management, refers to the process of analyzing and categorizing data related to products in order to gain insights and enhance decision making. It involves gathering, organizing, and evaluating product data from various sources to understand its quality, completeness, and consistency. Data profiling allows product managers to assess the accuracy and reliability of product data, ensuring that it meets the specific requirements and standards of the organization. By examining different attributes of the data, such as product descriptions, specifications, pricing, and availability, product managers can identify any inconsistencies, anomalies, or errors that might exist. Through data profiling, product managers can understand the characteristics and patterns of product data, helping them identify opportunities for improvement or optimization. For example, they can identify missing or incomplete data that needs to be filled in, ensuring that product information is comprehensive and informative for customers. Another key aspect of product data profiling is ensuring data integrity. Product managers need to ensure that the data is accurate, up-to-date, and valid. By identifying and resolving data quality issues, such as duplicate entries, inconsistencies, or outdated information, product managers can maintain a high level of data integrity. Additionally, product data profiling enables product managers to identify any regulatory or compliance requirements related to product information. This is particularly important in industries where product data needs to adhere to specific guidelines, such as medical devices or food products.

By profiling the data, product managers can ensure that it meets the required standards and avoids any potential legal or compliance issues.

Product Data Quality Assessment Tool Usage

A Product Data Quality Assessment Tool refers to a software or solution that is used by Product Managers to evaluate and measure the accuracy, consistency, completeness, and validity of product data. This tool plays a crucial role in ensuring that product information is reliable, up-to-date, and error-free, thereby supporting effective decision-making and enhancing customer satisfaction. Product Managers need to assess the quality of product data to ensure that it meets the required standards and aligns with the company's overall goals and objectives. This assessment involves checking various aspects of the data, including attributes, descriptions, specifications, pricing, images, and categorization. By utilizing a Product Data Quality Assessment Tool, Product Managers can evaluate the data against predefined criteria to identify any discrepancies, inconsistencies, or errors that may exist. The tool typically offers functionalities such as data profiling, data cleansing, data enrichment, and data validation. Data profiling allows Product Managers to analyze the characteristics of the data, such as its structure, format, and completeness. This helps in identifying any anomalies or patterns that may indicate data quality issues. Data cleansing enables Product Managers to identify and remove duplicates, inaccuracies, or outdated information to maintain data integrity. Data enrichment involves enhancing the product data by adding missing information or standardizing it according to industry standards. Data validation ensures that the data meets the required business rules and constraints. By leveraging a Product Data Quality Assessment Tool, Product Managers can obtain an accurate and comprehensive view of the product data, enabling them to make informed decisions regarding product strategy, pricing, promotions, and inventory management. Moreover, this tool facilitates collaboration among cross-functional teams by providing a centralized platform for data assessment and correction. In conclusion, a Product Data Quality Assessment Tool is an essential component of Product Management, as it enables Product Managers to evaluate, improve, and maintain the quality of product data. Utilizing this tool ensures that accurate and reliable information is available to support decision-making, enhance customer satisfaction, and drive business success.

Product Data Quality Assessment

Product Data Quality Assessment refers to the process of evaluating the accuracy, completeness, consistency, and reliability of product data in order to ensure its integrity and usefulness for effective product management. It involves analyzing the quality of product data based on predefined criteria and metrics to identify any issues or inconsistencies that may impact decision-making and business processes. In product management, data plays a crucial role in making informed decisions, driving innovation, and delivering high-quality products to the market. However, with the increasing complexity and volume of product data across various systems and sources, ensuring data quality becomes a critical task. Product Data Quality Assessment provides a systematic approach to evaluate the quality of product data and ensure it meets the required standards and business objectives.

Product Data Quality Control Process

A product data quality control process refers to the systematic approach taken by product management teams to ensure that product data is accurate, complete, consistent, and up-to-date. It involves various steps and checks to verify the quality and reliability of product data, helping to maintain the overall integrity and usefulness of the data within the organization. At the core of a product data quality control process lies the identification and resolution of any issues or errors that might exist in the product information. This includes checking for inaccuracies in product specifications, pricing, descriptions, and images, among others. Additionally, it involves assessing the consistency of data across various channels, such as online platforms, physical stores, or third-party vendors, to ensure a unified and cohesive representation of the product.

Product Data Quality Control

Product data quality control refers to the process of ensuring that the data related to a product is accurate, complete, consistent, and relevant. It involves verifying and validating the information associated with a product to minimize errors, discrepancies, and inaccuracies. The aim is to provide reliable and trustworthy product data to various stakeholders, such as customers, suppliers, and internal teams. In the context of product management, data quality control is crucial for several reasons. Firstly, accurate product data is essential for making informed decisions regarding pricing, inventory management, and marketing strategies. Incorrect or incomplete data can lead to inefficiencies and potential financial losses for the company. Secondly, reliable product data is necessary for delivering accurate and up-to-date information to customers. This includes product descriptions, specifications, images, and pricing details, which greatly influence potential buyers' purchasing decisions. The process of product data quality control typically involves several steps. Firstly, data collection is carried out using various sources, such as suppliers, manufacturers, and internal databases. It is important to ensure that the collected data is correct and complete. This can be achieved by setting up validation rules, conducting data cleansing, and using automated tools to detect and correct errors. Secondly, data is stored in a centralized system or database, where it can be easily accessed and managed. Thirdly, data integration is performed to consolidate information from different sources and ensure consistency across all data points. This step involves mapping and aligning data attributes to maintain a standardized format. Once the data is collected, stored, and integrated, it undergoes continuous monitoring and maintenance to ensure its accuracy and relevance. This includes regular updates, data audits, and validation checks. Additionally, implementing data governance practices and establishing data quality metrics can help track the effectiveness of the quality control process. Lastly, data quality control should be an ongoing process, as product data is subject to change due to factors such as product updates, new releases, and market trends.

Product Data Quality

Product Data Quality refers to the level of accuracy, completeness, consistency, and reliability of the data associated with a product in the realm of Product Management. It encompasses the overall quality and correctness of the data collected, stored, and maintained throughout the product lifecycle. Accurate product data is crucial for effective decision-making, efficient product development, and successful marketing and sales initiatives. It ensures that the information presented to customers, stakeholders, and internal teams is correct, reliable, and up-to-date. Inaccurate or inconsistent data can lead to misunderstandings, wasted resources, poor customer experiences, and ultimately, financial losses for the company. Completeness of product data involves having all the necessary and relevant information available for a product. This includes attributes such as product name, description, features, specifications, pricing, availability, and related images or documentation. Incomplete data can lead to confusion, delays in product launches, and missed opportunities for cross-selling or upselling. Consistency of product data ensures that the information remains uniform and standardized across different channels, platforms, and touchpoints. It means that there are no contradictions or discrepancies in the data displayed on a company's website, mobile app, social media, print materials, or point-of-sale systems. Consistent data enhances brand credibility, customer trust, and overall user experience. Reliability of product data refers to its dependability and trustworthiness. It means that the data is sourced from reliable and authoritative channels, such as official product documentation, manufacturer specifications, or trusted third-party sources. Reliable data builds customer confidence, minimizes returns or complaints, and supports informed purchasing decisions. Ensuring high-quality product data requires implementing robust data governance practices, including data validation, data cleansing, and regular data audits. These processes involve identifying and rectifying any errors, inconsistencies, redundancies, or omissions in the product data. It may involve leveraging data management tools, employing data quality standards, implementing data governance frameworks, and establishing data stewardship roles and responsibilities. In conclusion, Product Data Quality plays a crucial role in Product Management by ensuring accurate, complete, consistent, and reliable product information. It is essential for driving effective decision-making, streamlining processes, enhancing customer experiences, and achieving overall business success.

Product Data Query Language

Product Data Query Language (PDQL) is a structured query language specifically designed for product management. It allows product managers to retrieve, filter, and manipulate product data stored in databases or other data repositories. PDQL provides a standardized way to access and analyze product information, enabling product managers to make informed decisions based on accurate and up-to-date data. With PDQL, product managers can easily retrieve specific product attributes or combinations of attributes, such as product name, SKU, price, availability, and more. PDQL follows a syntax similar to other query languages, such as SQL, but with a focus on product-centric data. It employs keywords and operators to perform searches, filtering, and sorting operations on product data. PDQL supports a range of functionalities including querying, aggregating, grouping, and joining product data. One of the key advantages of using PDQL is its ability to handle large volumes of product data efficiently. Product managers can write complex queries to retrieve data based on specific conditions, such as filtering products by category, location, or sales performance. PDQL also allows managers to combine multiple queries or subqueries to obtain the desired product data results. Furthermore, PDQL supports the integration of external data sources, enabling product managers to enrich their product data with additional information from third-party systems. This integration can provide valuable insights, such as market trends, customer demographics, or competitor analysis, which can inform product strategy and decision-making. In summary, Product Data Query Language (PDQL) is a specialized query language used by product managers to retrieve, filter, and manipulate product data. It offers a standardized and efficient way to access and analyze product information, enabling informed decision-making and facilitating the integration of external data sources to gain additional insights.

Product Data Recovery

Product Data Recovery refers to the process of retrieving and restoring lost or corrupted data associated with a product. It is a crucial aspect of Product Management as it ensures the availability and accuracy of product-related information, which is essential for decision-making, customer support, and overall product performance. In the context of Product Management, data recovery involves various steps and techniques to recover product data from different sources such as databases, cloud storage, logs, and backups. These steps typically include: 1. Identification and assessment: This step involves identifying the extent of data loss or corruption and assessing the potential impact on the product and its stakeholders. It helps in setting priorities and allocating resources for data recovery efforts. 2. Data retrieval: Once the affected data is identified, the next step is to retrieve it from the available sources. This may involve using specialized software tools or engaging professionals with expertise in data recovery methods. 3. Data restoration: After retrieving the lost or corrupted data, the focus shifts to restoring it to its original state. This may include cleaning up any inconsistencies or errors in the recovered data and ensuring its compatibility with the product's underlying systems and infrastructure. 4. Data validation: Once the data is restored, it needs to be validated for accuracy and completeness. This involves performing checks and tests to ensure that the recovered data is reliable and can be trusted for further use. By effectively managing the process of product data recovery, Product Managers can minimize potential disruptions caused by data loss or corruption. They can also ensure that the product operates smoothly, meets the needs of customers, and enables informed decision-making based on reliable and up-to-date information.

Product Data Reporting

Product Data Reporting refers to the process of collecting, organizing, and analyzing data related to a product in order to make informed decisions and drive product strategy. It is an essential aspect of product management, as it allows product managers to gain insights into the performance and usage of their products, identify areas for improvement, and make data-driven decisions to maximize product success. The primary objective of Product Data Reporting is to provide a comprehensive view of how a product is performing in the market and how it is being used by customers. This includes tracking various metrics such as sales figures, revenue, customer feedback, user engagement, and other relevant data points. By analyzing this data, product managers can gain valuable insights into the effectiveness of their product strategy, identify trends, and understand customer preferences and behavior. This enables them to make informed decisions about product development, marketing strategies, and overall product roadmap. Product Data Reporting involves the use of various tools and technologies to collect and analyze data. These may include analytics platforms, customer relationship management systems, user surveys, feedback channels, and other data collection methods. The data is then aggregated and organized into meaningful reports and dashboards, which provide a visual representation of the product's performance and key metrics. These reports can be used to communicate insights to stakeholders, such as executives, marketing teams, and development teams, to align efforts and make data-driven decisions. In addition to monitoring and tracking product performance, Product Data Reporting also plays a crucial role in identifying opportunities for product improvement and innovation. By analyzing customer feedback, usage patterns, and market trends, product managers can identify pain points, unmet needs, and emerging market trends that can be leveraged to enhance the product and stay ahead of the competition. In conclusion, Product Data Reporting is a vital process that enables product managers to gain insights into the performance and usage of their products. By collecting and analyzing data, product managers can make informed decisions, identify areas for improvement, and drive product strategy to maximize success in the market.

Product Data Reservoir Architecture

A Product Data Reservoir Architecture refers to the overall structure and design of a system or platform used by Product Managers to manage and store product-related data. It encompasses the various components, technologies, and processes involved in collecting, organizing, storing, and accessing product data. At its core, a Product Data Reservoir Architecture aims to provide a robust and scalable infrastructure to handle large volumes of data generated from various sources, such as customer feedback, sales data, market research, and production metrics. It serves as a central repository where Product Managers can access and analyze data to make informed decisions regarding product strategy, development, and marketing.

Product Data Reservoir

A Product Data Reservoir is a centralized repository that stores and manages all relevant data related to a product throughout its lifecycle. It serves as a comprehensive and reliable source of information for product managers, allowing them to make informed decisions and drive product strategies. Product managers rely on various types of data to understand customer needs, market trends, competitor analysis, and performance metrics. These data sources may include customer feedback, sales data, user analytics, market research, and more. The Product Data Reservoir aggregates and organizes this information in a structured manner, providing a holistic view of the product's performance and its impact on the business. The primary purpose of a Product Data Reservoir is to enable data-driven decision-making. By centralizing data from multiple sources, it eliminates the need for product managers to search through different systems or departments for relevant information. They can access the reservoir to retrieve the data they need, saving time and effort. In addition to serving as a storage for data, the Product Data Reservoir also facilitates data analysis and reporting. It often includes tools and capabilities for data mining, visualization, and reporting, allowing product managers to extract insights and communicate them effectively to stakeholders. The Product Data Reservoir is a valuable asset for product managers to track product performance, identify areas for improvement, and spot emerging market trends. It provides a historical record of product data, allowing product managers to analyze trends over time and make data-supported decisions for future product iterations or enhancements. Overall, the Product Data Reservoir plays a crucial role in enabling effective product management by providing a centralized, comprehensive, and accessible repository of product-related data. It empowers product managers to make informed decisions, optimize product strategies, and drive business growth.

Product Data Resilience Strategy

A product data resilience strategy refers to a structured approach or plan implemented by product managers to ensure the durability and availability of data associated with a specific product. This strategy focuses on mitigating the risks and challenges related to data loss, corruption, or unavailability, which could have a direct impact on the functionality and success of a product. The purpose of a product data resilience strategy is to safeguard and protect the data that is crucial for the proper functioning of a product throughout its lifecycle. This includes data related to user preferences, configurations, transactions, and any other information that is necessary for the product to deliver its intended value. The first step in developing a product data resilience strategy is to identify and assess potential risks that could impact the availability and integrity of the product's data. These risks could arise from hardware or software failures, natural disasters, cyber-attacks, human errors, or any other unforeseen events. Once the risks are identified, appropriate measures can be put in place to minimize their impact. An effective strategy should include measures for data backup and recovery. This involves creating regular backups of critical data and storing them in secure locations or cloud-based storage systems. Backup processes should be automated to ensure consistency and reliability. Additionally, testing the backup and recovery procedures periodically is essential to validate their effectiveness and identify any potential shortcomings. Another crucial aspect of a product data resilience strategy is data security. Product managers must implement robust security measures, such as data encryption, access controls, and authentication mechanisms, to protect data from unauthorized access or tampering. Regular security assessments should be conducted to identify vulnerabilities and apply appropriate patches or updates to address them. Furthermore, a resilient strategy should prioritize the performance and scalability of data-intensive operations. This includes optimizing data storage systems, implementing caching mechanisms, and leveraging technologies that enable efficient data retrieval and processing. By ensuring the scalability and performance of data operations, product managers can prevent bottlenecks and ensure the seamless functioning of the product.

Product Data Resilience

Product Data Resilience refers to a product's ability to maintain the integrity, availability, and consistency of its data throughout its lifecycle, particularly in the face of unexpected disruptions or failures. It involves implementing measures and mechanisms to ensure that product data remains secure, accurate, and accessible, even in the event of system failures, hardware malfunctions, software errors, or cybersecurity threats. In the context of Product Management, ensuring product data resilience is essential for several reasons. Firstly, product data is the lifeblood of any product, containing critical information such as specifications, configurations, pricing, customer data, and sales history. This data is utilized by various stakeholders, including development teams, marketing teams, sales teams, and customer support teams, to effectively manage and enhance the product's lifecycle. Secondly, product data resilience is closely tied to customer satisfaction and trust. If product data is compromised or inaccessible, it can result in delays, errors, or inconsistencies in product delivery, support, or communication. This, in turn, can lead to frustrated customers, lost sales opportunities, damaged reputation, and potential legal implications. Therefore, implementing robust data resilience strategies is crucial for maintaining customer confidence and delivering a positive customer experience. In practice, ensuring product data resilience requires a multi-faceted approach. This may involve implementing redundant systems, backup mechanisms, and failover capabilities to ensure continuous access to product data even during system failures. It may also involve implementing stringent data security measures, including encryption, access controls, and intrusion detection systems, to safeguard product data from unauthorized access or tampering. Furthermore, regular data backups, version control, and synchronization mechanisms can help protect against data loss or corruption. Comprehensive testing, monitoring, and logging practices can aid in identifying and addressing any potential issues or vulnerabilities before they escalate into major problems. In summary, product data resilience is a critical aspect of effective product management. It ensures the integrity, availability, and consistency of product data, driving customer satisfaction, trust, and overall business success.

Product Data Retention Policy Definition

A Product Data Retention Policy is a formal framework or set of rules implemented by a company to govern the retention and storage of data related to its products throughout their lifecycle. This policy is developed and enforced by the Product Management department to ensure that data generated or collected during the development, launch, and usage of a product is handled in a compliant and secure manner. The primary objective of a Product Data Retention Policy is to define the timeframes, storage locations, access controls, and disposal procedures for product-related data. The policy aims to strike a balance between retaining data for future analysis, support, and compliance purposes, while also addressing privacy and data protection concerns. The policy typically includes guidelines on how different types of product data should be retained and for how long. This may include customer feedback, usage statistics, performance metrics, bug reports, sales data, product specifications, and any other relevant information that has been collected or produced during the product's lifecycle. The Product Data Retention Policy also outlines the responsibilities and roles of various stakeholders involved in managing and safeguarding the data. It establishes protocols for regular data backups, access controls, data encryption, and secure storage practices to protect sensitive information from unauthorized access or loss. Besides data retention guidelines, the policy may also address data disposal procedures, including data destruction or anonymization practices when retaining specific data is no longer necessary or violates data protection regulations. By implementing a Product Data Retention Policy, companies ensure they conform to legal and industry-specific data retention requirements, safeguard sensitive information, and facilitate ongoing product improvement and customer support. It helps product managers make informed decisions based on historical data, track product performance, and identify areas for optimization, all while maintaining the trust and privacy of their customers.

Product Data Retention Policy

A product data retention policy is a formal document that outlines the guidelines and procedures for managing and storing the data associated with a particular product or service throughout its lifecycle. It establishes the timeframe for retaining various types of data, as well as the mechanisms for securely storing and disposing of that data. The primary purpose of a product data retention policy is to ensure that data related to a product is kept for the appropriate length of time, in compliance with legal and regulatory requirements. It also helps to protect the privacy of customers and users by ensuring that their personal data is handled in a secure and responsible manner.

Product Data Retention

Product Data Retention refers to the practice of storing and maintaining historical data related to a product throughout its lifecycle. This data can include information such as customer feedback, sales figures, user behavior, and product performance. In the context of Product Management, data retention is essential for several reasons. First, it allows product managers to track and analyze the success of their products over time. By storing data on product usage, customer satisfaction, and sales trends, they can identify patterns and make informed decisions about product improvements or adjustments to marketing strategies. Second, data retention enables product managers to understand user behavior and preferences. By analyzing historical data, they can gain insights into how customers interact with the product, what features they value most, and where there may be opportunities for optimization or new feature development. Furthermore, retaining product data is crucial for compliance and legal purposes. Many industries have strict regulations concerning data privacy and security, requiring companies to store and protect customer information for a specified period. Product managers must ensure that they are in compliance with these regulations and have appropriate data retention policies in place. In addition to these benefits, product data retention also facilitates knowledge transfer and collaboration within an organization. When product managers leave a company or move to a different role, their successors can use the stored data to understand the product's history, challenges, and successes. This knowledge continuity helps maintain a consistent product strategy and prevents valuable insights from being lost. In summary, product data retention is the practice of storing and maintaining historical data related to a product's lifecycle. It allows product managers to track performance, understand user behavior, ensure compliance, and facilitate knowledge transfer. By leveraging this data, product managers can make data-driven decisions, optimize their products, and improve the overall customer experience.

Product Data Science Workflow Tool

A Product Data Science Workflow Tool is a software solution designed to assist product management teams in analyzing and utilizing data to make informed decisions and drive product development. It provides a structured workflow, tools, and processes to effectively gather, clean, organize, analyze, and visualize data related to a product's performance, user behavior, market trends, and other relevant metrics. The primary goal of a Product Data Science Workflow Tool is to enable product managers to leverage data to better understand customer needs, identify opportunities for improvement, and prioritize product enhancements and feature developments. The tool facilitates data-driven decision-making, helping product managers to identify patterns, trends, and correlations within the data that can inform product strategy. The workflow in a Product Data Science Workflow Tool typically comprises several stages, including data collection, data preprocessing, exploratory data analysis, statistical modeling, and data visualization. The tool provides a user-friendly interface and a range of built-in features to streamline and automate these stages, reducing the manual effort required to extract insights from data. A Product Data Science Workflow Tool allows product managers to define key performance indicators (KPIs) and track their progress over time. It enables them to delve deep into the data to identify factors influencing product metrics, conduct segmentation analysis, and perform A/B testing to evaluate the impact of different product variations or features. In addition to analysis and modeling capabilities, a Product Data Science Workflow Tool often includes collaboration features that facilitate knowledge sharing and cross-functional teamwork. It allows product managers to share data insights, reports, and visualizations with stakeholders, such as executives, engineering teams, and marketing departments, to align product strategy with business objectives. In summary, a Product Data Science Workflow Tool is a software solution that empowers product management teams to gather, process, analyze, and visualize data to drive informed decision-making and enhance product development. It provides a structured workflow and a range of features to enable product managers to uncover valuable insights, make data-driven decisions, and collaborate effectively with other stakeholders.

Product Data Science

Product Data Science is a discipline within Product Management that combines data analysis and scientific methods to inform product decision-making and drive product innovation. It involves the application of statistical and machine learning techniques to turn raw data into actionable insights, and to identify patterns and trends that can help optimize product performance and user experience. Product Data Science encompasses a range of activities, including data collection, data cleaning and preprocessing, exploratory data analysis, statistical modeling, and predictive analytics. It leverages tools and technologies such as data warehouses, data lakes, data visualization tools, and programming languages like Python or R to analyze and interpret large volumes of data. At its core, Product Data Science aims to answer key questions related to product development, user behavior, and market dynamics. It helps product managers understand user needs and preferences, track and measure product metrics, identify opportunities for product improvement, and make informed decisions based on data-driven insights. One of the key responsibilities of a Product Data Scientist is to design and conduct experiments to test product hypotheses and evaluate the impact of product changes. They may use A/B testing or multivariate testing methodologies to assess the effectiveness of different product variations and features. The insights gained from these experiments can help prioritize product roadmap items, optimize product features, and drive overall product strategy. Another important aspect of Product Data Science is user segmentation and personalization. By analyzing user data, Product Data Scientists can identify distinct user groups based on demographics, behavior, or preferences. This enables product managers to tailor their product offerings and marketing strategies to different user segments, maximizing user satisfaction and engagement. In summary, Product Data Science is a critical component of Product Management, leveraging data-driven techniques to support decision-making and drive product innovation. By applying scientific methods and data analysis, product managers can gain valuable insights into user behavior, optimize product performance, and ultimately build better products that meet user needs and drive business growth.

Product Data Security Policy Implementation

A Product Data Security Policy Implementation is a formal set of guidelines and procedures that are established within a product management framework to ensure the secure handling, storage, and transmission of data related to a specific product or service. This policy is designed to protect sensitive information from unauthorized access, use, or disclosure, and to mitigate the risk of data breaches, identity theft, and other security incidents. It sets forth the responsibilities and requirements for both internal product teams and external stakeholders who handle or have access to product data.

Product Data Security Policy

A Product Data Security Policy is a formal document that outlines the procedures, guidelines, and protocols for safeguarding and protecting the data associated with a product throughout its lifecycle. It governs how data is collected, stored, processed, and managed to ensure the confidentiality, integrity, and availability of the product's data. The policy is designed to address potential vulnerabilities, risks, and threats to the product's data security. It establishes a framework that defines roles, responsibilities, and controls to mitigate these risks and protect

115

against unauthorized access, disclosure, alteration, or destruction of data.

Product Data Security

Product Data Security refers to the measures and practices taken to protect the data associated with a product throughout its lifecycle. It encompasses various strategies and tactics to safeguard the confidentiality, integrity, and availability of the data that is generated, processed, stored, or transmitted by the product. The primary objective of Product Data Security is to prevent unauthorized access, disclosure, alteration, or destruction of sensitive information and assets related to the product. This includes protecting customer data, intellectual property, proprietary information, and any other confidential or classified data that the product handles. Data security starts at the design stage of the product, ensuring that the necessary security controls and mechanisms are incorporated into the system architecture. This includes authentication, authorization, encryption, and access control mechanisms to enforce proper user authentication and restrict unauthorized access to data. During the development and testing phases, Product Data Security involves rigorous testing and vulnerability assessments to identify and remediate any security vulnerabilities or weaknesses in the product. This helps ensure that the product is free from common security flaws and can withstand potential attacks. In the deployment and operation stage, continuous monitoring and logging mechanisms are put in place to track and detect any suspicious or malicious activities within the product's environment. Additionally, regular software updates and patches are applied to address newly discovered security vulnerabilities. Furthermore, Product Data Security also extends to the product's end-of-life stage, where proper data sanitization and disposal procedures are implemented to prevent unauthorized access to residual data or the reuse of storage media. To achieve effective Product Data Security, product managers need to work closely with cross-functional teams, including software developers, security experts, and privacy professionals. They must also stay up to date with the latest security threats and industry best practices, ensuring that their products adhere to relevant regulations and standards.

Product Data Storage

Product Data Storage refers to the management and organization of data related to a product throughout its lifecycle. It involves collecting, storing, and retrieving various types of information about a product, including specifications, features, pricing, inventory, sales data, and customer feedback. This data is crucial for product managers as it enables them to make informed decisions and drive product strategy. They can analyze the data to understand customer preferences, identify market trends, and determine areas for improvement or innovation.

Product Data Synchronization Method

Product Data Synchronization Method refers to the process of ensuring that consistent and accurate data related to products is maintained and updated across all relevant systems and channels within an organization. This method involves the synchronization of product data across various platforms, such as e-commerce websites, mobile apps, ERP systems, and offline stores, to provide a seamless and unified experience for both customers and internal stakeholders. The main objective of product data synchronization is to eliminate discrepancies and inconsistencies in product information, such as pricing, inventory levels, descriptions, images, and specifications, that may arise due to multiple sources of data and frequent updates. By implementing a robust and efficient synchronization method, companies can avoid customer dissatisfaction, operational inefficiencies, and sales losses caused by outdated or incorrect product information. There are several techniques and tools available for product data synchronization, depending on the complexity and scale of the organization's product catalog. These methods generally involve the integration of different systems and the implementation of data validation and transformation processes. Some common approaches include: 1. Batch Synchronization: This method involves scheduled updates or batch processing to synchronize product data at regular intervals. It is suitable for organizations with a large number of products and slower data update frequencies. 2. Real-time Synchronization: In this method, product data is synchronized instantaneously as soon as changes occur. It requires real-time integration between various systems and is commonly used in industries or channels with high data volatility and rapid updates. 3. Delta Synchronization: In delta synchronization, only the changes or updates since the last synchronization are applied, reducing the processing time and resource requirements. This method is useful for organizations with frequent product data updates or limited processing capabilities. Product data synchronization methods may also involve data mapping, data cleansing, and data transformation steps to ensure compatibility and consistency across different systems and formats. It is essential for organizations to establish clear data governance policies, define data quality standards, and implement monitoring mechanisms to ensure the effectiveness and accuracy of the synchronization process.

Product Data Synchronization

Product Data Synchronization is the process of harmonizing and updating product information across different systems or platforms within an organization. It involves the efficient and accurate exchange of product data, ensuring consistency and integrity throughout the product management lifecycle. Product data typically includes attributes such as product name, description, pricing, specifications, images, and various other details that provide a comprehensive overview of a product. In an organization, this data is often stored in multiple databases, systems, or software, such as Enterprise Resource Planning (ERP), Customer Relationship Management (CRM), Product Information Management (PIM), and e-commerce platforms. The goal of Product Data Synchronization is to ensure that all systems and platforms within an organization have up-to-date and accurate product information. This synchronization enables better decision-making, reduces errors, improves operational efficiency, and enhances the overall customer experience. The process of Product Data Synchronization typically involves the following steps: 1. Extracting product data from various sources: The first step is to extract relevant product data from different systems, databases, or platforms within the organization. This data may be stored in different formats or structures. 2. Transforming and mapping data: Once the data is extracted, it needs to be transformed and mapped to a standardized format that can be easily understood and processed by all systems. This step ensures consistency and compatibility of the data across various platforms. 3. Updating and synchronizing data: After transformation, the updated product data is synchronized across all relevant systems. This involves updating existing data, adding new data, or deleting obsolete data. The synchronization process may be automated or manual, depending on the organization's needs and capabilities. 4. Data validation and quality control: Once the data is synchronized, it needs to be validated for accuracy, completeness, and consistency. This step involves identifying and resolving any data discrepancies, errors, or missing information. 5. Continuous monitoring and maintenance: Product Data Synchronization is an ongoing process that requires continuous monitoring and maintenance. As new products are introduced or existing products are updated, the synchronized data needs to be kept up to date to ensure accuracy and consistency across all systems. Overall, Product Data Synchronization plays a critical role in effective product management by ensuring that all relevant systems and platforms within an organization have access to accurate, up-to-date, and consistent product information, thereby enabling efficient operations and enhancing the customer experience.

Product Data Transformation Tool

A Product Data Transformation Tool refers to a software solution that is designed to facilitate the conversion, mapping, and integration of product data across various systems and formats within a product management context. Product management involves overseeing the entire lifecycle of a product, which includes gathering, organizing, and managing product data. This data can come from multiple sources such as suppliers, manufacturers, or internal departments, and may exist in different formats like spreadsheets, databases, or XML files. The purpose of a Product Data Transformation Tool is to standardize and consolidate product data from diverse sources into a unified format that can be easily understood, manipulated, and shared across the organization. This tool enables product managers to efficiently handle large volumes of data, reduce errors or inconsistencies, and improve the overall data quality. Key features of a Product Data Transformation Tool include data extraction, transformation, and loading capabilities. Data extraction involves retrieving product data from various sources, while transformation encompasses mapping, conversion, and validation of the data. Loading refers to the process of uploading the transformed data into the target system or repository. A Product Data Transformation Tool typically offers a user-friendly interface that allows product managers to configure data transformation rules, define mapping relationships, and specify data validation criteria. It may also provide functionalities like data cleansing, deduplication, enrichment, or synchronization. By using a Product Data Transformation Tool, product managers can streamline their data management processes, enhance data accuracy and consistency, and accelerate time-to-market for new products. It eliminates the manual effort and reduces the risk of human errors that are associated with handling data in disparate formats. In conclusion, a Product Data Transformation Tool is a vital tool for product managers to effectively manage and integrate product data across different systems and formats, ensuring data accuracy, consistency, and efficiency throughout the product lifecycle.

Product Data Transformation

A product data transformation refers to the process of converting and reformatting product data from one structure or format to another, facilitating its management and utilization in product management systems. It involves the extraction, manipulation, and organization of product information to ensure consistency, accuracy, and compatibility across various platforms, channels, and applications. This transformation process plays a crucial role in product management as it enables effective data integration, streamlines workflows, and enhances the overall efficiency of managing product information. By transforming product data into a standardized and structured format, it becomes easier to navigate, search, and analyze, resulting in improved decision-making and better customer experiences. One aspect of product data transformation is data cleansing, which involves identifying and rectifying any inconsistencies, errors, or redundancies in the data. This may include removing duplicate entries, addressing missing or incomplete information, and standardizing units of measurement, categories, or attributes. By ensuring the accuracy and completeness of product data, organizations can avoid costly mistakes, minimize customer dissatisfaction, and maintain a high level of data quality. Additionally, product data transformation often includes data enrichment, which involves enhancing the existing data with additional information or attributes. This could involve enriching product descriptions with images, videos, or customer reviews, or adding relevant metadata such as brand, manufacturer, or compatibility information. By enriching product data, organizations can provide more detailed and comprehensive information to customers, ultimately improving product discoverability and increasing sales. The transformed product data can then be utilized in various product management activities, such as catalog management, inventory management, pricing optimization, or omnichannel distribution. It enables organizations to efficiently manage their product portfolios, update price lists, track stock levels, and synchronize product information across different sales channels or platforms. In conclusion, product data transformation is a critical process in product management that involves converting, cleaning, and enriching product data to ensure consistency, accuracy, and compatibility. It enables organizations to effectively manage and utilize product information, leading to improved decision-making, enhanced customer experiences, and increased operational efficiency.

Product Data Virtualization Solution

A product data virtualization solution is a software tool or platform that enables product managers to aggregate and integrate data from various sources, such as internal systems, external vendors, and third-party applications, into a centralized virtual database. This centralized database can then be accessed and used by product managers to gain insights, make data-driven decisions, and provide accurate and up-to-date product information to stakeholders. By virtualizing and consolidating product data from multiple sources, a product data virtualization solution enables product managers to have a unified and comprehensive view of their product information. It eliminates the need to manually gather and reconcile data from disparate sources, saving time and reducing the risk of errors or inconsistencies.

Product Data Virtualization

Data Virtualization is a software technology that enables organizations to create a virtual, unified view of product data from multiple sources, without physically moving or duplicating the data. It provides a layer of abstraction that allows product managers to access and analyze data from various systems, such as ERP (Enterprise Resource Planning), CRM (Customer Relationship Management), and PLM (Product Lifecycle Management), in a consistent and simplified manner. Product Data Virtualization combines data integration, data federation, and data abstraction techniques to provide a real-time, holistic view of product information. It leverages advanced querying capabilities and metadata-driven transformations to transform and aggregate data from disparate sources on the fly, making it available for analysis and reporting purposes.

Product Data Visualization

Product data visualization refers to the practice of representing product-related information in a visual format, such as charts, graphs, and dashboards, to facilitate better understanding and decision-making in product management. Data visualization plays a crucial role in product management as it allows product managers to analyze and interpret extensive amounts of data quickly and efficiently. By visually representing complex product data, product managers can identify patterns, trends, and insights that may not be apparent in raw data or text-based reports.

Product Data Warehouse

A product data warehouse is a centralized database that stores and integrates data related to product management. It serves as a comprehensive repository of information about products, including their characteristics, performance, pricing, inventory, and sales data. By consolidating and organizing product data from various sources, the data warehouse provides product managers with a holistic view of the entire product portfolio. This data warehouse collects and integrates data from different systems and sources, such as inventory management systems, sales trackers, marketing platforms, and customer feedback systems. It ensures that all relevant product data is captured, stored, and made accessible to product managers for analysis and decision-making purposes. The primary purpose of a product data warehouse is to enable product managers to make informed decisions about their products. By analyzing the data stored in the warehouse, product managers can gain insights into product performance, customer preferences, market trends, and competitive analysis. This information helps them understand how their products are performing in the market and identify areas for improvement or growth. The data stored in the product data warehouse is typically organized and structured in a way that facilitates analysis and reporting. It allows product managers to generate reports, dashboards, and visualizations to track key performance indicators (KPIs), monitor product metrics, and evaluate product strategies. The warehouse may also provide tools for data mining and predictive analytics, enabling product managers to forecast future product demand, identify potential product issues, and make data-driven decisions. In addition to supporting strategic decision-making, a product data warehouse also plays a crucial role in operational product management. It provides real-time visibility into product inventory, availability, and sales data, allowing product managers to manage product lifecycles, make pricing decisions, and optimize inventory levels. The warehouse may also integrate with other systems, such as order management or customer relationship management (CRM) platforms, to facilitate seamless product information flow and streamline processes.

Product Data Wrangling Tool

A product data wrangling tool is a software application that is specifically designed for product management professionals to effectively manage and organize large volumes of product data. The tool enables product managers to streamline the process of collecting, cleaning, transforming, and organizing product data from various sources, such as suppliers, manufacturers, and internal systems. With a product data wrangling tool, product managers can easily import and aggregate product data from different data sources, including spreadsheets, databases, and e-commerce platforms. The tool provides a user-friendly interface that allows users to map and match product attributes, eliminate duplicates, and ensure data consistency and accuracy. The tool offers a range of features that facilitate data cleansing and transformation activities. Product managers can use built-in algorithms and functions to standardize product names, categorize products into hierarchies, and enrich product data with additional attributes and metadata. The tool also provides capabilities for data validation, allowing product managers to identify and resolve inconsistencies and errors in the data. Furthermore, a product data wrangling tool enables product managers to collaborate with other stakeholders, such as marketing teams, sales teams, and suppliers. The tool supports data sharing and collaboration workflows, allowing multiple users to access and work on product data simultaneously. Product managers can define access permissions, track changes, and merge data edits to ensure data integrity and version control. In addition to data management and collaboration features, a product data wrangling tool often includes advanced analytics and reporting capabilities. Product managers can generate insights and reports on product performance, sales trends, and customer preferences based on the organized and clean product data. These insights can drive informed decision-making and support strategic product planning and development.

Product Data Wrangling

Product Data Wrangling refers to the process of collecting, cleaning, organizing, and transforming product-related data in order to create meaningful insights and drive informed decision-making in product management. Product managers are responsible for understanding customer needs, translating them into product requirements, and overseeing the development and launch of new products. In order to effectively perform these tasks, it is crucial for product managers to have access to accurate and reliable data about their products, customers, and market trends. Data wrangling begins with the collection of relevant product data from various sources including customer feedback, sales data, user analytics, and market research. This data is often stored in different formats across multiple databases, making it necessary to consolidate and integrate the data into a single, unified dataset. Once the data is collected, the next step in the wrangling process is cleaning and preprocessing the data. This involves identifying and correcting any errors or inconsistencies in the data, removing duplicate or irrelevant entries, and handling missing values. Data cleaning ensures that the data is reliable and accurate, which is essential for making informed product decisions. After cleaning, the product data is organized and structured in a way that is easy to analyze and interpret. This involves categorizing and tagging the data based on different attributes such as product features, customer segments, and market segments. Organizing the data allows product managers to quickly retrieve and analyze specific subsets of data, enabling them to gain insights into customer preferences, identify market trends, and evaluate the performance of existing products. The final step in the data wrangling process is transforming the data into a format that can be used for further analysis and visualization. This may involve aggregating the data, calculating metrics and KPIs, and creating visual representations such as charts and graphs. Data transformation enables product managers to identify patterns, trends, and associations in the data, which can inform product strategy and decision-making processes. In conclusion, product data wrangling is an essential process in product management that involves collecting, cleaning, organizing, and transforming product-related data. By effectively wrangling the data, product managers are able to gain valuable insights, make informed decisions, and drive the success of their products in the market.

Product Decision-Making

Product Decision-Making refers to the process of evaluating various options and making informed choices to determine the features, pricing, positioning, and overall strategy of a product in order to meet the needs and desires of target customers while achieving the goals and objectives of the organization. In the field of Product Management, decision-making plays a crucial role in the success of a product. It involves gathering and analyzing relevant market, customer, and competitive data to identify opportunities and threats. Product managers use this information to assess the feasibility and potential impact of different decision options. The first step in product decision-making is to define the product vision, goals, and strategy. This involves understanding the target market, customer needs, and business objectives. The product manager then determines the key features and functionalities that will differentiate the product and provide value to customers. Once the product vision is established, the product manager evaluates pricing options. This includes analyzing market trends, competitive positioning, production costs, and customer willingness to pay. The chosen pricing strategy should align with the value proposition of the product and support revenue goals. Another important aspect of product decision-making is positioning. Product managers need to determine the unique selling proposition and create a compelling marketing message that resonates with the target audience. This involves understanding customer preferences, conducting market segmentation, and developing a positioning strategy that highlights the product's strengths and benefits. During the decision-making process, product managers also need to consider the product roadmap and prioritize features based on customer feedback, market trends, and business objectives. They must evaluate the trade-offs between different features and make decisions that will maximize customer satisfaction and competitive advantage. Finally, product decision-making involves developing a go-to-market strategy and identifying the most suitable distribution channels. This includes selecting sales channels, creating marketing campaigns, and determining the optimal launch plan to reach the target customers effectively. In summary, product decision-making in the context of Product Management is the process of evaluating various options and making informed choices regarding the features, pricing, positioning, and overall strategy of a product. It encompasses the analysis of market data, customer insights, and competitive factors to determine the most effective and successful approach to meet customer needs and achieve organizational goals.

Product Defect Reporting

Product Defect Reporting is a formal process within Product Management that involves the identification, documentation, and communication of product defects or faults. It plays a vital role in ensuring product quality, customer satisfaction, and the overall success of a product. When a defect is identified in a product, it is important to promptly report it through the appropriate channels to initiate the necessary actions for resolution. The defect reporting process typically follows the steps outlined below: The first step in defect reporting is identification. This involves recognizing and documenting any issues or non-conformities in the product that can affect its functionality, performance, or user experience. Defects can manifest in various forms, such as software bugs, hardware malfunctions, design flaws, or usability problems. After identification, the defect needs to be documented in detail. This includes capturing the specific symptoms or behaviors of the defect, steps to reproduce it, and any relevant supporting information. Clear and concise documentation is crucial to enable effective communication and understanding of the defect by all stakeholders involved in the resolution process. Once the defect is documented, it needs to be communicated to the appropriate parties, such as the development team, quality assurance team, or stakeholders responsible for defect resolution. This can be done through defect tracking systems, project management tools, or other established communication channels within the organization. Upon receiving the defect report, the responsible parties will analyze and prioritize the defect based on its severity, impact on users, and business priorities. This evaluation helps in determining the appropriate course of action, such as assigning resources, scheduling fixes, or applying temporary workarounds. Throughout the defect resolution process, regular updates and status reports are shared with all stakeholders to keep them informed about the progress and expected timelines for resolution. Once the defect is fixed, the resolution is verified through rigorous testing to ensure that it has been effectively addressed. Overall, Product Defect Reporting is a critical aspect of Product Management as it enables the timely detection and resolution of product defects, leading to improved product quality and customer satisfaction. It ensures that organizations can address any issues that arise promptly, maintain a good reputation in the market, and continually improve their products for long-term success.

Product Design Reviews

A product design review is a formal evaluation process conducted by the product management team to assess the design of a product at different stages of its development. It involves gathering feedback from various stakeholders, such as customers, engineers, and designers, to ensure that the product meets the desired requirements and objectives. The purpose of a product design review is to identify any shortcomings, potential risks, or areas of improvement in the design of a product. It aims to ensure that the product is functional, user-friendly, scalable, and aligns with the overall product strategy and vision. By conducting regular design reviews, product managers can address any issues early on in the development process and make any necessary adjustments to enhance the product's quality and performance.

Product Design Thinking

Product design thinking refers to a systematic and collaborative approach used in product management to identify, understand, and address the needs and preferences of consumers. It involves applying design principles and methodologies to create innovative and user-centric solutions. At its core, product design thinking focuses on empathizing with users, defining their problems, ideating potential solutions, prototyping, and testing. It places heavy emphasis on understanding the end-user and utilizing consumer insights to drive product development.

Product Design Validation

Product design validation is a critical process in product management that involves testing and evaluating a product's design to ensure its effectiveness, usability, and alignment with user needs and business goals. It is a systematic and objective approach used to validate design decisions and mitigate risks before moving into production or launch. During product design validation, various methods are used to gather feedback and insights from users, stakeholders, and experts. These methods can include user testing, surveys, interviews, focus groups, and usability studies. The goal is to uncover any potential issues, identify areas for improvement, and validate that the design meets the requirements and expectations of its intended users. By conducting product design validation, product managers can gain valuable insights and make informed decisions on design iterations or necessary changes. This process helps to identify and address any usability or functionality issues early on, saving both time and resources in the long run. Furthermore, product design validation plays a crucial role in ensuring the product's market fit and competitiveness. By involving users and stakeholders in the validation process, product managers can better understand their needs, preferences, and pain points. This information can then be used to optimize the product design and enhance its value proposition. In addition, product design validation enables product managers to assess the feasibility and viability of the design. It allows for the identification of any technical or manufacturing constraints that may impact the product's quality, cost, or timeline. By validating the design, product managers can minimize the risks of manufacturing or production issues, ultimately improving the overall product quality and customer satisfaction. In summary, product design validation is a critical step in the product management process that involves testing, gathering feedback, and evaluating a product's design to ensure its alignment with user needs, business goals, and market demands. It helps identify potential issues and validates the design's usability, effectiveness, and functionality. By conducting thorough design validation, product managers can optimize the product's design, mitigate risks, and enhance its market fit and competitiveness.

Product Design Verification

Product design verification is an essential process in product management that aims to ensure that a product meets specified design requirements and is ready for market release. It involves assessing and validating the design of a product to ensure it is functional, reliable, safe, and user-friendly. During the product design verification process, the focus is on confirming that the product design meets the intended specifications and that it can perform its intended functions effectively. The verification process typically involves testing the product design against predetermined criteria, including performance, functionality, durability, and safety. Verification activities may include conducting various tests, such as functional testing, stress testing, environmental testing, and usability testing. These tests help identify any design flaws, weaknesses, or potential risks that may arise during product use. By uncovering these issues early in the design phase, product designers and managers can address them before the product reaches the market. The design verification process also plays a crucial role in ensuring that the product meets regulatory and compliance standards. Depending on the industry and the nature of the product, there may be specific regulations and standards that the product must adhere to. The verification process helps confirm that the product design complies with these requirements, reducing the risk of non-compliance or potential legal issues. In addition to functional and regulatory aspects, product design verification also considers user experience and usability factors. Usability testing involves evaluating how easily and efficiently users can interact with the product, ensuring that it is intuitive, user-friendly, and meets the expectations of the target audience. In summary, product design verification is the process of evaluating and validating a product design against specified requirements, considering factors such as functionality, reliability, safety, compliance, and user experience. By verifying the design early in the product development lifecycle, product managers can identify and address any design flaws or potential risks, ensuring a high-quality, market-ready product.

Product Design

Product design is a crucial aspect of the product management process that involves conceptualizing, creating, and refining a product's physical and visual attributes to meet specific user needs and business goals. It encompasses the entire lifecycle of product development, including ideation, research, prototyping, testing, and finalizing the design. The primary objective of product design is to deliver a high-quality, functional, and aesthetically pleasing product that satisfies customer requirements and expectations. It requires a deep understanding of user behavior, market trends, and technological advancements to ensure that the final product stands out in the competitive landscape.

Product Development Collaboration

Product development collaboration refers to the process of working together with various stakeholders, both internal and external, in order to create, design, and bring a new product to market. It is an essential aspect of product management, as it involves coordinating and integrating efforts from different teams and individuals throughout the entire product development lifecycle. In a collaborative product development approach, cross-functional teams from different departments, such as engineering, design, marketing, and sales, work together to define the product's concept, features, and specifications. This collaborative effort ensures that all aspects of the product are considered and optimized for success in the market. Collaboration in product development involves open and frequent communication, sharing of ideas, and collective decision-making. It fosters a culture of collaboration and innovation, where every team member's input and expertise are valued and utilized. By bringing together diverse perspectives and skills, collaboration promotes the generation of unique and creative ideas that can lead to breakthrough products. Effective collaboration in product development also relies on the use of collaborative tools and technologies. These tools enable teams to work together seamlessly, regardless of geographical location. Examples of such tools include project management software, virtual meeting platforms, and cloud-based document sharing systems. These tools facilitate real-time communication, document version control, task tracking, and collaboration across different time zones and locations. Product development collaboration is not limited to internal stakeholders. It also involves external collaboration with suppliers, partners, and even customers. Collaborating with suppliers ensures that the necessary materials, components, or services are available and meet the required specifications. Partnering with external organizations can bring in specialized expertise, access to new markets, or additional resources that can accelerate the product development process. In some cases, involving customers in the product development process through techniques like co-creation or user feedback can lead to products that better meet customer needs and preferences. In conclusion, product development collaboration is a critical aspect of product management, enabling teams to leverage diverse skills, perspectives, and resources to create successful products. It involves coordination and integration of efforts from internal and external stakeholders throughout the entire product development lifecycle, with the goal of delivering innovative, market-driven products.

Product Development Phases

In the context of Product Management, product development can be divided into several distinct phases. These phases represent a systematic approach to creating, improving, and launching products. The key phases of product development include: 1. Ideation: This phase involves generating and exploring ideas for new products or enhancements to existing ones. It often includes brainstorming sessions, market research, and feedback from customers and stakeholders. The goal is to identify potential opportunities and determine the best ideas to pursue further. 2. Concept Development: Once a promising idea is identified, the concept development phase begins. This phase involves defining the product's scope, features, and target market. It includes creating prototypes or mock-ups to visualize the product and gathering feedback to refine the concept. 3. Design and Engineering: In this phase, detailed designs are created based on the approved product concept. The design and engineering team works on translating the concept into a technically feasible product, considering factors such as functionality, performance, materials, and manufacturing processes. This phase includes activities like creating detailed specifications, conducting feasibility studies, and developing prototypes. 4. Testing and Validation: Once the design is complete, the product goes through rigorous testing and validation to ensure it meets the intended requirements and standards. This phase includes different types of testing, such as functional testing, performance testing, usability testing, and compliance testing. The feedback and data gathered during this phase help identify and address any potential issues or improvements needed before launching the product. 5. Manufacturing and Production: After successful testing and validation, the product moves into the manufacturing and production phase. This involves setting up the production line, procuring raw materials, and implementing quality control processes. The goal is to ensure that the product is manufactured efficiently, at the desired quality level, and in the required quantities to meet market demands. 6. Launch and Commercialization: The final phase of product development is the launch and commercialization of the product. This involves creating marketing and sales strategies, preparing promotional materials, and developing distribution channels. The goal is to effectively introduce the product to the market and generate customer awareness and demand. Each of these product development phases is crucial for ensuring successful product management. By following a systematic and structured approach, organizations can increase their chances of creating innovative, high-quality products that meet customer needs and expectations.

Product Development Team

A product development team, in the context of product management, is a group of individuals responsible for the ideation, creation, and introduction of new products or the enhancement of existing products within a company or organization. The primary objective of a product development team is to take a concept or idea and transform it into a tangible, marketable product that aligns with the company's overall business goals and customer needs. This involves a collaborative and multidisciplinary approach, with team members from various functional areas bringing their expertise and skills to the table. Key responsibilities of a product development team include conducting market research and analysis to identify customer needs and market opportunities, brainstorming and generating innovative product ideas, conducting feasibility studies to assess the technical and financial viability of the proposed product, creating detailed product specifications and design plans, coordinating and facilitating the actual development process, and working closely with cross-functional teams such as engineering, marketing, and sales to ensure successful product launch and commercialization. The product development team plays a crucial role in ensuring that the final product meets customer expectations and contributes to the company's overall growth and success. They are tasked with understanding market trends, customer preferences, and competitive landscape to develop products that not only meet the needs of the target market but also have a competitive edge. This requires a deep understanding of the customers and their pain points, as well as the ability to anticipate future market demands. Effective communication, collaboration, and project management skills are essential for a product development team to succeed. The team members must work together seamlessly, leveraging their unique perspectives and expertise to drive the product from concept to market. They must also navigate potential obstacles and challenges, adjusting plans and priorities as needed to ensure timely delivery of high-quality products.

Product Development

Product development refers to the process of creating and evolving a new product or enhancing an existing product to meet the needs and preferences of customers. It involves multiple stages, starting from the ideation phase, where ideas for a new product or product improvement are generated, to the final launch of the product in the market. The product management team plays a vital role in overseeing the product development process. They are responsible for identifying customer needs and market trends, conducting market research and analysis, and collaborating with various stakeholders, such as engineers, designers, and marketing teams, to develop and bring the product to market.

Product Differentiation

Product differentiation is a strategic approach used in product management to distinguish a particular product or service from its competitors. It involves developing unique features, characteristics, or benefits that set the product apart from others in the market. The aim of product differentiation is to create perceived value and to establish a competitive advantage that attracts and retains customers. There are several ways in which product differentiation can be achieved. One common method is through physical attributes or design. This can involve incorporating innovative features, using higher quality materials, or creating a visually appealing product. By offering something distinct in terms of appearance or functionality, the product can stand out from similar offerings in the market. Another approach to product differentiation is through branding and positioning. This involves creating a strong brand identity and associating the product with certain attributes or values that resonate with the target market. By establishing a unique brand image, the product can appeal to specific consumer segments and differentiate itself from competitors who may offer similar products. Product differentiation can also be achieved through service or customer experience. By providing exceptional customer service, offering personalized support, or creating a seamless user experience, a product can differentiate itself based on the level of service it provides. This can be particularly effective in industries where customer relationships and satisfaction play a significant role in purchasing decisions. Additionally, product differentiation can be achieved through pricing strategies. This can involve offering the product at a higher or lower price point compared to competitors, or providing different pricing options or bundles. By positioning the product as more affordable or as a premium offering, it can attract customers who are looking for specific price points or value propositions. In conclusion, product differentiation is a key concept in product management that involves creating unique features, branding, service, or pricing strategies to set a product apart from competitors. By offering something distinct, a product can capture the attention and loyalty of customers, leading to increased market share and profitability.

Product Discovery Framework Resources

A Product Discovery Framework is a structured and iterative approach used by product managers to identify, define, and prioritize product opportunities. It is a framework that guides the product management team in understanding customer needs, market trends, and competitive landscapes to develop innovative and successful products. The framework typically consists of several key stages, including problem identification, idea generation, validation, and prioritization. In the problem identification stage, product managers collaborate with cross-functional teams to gather insights and understand user pain points. This involves conducting user research, analyzing market data, and evaluating existing solutions. The idea generation stage aims to generate a wide range of potential solutions to the identified problems. Product managers facilitate brainstorming sessions and leverage various ideation techniques, such as mind mapping or storyboarding, to encourage creativity and generate innovative ideas. The validation stage involves testing and refining the generated ideas. Product managers create prototypes or minimum viable products (MVPs) to gather feedback from users through user testing or beta testing. This iterative process helps validate ideas, gather insights, and iterate on the product concept. Once the ideas are validated, the prioritization stage comes into play. Product managers assess the potential impact, feasibility, and effort required for each idea. They collaborate with stakeholders, such as developers and designers, to evaluate technical feasibility and estimate resource requirements. This stage aims to identify the most promising ideas that align with strategic goals and have a high likelihood of success. Throughout the product discovery framework, product managers continuously engage with customers, stakeholders, and subject matter experts to gather insights and validate assumptions. They use various tools and techniques, such as user interviews, surveys, analytics, and market research, to inform decision-making and ensure that the final product meets user needs and aligns with business objectives.

Product Discovery Frameworks

A Product Discovery Framework is a structured approach or methodology used in Product Management to identify, evaluate, and prioritize potential product opportunities or ideas. It provides a systematic way to explore, validate, and refine ideas before investing significant resources into development. Product Discovery Frameworks typically involve a series of steps or stages that guide the product team through various activities, such as user research, problem identification, solution brainstorming, prototyping, and testing. The main goal is to uncover valuable insights about user needs, pain points, and preferences, as well as to ensure that the proposed solutions effectively address those needs.

Product Distribution Channels

Product distribution channels refer to the various methods and channels through which a company sells and delivers its products to the end consumers. These channels play a crucial role in product management as they determine how the product reaches its target market and how effectively it can be distributed to meet customer demand. A well-designed distribution channel can greatly impact a company's sales and market share. There are different types of distribution channels available to companies, and the choice of channel depends on various factors such as the type of product, target market, competition, and company capabilities. The four main types of distribution channels are direct, indirect, dual, and multi-channel distribution.

Direct distribution channels involve selling products directly to the end consumers, without the involvement of intermediaries. This can be done through company-owned physical stores, e-commerce websites, or direct sales representatives. Direct distribution provides the company with greater control over the customer experience and allows for closer relationships with customers. However, it can also be more costly to set up and manage. Indirect distribution channels involve the use of intermediaries to sell and deliver products to the end consumers. These intermediaries can include wholesalers, retailers, distributors, and agents. Indirect distribution allows companies to reach a wider customer base and tap into the expertise and resources of these intermediaries. However, it can also reduce the company's control over the customer experience and increase the cost of distribution. Dual distribution channels involve using both direct and indirect channels simultaneously. This allows companies to leverage the benefits of both approaches and reach customers through multiple channels. Dual distribution can be useful when targeting different customer segments or when trying to maximize market coverage. Multi-channel distribution involves using multiple channels, both online and offline, to sell and deliver products to customers. This can include a combination of direct sales, e-commerce, retail stores, and other distribution methods. Multi-channel distribution allows companies to cater to the preferences and convenience of different customer segments, and it can help increase sales and market reach.

Product Distribution

Product Distribution refers to the process of getting a product from the manufacturing plant or warehouse to the end user or consumer. It encompasses all activities involved in ensuring that the product is available for purchase and consumption by the target market. This includes transportation, storage, and handling of the product as it moves through the supply chain. In product management, distribution plays a crucial role in the success of a product. It is a key component of the marketing mix and directly affects the reach and availability of the product to the target market. A well-planned and executed distribution strategy can help a company gain a competitive advantage and maximize sales.

Product Documentation Management

Product Documentation Management refers to the process of creating, organizing, updating, and distributing product documentation in order to support the successful development, launch, and maintenance of a product. It involves capturing all relevant information about the product, such as specifications, user guides, release notes, and troubleshooting manuals, and ensuring that this information is easily accessible to all stakeholders. Effective product documentation management is crucial for a variety of reasons. Firstly, it helps ensure that all relevant information about the product is readily available to the product team, as well as to other teams within the organization. This enables everyone involved in the product development process to have a clear understanding of the product's features, capabilities, and limitations, which in turn helps improve decision-making and collaboration. Additionally, product documentation management plays a key role in facilitating product support and customer satisfaction. By creating comprehensive user guides and troubleshooting manuals, product teams can provide customers with the necessary information to effectively use and troubleshoot the product. This not only helps customers derive maximum value from the product but also reduces their reliance on customer support, resulting in cost savings for the organization. Furthermore, product documentation management ensures that product information is kept up to date. Products often undergo changes and updates, whether it be in terms of features, functionalities, or bug fixes. By maintaining a centralized repository of product documentation and employing a systematic approach to updating and versioning, the product team can ensure that all stakeholders have access to the latest and most accurate information, thereby minimizing confusion and errors. In summary, product documentation management is the process of creating, organizing, updating, and distributing product documentation to support the successful development, launch, and maintenance of a product. It is critical for fostering collaboration, enabling effective product support, and ensuring that accurate and up-to-date information is available to all stakeholders.

Product Documentation

Product documentation refers to the collection of written materials that provide detailed information about a product, its features, functionality, and usage. It is an essential component of the product management process, serving as a comprehensive guide for both internal teams and external stakeholders. The main purpose of product documentation is to ensure effective understanding and utilization of the product. It encompasses various forms of written content, including user manuals, installation guides, release notes, API documentation, and technical specifications. These materials are created and maintained by the product management team, in collaboration with other relevant teams such as development, testing, and customer support. The content of product documentation typically covers the following aspects: 1. Product Overview: This section provides a high-level description of the product, its purpose, and its target audience. It outlines the key features and benefits of the product, giving users a brief introduction before delving into the specifics. 2. User Guides: User guides are detailed instructions on how to use the product effectively. They provide step-by-step explanations, often accompanied by diagrams or screenshots, to help users navigate through different features and perform specific tasks. User guides are crucial for both new users and experienced ones who need assistance with advanced functionalities. 3. Technical Specifications: These documents provide in-depth technical details about the product. They describe the hardware or software requirements, compatibility guidelines, and technical limitations. Technical specifications are essential for IT administrators, developers, and other technical users who require a deeper understanding of the product's technical aspects. 4. API Documentation: For products that have an application programming interface (API), API documentation explains how to integrate and utilize the product's API effectively. It includes information on endpoints, request/response formats, authentication methods, and available functionalities. API documentation is crucial for developers and system integrators who need to interact with the product programmatically. In conclusion, product documentation acts as a comprehensive reference for users and stakeholders, providing them with the necessary information to understand, install, configure, and effectively use the product. It plays a vital role in ensuring a positive user experience, reducing support requests, and enabling efficient collaboration between different teams involved in the product's lifecycle.

Product Durability

Product durability, in the context of product management, refers to the ability of a product to withstand wear and tear, maintain its functionality, and retain its overall quality over an extended period of time. When a product is considered durable, it means that it can withstand the rigors of regular use, resist damage, and remain in good working condition for a significant duration. Durability is a key attribute that customers often seek while making buying decisions, as it is closely related to the product's longevity and value for money.

Product End User Training

Product end user training is a formal process that aims to educate and inform individuals or groups on how to effectively use a particular product. It is a crucial aspect of product management, as it plays a significant role in ensuring customer satisfaction and maximizing the product's potential. This training is designed to equip end users with the necessary knowledge and skills to navigate, operate, and utilize the features and functionalities of the product. It typically includes comprehensive instructions, demonstrations, and practical exercises that allow users to engage with the product in a hands-on manner.

Product End Of Life (EOL)

Product End of Life (EOL) in the context of Product Management refers to the stage in a product's lifecycle when it is no longer viable for continued support or production. At this point, the product is considered obsolete and is no longer actively marketed or sold to customers. EOL can occur for various reasons, including technological advancements, changing market demands, or the introduction of newer and more advanced products. It signifies the end of the product's usefulness and the need for customers to transition to alternative solutions or newer versions offered by the company.

Product Environmental Testing

Product Environmental Testing is the process of evaluating and analyzing the impact of a product on the environment throughout its lifecycle. It involves conducting various tests and assessments to measure the product's compliance with environmental standards, regulations, and requirements. The purpose of Product Environmental Testing is to ensure that a product is environmentally friendly and does not pose any harm or risk to the environment during its manufacturing, use, and disposal stages. It helps identify any potential environmental impacts and allows product managers to make informed decisions about the product's design, materials, and manufacturing processes.

Product Factory Production

Product Factory Production refers to the process of manufacturing products in a factory setting. It involves the transformation of raw materials and components into finished goods that are ready for sale in the market. Product Factory Production is a critical aspect of Product Management, as it directly influences the availability, quality, and cost of products. In Product Management, Product Factory Production is responsible for ensuring efficient and seamless manufacturing operations. This includes planning, coordinating, and executing all activities related to the production process, such as procurement of raw materials, scheduling of production runs, monitoring of production lines, quality control, and inventory management.

Product Failure Analysis

A product failure analysis is a formal evaluation conducted by product management teams to assess the reasons behind the failure of a product. It involves a systematic examination of various factors including market dynamics, product design, development processes, marketing strategies, and customer feedback to identify the root causes of the failure. Product failures can occur for a variety of reasons, such as inadequate market research, poor product-market fit, incorrect pricing, subpar quality, ineffective marketing campaigns, or competitive challenges. The purpose of conducting a product failure analysis is to gain insights into these factors to improve future product development and avoid similar failures in the future.

Product Features

Product features refer to the specific characteristics and functionalities of a product that differentiate it from other offerings in the market. These features are designed to address the needs and preferences of the target customers and provide them with unique value. As a crucial aspect of product management, defining and prioritizing product features is essential for the success of a product. Product managers work closely with cross-functional teams, including engineering, design, and marketing, to identify, analyze, and prioritize the features that will be included in the product. They conduct thorough market research to understand customer needs and preferences, industry trends, and competitive offerings. Based on this research, product managers define a set of features that align with the product's overall vision and strategy.

Product Feedback Analysis

Product Feedback Analysis is the process of gathering, analyzing, and interpreting feedback from customers or users to gain insights and make data-driven decisions to improve a product or service. In the field of Product Management, feedback is a crucial element in the iterative process of developing and enhancing a product. It provides valuable information about customer perceptions, preferences, and pain points, which can be used to optimize features, user experience, and overall satisfaction.

Product Field Testing

Product field testing is a critical phase of the product management process that involves evaluating a new product or feature in real-world conditions before its official launch. It allows product managers to gain insight into how the product performs, how users interact with it, and whether it meets the intended objectives and expectations. During product field testing, the product or feature is deployed to a limited number of users who are representative of the target market. These users are selected based on specific criteria, such as demographics, location, or usage patterns, to ensure the test results are relevant and reliable. The primary goal of product field testing is to uncover any potential issues or shortcomings that may have gone unnoticed during the development and testing phases. By involving users in the testing process, product managers can gather valuable feedback on various aspects of the product, including its usability, functionality, performance, and overall user experience. Feedback from users is collected through different means, such as surveys, interviews, usage logs, or direct observations. This data is then analyzed and used to identify areas for improvement or refinement before the product is officially launched. Field testing also helps in validating assumptions, identifying potential market fit, and making informed decisions about the product's future direction. Product field testing provides several benefits to product managers and organizations. Firstly, it minimizes the risk of launching a product that is poorly received or fails to meet user expectations. It allows product managers to fine-tune the product based on real-world user feedback, aligning it more closely with user needs and preferences. Secondly, product field testing helps in building customer trust and loyalty. By involving users in the testing process, the organization demonstrates that it values their opinion and is committed to delivering a high-quality product. This can lead to increased customer satisfaction and a positive brand image. In conclusion, product field testing plays a crucial role in ensuring the success of a new product or feature. It enables product managers to gather user feedback, identify potential issues, and make necessary improvements before the official launch. By incorporating real-world testing and user validation, organizations can increase the chances of creating a successful and well-received product.

Product Green Design

Product Green Design refers to the practice of incorporating environmentally friendly and sustainable principles in the design and development of products. It involves considering the entire lifecycle of a product, from raw material acquisition to manufacturing, distribution, use, and disposal. The goal of Product Green Design is to minimize the negative impact of products on the environment and maximize their positive contributions to sustainability. In the context of Product Management, incorporating Product Green Design principles requires a holistic approach that considers not only the environmental impact of the product itself but also the entire value chain. Product Managers play a key role in driving sustainable product development by collaborating with cross-functional teams, including designers, engineers, supply chain professionals, and marketing experts. The first step in implementing Product Green Design is to assess the environmental impact of the product throughout its lifecycle. This includes conducting a life cycle assessment (LCA) to identify areas where improvements can be made. Product Managers need to consider factors such as energy consumption, material selection, waste generation, and emissions. They also need to evaluate the potential impact on air, water, and soil quality, as well as the overall ecological footprint. Based on the findings of the LCA, Product Managers can work with designers and engineers to identify and implement sustainable design strategies. This may involve incorporating renewable or recyclable materials, reducing energy consumption, improving product durability, or optimizing packaging for efficient transportation and storage. Product Managers also need to consider end-of-life considerations, such as designing products that are easily recyclable or biodegradable. Product Green Design is not only about minimizing negative impacts but also about creating products that offer environmental benefits. For example, Product Managers can focus on developing energy-efficient products, such as appliances or vehicles that consume less electricity or fuel. They can also explore opportunities for incorporating renewable energy sources, such as solar panels or wind turbines, into the product design. In summary, Product Green Design involves integrating environmentally friendly and sustainable principles into the design and development of products. This requires a comprehensive understanding of the product's lifecycle and collaboration with cross-functional teams. By incorporating Product Green Design principles, Product Managers can help minimize the negative environmental impact of products and create more sustainable and eco-friendly solutions.

Product Idea Incubation

Product Idea Incubation refers to the process of nurturing and developing new product ideas from concept to market-readiness. It involves thoroughly evaluating the feasibility, market potential, and viability of the proposed product before investing resources into its development. During the product idea incubation phase, cross-functional teams, typically comprising product managers, designers, engineers, and marketers, collaborate to refine the initial concept and validate its potential. This process often includes conducting thorough market research, customer interviews, and competitor analysis to understand market demand and size, identify target customers, and assess potential barriers to entry. The incubation phase also involves assessing the technical feasibility of the product idea, considering factors like required resources, technical expertise, and development timelines. This evaluation helps determine if the proposed product aligns with the organization's capabilities and goals. In addition to evaluating the market potential and technical feasibility, product managers also consider the financial viability of the product idea. This entails estimating the potential return on investment, projected revenue, and cost of development, production, and marketing. Throughout the product idea incubation process, cross-functional teams collaborate to further refine the proposed product by iterating on the initial concept, designing prototypes, and gathering feedback from potential customers. This iterative approach helps validate the product idea, identify potential improvements, and minimize risks associated with development. The output of the product idea incubation phase includes a thoroughly evaluated and refined product concept, along with a comprehensive business case that outlines the market opportunity, target customers, competitive analysis, financial projections, and development plan. This output serves as the foundation for subsequent stages of product development, such as design, engineering, and commercialization.

Product Ideation Workshops

A Product Ideation Workshop is a structured session conducted by Product Managers to generate and refine new product ideas. It involves bringing together a diverse group of stakeholders, including cross-functional team members, customers, and subject matter experts, to brainstorm and collaborate on potential solutions to address specific user needs or business opportunities. The objective of a Product Ideation Workshop is to foster creativity, encourage innovative thinking, and explore various perspectives to generate a wide range of ideas. The workshop typically follows a facilitated process that includes specific steps and techniques to stimulate idea generation and stimulate participants' creativity. During the workshop, the Product Manager sets the context by presenting the problem statement or opportunity that the team is aiming to address. This establishes a common understanding and focus for the ideation session. Participants are encouraged to think beyond existing constraints and explore unconventional ideas. The workshop facilitator employs various brainstorming techniques, such as mind mapping, analogies, role-playing, or scenario analysis, to prompt participants to generate ideas. The focus is on quantity rather than quality at this stage, as the goal is to generate a large pool of ideas without judgment or criticism. Once the initial ideation phase is complete, the group engages in a structured evaluation and refinement process. The facilitator leads discussions to help identify promising ideas, considering factors such as feasibility, desirability, and viability. Participants may employ ranking or voting techniques to prioritize the ideas that have the most potential. By the end of the Product Ideation Workshop, the team should have a shortlist of well-defined product ideas that align with business goals and user needs. These ideas can then be further evaluated, prototyped, and tested to determine their potential for development into viable products or features.

Product Ideation

Product ideation refers to the process of generating and developing new product ideas for a company or organization. It is a crucial step in the product management lifecycle, as it lays the foundation for innovation, growth, and competitive advantage. The goal of product ideation is to identify and explore potential market opportunities, customer needs, and pain points that can be addressed through the creation of new products or enhancements to existing ones. This involves brainstorming, researching, and analyzing various sources of inspiration, such as customer feedback, market trends, emerging technologies, and competitive offerings.

Product Improvement

Product Improvement is the continuous process of enhancing a product in order to meet the changing needs and demands of customers, maximize its usability and functionality, and ultimately increase its value in the marketplace. This process involves identifying and understanding the pain points and shortcomings of the existing product, soliciting feedback from customers and stakeholders, conducting market research, and analyzing industry trends and competitors' offerings. Through this analysis, product managers gain insights into what changes, updates, or additions should be made to the product to make it more appealing and competitive. Once areas of improvement have been identified, product managers collaborate with cross-functional teams including designers, engineers, and marketers to develop and implement strategies to address these issues. This may involve refining the product's features and functionalities, enhancing the user experience, improving performance, or adding new capabilities. Throughout the product improvement process, it is essential for product managers to prioritize enhancements based on their potential impact and feasibility. This requires evaluating the cost of implementing changes, the resources and time required, and the potential benefits in terms of increased customer satisfaction, retention, and revenue. Effective product improvement also involves testing and validating the proposed changes before implementing them. Product managers utilize various methods such as user testing, prototyping, and A/B testing to ensure that the intended improvements actually deliver the desired outcomes and do not inadvertently introduce new issues or challenges. Furthermore, product managers continually monitor and evaluate the success of the implemented improvements, collecting data and feedback to measure the impact of the changes on key performance indicators such as customer satisfaction, sales, and market share. This information is then used to inform future product improvement initiatives and iterate on the product development process. In conclusion, product improvement is a critical aspect of product management that involves analyzing customer needs, identifying areas for enhancement, implementing changes, and evaluating the impact. This iterative process allows products to stay relevant, competitive, and valuable in the marketplace.

Product Innovation

Product innovation refers to the process of creating and introducing new products or enhancing existing products in order to meet the changing needs and desires of customers, and to gain a competitive advantage in the market. In the field of product management, product innovation plays a critical role in driving business growth and success. It involves conducting extensive research and analysis to identify customer needs and market trends, and then utilizing this information to develop and launch new products or improve existing ones.

Product Intellectual Property (IP)

Product Intellectual Property (IP) refers to the legal rights and protections that are granted to the creators or owners of a product. It encompasses the exclusive rights to use, sell, manufacture, or distribute the product and its associated features, design, or technology. In the context of Product Management, IP plays a crucial role in ensuring the competitiveness and profitability of a product. It provides a means to protect and monetize the unique aspects and innovations that differentiate the product from competitors in the market. By obtaining IP rights, such as patents, trademarks, copyrights, or trade secrets, Product Managers can safeguard their product's value and prevent unauthorized use or replication by others.

Product Intellectual Property

Product Intellectual Property refers to the legal rights and protections assigned to the creations, inventions, or designs that are associated with a product. It includes any original or unique aspects of the product that provide a competitive advantage or have commercial value. These rights safeguard the interests of the creators or owners and prevent others from utilizing, selling, or copying the protected aspects of the product without permission. In the context of Product Management, understanding and managing Product Intellectual Property is crucial for several reasons. Firstly, it allows the product management team to assess the potential value and marketability of a product by identifying its unique features or design elements that can be protected. By ensuring that a product has Intellectual Property protection, the company can establish a competitive edge and capitalize on its innovations. Additionally, managing Product Intellectual Property helps in maintaining a strong brand identity and reputation. By securing trademarks, logos, or unique product names, a company can prevent competitors from using similar branding elements that might confuse customers or dilute the brand's equity. It also allows the product management team to enforce quality standards and protect against counterfeit or low-quality imitations that may harm the brand's reputation. Moreover, having a thorough understanding of Product Intellectual Property enables the product management team to effectively manage partnerships and collaborations. It ensures that licenses or agreements are in place to protect proprietary technology or other Intellectual Property assets shared with partners, suppliers, or vendors. By carefully managing and preserving these rights, the company

131

can maintain control over its innovations and avoid potential conflicts or disputes. In summary, Product Intellectual Property refers to the legal rights and protections that safeguard the unique aspects of a product, providing a competitive advantage and commercial value. Understanding and effectively managing these rights is crucial for product management teams to assess value, protect the brand's identity, and maintain control over proprietary technologies or collaborations.

Product Inventory Management

Product Inventory Management is the process of overseeing and controlling the flow of items from the point of production to the point of consumption. It involves keeping track of inventory levels, ordering new stock, and ensuring that sufficient quantities of products are available to meet customer demand. In the context of Product Management, effective inventory management is essential for maximizing profitability and customer satisfaction. It enables efficient allocation of resources, reduces carrying costs, minimizes stockouts, and avoids excess inventory. By carefully managing inventory, organizations can optimize the balance between supply and demand, minimize production delays, and improve overall operational efficiency.

Product Just-In-Time (JIT)

Just-In-Time (JIT) in the context of product management refers to a methodology that aims to optimize the production and delivery of products by reducing waste and improving efficiency. JIT emphasizes on producing and delivering products only when they are needed, in the right quantities, and at the right time. This approach helps businesses minimize their inventory holding costs, reduce lead times, and increase overall productivity. It also enables companies to respond quickly to changing customer demands and market trends.

Product KPIs

Product KPIs, or Key Performance Indicators, in the context of Product Management, are measurable values that indicate the success of a product in achieving its goals and objectives. These indicators are used to track the performance of a product and provide actionable insights to drive decision-making and improve the overall product strategy. Product KPIs are crucial for Product Managers to define and monitor, as they help in assessing the product's performance against set targets and benchmarks. These KPIs can vary depending on the nature of the product, the industry, and the specific goals of the organization. However, there are some commonly used KPIs in Product Management that are relevant across different contexts: 1. Revenue: One of the primary KPIs for measuring the success of a product is its revenue generation. This can be measured through various metrics, such as total sales, average revenue per user, or average transaction value. Revenue KPIs help Product Managers understand the product's financial performance and its impact on the organization's bottom line. 2. Customer Acquisition and Retention: These KPIs focus on the ability of a product to attract and retain customers. Metrics like customer acquisition cost, customer churn rate, or customer lifetime value provide insights into the effectiveness of the product's marketing and sales strategies, as well as its ability to deliver value and satisfy customer needs. 3. User Engagement: User engagement KPIs measure the level of interaction and involvement of users with the product. Metrics like active users, session duration, or user retention rate help Product Managers assess the product's ability to captivate and retain user attention. These KPIs are particularly important for digital products, where user engagement directly impacts the success of the product. 4. NPS (Net Promoter Score): NPS is a widely used KPI that measures customer satisfaction and loyalty. It gauges customers' likelihood to recommend the product to others, indicating their overall satisfaction and perception of the product's quality. NPS helps Product Managers understand customer sentiment and identify areas for improvement. 5. Time to Market: This KPI measures the time it takes to develop and launch a product or feature. It provides insights into the product's speed to market, which is crucial in highly competitive industries where the ability to deliver new features and updates quickly can drive product success. By monitoring and analyzing these KPIs, Product Managers can gain valuable insights into the performance of their products and make data-driven decisions to optimize their strategies, improve user experience, and ultimately drive business growth.

Product Kanban Method

The Product Kanban Method is a visual project management technique used in product management to visualize and manage the flow of work. This methodology follows the principles of the Kanban system, which originated from Lean Manufacturing and has been adapted for software development and project management. In the Product Kanban Method, work items are represented as cards or notes on a Kanban board, which consists of columns that represent different stages of the workflow. Each column represents a specific state or phase of the product development process, such as backlog, analysis, design, development, testing, and deployment. When a new work item or task is identified, it is added to the first column, typically called the backlog or to-do column. As the team progresses, each work item is moved across the board from left to right, with each column representing a step closer to completion. This visual representation allows team members and stakeholders to have a clear understanding of the progress of the work and the status of each task. The Product Kanban Method also incorporates the concept of limiting work in progress (WIP). Each column on the Kanban board has a WIP limit, which determines the maximum number of work items that can be in that specific column at any given time. This limitation helps to identify bottlenecks and prioritize work, ensuring that team members are not overwhelmed with too many tasks and that they can focus on completing one task before moving on to the next. Through the use of the Product Kanban Method, product managers are able to effectively manage and prioritize their product development process. They can visualize and identify potential issues or bottlenecks, and make data-driven decisions to improve the flow and efficiency of the development cycle. By visualizing and limiting work in progress, the Product Kanban Method helps to reduce waste, improve collaboration and communication, and deliver value to customers in a timely manner. The Product Kanban Method is a flexible and adaptable approach to product management, allowing teams to easily adjust and optimize their workflow. With its emphasis on visual representation and continuous improvement, it has become a popular method among product managers seeking to enhance their team's productivity and efficiency.

Product Knowledge Sharing Platforms

A product knowledge sharing platform is an online software tool or platform that facilitates the exchange of product-related information and knowledge among product management teams and other stakeholders. It serves as a centralized hub for storing, organizing, and disseminating information about products, including their features, specifications, use cases, and best practices. Product knowledge sharing platforms provide a collaborative environment where product managers, developers, marketers, and other team members can contribute and access up-to-date information about products. They typically offer a range of features to support knowledge sharing, such as: 1. Content Creation and Management: Users can create and upload product-related content, such as product descriptions, user manuals, training videos, and case studies. The platform allows them to organize and categorize the content for easy searching and retrieval. 2. Document Versioning and Control: The platform ensures that only the latest and approved versions of documents are available to users. It tracks changes and updates, allowing users to access the most recent information about products. 3. Search and Discovery: Users can search for specific product information using keywords or filters. The platform provides advanced search capabilities to quickly locate relevant content and resources. 4. Collaboration and Feedback: Product knowledge sharing platforms foster collaboration among team members by enabling them to provide comments, give feedback, and engage in discussions. This promotes cross-functional information exchange and improves decision-making. 5. Analytics and Reporting: The platform may include analytics and reporting features to track user engagement, content popularity, and overall knowledge sharing effectiveness. These insights help product management teams identify knowledge gaps and optimize their knowledge sharing strategies. By leveraging a product knowledge sharing platform, product management teams can enhance their productivity, accelerate product development cycles, and improve overall product quality. The platform enables efficient knowledge transfer, minimizes information silos, and ensures that everyone involved in product development and management has access to the most relevant and accurate product information. It also helps onboard new team members quickly and fosters a culture of continuous learning and improvement.

Product Knowledge Sharing

Product Knowledge Sharing is the process of disseminating comprehensive and accurate information about a product to the various stakeholders involved in product management. It involves sharing detailed insights and knowledge about the product's features, specifications, benefits, and applications to enhance the understanding and awareness of everyone involved. This sharing of product knowledge is crucial for effective product management as it enables the stakeholders, such as product managers, sales teams, marketing professionals, and customer support representatives, to have a deep and holistic understanding of the product. By having a thorough knowledge of the product, they can better communicate its value proposition, address customer queries and concerns, make informed decisions, and effectively promote and sell the product in the market.

Product Knowledge Transfer

Product Knowledge Transfer in the context of Product Management refers to the process of sharing information, expertise, and understanding of a product from one individual or group to another. It is essential for ensuring a smooth transition between different phases of a product's lifecycle, such as development, launch, and maintenance. The main goal of Product Knowledge Transfer is to transfer a comprehensive understanding of the product, including its features, functionality, target market, competitive landscape, and value proposition. It helps stakeholders, including product managers, developers, marketers, and sales teams, to gain the necessary knowledge and skills to effectively manage and promote the product.

Product Labeling

Product labeling in the context of product management refers to the process of creating and displaying information on a product in a clear and concise manner. It involves the use of labels or tags on the packaging or the product itself to provide important details and instructions to consumers, retailers, and distributors. The purpose of product labeling is to communicate relevant information about the product to various stakeholders, including its features, specifications, usage instructions, warnings, and any legal requirements or certifications. It serves as a form of communication between the product and its users, enabling them to make informed decisions about its purchase and usage.

Product Launch Budget

The product launch budget refers to the financial resources allocated for the successful introduction of a new product to the market. It is an essential part of the product management process, as it helps determine the necessary expenses to create awareness, generate demand, and achieve sales targets. The product launch budget encompasses various aspects, including research and development, manufacturing, marketing, and sales activities. It involves estimating and planning for the costs associated with product design, prototyping, production, packaging, distribution, promotion, and sales support. Additionally, it may also include expenses related to market research, competitive analysis, branding, advertising, public relations, and event management. The product launch budget serves as a guideline for the product manager and the entire cross-functional team involved in bringing the product to market. It helps prioritize and allocate resources effectively, ensuring that sufficient funds are available for each stage of the product launch process. The budgeting process typically starts with a thorough assessment of the market potential and the competitive landscape. This analysis helps determine the overall financial goals and objectives for the product launch. The budget is then developed by estimating the costs for each activity or expense category, taking into account factors such as timeframes, resource requirements, and expected outcomes. Once the budget is finalized, it is used as a benchmark for tracking and controlling expenditures throughout the product launch process. Regular monitoring and review of actual expenses against the budget help identify any deviations and allow for corrective actions to be taken. The product launch budget is crucial for ensuring the success of a new product introduction. It helps prevent overspending, assists in making informed financial decisions, and maximizes the return on investment. By effectively managing the budget, product managers can optimize resource allocation and enhance the overall efficiency and effectiveness of the product launch activities. In conclusion, the product launch budget is a financial plan that outlines the projected expenses associated with introducing a new product to the market. It serves as a roadmap for managing resources and achieving the desired outcomes during the product launch process. Proper budgeting and control are essential for achieving successful product launches and meeting business objectives.

134

Product Launch Checklist

A product launch checklist is a comprehensive and structured list of tasks and activities that need to be completed before and during the launch of a new product. It is an essential tool for product managers to ensure a smooth and successful launch, as well as to minimize risks and mistakes. The product launch checklist serves as a guide and reminder for product managers, helping them stay organized and focused during the launch process. It outlines all the necessary steps and considerations to be taken into account, ensuring that no important task is overlooked or neglected.

Product Launch Email Campaign

A product launch email campaign is a strategic marketing initiative undertaken by a product management team to introduce a new product or service to the target audience through a series of emails. It is designed to create awareness, generate interest, and drive conversions among prospective customers. The goal of a product launch email campaign is to effectively communicate the value proposition, benefits, and features of the new product to the target audience. It aims to build anticipation and excitement around the launch, leading to increased brand awareness and customer engagement.

Product Launch Event Planning

A product launch event refers to the planning and execution of an event to introduce a new product to the market. It is an important aspect of product management, as it aims to create awareness, generate excitement, and drive sales for the newly launched product. The process of planning a product launch event involves several key elements. Firstly, the objectives and goals of the event need to be defined. This includes determining the target audience, understanding their needs and preferences, and aligning the event objectives with the overall product strategy. Once the objectives are set, the next step is to plan the logistics of the event. This includes selecting a suitable venue, scheduling the date and time, and organizing the necessary equipment and resources. Additionally, the event planning team should also consider factors such as budget, decor, catering, and transportation to ensure a seamless and memorable experience for the attendees. Another crucial aspect of product launch event planning is the creation of promotional materials and communication strategies. This involves designing invitations, creating press releases, developing social media campaigns, and coordinating with the marketing team to ensure consistent messaging and branding. The goal is to generate buzz and excitement around the product and encourage attendance and coverage from the media and key influencers. During the event, product managers should focus on creating an engaging and immersive experience for the attendees. This can be achieved through interactive product demonstrations, live presentations, and networking opportunities. It is also important to gather feedback from attendees to gauge their reactions, identify areas for improvement, and gather insights for future product development. Overall, a well-planned product launch event can greatly contribute to the success of a new product. It helps to create excitement, generate awareness, and build anticipation among the target audience. By carefully considering the objectives, logistics, promotional materials, and attendee experience, product managers can maximize the impact of their product launch event and increase the chances of a successful market introduction.

Product Launch Event

A product launch event in the context of product management refers to a carefully planned and executed event to introduce a new product or service to the market. It serves as an opportunity for the company to generate excitement, build anticipation, and create awareness among its target audience. The purpose of a product launch event is to showcase the features, benefits, and unique selling points of the new product. It allows the company to demonstrate its innovation, expertise, and commitment to meeting customer needs. The event may include presentations, demonstrations, hands-on experiences, and opportunities for attendees to ask questions and provide feedback.

Product Launch Metrics

Product Launch Metrics are quantitative and qualitative measures used to evaluate the success

135

of a product launch in the context of Product Management. These metrics provide insights into the performance, impact, and effectiveness of the launch, allowing product managers to assess whether the launch objectives have been achieved and to identify areas for improvement. Quantitative metrics in product launch often include measures such as sales revenue, market share, customer adoption rate, and customer satisfaction. These metrics help assess the financial success of the launch, the extent to which the product has captured the target market, and how well it has satisfied customer needs. Sales revenue, for example, indicates the product's financial performance and overall market demand. Market share shows the product's competitive position in relation to other offerings in the market. Customer adoption rate reflects how quickly and widely customers are adopting and using the product. Customer satisfaction gauges the level of customer contentment and loyalty towards the product. Qualitative metrics, on the other hand, provide insights into the customer experience, brand perception, and market feedback. These metrics often encompass customer feedback surveys, online reviews, social media sentiment analysis, and customer testimonials. Qualitative metrics help product managers understand how customers perceive the product, identify areas of improvement, and gauge overall customer satisfaction. Customer feedback surveys, for instance, provide direct input from customers regarding their experience with the product, highlighting areas for improvement or satisfaction. Online reviews and social media sentiment analysis can uncover positive or negative sentiment towards the product, enabling product managers to address concerns or leverage positive feedback. Customer testimonials give insights into the overall satisfaction and value derived from the product.

Product Launch Plan

A product launch plan, in the context of Product Management, refers to a detailed and structured strategy that outlines the necessary steps and activities required to successfully introduce a new product into the market. It encompasses the entire process from the initial conception of the product to its launch, ensuring that all aspects of the launch are carefully planned and executed. The purpose of a product launch plan is to create a systematic approach that minimizes risks and maximizes the chances of success during the product launch phase. It serves as a roadmap that guides the product team on how to effectively introduce the new product to the target market, attract customers, and generate sales. By following a well-defined product launch plan, product managers can mitigate challenges, address potential issues, and optimize resources to drive the desired business outcomes.

Product Launch Press Release

A product launch press release is a formal announcement issued by a company's product management team to inform the public, media, and industry about the launch of a new product or a significant update to an existing product. The press release is typically distributed to various media outlets, including newspapers, magazines, websites, and blogs, to generate awareness and interest among the target audience. The purpose of a product launch press release is to create a buzz around the new product and generate media coverage, which in turn helps to generate publicity, increase brand visibility, and attract potential customers. It is an important tool for product management professionals to communicate the key features, benefits, and value proposition of the product to the target market.

Product Launch Strategy

A product launch strategy refers to the overall plan and approach that a product manager takes when introducing a new product to the market. It involves a series of strategic decisions and actions that aim to maximize the success of the product launch and achieve the desired business objectives. The product launch strategy typically begins with market research and analysis to identify the target customers, understand their needs and preferences, and assess the competitive landscape. This information is used to develop a clear positioning statement for the product and to define the key features and benefits that differentiate it from competing offerings. Once the positioning and key messaging have been established, the product manager creates a comprehensive marketing plan that outlines the specific tactics and channels to be used to generate awareness and drive demand for the new product. This may include traditional advertising and promotion, online marketing activities, social media campaigns, and other innovative strategies to reach the target audience. In addition to the marketing plan, the product launch strategy also encompasses the operational and logistical aspects of bringing the product to market. This includes coordinating with cross-functional teams such as manufacturing, supply chain, sales, and customer service to ensure that all necessary preparations and resources are in place for a successful launch. Throughout the product launch process, the product manager closely monitors key performance indicators and gathers feedback from customers and stakeholders. This information is used to make necessary adjustments and refinements to the product, messaging, and marketing activities to optimize the chances of success. In summary, a product launch strategy is a comprehensive plan that guides the product manager in introducing a new product to the market. It encompasses market research, positioning, marketing tactics, operational preparations, and continuous feedback and improvement. By following a well-defined launch strategy, product managers can increase the likelihood of achieving their business goals and maximizing the success of the new product.

Product Launch Teasers

Product launch teasers are marketing strategies used by product management teams to generate interest and anticipation for a new product or service prior to its official launch. These teasers are usually implemented through various channels, such as social media, email campaigns, and advertisements, with the aim of creating a buzz and building excitement among the target audience. The purpose of product launch teasers is to ignite curiosity and capture the attention of potential customers. By providing glimpses of the upcoming product or service, these teasers aim to generate interest and intrigue, prompting individuals to seek more information or eagerly anticipate the official launch. This strategy can effectively create a sense of exclusivity and urgency, enticing customers to be among the first to purchase or experience the product.

Product Launch

A product launch refers to the process of introducing a new product to the market, with the aim of generating awareness, interest, and sales. It is a critical stage in the product lifecycle and requires careful planning, coordination, and execution. The product launch process typically starts with market research and analysis to identify customer needs and preferences. This information is used to develop a product that meets or exceeds those expectations. Once the product is ready, a launch plan is developed, outlining the strategies and tactics to be used to introduce the product to the target market. The launch plan typically includes a marketing campaign, which may include various elements such as advertising, public relations, social media, and events. These activities are aimed at building buzz and generating excitement around the product. The goal is to create a strong brand image and position the product as a desirable solution to customers' problems or needs. In addition to the marketing campaign, the product launch process also involves logistics planning. This includes ensuring that the product is available in the right quantities and at the right locations, coordinating distribution channels, and training sales personnel. It is important to have a smooth and efficient supply chain to meet customer demand and avoid stockouts or delays. During the product launch, it is crucial to monitor and evaluate the performance of the marketing activities and adjust the strategies as needed. This may involve gathering feedback from customers and making improvements based on their input. It is also important to track sales and other performance indicators to gauge the success of the launch and make informed decisions for future product updates or expansions. In conclusion, a product launch is a strategic process that involves introducing a new product to the market with the aim of generating awareness, interest, and sales. It requires careful planning, coordination, and execution of marketing and logistics activities. By effectively managing the product launch process, companies can increase their chances of success and establish a strong presence in the market.

Product Lean Development

Product Lean Development, also known as Lean Product Development, is an iterative and problem-solving approach in Product Management that focuses on continuously delivering value to customers, reducing waste, and maximizing efficiency. The concept of Lean Development originated from Lean Manufacturing and the Toyota Production System. It emphasizes the systematic elimination of waste and inefficiencies in order to optimize processes and improve overall product development outcomes.

Product Lean Manufacturing

Product Lean Manufacturing is a systematic approach to product development and production that aims to eliminate waste and maximize efficiency. The core principle of Product Lean Manufacturing is to deliver the highest value to end customers while reducing costs and minimizing resources. This methodology focuses on continuously improving processes, increasing productivity, and reducing lead time from ideation to delivery.

Product Legal Requirements

Product Legal Requirements refer to the set of laws, regulations, standards, and specifications that a product must comply with in order to be legally sold, distributed, and used in a particular market or jurisdiction. These requirements are designed to ensure the safety, quality, and reliability of products, as well as protect consumers and the environment. Compliance with product legal requirements is a crucial aspect of product management, as failure to meet these requirements can result in serious legal and financial consequences for both the manufacturer and the seller. It is the responsibility of the product manager to understand and navigate the complex web of legal requirements that apply to their product and ensure that all necessary measures are taken to maintain compliance throughout the product lifecycle.

Product Liability

Product Liability in the context of Product Management refers to the legal responsibility and obligation of manufacturers, sellers, and distributors for any harm or injuries caused by their products to consumers or users. It is a crucial aspect of ensuring consumer safety and protection. When a product is found to be defective, dangerous, or fails to meet the expected standards of safety, the manufacturer or any party involved in the distribution chain can be held liable for any injuries or damages caused. The concept of product liability is based on the principle that those who profit from selling or distributing a product should bear the responsibility for any harm it may cause, rather than the injured party alone.

Product Licensing

Product Licensing is a formal agreement between two parties, the licensor and the licensee, granting the licensee the right to produce, distribute, or sell a product under the licensor's brand, trademark, or patent. This agreement allows the licensee to benefit from the established reputation, customer base, and intellectual property of the licensor, while the licensor earns revenue through royalties or upfront fees. Licensing offers several benefits for both the licensor and the licensee. For the licensor, it provides an opportunity to expand their product reach without bearing the costs of production, distribution, and marketing. By granting licenses, the licensor can leverage the licensee's expertise in specific markets or regions, allowing them to tap into new customer segments or geographic areas. Licensing can also serve as a way to generate additional revenue streams, as the licensor receives a portion of the licensee's profits in the form of royalties. On the other hand, for the licensee, product licensing offers a way to enter new markets or industries without having to invest in research and development or build a brand from scratch. It allows them to leverage the established reputation and customer loyalty associated with the licensor's brand, significantly reducing the time and effort required to establish themselves in the market. Additionally, the licensee can benefit from the licensor's support and resources, such as access to manufacturing facilities, marketing materials, or training programs. Product licensing agreements typically include terms and conditions regarding the scope of the license, the payment structure (e.g., upfront fees, royalties), geographic limitations, quality control standards, and any exclusivity provisions. These agreements are legally binding and require careful negotiation and drafting to ensure that both parties' interests are protected. It is crucial for product managers to thoroughly understand the licensing agreement and its implications to effectively manage the licensed product and maintain a successful partnership between the licensor and licensee.

Product Lifecycle Assessment

A Product Lifecycle Assessment (PLA) is a strategic tool used in Product Management to evaluate the environmental and social impact of a product throughout its entire life cycle, from raw material extraction to disposal. It aims to identify opportunities for improvement and

138

minimize negative impacts, while also considering the economic aspects of the product. The PLA is conducted by analyzing various stages of the product's life cycle, including raw material acquisition, manufacturing, distribution, usage, and end-of-life. Each stage is assessed based on its energy consumption, carbon emissions, waste generation, and other environmental and social factors. The data collected is then used to calculate the product's overall environmental footprint. The purpose of conducting a PLA is twofold. Firstly, it helps product managers to identify potential sustainability issues and opportunities for optimization. By understanding the environmental and social impacts of a product, managers can make informed decisions about its design, materials, manufacturing processes, and supply chain management. This enables them to reduce resource consumption, waste generation, and emissions, leading to cost savings and a more favorable brand image. Secondly, a PLA allows product managers to communicate the environmental performance of their products to customers, stakeholders, and regulatory bodies. Through proper labeling and disclosure, they can provide transparent information and promote the product's sustainability credentials. This helps companies differentiate themselves from competitors and meet the growing demand for eco-friendly products, thereby enhancing their market position. In conclusion, a Product Lifecycle Assessment is a crucial tool for Product Managers to evaluate the sustainability impact of their products throughout their entire life cycle. By identifying areas for improvement and communicating the environmental performance of their products, managers can make informed decisions, reduce negative impacts, and enhance their brand image in the marketplace.

Product Lifecycle Management

Product Lifecycle Management (PLM) is a strategic approach to product management that encompasses the entire lifespan of a product, from its conception through its development, manufacturing, and end-of-life phases. It involves the coordination and integration of all aspects of a product's lifecycle, including design, engineering, manufacturing, marketing, sales, and support. PLM aims to optimize the value and performance of a product by managing and controlling the information related to its creation, evolution, and disposal. It ensures that all stakeholders have access to the accurate and up-to-date information they need to make informed decisions throughout the product lifecycle. The PLM process begins with the identification of product requirements and the generation of innovative ideas for new or improved products. These ideas are then refined and evaluated to determine their feasibility and potential for success in the market. Once a product concept is approved, detailed design and development activities are undertaken, including prototyping, testing, and validation. During the manufacturing phase, PLM involves ensuring that the production processes are efficient and cost-effective, while meeting quality standards and regulatory requirements. It also involves managing the supply chain to ensure timely delivery of raw materials and components, as well as the proper disposal of waste products. Throughout the product's lifecycle, PLM also encompasses marketing and sales activities, such as pricing, promotion, and distribution strategies. It involves gathering and analyzing customer feedback and market data to continuously improve the product and meet changing customer needs and preferences. Finally, PLM addresses the end-of-life phase of a product, including its decommissioning, recycling, or disposal. It ensures that environmental and regulatory requirements are met, and that any relevant intellectual property rights are protected.

Product Lifecycle

The product lifecycle is a concept used in product management to describe the stages that a product goes through from its inception to its eventual discontinuation. It is a tool that helps product managers plan, develop, and manage products effectively throughout their lifecycle. The product lifecycle consists of four main stages: introduction, growth, maturity, and decline. In the introduction stage, a product is launched into the market. The focus during this stage is on promotion and building awareness among potential customers. Marketing efforts are often high, and sales volumes are typically low. Product managers need to closely monitor customer feedback and make any necessary adjustments to the product based on that feedback. The growth stage is characterized by an increase in sales and market acceptance. Customers become aware of the product, and demand starts to rise. The focus for product managers in this stage is on improving the product, expanding distribution channels, and capturing as much market share as possible. This stage usually presents opportunities for product line extensions or variations to target different customer segments. In the maturity stage, the product experiences a peak in sales as it reaches market saturation. Competition becomes intense, and price becomes a significant factor in purchasing decisions. Product managers need to focus on maintaining market share, defending against competitors, and finding ways to differentiate the product from others in the market. They may also look for opportunities to extend the product's lifecycle through product upgrades or new features. In the decline stage, sales start to decline as the product becomes obsolete or is replaced by newer, more innovative products. Product managers may consider discontinuing the product or finding ways to reposition it in the market. They need to analyze the reasons behind the decline and make tough decisions about the product's future. It is also essential to manage inventory and ensure a smooth transition to new products.

Product Load Testing

Product Load Testing is a crucial aspect of Product Management that involves simulating real-life usage scenarios and conducting performance tests on a product under heavy load. It is aimed at assessing the product's ability to handle a high volume of users, transactions, or data, ensuring its optimal performance and reliability. Load testing is typically carried out to identify and rectify potential bottlenecks and weaknesses in the product's architecture, infrastructure, or codebase. By subjecting the product to a heavy workload, Product Managers can uncover any issues related to scalability, response time, throughput, resource utilization, or stability, and take appropriate measures to mitigate them.

Product Maintenance

Product maintenance refers to the ongoing activities and tasks carried out to ensure the smooth functioning, reliability, and customer satisfaction of a product throughout its lifecycle. It is an essential aspect of product management that involves managing and addressing the various issues, bugs, and enhancements that arise after the product is launched. The primary goal of product maintenance is to keep the product in good working condition, improve its performance, and meet the evolving needs and expectations of the customers. It involves a systematic approach to identifying, prioritizing, and resolving issues, as well as implementing updates, patches, and upgrades to enhance the product's functionality and usability.

Product Management

Product management is a discipline within an organization that focuses on the strategic planning and development of products or services. It involves overseeing the entire lifecycle of a product, from its conceptualization to its launch and ongoing growth. The product manager is responsible for guiding the product through each stage, ensuring its success in the market. The primary objective of product management is to meet the needs and desires of customers while aligning with the overall goals of the company. This requires a deep understanding of the target market, including their preferences, pain points, and buying behaviors. By gathering and analyzing customer insights, the product manager can make informed decisions on product features, pricing, and positioning. As part of their role, product managers collaborate closely with cross-functional teams, including engineering, design, marketing, and sales. They act as a bridge between these teams, ensuring effective communication and coordination to deliver a high-quality product on time and within budget. This involves setting clear goals and priorities, defining project timelines, and managing resources effectively. Throughout the product development process, product managers regularly assess and refine the product strategy. They monitor market trends and competitive landscapes to identify opportunities for product improvement or expansion. They also evaluate the product's performance against key performance indicators (KPIs), such as sales, customer satisfaction, and market share, making data-driven decisions to drive continuous improvement. In summary, product management is the strategic discipline that guides the end-to-end process of developing and launching products or services. It involves understanding customer needs, coordinating cross-functional teams, and continuously improving the product to meet market demands. A successful product manager possesses a blend of technical, business, and leadership skills to ensure the product's success and drive business growth.

Product Management Software

Product Management Software refers to a digital tool or application specifically designed to facilitate and streamline the processes involved in product management. It offers a centralized platform for product managers to plan, organize, and track various aspects of a product's lifecycle, from conception to launch and beyond. The primary purpose of Product Management Software is to provide a comprehensive set of features and functionalities that enable product managers to efficiently manage and execute their responsibilities. These responsibilities typically include market research, product planning, requirement gathering, product development, product launch, market analysis, and ongoing product iterations. A key feature of Product Management Software is its ability to capture and organize all relevant information regarding the product's lifecycle. This includes market trends, customer feedback, competitive analysis, market segmentation, product specifications, project timelines, and team collaboration. By centralizing this information, the software allows product managers to make informed decisions, prioritize tasks, and ensure effective communication and collaboration across teams. Another crucial aspect of Product Management Software is its ability to establish and maintain a clear product roadmap. This involves defining product goals and objectives, prioritizing features and enhancements, and aligning the product strategy with business objectives. The software enables product managers to create and communicate a visual representation of the product roadmap, which helps stakeholders understand the product's direction and milestones. Furthermore, Product Management Software often includes tools for gathering and analyzing customer feedback and market data. This enables product managers to obtain valuable insights into customer preferences, market demands, and emerging trends. By leveraging this information, product managers can make data-driven decisions, refine product strategies, and identify opportunities for innovation and product differentiation. In summary, Product Management Software provides product managers with a comprehensive digital solution to effectively plan, execute, and oversee all stages of a product's lifecycle. It offers a centralized platform for information management, team collaboration, and decision-making, ultimately helping product managers achieve their objectives in an efficient and informed manner.

Product Management Tools

A product management tool is a software application or platform that helps product managers and their teams streamline and centralize the various tasks and processes involved in product development and management. This tool provides a centralized hub for product managers to track and manage product requirements, prioritize and plan product roadmaps, collaborate with cross-functional teams, and monitor the progress and success of their products. Product management tools offer a wide range of features and functionalities that support different stages of the product lifecycle. These tools typically include capabilities such as: - Requirements Management: Product managers can capture and organize product requirements, defining the features and functionality that the product should have. They can also track changes and updates to requirements throughout the development process. - Roadmap Planning: These tools allow product managers to create and visualize product roadmaps, outlining the strategic direction and timeline for the product. They can prioritize features, allocate resources, and communicate the product vision to stakeholders. - Team Collaboration: Product management tools facilitate collaboration and communication among cross-functional teams, including product managers, designers, developers, marketers, and sales teams. They provide a platform for sharing updates, feedback, and documents, ensuring everyone is aligned and working towards a common goal. - Agile Development Support: Many product management tools integrate with agile development methodologies, enabling product managers to manage and track tasks, sprints, and user stories. This ensures that product development remains iterative, with regular feedback and adjustments based on user needs. - Analytics and Reporting: These tools offer built-in analytics and reporting capabilities, allowing product managers to monitor key product metrics, track user behavior, and measure the success of product features. They provide insights that help inform product decisions and identify areas for improvement. In summary, product management tools serve as a central hub for product managers, providing a platform to manage and streamline the various tasks and processes involved in product development and management. These tools enable product teams to collaborate effectively, prioritize and plan product roadmaps, and measure the success of their products.

Product Manager

A Product Manager is a role within the field of Product Management that is responsible for the strategy, development, and execution of a product or product line. They serve as the central point of contact and decision-maker for all aspects of the product, from conception to launch and beyond. Product Managers are the driving force behind the success of a product or product line. They work closely with cross-functional teams, including engineering, design, marketing, and sales, to define and deliver a product that meets the needs of the target market and achieves business goals. The primary responsibilities of a Product Manager include: - Developing a deep understanding of customer needs and market trends through research and data analysis. - Defining the product vision and strategy based on customer insights and business objectives. - Gathering and prioritizing product requirements, both from internal stakeholders and external customers. - Collaborating with engineering and design teams to develop and deliver new features and enhancements. - Ensuring the product meets quality standards and is delivered on time and within budget. - Leading product launches and driving adoption and usage among the target market. - Monitoring product performance and gathering feedback to iterate and improve the product over time. Product Managers must possess a unique blend of technical, business, and interpersonal skills. They must be able to understand complex technical concepts, articulate a clear product vision, and effectively communicate with stakeholders at all levels of the organization. In summary, a Product Manager is responsible for guiding the development and success of a product or product line. They act as the bridge between the customer, business, and technical teams, ensuring the right product is built to meet customer needs and achieve business objectives.

Product Manufacturing Automation

Product manufacturing automation is the process of utilizing advanced technologies and machinery to streamline and optimize the production and assembly of products. It involves automating various aspects of the manufacturing process, such as the use of robotics, computer-aided design (CAD), computer numerical control (CNC) machines, and automated material handling systems. With product manufacturing automation, companies are able to increase efficiency, reduce production costs, improve quality control, and shorten production lead times. By automating repetitive tasks and eliminating human error, manufacturers can achieve higher levels of accuracy and consistency in the production of goods. This ultimately leads to lower defect rates and higher customer satisfaction. One of the key benefits of product manufacturing automation is the ability to scale production capacity without significantly increasing labor costs. With automated systems in place, manufacturers can easily adjust production volume to meet changing market demands, without the need to hire and train additional workers. This flexibility allows companies to respond quickly to market fluctuations and maintain a competitive edge. In addition to improving efficiency and reducing costs, product manufacturing automation also enables manufacturers to enhance product customization. Automation technologies can be used to quickly reconfigure production lines and adapt to changing customer preferences. This level of flexibility allows companies to offer a wider range of product variations and options, catering to individual customer needs and preferences. Overall, product manufacturing automation plays a crucial role in modern product management by enabling companies to meet the demands of a rapidly changing market. By automating repetitive tasks, reducing errors, and improving efficiency, manufacturers can produce high-quality products at a lower cost, while also maintaining the ability to quickly adapt to market demands. In an increasingly competitive business environment, product manufacturing automation is essential for companies looking to stay ahead of the competition and deliver value to their customers.

Product Manufacturing Processes

Product Manufacturing Processes refers to the series of steps and procedures involved in transforming raw materials and components into finished products. These processes are designed to ensure efficiency, quality, and cost-effectiveness throughout the production cycle. One of the key aspects of product manufacturing processes is the selection of the appropriate manufacturing method. This decision is based on factors such as the product design, required production volume, available resources, and budget. Some common manufacturing methods include casting, molding, forming, machining, and assembly. The first step in the manufacturing process is typically material preparation. This involves sourcing and ordering the necessary raw materials and components, as well as inspecting and testing them for quality and consistency. Once the materials are approved, they are prepared for production by cutting, shaping, or treating them as required. Next, the materials are processed using the chosen manufacturing method. For example, in casting, the molten material is poured into a mold to obtain the desired shape. In molding, the material is injected into a mold under high pressure. In forming, the material is shaped by bending or stretching. Machining involves removing excess material through cutting, drilling, or grinding. After the primary manufacturing process, additional steps may be required, such as surface finishing, coating, or painting. These steps are essential for enhancing the appearance and durability of the product. Quality control measures are integrated throughout the manufacturing process to ensure that each product meets the required specifications and standards. Once the products are manufactured, they undergo a final inspection and are packaged for distribution. This includes labeling, barcoding, and adding necessary instructions or manuals. The products are then ready to be delivered to customers or to be stored in a warehouse until further distribution. In conclusion, product manufacturing processes encompass the various stages involved in converting raw materials and components into finished products. It involves a careful selection of manufacturing methods, material preparation, primary manufacturing processes, additional treatments, quality control measures, and packaging. The goal is to achieve efficient, cost-effective, and high-quality production to meet customer demands and expectations.

Product Manufacturing Quality

Product manufacturing quality refers to the level of excellence and consistency achieved in the production of a product. It is a critical aspect of product management as it directly affects the satisfaction of customers and the success of the business. When a product is manufactured with high quality, it meets or exceeds the expectations of customers and performs its intended functions effectively and reliably. This is achieved through a combination of various factors, including the use of high-quality materials, adherence to strict manufacturing processes, and quality control measures.

Product Manufacturing

Product manufacturing is the process of creating physical goods by combining raw materials, components, and resources through a series of coordinated activities. It involves the conversion of ideas, designs, and specifications into tangible products that are ready for distribution and use by customers. The product manufacturing process begins with product design and development, where concepts and ideas are transformed into detailed plans and specifications. This stage often involves market research, prototyping, and testing to ensure that the product meets the desired requirements and customer needs. Once the design is finalized, the manufacturing process moves on to sourcing and procurement, where the necessary raw materials, components, and equipment are identified and acquired. This may involve negotiating with suppliers, establishing partnerships, and ensuring the availability of resources to support the production process. Next, the actual production takes place, which may involve various techniques such as assembly, fabrication, molding, or machining, depending on the type of product being manufactured. This stage requires the coordination of different manufacturing operations, such as quality control, inventory management, and production scheduling, to ensure efficient and timely production. After the product is manufactured, it undergoes thorough testing and quality assurance procedures to ensure that it meets the required standards and specifications. This may include performance testing, durability testing, and compliance with industry regulations and safety standards. Once the products pass the quality assurance stage, they are prepared for distribution and shipment. This involves packaging, labeling, and organizing the products for transport to distribution centers or directly to customers. The manufacturing process also includes the management of logistics, transportation, and fulfillment to ensure that products reach their intended destinations in a timely manner. In conclusion, product manufacturing is a crucial aspect of product management that involves the transformation of ideas and designs into tangible products through a series of coordinated activities. It encompasses various stages, from product design and development to production, quality assurance, and distribution. Effective product manufacturing requires careful planning, coordination, and management of resources to ensure the timely production of high-quality products that meet customer needs and expectations.

Product Market Decline

A product market decline, in the context of product management, refers to a situation where the demand for a particular product or a category of products decreases significantly over time. This decline can occur due to various factors such as changing customer preferences, technological advancements, market saturation, or the emergence of substitute products. When a product market experiences a decline, it means that the product is no longer able to attract and retain sufficient customers to sustain its growth and profitability. This decline usually leads to a decrease in sales, market share, and overall revenue for the product or category of products.

Product Market Entry Strategy

A product market entry strategy refers to the plan and approach that a company employs to introduce a new product into the market. It involves a series of steps and decisions aimed at positioning the product effectively, establishing a customer base, and achieving business objectives. The first step in developing a product market entry strategy is to conduct comprehensive market research. This involves analyzing the target market's characteristics, demographics, preferences, and buying behavior. This information helps the company understand the market landscape and identify potential opportunities and challenges. Based on the market research findings, the company can then determine the target market segment that it wants to focus on. This involves identifying the specific group of customers who are most likely to be interested in and benefit from the product. By selecting a target market segment, the company can develop a more tailored marketing and promotional strategy. Once the target market segment is identified, the company needs to decide on the positioning and differentiation strategy for the product. This involves determining how the product will be perceived by customers in relation to competitors' offerings. The company needs to highlight the unique features and benefits of the product to create a competitive advantage. Another crucial aspect of the product market entry strategy is pricing. The company needs to establish a pricing strategy that aligns with the target market's perceived value, while ensuring profitability. Factors such as production costs, competition, and customer willingness to pay need to be considered when determining the product's price. Furthermore, the company needs to develop a distribution strategy for the product. This involves identifying the most appropriate channels and intermediaries to reach the target market. Distribution channels can include direct sales, online platforms, wholesalers, retailers, and partnerships. In addition to these key elements, the product market entry strategy also encompasses marketing communication and promotional activities. Companies need to create awareness and generate interest in the product through advertising, public relations, social media, and other marketing channels. The company should also develop a comprehensive sales plan to support the product's launch and ongoing marketing efforts.

Product Market Exit Plans

Product Market Exit Plans refer to the strategic plans made by product managers to discontinue a product from the market. It involves the decision-making process and actions taken to terminate the production, distribution, and sales of a specific product. These exit plans are typically developed when a product reaches the end of its life cycle or is no longer aligned with the company's objectives and target market. The goal of such plans is to minimize losses and maximize the utilization of resources during the exit process.

Product Market Exit Strategy

A product market exit strategy is a formal plan or approach developed by product management teams to discontinue a particular product or service from the market. It is a strategic decision made when a company decides to stop producing, selling, or supporting a specific product in order to allocate resources more efficiently or refocus efforts on other products that have better market potential. To establish a product market exit strategy, product managers must carefully evaluate several factors, such as the product's profitability, customer demand, market saturation, competitive landscape, and overall business objectives. This assessment helps determine if discontinuing the product is the most feasible and beneficial course of action. There are various reasons why a company may consider implementing a product market exit strategy. Some of these include: 1. Declining or insufficient demand: If a product experiences a significant decline in sales or lacks sufficient customer demand, it may no longer be economically viable to continue investing resources in its production and marketing. 2. Technological advancements:

144

The emergence of new technologies or alternative solutions may render a product obsolete or less attractive to customers. In such cases, discontinuing the product may prevent further losses and enable the company to focus on developing more innovative offerings. 3. Market saturation or intense competition: When a market becomes overcrowded with similar products or experiences intense competition, it may be challenging for a company to maintain a competitive edge or generate sufficient revenues. In such situations, an exit strategy allows the company to reallocate resources to more promising markets. 4. Changing customer preferences or needs: If customer preferences shift or their needs evolve, a product may become less relevant or effective. By discontinuing the product and reallocating resources to address the changing market dynamics, a company can better meet customer demands and improve its market position. 5. Regulatory or legal constraints: Changes in regulations or legal requirements can sometimes make it impractical or impossible to continue manufacturing or selling a product. In such cases, a product market exit strategy helps the company avoid non-compliance or legal issues. Regardless of the reasons, implementing a product market exit strategy requires careful planning and execution. It involves identifying the best approach for withdrawing the product, managing customer relationships, communicating the decision effectively, and minimizing any negative impact on the company's reputation and financial performance. By executing a well-defined exit strategy, product management teams can optimize resource allocation and focus on products with higher growth potential.

Product Market Expansion

Product market expansion refers to the strategic initiative taken by a company to extend the reach and penetration of its existing products or services into new markets. This expansion can occur through various approaches such as entering new geographic regions, targeting different customer segments, or diversifying into related industries. The primary objective of product market expansion is to capitalize on untapped market opportunities and generate additional revenues and market share. By expanding into new markets, companies can reduce their reliance on a single market and mitigate risks associated with market saturation or economic downturns in their existing markets.

Product Market Fit

Product Market Fit is a concept in Product Management that refers to the degree to which a product satisfies the needs and demands of its target market. It is a measure of how well a product fits into the market and resonates with customers, ultimately determining the success or failure of a product. Product Market Fit is achieved when a product fulfills the market's requirements and provides unique value to its customers, creating a strong demand and high customer satisfaction. It signifies a perfect alignment between the product being offered and the market needs, resulting in a positive customer experience and loyalty. To determine if a product has achieved Product Market Fit, several factors can be considered. One of the key indicators is customer adoption and retention rates. If customers are consistently using and returning to the product, it suggests that the product is meeting their needs effectively. Additionally, feedback from customers and market research can provide valuable insights into the product's fit within the market. When a product achieves Product Market Fit, it positions itself as a market leader, gaining a competitive advantage over other similar products. It also opens up opportunities for growth and expansion, as satisfied customers become advocates for the product, leading to organic word-of-mouth promotion. On the other hand, a product that lacks Product Market Fit may struggle to gain traction in the market. It may face low customer adoption rates, low customer satisfaction, and high customer churn. These are indicators that the product does not meet the needs or expectations of the market, requiring adjustments or even a pivot in the product strategy. In conclusion, achieving Product Market Fit is a crucial milestone in Product Management. It signifies that a product is well-suited to its target market, leading to customer satisfaction, increased adoption rates, and a competitive advantage. It requires careful research, customer understanding, and constant iteration to ensure that the product aligns with market needs and demands.

Product Market Growth

Product market growth refers to the increase in demand and consumption of a specific product or service within a given market over time. It is a key measurement used in product management to evaluate the success and potential of a product in the market. The growth of a product market is influenced by various factors, such as changes in customer preferences, technological advancements, market competition, and economic conditions. Understanding and analyzing product market growth is essential for product managers in making informed decisions about product strategy, marketing initiatives, and resource allocation.

Product Market Research

Product market research is a critical aspect of product management, aimed at gathering and analyzing data to understand the market dynamics, consumers' preferences, and competitors' offerings. It involves conducting systematic research to gain insights on consumer behavior, market trends, and potential demand for a product or service. This information helps product managers make informed decisions about product development, positioning, pricing, and marketing strategies. The primary goal of product market research is to identify and validate opportunities for creating or improving products that meet customers' needs and preferences. By understanding market demands and consumer behavior, product managers can develop products that are more likely to succeed in the marketplace. Product market research involves various methods of data collection, such as surveys, interviews, focus groups, and market experiments. These methods help gather both quantitative and qualitative data, providing a comprehensive understanding of the market and customer preferences. Quantitative research involves gathering numerical data that can be analyzed statistically. This includes collecting data on market size, growth rates, customer demographics, purchasing patterns, and market segmentation. It provides valuable insights into the size of the target market, potential market share, and customer segments that need to be targeted. Qualitative research, on the other hand, focuses on understanding consumer motivations, preferences, and perceptions. This involves gathering non-numerical data through interviews, observation, and open-ended questions. Qualitative research helps product managers uncover underlying consumer needs, pain points, and opportunities for differentiation. Product market research also involves analyzing competitive landscape and understanding competitors' offerings, pricing strategies, and market positioning. This enables product managers to identify gaps in the market and potential competitive advantages for their own products. Overall, product market research plays a crucial role in informing product strategy and decision-making. By gathering and analyzing data on market dynamics, consumer preferences, and competitors' offerings, product managers can make informed decisions that increase the likelihood of a product's success in the market.

Product Market Saturation

Product market saturation is a term used in product management to describe the level of market penetration or adoption that a product has achieved within a specific market or customer segment. It refers to the point at which the market is fully saturated or saturated to the extent that further growth and expansion becomes difficult. When a product reaches saturation, it means that the majority of potential customers in the target market have already purchased or adopted the product. At this point, the market becomes highly competitive, with numerous players vying for a limited number of new customers or trying to maintain their existing customer base.

Product Marketing Analytics

Product Marketing Analytics refers to the process of gathering, analyzing, and interpreting data related to the performance and impact of marketing efforts on a product. It involves the collection and examination of various metrics and KPIs to gain insights and make informed decisions about marketing strategies and campaigns. Through the use of data and analytics, product marketers can assess the effectiveness of their promotional activities, understand customer behavior and preferences, and identify areas of improvement or opportunities for growth. By analyzing marketing data, product managers can evaluate the success of different marketing channels, campaigns, and messaging, and make data-driven decisions to optimize their marketing strategies and drive product success.

Product Marketing Collaboration

Product Marketing Collaboration refers to the process of collaboration between product marketing teams and other cross-functional teams within an organization to develop, launch, and promote products effectively in the market. Product marketing teams play a crucial role in understanding the market, customers, and competition. They are responsible for developing the go-to-market strategy and messaging for new products, as well as driving their successful adoption and growth in the market. However, product marketing cannot exist in isolation and requires collaboration with various other teams in order to achieve its objectives. The collaboration between product marketing and other cross-functional teams begins at the early stages of product development. Product marketing works closely with product management teams to gather market insights and feedback, understand customer needs and pain points, and ensure that the product being developed aligns with market demand. This collaboration helps in the creation of a product that is truly valuable and addresses the needs of the target market. Furthermore, product marketing collaborates with the sales team to develop effective sales enablement materials, such as product presentations, case studies, and competitive analysis, to help the sales team effectively position and sell the product. The collaboration also involves training the sales team on the product's unique value proposition, key features, and benefits, so that they can effectively communicate these to potential customers. In addition to product management and sales, product marketing also collaborates with the marketing communications team to develop compelling marketing campaigns and messaging that effectively communicate the value of the product to the target audience. This collaboration involves aligning marketing efforts with the go-to-market strategy, identifying appropriate marketing channels, and creating engaging content, such as product videos, whitepapers, and blog posts. Overall, product marketing collaboration is a vital aspect of successful product management. It enables cross-functional teams to work together effectively, leveraging their diverse expertise and perspectives to ensure that products are developed, launched, and promoted in a way that resonates with the target market and drives business growth.

Product Marketing Collateral

Product marketing collateral refers to various types of content and materials that are created to support the marketing and sales efforts of a product. These materials provide information and education about the product, its features and benefits, and help in promoting and positioning the product in the market. The purpose of product marketing collateral is to create awareness and generate interest in the product among potential customers. It is designed to communicate the value proposition of the product and convince customers that the product can meet their needs and solve their problems. The types of product marketing collateral can vary depending on the nature of the product, the target audience, and the marketing strategy. Some common types of collateral include product brochures, datasheets, white papers, case studies, product demos, videos, and customer testimonials. Product brochures are typically used to provide a high-level overview of the product, its key features, and benefits. They are often used during sales meetings, trade shows, and other marketing events to give potential customers a quick snapshot of the product. Datasheets, on the other hand, provide more detailed technical information about the product. They are often used by technical decision-makers and engineers who need specific information about the product's capabilities and specifications. White papers are in-depth reports that explore a specific topic related to the product or the industry it operates in. They are designed to provide thought leadership and educate potential customers about the challenges and opportunities in the market, and how the product can address those challenges. Product demos and videos are powerful tools that allow potential customers to see the product in action. They can showcase the product's key features, benefits, and use cases, and help in building confidence and trust among potential customers. Case studies and customer testimonials provide real-world examples of how the product has helped other customers solve their problems and achieve their goals. They can help in building credibility and trust, and give potential customers confidence that the product can deliver on its promises. In summary, product marketing collateral is a collection of materials and content that are created to support the marketing and sales efforts of a product. These materials provide information, education, and persuasion to potential customers, and help in promoting and positioning the product in the market.

Product Marketing Dashboards

Product Marketing Dashboards refer to data visualization tools used by product management teams to track and analyze various metrics related to the marketing of a product or service.

147

These dashboards provide a comprehensive view of key performance indicators (KPIs) and help product managers track the success of their marketing efforts and make data-driven decisions. Product Marketing Dashboards typically display a range of metrics such as customer acquisition rates, conversion rates, revenue generated, customer feedback scores, and website traffic. They can also include more granular data points such as the performance of specific marketing campaigns, the effectiveness of different marketing channels, and the impact of individual marketing strategies.

Product Marketing Metrics

Product marketing metrics refer to the quantifiable measures used by product managers to evaluate the success and performance of their products in the market. These metrics provide valuable insights into various aspects of the product's performance, customer adoption, and revenue generation, and help product managers make data-driven decisions to improve the product's market position. There are several key product marketing metrics that play a crucial role in assessing the product's success. One such metric is the market share, which measures the percentage of the total market that a product or brand captures. A higher market share indicates a stronger market presence and greater customer acceptance. Another important metric is customer satisfaction, which measures the level of customer happiness and loyalty towards the product. Product managers use surveys, Net Promoter Score (NPS), and other customer feedback mechanisms to assess customer satisfaction. Higher customer satisfaction scores indicate higher customer retention rates and a higher likelihood of word-of-mouth referrals. Revenue metrics also play a significant role in product marketing. Metrics such as revenue growth rate, average revenue per user (ARPU), and customer lifetime value (CLTV) help product managers gauge the financial performance and profitability of their products. These metrics enable them to identify opportunities for upselling, cross-selling, and optimizing pricing strategies. Customer acquisition cost (CAC) is another important metric that measures the cost incurred in acquiring a new customer. This metric helps product managers optimize their customer acquisition strategies and evaluate the ROI of their marketing efforts. By comparing CAC with customer lifetime value, product managers can determine the profitability of their customer acquisition channels. Furthermore, product managers also track metrics such as product adoption rate and churn rate. Product adoption rate measures the speed at which customers embrace and start using the product. On the other hand, churn rate measures the rate at which customers stop using the product or switch to a competitor. These metrics provide insights into the product's stickiness and customer retention efforts. In summary, product marketing metrics are critical for product managers to assess and measure the success of their products in the market. These metrics help them understand customer behavior, drive product improvements, optimize marketing strategies, and ultimately achieve product-market fit.

Product Marketing Planning

Product marketing planning is a systematic process that involves developing and implementing a strategic plan for launching and promoting a product or service in the market. It encompasses the activities and strategies needed to effectively position, sell, and distribute the product to the target audience. The primary goal of product marketing planning is to create a roadmap that outlines the steps and initiatives required to achieve optimal market penetration, customer adoption, and revenue generation. This process requires a deep understanding of the target market, customer needs, and competitive landscape. It involves conducting market research, identifying customer segments, and defining the unique value proposition of the product. Product marketing planning begins with market analysis, where the product manager assesses the market size, growth potential, and competitive dynamics. This information helps in identifying market trends, customer preferences, and potential barriers to adoption. Based on this analysis, the product manager develops a comprehensive marketing strategy that includes product positioning, pricing, distribution channels, and promotion tactics. Product positioning is a key component of product marketing planning. It involves defining the unique selling proposition (USP) of the product and differentiating it from competitors. The product manager identifies the target audience and develops messaging strategies that effectively communicate the value proposition to the customers. This includes creating compelling product descriptions, benefits, and features that resonate with the target market. Pricing is another critical element of product marketing planning. The product manager conducts pricing analysis to determine the optimal price that maximizes revenue and profitability. This involves considering factors such as production costs, competitive pricing, and customer willingness to pay. The pricing strategy should align with the perceived value of the product and the pricing expectations of the target market. Furthermore, product marketing planning involves selecting appropriate distribution channels to ensure efficient product delivery and availability. The product manager evaluates various options such as direct sales, retail partnerships, or online channels based on factors like customer accessibility and cost-effectiveness. The chosen distribution strategy should enable the product to reach the intended customers effectively. Lastly, product marketing planning includes developing promotional campaigns and marketing materials to create awareness, generate interest, and stimulate demand for the product. This may involve designing advertisements, organizing events, or utilizing digital marketing tactics to reach the target market. The product manager continuously monitors and evaluates the effectiveness of these marketing activities to make necessary adjustments and drive desired outcomes.

Product Marketing Roadmaps

A product marketing roadmap is a strategic planning tool that outlines the goals, tasks, and timelines for marketing a specific product or service. It serves as a framework for product managers to align their marketing efforts with the overall business objectives and ensure a cohesive and well-executed marketing strategy. At its core, a product marketing roadmap provides a roadmap for how a company plans to bring a product to market, from initial product development to launch and beyond. It outlines the key marketing activities that need to be completed at each stage of the product's lifecycle and helps to ensure that all necessary tasks are identified and assigned to the appropriate teams or individuals.

Product Marketing Strategy

Product Marketing Strategy is a key component of Product Management that focuses on creating and implementing a comprehensive plan to effectively promote and sell a product to its target market. It involves in-depth research and analysis of the market, customers, and competitors in order to develop strategic initiatives that will drive product adoption and sales.The primary goal of a Product Marketing Strategy is to position the product in a way that it stands out from competing products and meets the needs and desires of the target market. This involves identifying the target market segments and creating a value proposition that clearly communicates the unique selling points of the product.

Product Marketing Technology Stack

A product marketing technology stack refers to a combination of software tools and platforms that are used by product management teams to streamline and enhance their product marketing efforts. This stack often includes a variety of tools that help manage various aspects of the product lifecycle, from ideation and development to launch and post-launch activities. The product marketing technology stack is designed to support product managers in their day-to-day tasks by providing them with the necessary tools to analyze market trends, gather customer insights, track competition, and effectively communicate and promote their products to target audiences. The stack typically consists of different types of software and platforms, each serving a specific purpose within the product management process. One of the key components of a product marketing technology stack is a customer relationship management (CRM) system. A CRM system helps product managers centralize and organize customer data, track interactions and engagements, and gain insights into customer behavior and preferences. This information is critical for product managers to understand their target audience and make data-driven decisions when it comes to product development and marketing strategies. Another important tool within the product marketing technology stack is a product analytics platform. This platform allows product managers to track and measure the performance of their products across various metrics, such as user engagement, retention, and revenue. By analyzing these metrics, product managers can identify areas of improvement and refine their product strategies to better meet customer needs and drive business growth. Additionally, a product management platform is often included in the stack to help product managers collaborate and manage tasks more efficiently. This platform typically includes features such as project management, task tracking, and communication tools, allowing product teams to work together seamlessly and stay on top of product development timelines and milestones. In conclusion, a product marketing technology stack is a collection of software tools and platforms that enable product managers to effectively manage and market their products. It encompasses various tools such as CRM systems, product analytics platforms, and product management platforms, all working together to support product managers in their efforts to create, launch, and promote successful products.

Product Marketing

Product marketing in the context of product management refers to the activities and strategies undertaken to promote and sell a particular product in the market. It involves analyzing the target audience, identifying their needs and preferences, and then creating and implementing a marketing plan to effectively communicate and demonstrate the value and benefits of the product to the customers. The ultimate goal of product marketing is to generate demand and drive sales for the product. Product marketing plays a crucial role in the overall success of a product. It bridges the gap between product development and customer acquisition by positioning the product in the market and ensuring that it meets the needs and expectations of the target audience. Product marketers work closely with product managers, sales teams, and other stakeholders to develop a deep understanding of the product's features, competitive landscape, and market trends. This enables them to develop compelling messaging and positioning strategies that differentiate the product from competitors and resonate with the target customers. In addition to creating marketing content and collateral, product marketers also play a vital role in pricing and packaging decisions. They conduct market research to determine the optimal price point for the product based on factors such as the perceived value, competitor pricing, and market demand. They also collaborate with product managers to define the product's packaging and pricing tiers, ensuring that the offerings align with customer needs and the overall business objectives. Product marketing is an iterative process that requires continuous monitoring and analyzing of market trends, customer feedback, and competitor activities. This helps product marketers to refine their marketing strategies and messaging to stay aligned with changing customer needs and market dynamics. They also work closely with sales teams to provide them with the necessary resources, training, and support to effectively sell the product and address customer inquiries or objections. Overall, product marketing serves as a critical link in the product management lifecycle, helping to drive product adoption, market growth, and revenue generation. It combines a deep understanding of the product, target audience, and market dynamics with effective messaging and positioning to create a compelling value proposition that motivates customers to choose and advocate for the product.

Product Material Selection

Product Material Selection in the context of Product Management refers to the process of selecting the most suitable materials to be used in the manufacturing or development of a product. The chosen materials can significantly impact the performance, quality, cost, and overall success of the product. During the product development phase, the choice of materials is a crucial decision that requires consideration of various factors such as functionality, aesthetics, durability, safety, and cost-effectiveness. The right materials need to be selected to ensure that the product meets the desired specifications and requirements, while also aligning with the target market and customer expectations.

Product Material Testing

Product Material Testing is a critical aspect of Product Management that involves evaluating the quality, durability, and performance of materials used in the manufacturing of a product. The primary purpose of Product Material Testing is to ensure that the materials used in the production of a product meet the required standards and specifications. This testing process helps in determining the suitability of materials for the intended use and ensures that the product will perform as expected throughout its lifecycle.

Product Materials

Product materials refer to the physical components, substances, and resources that are used in the manufacturing and production of a product. These materials can include raw materials, components, packaging materials, and other resources that are essential for the creation and functionality of a product. Product materials play a crucial role in the overall quality, durability, and functionality of a product. They determine the strength, performance, and aesthetic appeal of the final product, and therefore, have a direct impact on customer satisfaction and market acceptance. The selection of product materials is a critical decision in product management. Product managers need to consider various factors such as cost, availability, sustainability, and regulatory compliance when choosing the materials for a product. They must also ensure that the chosen materials align with the product's design, performance requirements, and target market preferences. Product materials are often sourced from multiple suppliers and manufacturers, and managing the supply chain is an integral part of product management. Product managers need to establish strong relationships with suppliers, negotiate pricing and terms, and ensure the timely delivery of materials to meet production schedules and customer demands. Furthermore, product managers need to continually assess the quality, availability, and cost-effectiveness of product materials. They must stay updated with advancements in materials technology and industry trends to identify opportunities for improvement and innovation in the product's design and production processes. In summary, product materials are the physical components and resources that are used in the creation and production of a product. They impact the quality, functionality, and customer satisfaction of the final product. Product managers play a crucial role in selecting, managing, and improving the materials used in their products to ensure competitiveness in the market.

Product Metrics Dashboards

Product Metrics Dashboards refer to a collection of visual representations and data summaries that provide crucial insights into the performance and success of a product. These dashboards enable product managers to monitor key metrics, track progress, and make informed decisions to drive product improvement and achieve business objectives. With the increasing complexity of products and the need to measure various aspects of their performance, product managers rely on metrics to evaluate their products' health and impact. Product Metrics Dashboards serve as a central hub where these metrics are displayed in a clear and concise manner, facilitating easy understanding and analysis.

Product Metrics Tracking

Product Metrics Tracking refers to the process of measuring, analyzing, and evaluating the performance and effectiveness of a product using various quantitative and qualitative metrics. This practice is an essential component of product management, as it allows product managers to assess the success and impact of their products and make data-driven decisions to drive improvements. Product metrics tracking involves the collection and analysis of data related to various aspects of a product, including user engagement, customer satisfaction, revenue, conversion rates, and user behavior. By tracking these metrics, product managers can gain insights into how well the product is performing and identify areas that need attention or optimization.

Product Metrics

Product Metrics can be defined as quantitative measurements used to evaluate the performance and success of a product in the market. These measurements provide valuable insights and data that help product managers make informed decisions and drive improvements. Product Metrics typically focus on various aspects of a product, including its usage, customer satisfaction, revenue generation, and market share. By analyzing these metrics, product managers can understand how well a product is meeting customer needs, identify areas for improvement, and track the impact of product changes or updates.

Product Owner Responsibilities

A Product Owner is a key role in Product Management who is responsible for maximizing the value of a product and its development team. They act as the bridge between the stakeholders and the development team, ensuring that the product aligns with the goals and needs of the business. The Product Owner's responsibilities span the entire product development lifecycle, from conception to release. They are responsible for defining and prioritizing the product backlog, which is a prioritized list of features, enhancements, and bug fixes. They work closely with stakeholders such as customers, users, business analysts, and developers to gather requirements and define the product vision. The Product Owner works closely with the development team to ensure that they have a deep understanding of the product vision and requirements. They collaborate with the team on a daily basis, answering questions, providing clarifications, and ensuring the product is on track. They are responsible for making effective decisions and trade-offs, balancing the needs of the business with technical feasibility and constraints. The Product Owner is also responsible for validating and accepting completed work from the development team. They review and provide feedback on deliverables, ensuring they meet the defined acceptance criteria and quality standards. They may also conduct user acceptance testing to verify that the product meets the needs of the end-users. Furthermore, the Product Owner is responsible for communicating the product vision, progress, and updates to stakeholders. They conduct regular meetings, such as sprint planning, backlog refinement, and sprint reviews, to ensure alignment and gather feedback. They act as the main point of contact for any product-related inquiries or issues. In summary, the Product Owner plays a crucial role in Product Management by driving the success of the product. Their responsibilities include defining the product vision, prioritizing and managing the product backlog, collaborating with the development team, accepting completed work, and communicating with stakeholders. They serve as the link between the business and the development team, ensuring the product meets the needs of the users and the organization.

Product Owner Role Descriptions

A Product Owner is a key role in Product Management, responsible for defining and prioritizing the features and functionality of a product or service. They work closely with stakeholders, including customers, users, and development teams, to understand their needs and translate them into actionable requirements. The Product Owner is responsible for managing the product backlog, which is a prioritized list of features and user stories that define the scope of the product. They work closely with the development team to ensure that the backlog is refined, estimated, and ready for implementation. The Product Owner works closely with stakeholders to understand their needs and prioritize the backlog based on value and impact. They continuously gather feedback from customers and users to ensure that the product is meeting their needs and delivering value. They communicate the product vision and roadmap to stakeholders, ensuring alignment and buy-in from all parties involved. The Product Owner is also responsible for ensuring that the development team has a clear understanding of the requirements and user stories. They work closely with the team during the sprint planning, providing guidance and clarifications as needed. They participate in daily stand-up meetings, sprint reviews, and retrospectives to provide feedback and ensure that the product is on track. In addition to their role in defining and prioritizing the product backlog, the Product Owner is also responsible for managing the release planning and coordination. They work closely with the development team to plan the release schedule, ensuring that all necessary features and functionality are delivered on time and within budget. The Product Owner is a key advocate for the product, representing the needs of the customers and users throughout the development process. They work closely with the development team to ensure that the product is delivered to the highest quality standards and meets the defined requirements and user stories. In summary, the Product Owner is responsible for defining and prioritizing the features and functionality of a product or service, working closely with stakeholders and development teams to ensure that the product is meeting the needs of customers and users. They are accountable for the product backlog, release planning, and coordination, and serve as the key advocate for the product throughout the development process.

Product Owner

A Product Owner is a key role in Product Management, responsible for defining and prioritizing the features and capabilities of a product. They work closely with stakeholders, development teams, and other members of the product management team to ensure that the product meets the needs of the customers and the business. The Product Owner is responsible for creating and maintaining the product backlog, which is a prioritized list of user stories or tasks that need to be completed to deliver the product. They use their knowledge of the market, customer needs, and business goals to define the requirements and decide which features to include in the product and when they should be delivered.

Product PLM Software

A Product PLM (Product Lifecycle Management) software is a tool used by product managers to manage all stages of a product's lifecycle, from conception to retirement. It provides a centralized platform for product-related information, allowing teams to collaborate and make informed decisions throughout the product development process. With a Product PLM software, product managers can effectively track and manage product data, documents, and workflows. They can create and maintain a comprehensive product record, including specifications, requirements, and design files. This helps ensure that all stakeholders have access to accurate and up-to-date information, reducing the risk of errors and miscommunication.

Product Packaging Design

Product packaging design refers to the process of creating and conceptualizing the visual appearance and layout of a product's packaging. It is an essential component of product management that aims to enhance the appeal and functionality of a product's packaging, while also effectively communicating its brand identity, value proposition, and key information. The primary goal of product packaging design is to attract and engage consumers, differentiate the product from competitors, and ultimately drive sales and customer satisfaction. It involves various elements such as the choice of materials, colors, typography, graphics, and overall packaging structure and shape. These elements are strategically combined to create a visually appealing and impactful packaging design that aligns with the brand's image and resonates with the target market.

Product Packaging

Product Packaging refers to the process of designing and producing the physical container or wrapping for a product. It involves the use of various materials and techniques to create an external covering that not only protects the product but also communicates relevant information to consumers. In the context of product management, packaging plays a crucial role in several aspects, including branding, marketing, and product differentiation. It is an integral part of the product's overall presentation and influences consumer perceptions, purchasing decisions, and user experience.

Product Patch Management

Product Patch Management is the process of identifying, evaluating, and implementing updates or patches for a software product to ensure its functionality, security, and performance. As software products evolve, it is common for bugs, vulnerabilities, or performance issues to arise. To address these issues, product managers must monitor and assess the software regularly, and if necessary, develop and distribute patches to resolve these problems.

Product Patent

A product patent is a legally enforceable exclusive right granted by the government to the inventor or assignee of a new and useful product. It provides the holder with the sole authority to make, use, or sell the patented product for a specific period of time, usually 20 years from the priority filing date. This form of intellectual property protection aims to encourage innovation by granting inventors the opportunity to profit from their inventions without fear of competition. It allows them to recoup their investment in research and development, as well as generate profits from their invention.

Product Patents

A product patent is a legal protection granted to the inventor or assignee of a new product or technology. It provides exclusive rights to the patent holder, preventing others from making, using, selling, or importing the patented product without their permission for a limited period of time. In the context of product management, product patents play a crucial role in protecting and monetizing innovations. They are a form of intellectual property rights that give the patent holder a competitive advantage in the market by safeguarding their unique and novel products from being copied or imitated by competitors. Product managers need to be aware of the patent landscape to ensure that the products they manage do not infringe on existing patents. Conducting a thorough patent search and analysis is essential to identify any potential intellectual property conflicts and avoid legal disputes. Moreover, product patents can provide a strong differentiation strategy for a company. By obtaining patents for their innovative products, organizations can establish themselves as leaders in their respective industries. These patents not only protect the company's products from being copied but also serve as a barrier to entry for competitors, as they would need to navigate around the existing patents to bring similar products to market. However, it is important to note that product patents come with their own set of challenges and considerations. The process of obtaining a patent can be lengthy and expensive, requiring extensive documentation and legal expertise. Additionally, patents have a limited lifespan, typically 20 years from the date of filing, after which the product becomes part of the public domain and can be freely used by anyone. In conclusion, product patents are a vital tool in product management, offering legal protection and exclusivity for innovative products. They enable companies to monetize their inventions, differentiate themselves in the market, and create barriers to entry for competitors. However, careful navigation of the patent landscape and consideration of the associated challenges are essential for effective product management.

Product Performance Optimization

Product Performance Optimization refers to the process of continuously improving and enhancing a product's performance and efficiency to meet or exceed customer expectations. It involves analyzing and measuring various performance metrics, identifying areas for improvement, and implementing strategies to maximize the product's effectiveness. In the field of Product Management, Product Performance Optimization plays a crucial role in ensuring that a product remains competitive and relevant in the marketplace. It aims to drive customer satisfaction, increase customer loyalty, and ultimately contribute to the overall success of the product and the company.

Product Portfolio Management

Product Portfolio Management refers to the process of strategically managing a company's collection of products or services to optimize their overall performance and value in alignment with the organization's objectives and market dynamics. Its main goal is to ensure that the product portfolio meets the needs of target customers, generates maximum revenue, and delivers a competitive advantage in the marketplace. This management approach involves evaluating, prioritizing, and allocating resources to product development and marketing efforts based on their potential impact on business outcomes.

Product Portfolio

Product Portfolio refers to the collection of products or services offered by a company or organization. It is a strategic tool used in Product Management to manage and organize the products or services within a company's offering. A product portfolio includes all the products or services that a company currently offers or plans to offer in the future. It provides a comprehensive view of the range of products or services that a company has and helps in making decisions about the development, marketing, and management of these products. The product portfolio represents the company's investment in different products or services and reflects its overall business strategy. It includes both existing products or services as well as new products or services under development. The portfolio can be categorized based on various factors such as product type, market segment, customer needs, or business goals. Managing a product portfolio involves making decisions about which products to invest in, which products to discontinue, and which products to prioritize for development or marketing efforts. It also involves analyzing the performance of each product or service in the portfolio and making adjustments or improvements to ensure its success in the market. A well-managed product portfolio ensures that a company offers a diverse range of products or services to cater to different customer needs and market segments. It helps in maximizing the company's revenue and profit by identifying and capitalizing on new market opportunities. It also provides a solid foundation for innovation and growth by allowing the company to explore new product ideas and expand its offering. In conclusion, a product portfolio is a strategic tool used in Product Management to manage and organize the collection of products or services offered by a company. It plays a crucial role in decision-making, resource allocation, and market positioning of a company's products, ultimately contributing to the company's success and growth.

Product Positioning

Product positioning is a strategic process in product management that involves creating a distinct and valuable perception of a product in the minds of target customers. It is the process of defining and communicating a product's unique attributes, benefits, and value proposition to differentiate it from competitors and meet customer needs effectively. Product positioning is crucial for a company to gain a competitive advantage in the market and maximize its product's success. It helps marketers understand how their target customers perceive their product and how it compares to competitors' offerings. Through effective positioning, companies can influence customer perception and preferences, leading to increased sales and market share.

Product Presentation Skills

Product presentation skills refer to the ability of a product manager to effectively showcase a product to potential customers or stakeholders. It involves the demonstration of key features and benefits of the product in a clear and persuasive manner, with the goal of generating interest and driving sales. Product presentation skills are crucial for product managers as they play a vital role in the success of a product. A well-executed product presentation can significantly impact customer perception, increase product adoption, and ultimately contribute to business growth.

Product Presentation

A product presentation is a formal presentation or demonstration of a product to potential customers, stakeholders, or decision-makers in order to generate interest, educate, and persuade them to buy or support the product.Product presentations are an integral part of the product management process, as they help in introducing, promoting, and positioning a product in the market. The purpose of a product presentation is to effectively communicate the value proposition, features, benefits, and unique selling points of the product in an engaging and persuasive manner.

Product Pricing Strategy

Product pricing strategy refers to the methodology or approach used by a company to set the price of its products or services in the market. It is an essential element of product management as it directly influences the sales, profitability, and overall success of a product. The goal of a product pricing strategy is to find the optimal price point that maximizes the value perceived by the customers while generating sufficient revenue for the company. It involves analyzing various factors such as production costs, competition, target market, customer demand, and the perceived value of the product. There are several commonly used pricing strategies in product management, including: 1. Cost-based pricing: This strategy involves setting the price based on the production and distribution costs of the product, along with a desired profit margin. It ensures that the company covers its expenses and generates a reasonable profit. 2. Market-based pricing: With this strategy, the price is determined by considering the prevailing market conditions, including the prices charged by competitors for similar products. The goal is to position the product competitively in the market while still generating profit. 3. Value-based pricing: This approach focuses on setting the price based on the perceived value of the product to the customer. It takes into account factors such as quality, uniqueness, convenience, and the benefits offered by the product. The price is set to reflect the value provided, rather than the cost of production. 4. Penetration pricing: This strategy involves initially setting a lower price than competitors to gain market share and attract customers. The goal is to stimulate demand and create a customer base, which can then be leveraged for future sales and profit growth. 5. Skimming pricing: In contrast to penetration pricing, skimming pricing involves setting a higher price initially to target early adopters and customers willing to pay a premium for a new product. It is commonly used for innovative or technologically advanced products with limited competition. In conclusion, product pricing strategy plays a crucial role in product management as it determines the revenue, profitability, and market positioning of a product. By carefully analyzing the various factors and selecting an appropriate pricing strategy, companies can effectively maximize their product's success in the market.

Product Pricing

Product pricing is the strategic process of determining the price at which a product will be sold to customers. It involves analyzing various factors such as production costs, competition, market demand, and the perceived value of the product to the target market. Effective product pricing is essential for the success of a product. It plays a critical role in achieving business objectives, maximizing profitability, and ensuring customer satisfaction. Pricing decisions can significantly impact sales volume, revenue, market share, and overall company performance.

Product Procurement

Product procurement refers to the process of acquiring the necessary products or materials needed to develop and produce a specific product. It involves identifying and selecting suppliers, negotiating contracts, and managing the supply chain to ensure the availability of the required resources. Product procurement is a critical aspect of product management as it directly impacts the ability to meet customer demands and deliver high-quality products on time. Effective procurement strategies not only help streamline the supply chain but also help reduce costs, maximize profits, and minimize the risks associated with sourcing materials.

Product Production Control

Product Production Control refers to the process of efficiently managing and overseeing all aspects of the production of a product. It involves coordinating and controlling various activities, resources, and tasks to ensure the timely and cost-effective production of high-quality products that meet the customer's requirements. The primary goal of Product Production Control is to optimize the production process and maximize productivity, while minimizing waste and ensuring the consistent delivery of products that meet the company's quality standards. This is achieved through effective planning, organizing, coordinating, and controlling of all production activities.

Product Production Planning

Product production planning refers to the process of strategically organizing and optimizing the production of a product. It involves various activities such as determining the quantity and timing of production, allocating resources, and setting production schedules. Product production planning is a critical aspect of product management as it ensures that the product is manufactured efficiently and meets the demand in the market. It helps in avoiding underproduction or overproduction, which can lead to financial losses or missed opportunities.

Product Project Management

Product Project Management is the process of overseeing and managing all aspects of a product's development and delivery within an organization. It involves planning, coordinating, and directing various activities to ensure that a product is successfully developed, produced, and brought to market. The primary objective of Product Project Management is to deliver a high-quality product that meets customers' needs and expectations, is within budget and schedule, and is aligned with the organization's overall strategic goals. This requires effective communication and collaboration among cross-functional teams, including product managers, engineers, designers, marketing professionals, and other stakeholders. The first step in Product Project Management is defining the project's scope, goals, and requirements. This involves identifying the target market, conducting market research, and gathering customer feedback to understand their preferences and needs. Based on this information, a project plan is developed, which includes timelines, budgets, and resource allocation. Once the project plan is in place, the Product Project Manager works closely with the team to execute the plan. This involves coordinating and delegating tasks, tracking progress, and resolving any issues or obstacles that arise. The manager also ensures that the project stays within budget and timeline, and that all deliverables are met. Another crucial aspect of Product Project Management is risk management. The manager identifies and assesses potential risks and develops mitigation strategies to minimize their impact. This may involve conducting risk assessments, creating contingency plans, and monitoring and controlling risks throughout the project lifecycle. Throughout the project, the Product Project Manager acts as a liaison between various stakeholders, ensuring clear communication and alignment of expectations. They provide regular updates to management and other stakeholders, and solicit their feedback and input. Upon completion of the project, the Product Project Manager conducts a post-mortem to evaluate the project's success and identify areas for improvement. This includes analyzing project outcomes, measuring customer satisfaction, and capturing lessons learned. The insights gained from this analysis are then used to refine future product development processes and improve project management practices. In conclusion, Product Project Management is a critical function within product management, responsible for overseeing and managing all aspects of a product's development and delivery. It requires effective planning, coordination, and communication to ensure the successful delivery of high-quality products that meet customer needs and align with organizational goals.

Product Promotion Strategy

A product promotion strategy is a planned approach designed to increase awareness, generate interest, and drive sales for a specific product. It encompasses a range of activities and tactics aimed at effectively promoting the features, benefits, and value proposition of the product to the target audience. The goal of a product promotion strategy is to create a compelling and persuasive message that resonates with potential customers, highlighting the unique selling points of the product and demonstrating why it is superior to competitors. By effectively promoting the product, companies can generate demand, stimulate customer interest, and ultimately drive sales.

Product Promotion

Product Promotion refers to the strategic marketing activities undertaken by the product management team to create awareness, generate interest, and drive sales of a particular product or service. It involves a combination of promotional tactics and communication channels tailored to effectively reach the target audience and persuade them to make a purchase decision. Product promotion plays a crucial role in the success of a product and is an integral part of the overall product management process. It aims to increase product visibility, communicate its unique value proposition, and ultimately influence consumer behavior. The primary objectives of product promotion include: 1. Creating Awareness: Promotion efforts are designed to inform potential customers about the existence and benefits of the product. This is typically done through advertising campaigns, public relations activities, and online marketing strategies. The goal is to ensure that the target audience is aware of the product's features, advantages, and potential uses. 2. Generating Interest: Once awareness is established, the next step is to generate interest and enthusiasm in the product. This can be achieved through various promotional activities such as offering free samples, conducting product demonstrations, or organizing promotional events. By showcasing the product's unique selling points and highlighting its value proposition, product managers aim to capture the interest of the target audience and differentiate the product from competitors. 3. Driving Sales: The ultimate goal of product promotion is to drive sales and increase revenue. Product managers employ a range of tactics to encourage consumers to make a purchase, including limited-time discounts, special offers, or loyalty programs. By leveraging persuasive messaging and compelling calls-to-action, they aim to convert potential buyers into actual customers. Effective product promotion requires careful planning, market research, and an understanding of target customer needs and preferences. The product management team must identify the most relevant promotional channels and tailor their messaging to resonate with the target audience. This may involve using various marketing tools such as traditional advertising, digital marketing, social media campaigns, or influencer endorsements. In summary, product promotion is a critical component of product management, encompassing a range of activities that aim to create awareness, generate interest, and drive sales. By effectively promoting a product, the product management team can increase its visibility, communicate its unique value proposition, and ultimately influence consumer behavior, leading to increased market share and revenue.

Product Prototype

A product prototype is a preliminary version of a product that is used to test and validate its design, functionality, and user experience before it is manufactured and released to the market. It is an essential tool in the product development process and plays a crucial role in ensuring that the final product meets the needs and expectations of customers. A product prototype is typically built using materials and components that closely resemble the final product. It may be a physical model, such as a 3D-printed object or a scaled-down version of the product, or a digital representation, such as a computer-generated image or a virtual reality simulation. The choice of prototype depends on the type of product and the objectives of the testing phase. The main purpose of creating a product prototype is to gather feedback from stakeholders, including potential customers, investors, and internal teams, in order to identify and address any issues or shortcomings in the product. By providing a tangible or visual representation of the product, a prototype enables stakeholders to better understand its features, functionality, and overall value proposition. During the prototyping process, product managers work closely with designers, engineers, and other stakeholders to refine the product's design, functionality, and user interface. They collect feedback from user testing sessions, focus groups, and surveys to uncover insights and make informed decisions about the product's features, aesthetics, and market positioning. Furthermore, a product prototype allows product managers to test the product's feasibility, performance, and manufacturability. It helps them identify any technical or production-related challenges that may arise during the manufacturing process and enables them to make necessary adjustments to improve the product's quality and cost-effectiveness. In conclusion, a product prototype serves as a tangible representation of a product's design and functionality, enabling stakeholders to provide feedback and make informed decisions about its development. It plays a critical role in ensuring that the final product meets the needs and expectations of customers while also addressing technical and manufacturing considerations.

Product Prototyping Methods

Product prototyping methods are techniques used by product managers to create a physical or digital representation of a new product, allowing for testing, feedback, and iteration before the final product is developed and launched. These methods are employed to reduce the risk of failure and to validate the viability and desirability of a product. One commonly used method of product prototyping is the use of rapid prototyping tools and technologies. These tools, such as 3D printers or computer-aided design (CAD) software, allow for the quick creation of physical prototypes with minimal cost and time investment. Rapid prototyping enables product managers to physically assess the form, fit, and function of the product, gather feedback from potential users, and make necessary adjustments to the design before moving forward with production.

Product Prototyping Tools

Product prototyping tools are software or hardware tools used by product managers to create a prototype of a product, which is an early version that can be tested and evaluated before the final product is developed and launched. These tools provide a way for product managers to visualize and communicate their ideas, test different design concepts, and gather feedback from stakeholders. There are various types of prototyping tools available, each with its own set of features and capabilities. Some of the commonly used prototyping tools include: 1. Sketching tools: These tools allow product managers to quickly sketch out their ideas and concepts on paper or on a digital canvas. Sketching tools are useful for creating rough prototypes and exploring different design possibilities. 2. Wireframing tools: Wireframing tools enable product managers to create low-fidelity, static representations of the user interface and functionality of a product. These tools focus on the structure and basic interactions of the product, without detailed visual design elements. 3. Mockup tools: Mockup tools allow product managers to create high-fidelity, interactive prototypes that closely resemble the final product. These tools often include pre-designed UI elements and templates that can be easily customized, enabling product managers to create realistic representations of the product. 4. Prototyping tools: Prototyping tools provide advanced features for creating interactive and dynamic prototypes with realistic behaviors and animations. These tools allow product managers to simulate user interactions and test different scenarios to gather feedback and validate the product concept. In addition to these specific types of prototyping tools, product managers also use general design and collaboration tools such as graphic design software, project management tools, and communication tools to support the prototyping process.

Product Prototyping

Product prototyping is a crucial activity in product management that involves creating a physical or digital representation of a product idea or concept. It is a process of designing, building, and testing a prototype to validate its feasibility, functionality, and user experience before further development. The prototyping phase allows product managers to visualize and test the product's features, interactions, and overall design. It helps in identifying potential issues, refining the user experience, and gathering feedback from stakeholders and end-users. Through the prototype, product managers can iterate and make necessary adjustments to improve the product's functionality and usability. Prototyping can take various forms depending on the nature of the product and the available resources. It can range from low-fidelity prototypes, such as sketches or wireframes, to high-fidelity prototypes that closely resemble the final product. The choice of prototype depends on the specific goals of the project and the level of detail required to evaluate its viability. The prototyping process typically involves several stages. Firstly, product managers define the objectives, target users, and key features of the product. Then, they develop a conceptual design or storyboard that outlines the product's functionality and user flow. This serves as a foundation for creating the prototype. Next, product managers select the appropriate prototyping tools or methods based on the desired fidelity and level of interactivity. They may choose to use paper prototypes, clickable wireframes, interactive mockups, or even functional prototypes using coding or specialized software. The chosen prototype is then built and tested with a representative group of users. Feedback gathered from the prototype testing phase is invaluable for product managers. It helps them understand user preferences, pain points, and potential areas of improvement. Based on this feedback, they can refine the design, adjust features, or even pivot the product strategy if necessary. Prototyping plays a vital role in reducing risk and uncertainty during the product development process. It allows product managers to make informed decisions based on real user insights and market feedback, ultimately increasing the chances of success when the product is launched. In conclusion, product prototyping is a critical step in product management that involves creating and testing a physical or digital representation of a product idea. It helps product managers validate the feasibility, functionality, and user experience of the product before further development, leading to better-informed decisions and higher chances of success in the market.

Product Quality Control

Product quality control is a systematic process established within product management to ensure that the quality of a product or service meets or exceeds customer expectations. It involves monitoring and evaluating various aspects of the product throughout its lifecycle to identify and address any potential quality issues. The goal of product quality control is to deliver a product that is reliable, functional, safe, and meets all specifications and requirements. It involves setting quality standards, establishing quality control processes, conducting inspections and tests, and taking corrective actions to ensure that the product meets these standards. The first step in product quality control is setting quality standards. These standards are based on customer expectations, industry best practices, and regulatory requirements. They define the desired attributes and performance of the product, such as durability, accuracy, functionality, and safety. Quality standards serve as benchmarks for evaluating the product's quality and guiding the quality control process. Once the quality standards are established, quality control processes are put in place to monitor and evaluate the product's quality. This includes inspecting raw materials and components before production, conducting in-process inspections during manufacturing, and performing final inspections before the product is shipped to customers. Quality control processes may also involve conducting tests, such as stress tests, functionality tests, and safety tests, to ensure the product meets all requirements. If any quality issues are identified during the quality control process, corrective actions are taken to address them. This may involve adjusting production processes, replacing faulty components, reworking defective products, or making design changes. The goal is to eliminate or minimize quality problems and ensure that the product meets the established quality standards. Product quality control is an ongoing process that continues throughout the lifecycle of the product. It is essential for maintaining customer satisfaction, brand reputation, and competitiveness in the market. By consistently delivering high-quality products, companies can build trust and loyalty with customers, differentiate themselves from competitors, and achieve long-term success.

Product Rapid Prototyping

Rapid prototyping in the context of product management refers to the process of quickly creating a working model or prototype of a product to test and validate its design, functionality, and usability. This iterative approach allows product managers to gather feedback early on in the development cycle, identify potential issues or improvements, and make informed decisions to optimize the final product. It involves creating a simplified version of the product that closely resembles the final version, but may not have all the features or functionalities.

Product Recall

A product recall is a formal action taken by a company to remove a product from the market due to safety concerns, defects, or non-compliance with industry standards or regulatory requirements. It is a proactive measure intended to protect consumers from potential harm and maintain a company's reputation and brand image. A product recall typically occurs when a company becomes aware of a problem or potential issue with a product after it has been released to the market. This can be the result of internal testing or customer complaints, as well as reports from regulatory agencies or industry organizations. Once a safety concern is identified, the company initiates a recall process to effectively communicate the issue to customers, halt further sales and distribution of the product, and provide appropriate remedies to affected consumers. The recall process involves several key steps. First, the company must determine the scope and severity of the issue, including identifying specific product models or batches that are affected. This information is then communicated through various channels, such as press releases, direct notifications to retailers, and updates on the company's website or social media platforms. A recall may involve instructions to consumers on how to return or dispose of the product, and the company may offer refunds, replacements, or repairs to affected customers. In some cases, the company may collaborate with regulatory agencies to ensure compliance and coordination in addressing the safety concern. Throughout the recall process, clear and timely communication is essential to inform consumers about the issue, address their concerns, and restore confidence in the company and its products. Product recalls can have significant financial and reputational implications for companies. The costs associated with implementing a recall, including production halts, additional customer support, and potential legal expenses, can be substantial. Moreover, a poorly managed recall can damage a company's brand reputation and erode customer trust. Therefore, effective product management involves a proactive approach to quality control, testing, and monitoring to minimize the risk of safety issues and the need for recalls. Timely detection and appropriate handling of potential problems demonstrate a company's commitment to consumer safety and satisfaction, contributing to long-term success and competitiveness in the market.

Product Registration

Product Registration is a formal process used in Product Management to record and manage information about a product, its ownership, and its usage. It involves collecting and storing data related to a product's purchase, warranty, and technical specifications. This information is used by manufacturers and businesses to keep track of their products, ensure that warranties are honored, and provide better customer support. The primary purpose of Product Registration is to establish a direct line of communication between manufacturers or businesses and their customers. By registering a product, customers provide their contact information and other relevant details, allowing manufacturers to reach out to them in case of recalls, updates, or important announcements. It also enables manufacturers to gather valuable feedback and insights into customers' preferences, usage patterns, and satisfaction levels. Product Registration typically involves filling out an online or paper form provided by the manufacturer or business. This form requires customers to provide information such as their name, address, contact details, product serial number, purchase date, and proof of purchase. Once submitted, this data is stored in a database or CRM system, making it easily accessible for future reference. Product Registration offers several benefits for both customers and manufacturers. For customers, it ensures that their products are covered under warranty and enables them to receive timely support and updates. It also increases their engagement with the brand and enables them to provide feedback and suggestions for product improvement. On the other hand, manufacturers gain vital insights into their customer base, allowing them to tailor their marketing efforts and product development strategies more effectively. In conclusion, Product Registration is a crucial aspect of Product Management that helps manufacturers and businesses keep track of their products and engage with their customers. It serves as a valuable tool for communication, warranty management, and market research, ultimately resulting in improved customer satisfaction and business success.

Product Regulation

Product regulation in the context of product management refers to the set of rules, standards, and laws that govern the development, manufacturing, distribution, and sale of products. It is a crucial aspect of ensuring the safety, quality, and efficacy of products, as well as protecting consumers from potential harm or deception. Product regulation encompasses various areas, including but not limited to, product safety, labeling requirements, environmental impact, consumer protection, and industry-specific regulations. These regulations may be imposed by national or international bodies, such as government agencies or industry associations, and are intended to establish minimum standards that must be met by product manufacturers, distributors, and sellers.

Product Regulatory Testing

Product regulatory testing refers to the process of evaluating and assessing products to ensure they meet the required regulatory standards and comply with all applicable regulations and guidelines. It involves conducting various tests and analyses to determine the safety, quality, and compliance of the product with respect to the specific regulatory requirements imposed by authorities and industry standards. The purpose of product regulatory testing is to protect consumers, businesses, and the environment from potential hazards and risks associated with using or consuming the product. It helps to ensure that products are safe, reliable, and perform as expected, which enhances customer satisfaction and builds trust in the brand or company.

Product Release

A product release in the context of product management refers to the process of launching a new product or releasing an updated version of an existing product to the market. It involves all the activities and tasks necessary to make the product available for purchase by customers. The product release process typically starts with the planning stage, where the product manager works closely with cross-functional teams to define the product requirements, set goals, and establish a timeline for the release. During this stage, market research and analysis are conducted to determine the target market, identify customer needs and preferences, and assess the competition. Once the planning stage is complete, the product development phase begins, where the actual creation and testing of the product take place. This may involve designing the product, developing prototypes, and conducting user testing to ensure that the product meets the desired specifications and quality standards. Throughout the development phase, the product manager works closely with the development team to ensure that the product is progressing according to the set timeline and requirements. After the product development is complete, the product moves into the launch phase. During this stage, marketing strategies are developed to create awareness and generate interest in the product. This may include creating promotional materials, coordinating product demonstrations or events, and implementing advertising campaigns. The product manager also works with the sales team to provide them with the necessary tools and training to effectively sell the product. Once the product is ready for release, it is made available for purchase to customers through various channels such as online platforms, retail stores, or direct sales. The product manager monitors the sales performance and gathers feedback from customers to identify any areas for improvement or potential updates for future versions. This feedback is then used to inform product updates and enhancements for future releases. In conclusion, a product release in product management is the process of launching a new or updated product to the market. It involves planning, development, marketing, and sales activities to make the product available to customers and ensure its success in the market.

Product Reliability Testing

Product reliability testing is a crucial phase in the process of product management that involves evaluating and ensuring the effectiveness and dependability of a product. It is a systematic approach used to determine the extent to which a product can maintain its intended functionality and performance under various conditions and usage scenarios. The primary objective of product reliability testing is to identify any potential defects, weaknesses, or vulnerabilities that may undermine the product's performance or cause it to fail in real-world situations. By subjecting the product to different stress levels and environmental conditions, product managers can assess its ability to withstand a range of anticipated or unforeseen challenges.

Product Reliability

Product reliability refers to the ability of a product to consistently perform its intended function without failure or breakdown over a specified period of time under normal operating conditions. It is an essential aspect of product management as it directly impacts customer satisfaction, brand reputation, and overall business success. In the context of product management, product reliability encompasses several key components. Firstly, it involves the durability and robustness of the product. A reliable product should be able to withstand various environmental conditions, resist wear and tear, and maintain its performance over an extended period of use. This includes factors such as the quality of materials used, the manufacturing process, and adherence to industry standards and regulations. Secondly, product reliability also includes the consistency and accuracy of the product's performance. Customers expect a product to deliver consistent results, without any fluctuations or deviations from its intended purpose. For example, in the case of electronic devices, reliability refers to the ability to consistently provide accurate and precise readings or outputs. This depends on the product's design, engineering, and the implementation of quality control measures. Furthermore, product reliability involves the prevention and mitigation of potential failures or breakdowns. It requires proactive measures such as rigorous testing, identifying potential failure points, and implementing appropriate preventive maintenance procedures. By addressing potential issues before they occur, product managers can ensure that customers can rely on the product to function as expected, reducing the risk of negative experiences and customer dissatisfaction. In conclusion, product reliability is a critical aspect of product management that focuses on ensuring that a product consistently performs its intended function without failure or breakdown. It includes elements such as durability, consistency, accuracy, and preventive measures to enhance the overall customer experience and build a strong brand reputation.

Product Repair

Product Repair refers to the process of fixing or restoring a faulty or damaged product to its original working condition. It is an essential aspect of product management as it helps ensure customer satisfaction, maintain product quality, and increase product lifespan. Product repair involves diagnosing the issue, identifying the necessary repairs or replacements, and implementing the appropriate solutions. It requires technical expertise and knowledge of the product's design and components. The goal of product repair is to eliminate any defects or malfunctions that may hinder the product's performance or usability. In product management, product repair plays a significant role in maintaining customer loyalty and trust. When a product breaks down or fails to meet the expected standards, customers rely on effective repair services to resolve the issue. Timely and efficient repair services not only meet customers' immediate needs but also contribute to a positive product experience. Product repair also helps in reducing product returns and exchanges, which can be costly for both the manufacturer and the customer. By providing reliable repair services, product managers can minimize the number of defective products reaching customers and improve overall product quality. This, in turn, can lead to a decrease in warranty claims and associated costs. Furthermore, product repair enables product managers to gather valuable insights from repair data. By analyzing repair patterns and trends, product managers can identify recurring issues or design flaws that may require product modifications or improvements. This data-driven approach helps in making informed decisions about product enhancements and upgrades, ultimately leading to better customer satisfaction and market competitiveness. In summary, product repair is a crucial component of product management that focuses on rectifying product defects or damages. Effective repair services not only address customer concerns but also contribute to overall product quality improvement and customer satisfaction. By leveraging repair data, product managers can gain valuable insights for continuous product enhancements and stay ahead in the competitive market.

Product Requirements Collaboration

Product requirements collaboration refers to the process of gathering and consolidating input from multiple stakeholders in order to define and prioritize the features, functionality, and overall goals of a product. It involves bringing together individuals from various departments, such as product management, engineering, design, and marketing, to collectively determine the requirements that will guide the development and improvement of a product. Through collaboration, the goal is to ensure that all relevant perspectives and expertise are taken into account, in order to create a holistic and well-informed set of requirements. This collaborative process helps to align the vision and expectations of different teams and individuals, enabling

162

them to work towards a shared product roadmap and ultimate success.

Product Requirements Gathering

The process of product requirements gathering in the context of product management involves collecting and documenting the necessary information and specifications for developing a product or feature. This stage plays a crucial role in ensuring that the final product meets the needs and expectations of the target market. During the requirements gathering process, product managers work closely with stakeholders, including customers, users, sales teams, and internal subject matter experts. The goal is to gather a comprehensive understanding of what the product needs to achieve, its functionality, usability, and any other requirements that are vital to its success. Product managers employ various techniques to gather requirements, such as conducting interviews and surveys, organizing focus groups, and analyzing market research data. These methods help uncover insights about user needs, pain points, and desired features. Additionally, product managers collaborate with cross-functional teams, including developers, designers, and engineers, to ensure that technical requirements are considered and addressed. Once the requirements are gathered and documented, product managers prioritize them based on factors like user value, technical feasibility, and business goals. This helps in making informed decisions about which features should be developed and included in the product roadmap. It also enables the team to allocate resources effectively and efficiently. The requirements gathering process continues throughout the product lifecycle, as new insights and feedback emerge from user testing, customer interviews, and market trends. Product managers leverage these inputs to refine and update the product requirements, ensuring that the product remains relevant and aligns with customer needs and market dynamics. In conclusion, product requirements gathering is a vital step in product management that involves collecting and documenting the necessary information and specifications for developing a product. It ensures that the final product meets customer needs and aligns with the overall business strategy.

Product Requirements Traceability Solutions

Product requirements traceability solutions refer to the tools, processes, and methodologies that enable product managers to track and manage the relationship between product requirements and the subsequent stages of product development and delivery. These solutions help ensure that all customer needs and business objectives are effectively captured, translated into requirements, and then successfully implemented in the final product. Product requirements traceability solutions typically involve the use of specialized software and systems that allow product managers to document, organize, and track requirements throughout the entire product lifecycle. These tools typically provide a centralized repository where product managers can store, link, and trace requirements across different stages, such as concept development, design, testing, and deployment. By utilizing product requirements traceability solutions, product managers can achieve several benefits. Firstly, they can ensure that all customer needs and business objectives are captured accurately and completely. This helps avoid misunderstandings and miscommunication between different stakeholders involved in the product development process. Secondly, product requirements traceability solutions enable product managers to assess the impact of changes to requirements. They allow them to easily identify the dependencies between different requirements, as well as the potential ripple effects of any modifications. This helps mitigate the risk of introducing unintended consequences or breaking existing functionalities. Moreover, these solutions enhance collaboration and communication among product teams, stakeholders, and customers. By providing a centralized and transparent view of requirements, everyone involved in the product development process can easily access and understand the stated objectives and constraints. This fosters alignment, reduces misunderstandings, and enables effective decision-making. In conclusion, product requirements traceability solutions are crucial for product managers to successfully manage the complex and evolving relationship between customer needs, business objectives, and the product development process. By providing tools and processes for documenting, organizing, and tracking requirements, these solutions ensure that all stakeholders are on the same page and that the final product meets the desired outcomes.

Product Requirements Traceability

Product Requirements Traceability is a critical process within the field of Product Management.

It refers to the ability to trace and document the origin, purpose, and progress of every requirement throughout the lifecycle of a product. The fundamental purpose of Product Requirements Traceability is to ensure that there is a clear and transparent link between a product's requirements and its subsequent implementation, testing, and validation. This process facilitates effective communication between different stakeholders and allows for the identification of any gaps or inconsistencies in the product development process.

Product Requirements

Product Requirements refer to a detailed description and set of specifications that define the features, functionalities, and characteristics of a product. They are developed by a cross-functional team, including product managers, engineers, designers, and other stakeholders, and serve as a roadmap for product development. Product Requirements are a crucial part of the product management process as they help ensure that the final product meets the needs and expectations of the target users. They capture the objectives, goals, and constraints of the product and provide a clear direction for the development team.

Product Resilience

Product resilience refers to the ability of a product to withstand and recover from disruptions, changes, and challenges in its environment while continuing to fulfill its intended purpose and deliver value to its users and stakeholders.As a key concept in product management, resilience allows products to adapt, evolve, and remain relevant in dynamic markets and competitive landscapes. It encompasses various dimensions, including technical, operational, and strategic resilience.

Product Retirement

Product retirement, in the context of product management, refers to the process of discontinuing a product from the market due to various reasons such as declining sales, technological obsolescence, or strategic business decisions. It involves the careful planning and execution of activities aimed at phasing out the product and managing its end-of-life cycle. During the product retirement process, organizations assess the viability and profitability of the product in order to determine whether it should be discontinued. Factors such as market demand, competition, profitability, and the availability of resources play a crucial role in this evaluation. Once a decision to retire a product is made, a well-defined plan is put in place to ensure a smooth transition. The product retirement process typically involves several stages. The first stage is the notification phase, where customers, suppliers, and other stakeholders are informed about the decision to retire the product. This allows them to make necessary adjustments to their operations and plan for alternatives. Clear communication and transparency are key during this phase to maintain customer trust and loyalty. Next, the inventory management stage focuses on reducing the stock of the retiring product. This may involve offering attractive discounts, promotions, or incentives to encourage customers to make a final purchase or transition to a new product. Careful coordination between sales, marketing, and supply chain teams is crucial to ensure an efficient and timely reduction in inventory levels. In parallel, organizations need to develop and implement a support plan for existing customers. This involves addressing any concerns or issues related to the retiring product and providing guidance on product alternatives or upgrades. Timely and accurate customer support during this phase is essential to maintain customer satisfaction and minimize potential negative impacts on the company's reputation. Lastly, the product retirement process includes the disposal or recycling stage, where any remaining inventory or assets associated with the retiring product are managed. This may involve selling off excess stock, repurposing components, or safely disposing of hazardous materials. Organizations strive to minimize waste and environmental impact during this stage through responsible disposal practices. Overall, product retirement is a critical aspect of product management that requires careful planning, effective communication, and seamless execution to ensure a successful transition for both the organization and its stakeholders.

Product Risk Management

Product Risk Management refers to the systematic process of identifying, analyzing, assessing, and mitigating potential risks associated with a product throughout its lifecycle, in order to maximize its success and minimize negative impacts. It is an integral part of product management, as it helps to ensure that the product meets the desired objectives, complies with regulations, and is safe and reliable for its intended use. The first step in product risk management is the identification of potential risks. This involves analyzing the product's design, functionality, manufacturing process, and intended use, to determine any possible hazards or vulnerabilities. Risks can include technical failures, design flaws, safety hazards, regulatory non-compliance, market competition, and financial implications. Once the risks are identified, they need to be analyzed and assessed. This involves evaluating the likelihood and severity of each risk, considering factors such as historical data, expert opinions, customer feedback, and industry standards. Risks that are deemed high in likelihood and severity are given higher priority for mitigation. The next step is to develop strategies and measures to mitigate or control the identified risks. This may involve making design changes, implementing safety features, conducting additional tests and inspections, creating backup plans, addressing regulatory requirements, and establishing contingency plans. The goal is to minimize the impact of potential risks and enhance the product's overall performance, reliability, and safety. Furthermore, product risk management is an ongoing process that continues throughout the product's lifecycle. Regular monitoring and evaluation are essential to identify new risks that may arise as market conditions change, technology advances, or customer demands evolve. This allows for proactive risk management and enables timely adjustments and improvements to the product. In conclusion, product risk management is crucial for product managers to ensure the success and longevity of a product. By systematically identifying, analyzing, assessing, and mitigating potential risks, product risk management improves the overall quality, safety, and reliability of the product, while minimizing negative impacts and enhancing customer satisfaction.

Product Roadmap Alignment Platforms

A product roadmap alignment platform is a tool or software that helps product managers in aligning their product roadmap with the overall strategic goals and objectives of the organization. It provides a centralized platform where product managers can visualize and communicate their product strategies, prioritize initiatives, and track progress towards achieving the product vision. The main purpose of a product roadmap alignment platform is to ensure that the product roadmap reflects the strategic priorities and objectives of the organization. It helps product managers in making informed decisions about which features and initiatives to prioritize based on their alignment with the overall business goals. By providing a clear visualization of the product roadmap, it enables product managers to communicate their plans to stakeholders and get buy-in from cross-functional teams.

Product Roadmap Alignment

Product Roadmap Alignment refers to the process of ensuring that the strategic goals, objectives, and priorities of an organization are reflected in the product roadmap. It involves aligning the product roadmap with other organizational plans, such as the business strategy, marketing plan, and technology roadmap, to ensure a cohesive and consistent approach to product development and delivery. Product Managers play a crucial role in product roadmap alignment by serving as the bridge between various stakeholders, including executives, sales, marketing, engineering, and customer support. They gather input from these stakeholders and use it to define the strategic direction for the product. This involves understanding and balancing different priorities, constraints, and trade-offs to create a roadmap that aligns with the organization's overall goals and objectives.

Product Roadmap Visualization

A product roadmap visualization is a strategic planning tool used in product management to communicate the direction and progress of a product over time. It is a visual representation that outlines the key objectives, goals, and initiatives of a product, as well as the timeline in which they are expected to be achieved. The product roadmap provides a high-level overview of the product's development and helps align the efforts of the product team, stakeholders, and other relevant parties. The purpose of a product roadmap visualization is to provide transparency and clarity regarding the product's vision and strategy. It helps stakeholders understand the "big picture" and visualize how the product will evolve over time. By clearly articulating the product's goals and objectives, it helps ensure that everyone is working towards a common vision.

Product roadmaps typically consist of several components. The main element is the timeline, which depicts the different stages and milestones in the product's development. These can include major releases, feature enhancements, bug fixes, and other initiatives. The timeline provides a visual representation of how the product will progress over time and helps stakeholders understand when they can expect certain features or improvements. In addition to the timeline, a product roadmap visualization may include other elements such as themes or goals. These themes represent overarching areas of focus or strategic objectives for the product. They help guide the prioritization of features and initiatives, ensuring that they align with the overall strategy. A product roadmap visualization can take various formats, depending on the needs and preferences of the product manager and stakeholders. It can be a simple graphical representation using shapes and colors, or it can be a more detailed chart or graph. The key is to create a visual that is clear, concise, and easy to understand. Overall, a product roadmap visualization is a powerful tool that helps product managers communicate their vision and strategy, align stakeholders, and track the progress of a product over time. By providing a visual representation of the product's goals and timeline, it helps ensure that everyone is on the same page and working towards a common objective.

Product Roadmap

A product roadmap is a strategic document used in product management that outlines the goals, vision, and direction for a product or set of products over a specific time period. It serves as a communication tool between the product team, stakeholders, and other departments within an organization. The product roadmap typically includes information about the product's key features, enhancements, and updates that will be delivered in the future. It helps align the product team and stakeholders on what will be worked on and when, providing a clear plan of action for development and marketing efforts.

Product Root Cause Analysis

A product root cause analysis is a structured process used by product managers to identify and address the underlying issues or problems causing a negative impact on a product's performance or success. It involves thoroughly examining the product's features, functionality, usability, and overall user experience to determine the root cause of any deficiencies or limitations. The purpose of conducting a product root cause analysis is to gain a deep understanding of the factors that contribute to the product's shortcomings and to develop appropriate solutions or improvements. By identifying and addressing the underlying causes, product managers can enhance the product's competitiveness, customer satisfaction, and overall business value.

Product Safety

Product Safety refers to the measures and precautions taken by product managers to ensure that the products they develop, manufacture, and sell are safe for their intended use and pose minimal risk to consumers or end-users. In the context of product management, product safety encompasses a wide range of considerations and activities, including: 1. Compliance with Regulatory Standards: Product managers must understand and comply with applicable safety regulations and standards set by government authorities and industry bodies. This involves conducting thorough research, staying updated on changes in regulations, and ensuring that products meet all necessary requirements. 2. Risk Assessment: Product managers need to assess potential risks associated with their products and take steps to mitigate or eliminate them. This involves identifying and analyzing potential hazards, evaluating the severity and likelihood of harm, and implementing appropriate risk control measures. 3. Product Testing and Certification: Product managers are responsible for organizing and conducting rigorous testing procedures to validate the safety of their products. This may involve conducting internal tests, collaborating with third-party testing laboratories, or obtaining necessary certifications to demonstrate compliance with predetermined safety standards. 4. Quality Control: Product managers must establish quality control processes to ensure that all products manufactured and delivered to customers meet specified safety requirements. This may involve implementing quality checklists, conducting inspections during the production process, and monitoring the overall supply chain for potential safety issues. 5. Consumer Communication and Education: Product managers play a vital role in communicating relevant safety information to consumers.

This may include providing clear and accurate instructions for product assembly, use, and maintenance, as well as issuing product recalls or warnings in case of safety concerns. Overall, product safety is an essential aspect of product management as it helps build trust with consumers, protects a company's reputation, and mitigates potential legal and financial risks associated with product failures or accidents. By prioritizing product safety, product managers can ensure that their products meet the highest standards of quality and reliability, providing a safe and satisfactory experience for end-users.

Product Sales Collateral

Product sales collateral refers to a collection of marketing materials and resources that are specifically designed to support and facilitate the sales process of a product or service. It is typically created and utilized by product management teams to provide comprehensive information and persuasive content that can help sales representatives effectively communicate the value and benefits of a product to potential customers. The main purpose of product sales collateral is to educate, inform, and engage customers, with the ultimate goal of driving product adoption and increasing sales. These collateral materials are developed with a deep understanding of the product's features, functionalities, and target market, and are tailored to the specific needs and preferences of the customer base. The content of sales collateral may vary depending on the nature of the product and the target audience, but typically includes a combination of the following: - Product brochures and catalogs, which provide an overview of the product's features, benefits, and specifications. - Case studies and success stories, which demonstrate how the product has delivered value and solved real-world problems for existing customers. - Whitepapers and industry reports, which offer in-depth analysis, insights, and thought leadership on industry-related topics and trends. - Product presentations and demos, which showcase the product's capabilities and functionality in a visual and interactive manner. - Testimonials and customer reviews, which highlight positive experiences and endorsements from satisfied customers. - Pricing and packaging details, including pricing guides, comparison charts, and discounts or promotions that may be applicable. - FAQ and knowledge base, which provide answers to common customer queries and support self-service information retrieval. - Sales scripts and talking points, which offer guidance and suggestions for sales representatives to effectively communicate the value proposition and handle objections. - Product samples or trials, which allow potential customers to experience the product first-hand before making a purchase decision. Ultimately, product sales collateral serves as a vital tool for sales teams to effectively position and differentiate a product in a crowded and competitive market. It enables sales representatives to communicate product value, address customer pain points, and build trust and credibility with potential buyers. By leveraging various types of sales collateral, product management teams can increase the likelihood of successful sales conversions and drive overall business growth.

Product Sales Demos

Product Sales Demos in the context of Product Management refer to the presentation and demonstration of a product to potential customers or clients with the goal of showcasing its features, benefits, and value to ultimately drive sales. These demos are typically performed by sales representatives or product managers who are well-versed in the product's functionality and target market. The purpose of a product sales demo is to educate and convince potential customers about the value and potential of the product. It allows them to see the product in action and understand how it can address their specific needs or pain points. The demo is an opportunity to highlight the product's unique features, competitive advantages, and how it can solve real-life problems for the customer.

Product Sales Forecast

A product sales forecast is a prediction of the future sales volume and revenue generated by a specific product or product line within a specified time period. This forecast is based on various factors such as historical sales data, market trends, customer insights, and competitive analysis. The purpose of a product sales forecast is to help product managers and organizations make informed decisions regarding production, inventory management, marketing strategies, and overall business planning. Product managers use sales forecasts to estimate the demand for their product and to set achievable sales targets. By analyzing past sales data and conducting market research, they can identify patterns and trends that may impact future sales. This information is then used to determine the sales potential of the product and to develop a plan to achieve those sales targets. Market trends and external factors play a crucial role in the accuracy of a product sales forecast. Factors such as changes in consumer behavior, economic conditions, competitor actions, and technological advancements can significantly impact the demand for a product. Therefore, product managers need to continuously monitor the market and update their forecasts accordingly. A product sales forecast not only helps in predicting future sales volume but also provides insights into revenue projections. By multiplying the forecasted sales volume with the product's price, product managers can estimate the revenue that can be generated in the given time period. This information is vital for budgeting, resource allocation, and financial planning. Accuracy is a critical factor in a product sales forecast. Overestimating or underestimating the sales volume can lead to inventory shortages or excess stock, resulting in financial losses for the organization. Therefore, product managers need to consider various factors and use reliable data sources to create a realistic and achievable forecast. In conclusion, a product sales forecast is a prediction of future sales volume and revenue generated by a specific product. It helps product managers in making informed decisions, setting sales targets, and planning business strategies. It is essential to update the forecast regularly based on market trends and external factors to ensure accuracy and avoid potential financial risks.

Product Sales Funnel

A product sales funnel refers to the stages through which potential customers pass before making a purchase. It is a strategic framework that product managers use to guide their product development and marketing efforts. The sales funnel helps product managers understand the customer journey, identify areas for improvement, and align their sales and marketing strategies. The sales funnel typically consists of several stages, starting from awareness and ending with conversion. Each stage represents a different level of customer engagement and readiness to purchase. The stages often include: Awareness: At this stage, potential customers become aware of the product or brand, usually through marketing efforts such as advertising, content marketing, or referrals. Interest: Once customers are aware of the product, they develop an interest in learning more about its features, benefits, and value proposition. Product managers can nurture this interest by providing informative content, demonstrations, or samples. Consideration: At this stage, customers actively consider purchasing the product. They compare it with alternatives and evaluate its fit to their needs, budget, and preferences. Product managers can help facilitate the decision-making process by highlighting unique selling points and addressing potential concerns or objections. Intent: When customers reach the intent stage, they have a strong intention to purchase the product. They may seek additional information, such as pricing details, product specifications, or customer reviews. Product managers can support this intent by providing clear and accessible information on product websites or through sales representatives. Conversion: This is the final stage where customers make a purchase. Product managers need to ensure a seamless buying experience, convenient payment options, and prompt customer support. They can also consider implementing cross-selling or upselling strategies to maximize the value of each transaction. The sales funnel concept allows product managers to analyze and optimize each stage of the customer journey. By understanding customer behavior and preferences at each stage, product managers can identify potential bottlenecks, improve conversion rates, and enhance overall customer satisfaction.

Product Sales

Product Sales is a term used in the field of Product Management to refer to the total number of units or value of products sold within a given time period. It is a crucial metric for businesses as it directly impacts revenue and profit. Product sales provide insights into the demand for a product and its performance in the market. In Product Management, tracking sales is essential for various purposes, such as evaluating the success of a product, identifying trends, and making informed decisions regarding product improvements and marketing strategies. By analyzing sales data, Product Managers can gain a deeper understanding of customer behavior, preferences, and market dynamics.

Product Scalability Testing

Product scalability testing refers to the process of evaluating a product's ability to handle increased workloads and maintain optimal performance levels. It involves conducting tests to assess the product's responsiveness, stability, and efficiency under varying usage scenarios, with the goal of determining its capacity to scale seamlessly with growing user demands. In the context of product management, scalability testing is crucial for identifying potential bottlenecks and limitations that may hinder a product's ability to handle increased user loads or data volumes. By conducting scalability tests, product managers can gather empirical data on how the product performs and behaves under different stress levels, allowing them to make informed decisions on optimizing performance and capacity planning.

Product Scalability

Product scalability refers to the ability of a product to handle an increasing workload or accommodate a growing number of users without experiencing significant performance degradation or functional limitations. It requires the product to effectively handle larger data volumes, increased processing demands, and additional user interactions while maintaining the desired level of performance and user experience. In the context of product management, scalability is a crucial aspect to consider when developing and managing a product. As a product manager, it is essential to assess and plan for scalability right from the initial stages of product development to ensure that the product can grow and adapt to changing market dynamics and customer demands.

Product Scrum Methodology

Product Scrum Methodology is an agile framework that is widely used in Product Management to manage and develop products in a highly iterative and collaborative manner. It involves a cross-functional team working together in short timeframes called sprints to deliver incremental value to the product. In Product Scrum Methodology, the product owner is responsible for defining and prioritizing the product backlog, which consists of a list of user stories or features that need to be developed. The team then selects a subset of items from the product backlog to be included in the sprint backlog for the current sprint. During the sprint, which typically lasts for 2-4 weeks, the team works on developing and testing the selected items from the sprint backlog. Daily scrum meetings are held to ensure that everyone is aligned and any roadblocks or issues are addressed. At the end of the sprint, a potentially shippable product increment is delivered. The key principle of Product Scrum Methodology is to embrace change and adapt to feedback. The product owner continually assesses and reprioritizes the product backlog based on the changing needs of the market and customer feedback. This allows for flexibility and ensures that the product remains relevant and valuable. Product Scrum Methodology also promotes collaboration and transparency. The team works closely together, sharing knowledge and expertise to deliver the best possible product. The progress of the project is made visible through burndown charts, which show the remaining work and help track the team's velocity. Overall, Product Scrum Methodology provides a structured and iterative approach to product development. By breaking down the work into small, manageable chunks and focusing on delivering value in short timeframes, it enables teams to quickly respond to changing market conditions and customer needs.

Product Security Testing

Product Security Testing refers to the process of evaluating the security features, vulnerabilities, and risks associated with a product or system. It is an essential part of product management, as it helps to identify and mitigate potential security threats and ensure the overall security posture of the product. During product security testing, a team of experts conducts various tests and assessments to identify and address security weaknesses. These tests can include vulnerability scanning, penetration testing, code review, and security architecture review. The main objective is to identify any vulnerabilities that could be exploited by an attacker and to recommend appropriate controls and countermeasures to mitigate these risks.

Product Security

Product security in the context of product management refers to the measures and practices implemented to protect the integrity, confidentiality, and availability of a product or its components. It encompasses the strategies, processes, and controls used to identify, assess, and mitigate security risks throughout the entire product lifecycle. The main objective of product security is to ensure that the product and its associated data are safeguarded against unauthorized access, manipulation, or destruction. This involves considering various aspects, including software, hardware, communication channels, and user interactions.

Product Serialization

Product Serialization refers to the process of assigning a unique identification number or code to each unit of a product. This identification number helps in tracking the product throughout its entire lifecycle, from manufacturing to distribution, and even after it reaches the end consumer. The purpose of product serialization is to create a system of traceability and accountability. By assigning a unique code to each unit, companies can track the movement of their products at every stage of the supply chain. This allows them to have better control over inventory, reduce the risk of counterfeiting, and improve the overall efficiency of their operations.

Product Service Centers

Product Service Centers are specialized facilities or organizations that provide a range of services related to a particular product or product line. These centers play a crucial role in product management by offering support and assistance to customers, managing product repairs and returns, and providing technical guidance and expertise. Product Service Centers are typically set up by companies to ensure that their customers have access to comprehensive after-sales support. They serve as a central point of contact for customers who have questions, concerns, or issues with a product. The centers employ knowledgeable staff who are trained to provide accurate and timely assistance, ensuring customer satisfaction and loyalty.

Product Service Requests

Product Service Requests, in the context of Product Management, refer to the formal or informal requests made by customers or internal teams for modifications, enhancements, or assistance related to a particular product or service. These requests can come from various sources, including customer feedback, sales teams, support teams, or other stakeholders. They serve as a means for customers or internal teams to communicate their needs, concerns, or suggestions regarding a product or service.

Product Serviceability

Product serviceability refers to the ease and efficiency with which a product can be serviced or repaired throughout its lifecycle. It is a critical aspect of product management, as it directly impacts customer satisfaction, cost-effectiveness, and brand reputation. Serviceability encompasses a range of factors that contribute to the overall service experience for both customers and service technicians. These factors include accessibility, diagnostic capabilities, availability of spare parts, and ease of maintenance and repair.

Product Simulation

Product Simulation is a strategic approach used in Product Management to simulate and test the performance and success of a product within a controlled environment before its actual launch. It entails creating a virtual or physical representation of the product and its intended market, allowing product managers to make informed decisions based on realistic scenarios. In Product Simulation, product managers utilize various tools and techniques to assess the potential impact of different factors on the product's success. These factors often include market demand, pricing, competition, and customer preferences. By simulating different scenarios, product managers can evaluate the product's performance, identify potential risks, and make necessary adjustments to optimize its market fit.

Product Six Sigma

Six Sigma is a data-driven methodology used in product management to identify and eliminate defects or variations in the production process. It aims to minimize errors and improve the overall quality of a product by systematically analyzing and improving processes. The main goal of Six Sigma in product management is to achieve high levels of customer satisfaction by consistently delivering products that meet or exceed customer expectations. It provides a structured approach to identify and address the root causes of defects, thereby reducing waste, increasing efficiency, and driving continuous improvement.

Product Software Updates

Product software updates refer to the process of releasing new versions or iterations of a software product to customers or end users. These updates typically aim to improve the functionality, performance, usability, and security of the software, as well as address any bugs or issues that may have been identified in previous versions. Product management plays a crucial role in managing software updates throughout the product lifecycle. This involves identifying and prioritizing the feature enhancements, bug fixes, and other improvements to be included in each update, as well as coordinating the development, testing, and release processes.

Product Spare Parts Management

Product Spare Parts Management refers to the process of effectively managing and controlling the inventory of spare parts for a particular product. It involves the identification, procurement, storage, and distribution of spare parts to support the maintenance and repair activities of the product. Proper spare parts management is crucial for ensuring the availability of required spare parts when needed, minimizing downtime, and maximizing the product's lifespan. It involves determining the optimal inventory levels, establishing efficient storage and retrieval systems, and implementing effective replenishment strategies.

Product Stage-Gate Process

A Product Stage-Gate Process is a structured approach used in product management to guide the development of new products or services from ideation to launch. It is a system of sequential stages and decision-making gates that enable organizations to assess and mitigate risks, allocate resources effectively, and optimize the development and commercialization process. The Stage-Gate Process consists of a series of defined stages, each representing a significant milestone in the product development journey. These stages are typically divided into activities such as idea generation, concept development, prototype creation, market testing, and final launch. At the end of each stage, a gate review is conducted to evaluate the progress and viability of the project, and to make informed decisions about whether to proceed to the next stage, revise the project, put it on hold, or terminate it altogether. The gate reviews are critical decision points where cross-functional teams, comprised of representatives from various departments like marketing, finance, operations, and research and development, assess the project against pre-defined criteria. These criteria include market potential, technical feasibility, financial viability, strategic alignment, competitive landscape, and overall project objectives. The gatekeepers responsible for making the decisions weigh the information presented and determine the next steps for the project. A key benefit of the Stage-Gate Process is its inherent flexibility, allowing organizations to adapt and respond to market changes, customer feedback, and evolving business dynamics. It promotes a disciplined approach to product development, ensuring that resources are allocated to the most promising projects, and reducing the risk of investing in unsuccessful ideas. It also facilitates better communication and collaboration between different functions within the organization, fostering a cross-functional mindset and alignment of goals. In summary, the Product Stage-Gate Process serves as a roadmap for product managers, providing a structured framework for managing the development and launch of new products or services. It helps organizations make informed decisions, prioritize resources, and maintain a systematic approach to innovation, resulting in increased success rates and improved competitiveness in the market.

Product Stakeholders

A product stakeholder is a person or group of people who have a vested interest in the success of a product. These individuals contribute to the decision-making process and provide valuable insights and feedback throughout the product's lifecycle. Product stakeholders play a crucial role in product management, as they help shape and prioritize product features, ensure alignment with business objectives, and represent the needs and requirements of various stakeholders.

171

There are several types of product stakeholders, each with their own unique perspectives and responsibilities. The most common types of product stakeholders include: 1. Customers: Customers are the end-users of the product. They provide important feedback on product features, usability, and overall satisfaction. Their perspectives and needs are crucial in shaping the product to meet market demands and achieve success. 2. Product Managers: Product managers are responsible for defining the product vision, strategy, and roadmap. They gather inputs from various stakeholders, prioritize features and requirements, and oversee the product development process. Product managers work closely with other stakeholders to ensure that the product meets their needs and aligns with business objectives. 3. Development Team: The development team consists of designers, developers, and engineers who are responsible for building and delivering the product. They work closely with other stakeholders to understand the requirements and specifications, provide technical expertise, and deliver a high-quality product on time. 4. Executive Management: Executive management provides guidance, strategic direction, and resources for the product. They make high-level decisions regarding the product's budget, market positioning, and overall strategy. 5. Sales and Marketing: Sales and marketing teams play a critical role in promoting and selling the product. They provide insights on market trends, customer needs, and competitive landscape. Their feedback helps shape the product's positioning, pricing, and go-to-market strategy. 6. Support and Operations: Support and operations teams are responsible for maintaining the product and ensuring its smooth operation. They gather customer feedback, identify and resolve issues, and contribute to product improvements and enhancements. In summary, product stakeholders are individuals or groups who have a stake in the success of a product. They provide valuable insights, feedback, and expertise throughout the product's lifecycle, helping to shape and prioritize product features, ensure alignment with business objectives, and represent the needs and requirements of various stakeholders.

Product Strategy

Product strategy in the context of product management can be defined as a high-level plan or approach that outlines how a company will create, deliver, and sustain value with its products or services. It serves as a roadmap for aligning the product vision and goals with the overall business objectives, market needs, and customer expectations. The product strategy encompasses various elements, including market analysis, competitive positioning, target markets, pricing, distribution, and marketing tactics. It involves making crucial decisions regarding the direction and focus of the product portfolio to maximize market share, revenue, and customer satisfaction.

Product Stress Testing

Product stress testing is a crucial aspect of product management that involves subjecting a product to a series of rigorous tests and simulations to assess its performance and durability under extreme conditions or high-stress situations. This type of testing is conducted to identify any weaknesses, vulnerabilities, or limitations of the product with the aim of enhancing its overall quality and ensuring its reliability in real-world scenarios. During product stress testing, various scenarios are created to evaluate the product's response to adverse conditions, such as excessive load, extreme temperatures, power failures, network disruptions, or other challenging circumstances. The goal is to push the product to its limits and observe how it handles these stress factors. This helps product managers understand the product's resilience and uncover any potential areas for improvement.

Product Supplier Assessment

A product supplier assessment is a structured evaluation process conducted by a product management team to analyze and assess the suitability and capabilities of potential suppliers for a specific product or set of products. During a product supplier assessment, the product management team collects and analyzes data and information about suppliers, including their financial stability, manufacturing capacity, quality control processes, delivery capabilities, reputation, and adherence to regulatory requirements. The assessment is typically carried out using a predefined set of criteria or evaluation framework. The main objective of a product supplier assessment is to identify and select suppliers that can meet the product's requirements and deliver the desired quality, at competitive prices, within the specified timeline. By thoroughly evaluating suppliers, the product management team can make informed decisions regarding supplier selection, negotiation of contracts, and ongoing supplier management. Typically, a product supplier assessment involves multiple stages, starting with the identification and shortlisting of potential suppliers based on their suitability and alignment with the product's requirements. This may involve researching and gathering information about suppliers from various sources, such as trade directories, industry contacts, and online databases. Once potential suppliers are identified, the product management team conducts a detailed evaluation of each supplier's capabilities and suitability. This may involve site visits to assess the supplier's manufacturing facilities, discussions with key stakeholders, and a review of their past performance and track record. After gathering all the necessary data and information, the product management team uses it to score and rank the suppliers based on predefined evaluation criteria. The evaluation criteria could include factors such as price, quality, delivery reliability, financial stability, technical expertise, and compliance with industry standards and regulations. Based on the supplier assessment results, the product management team can then make an informed decision on supplier selection and proceed with the contracting and negotiation process. Ongoing supplier management and performance monitoring are also key aspects of the product supplier assessment process.

Product Supplier Collaboration

Product Supplier Collaboration refers to the strategic partnership and collaboration between a company and its suppliers in the context of product management. It involves the joint effort and coordination between the company and its suppliers to develop, produce, and deliver products that meet customer needs and drive business success. This collaboration is rooted in the recognition of the suppliers as key stakeholders in the product development and management process. It goes beyond a transactional relationship and focuses on building long-term partnerships based on trust, mutual benefit, and shared goals. The objectives of product supplier collaboration are to improve product quality, reduce time-to-market, increase supply chain efficiency, and enhance customer satisfaction. By involving suppliers early in the product development process, companies can benefit from their expertise and gain access to innovative solutions, technologies, and materials. This collaboration allows for the seamless integration of supplier capabilities, resources, and knowledge into the product design and manufacturing processes. Effective product supplier collaboration relies on open communication and information sharing between the company and its suppliers. This includes sharing product specifications, requirements, and customer feedback, as well as providing visibility into demand forecasts and production schedules. Such collaboration enables suppliers to align their operations and capacity planning with the company's needs, ensuring timely and efficient delivery of products. Additionally, product supplier collaboration encompasses collaborative decision-making processes, such as joint product planning, cost analysis, and risk assessment. By involving suppliers in these decision-making processes, companies can leverage their insights and perspectives to optimize product design, pricing, and sourcing strategies. In summary, product supplier collaboration is a strategic approach to product management that involves partnering with suppliers to jointly develop, produce, and deliver products that meet customer needs. It entails open communication, information sharing, and collaborative decision-making to enhance product quality, reduce time-to-market, improve supply chain efficiency, and drive business success.

Product Supply Chain

A product supply chain refers to the entire process of producing, distributing, and delivering a product to the end consumer. It involves all the activities, resources, and entities that are involved in transforming raw materials into a finished product and getting it into the hands of the customer. At a high level, a product supply chain can be divided into four main stages: procurement, manufacturing, distribution, and retail. The procurement stage involves sourcing the necessary raw materials and other inputs required for production. This can include anything from sourcing metals for manufacturing electronic goods to procuring fabric for clothing production. The manufacturing stage involves transforming the raw materials into a finished product. This can include activities such as assembly, fabrication, packaging, and quality control. Manufacturers employ various processes and technologies to convert the raw materials into a final product that meets the desired specifications and quality standards. Once the product is manufactured, it moves on to the distribution stage. This involves transporting the product from the manufacturing facility to various distribution centers or warehouses. Distribution may also involve third-party logistics providers who handle the transportation, warehousing, and inventory management on behalf of the manufacturer. Finally, the product reaches the retail stage, where it is made available for purchase by the end consumer. This can involve selling through physical stores, online marketplaces, or both. Retailers play a crucial role in marketing, merchandising, and selling the product to the target customers. In addition to these four main stages, a product supply chain also includes various supporting activities such as demand planning, inventory management, transportation management, and customer service. These activities ensure that the right products are available in the right quantities at the right time and place. Overall, a well-managed product supply chain is essential for ensuring the efficient production, distribution, and delivery of products. It helps minimize costs, reduce lead times, improve customer satisfaction, and drive business growth. By effectively managing the flow of materials, information, and funds across the entire supply chain, organizations can gain a competitive advantage in the marketplace.

Product Sustainability

Product sustainability refers to the practice of designing, producing, and managing products in a way that minimizes their negative environmental, social, and economic impacts throughout their lifecycle. It involves considering the entire product lifecycle, from raw material extraction and manufacturing to distribution, use, and disposal. Product sustainability aims to create products that are environmentally responsible, socially beneficial, and economically viable. In the context of product management, product sustainability encompasses various aspects. Firstly, it involves incorporating sustainability principles and criteria into product development and design processes. Product managers need to consider the environmental impact of the materials used, the energy consumption during production, and the potential for recycling or reusing the product at the end of its life. By designing products with sustainability in mind, product managers can reduce the overall environmental footprint and ensure that the products align with corporate sustainability objectives. Secondly, product sustainability entails implementing sustainable manufacturing practices. This includes adopting energy-efficient processes, reducing waste generation, and minimizing the use of hazardous substances. Product managers need to work closely with manufacturing teams to ensure that sustainable practices are followed throughout the production process, from sourcing raw materials to packaging the final product. By implementing sustainable manufacturing practices, companies can reduce their environmental impact and improve resource efficiency. Thirdly, product sustainability involves considering the social and ethical implications of a product. This includes ensuring fair labor practices throughout the supply chain, promoting diversity and inclusion, and respecting human rights. Product managers need to collaborate with suppliers and partners to ensure that the products are produced under ethical conditions and that workers are treated fairly. By prioritizing social responsibility, companies can build trust and enhance their reputation among customers and stakeholders. In conclusion, product sustainability in the context of product management involves designing, producing, and managing products in a way that minimizes their negative impacts on the environment, society, and economy. It requires considering the entire product lifecycle, incorporating sustainability principles into product development, implementing sustainable manufacturing practices, and addressing social and ethical considerations. By embracing product sustainability, companies can contribute to a more sustainable future while also meeting customer demands and staying competitive in the market.

Product Target Audience

A product target audience refers to the specific group of people for whom a product is designed and marketed. It comprises the individuals who are most likely to have a need or desire for the product, and are therefore most likely to purchase it. Identifying and understanding the target audience is a crucial aspect of product management. Product managers conduct extensive market research and analysis to determine the characteristics and preferences of the target audience. This includes factors such as demographics (age, gender, income, etc.), psychographics (interests, values, lifestyle, etc.), and behaviors (buying habits, usage patterns, etc.). By gathering and analyzing this information, product managers gain insights into the needs, wants, and motivations of the target audience.

Product Technical Support

174

Product Technical Support refers to the assistance provided to customers regarding technical issues or concerns related to a specific product. It is a vital component of product management, ensuring customer satisfaction and enhancing the overall product experience. Product Technical Support involves a team of knowledgeable professionals who possess deep expertise in the product and can effectively address customer queries and concerns. This support team acts as a bridge between the customers and the development team, facilitating effective communication and problem-solving.

Product Telemetry Analytics

Product Telemetry Analytics is a method of collecting, analyzing, and interpreting data related to the usage and performance of a product. It involves the systematic tracking and measurement of various metrics and parameters that provide insights into how a product is being used by customers, as well as its overall performance and effectiveness. The purpose of Product Telemetry Analytics is to inform product managers and teams about the real-world usage patterns and behaviors of their products. By collecting and analyzing data from various sources, such as user interactions, system logs, and customer feedback, product managers can gain valuable insights into how customers are using their products, the problems they encounter, and the features they find most valuable.

Product Telemetry Dashboards

Product telemetry dashboards are analytical tools used by product managers to measure and monitor the performance and usage of a product. These dashboards provide real-time, visual insights and metrics that help product managers make data-driven decisions, optimize product features and functionality, and improve overall user experience. The primary purpose of product telemetry dashboards is to collect, analyze, and visualize data related to how customers are interacting with a product. This includes tracking key performance indicators (KPIs), such as user engagement, conversion rates, customer satisfaction, and revenue generated. By monitoring these metrics, product managers can gain valuable insights into the product's strengths, weaknesses, and areas for improvement. Product telemetry dashboards typically display data in the form of charts, graphs, and tables, allowing product managers to easily interpret and understand the information. These visualizations can include metrics like user retention, user acquisition, feature adoption rate, and customer feedback ratings. Product managers can also segment the data based on various demographic and behavioral attributes to gain a deeper understanding of different user groups and their preferences. In addition to monitoring the product's performance, telemetry dashboards can also help product managers identify and diagnose any issues or bugs that users may be experiencing. By tracking error rates, response times, and other performance metrics, product managers can quickly identify and address any technical issues, ensuring a smooth and seamless user experience. Overall, product telemetry dashboards play a crucial role in product management by providing a comprehensive and data-driven view of a product's performance. By leveraging these insights, product managers can make informed decisions, drive product improvements, and ultimately deliver a better experience for their customers.

Product Telemetry Data

Product telemetry data refers to the information and insights that are collected from a product in use. It is a form of data analytics that involves tracking and analyzing various metrics related to a product's performance, usage, and user behavior. The data is typically collected automatically through the use of sensors, sensors, monitoring tools, and other data collection mechanisms embedded within the product. This data provides valuable insights into how customers are using a product, what features they are using most frequently or not using at all, how often they encounter issues or errors, and other usage patterns. It can help product managers make informed decisions and improvements to enhance the user experience, drive product adoption, and increase customer satisfaction.

Product Test Automation Best Practices

Product Test Automation Best Practices refers to the recommended methods, techniques, and guidelines followed in automating the testing process of a product throughout its development lifecycle. It involves using automated tools and scripts to execute tests, validate product functionalities, and assess its overall quality. Automation in product testing plays a crucial role in enhancing efficiency, productivity, and accuracy. By automating repetitive and time-consuming test cases, product teams can focus on critical aspects of testing, such as exploratory testing and test case design. It also helps in reducing the number of manual errors and allows scalability, especially when dealing with complex or large-scale software applications.

Product Test Automation Frameworks

A Product Test Automation Framework is a structured set of guidelines, tools, and components that enable product managers to automate the testing process of their products. It provides a systematic approach to creating and executing automated test scripts, allowing for efficient and comprehensive testing of various product functionalities. The main purpose of a Test Automation Framework is to streamline the testing process, improve test coverage, and enhance the overall quality of the product. This is achieved by providing a standardized set of practices, methodologies, and tools that enable product managers to automate repetitive and time-consuming testing tasks. The framework typically consists of various components, such as libraries, modules, utilities, and test scripts, which are designed to be reusable and modular. These components can be easily integrated and customized to suit the specific testing requirements of the product and its different features. By leveraging a Test Automation Framework, product managers can benefit from increased productivity, reduced testing time, and improved accuracy in identifying and fixing bugs or issues. It allows for the automation of regression testing, functional testing, performance testing, and other types of testing, ensuring that the product meets the desired quality standards. Additionally, a Test Automation Framework facilitates collaboration among different stakeholders involved in the testing process. It provides a common platform and set of guidelines that enable effective communication and coordination between product managers, developers, testers, and other team members. This encourages a cross-functional approach to testing and helps in identifying and resolving issues at an early stage of the development cycle. In conclusion, a Product Test Automation Framework is an essential tool for product managers to automate the testing process and ensure the delivery of high-quality products. It offers a structured and systematic approach to testing, improves efficiency, and enhances collaboration among team members. By leveraging a Test Automation Framework, product managers can optimize their testing efforts and deliver reliable and robust products to the market.

Product Test Automation Tools

Product Test Automation Tools refer to software applications that are used in the field of product management to automate the process of testing and quality assurance for a product. These tools are designed to streamline and accelerate the testing process, enabling product teams to identify and fix issues faster, and ultimately deliver high-quality products to the market. Product test automation tools offer a range of capabilities that help product managers automate various aspects of the testing process. These include test case generation, test execution, result analysis, and reporting. By automating these tasks, product teams can reduce the time and effort required for testing, enabling them to focus on other critical aspects of product development.

Product Test Automation

Product Test Automation refers to the process of automating the testing of a product throughout its development lifecycle, using software tools and frameworks to execute test cases and validate the product's functionality, performance, and quality. This automation involves the use of scripts or code to simulate user interactions and test various features and functionalities of the product. Test automation plays a critical role in product management as it helps streamline the testing process, increase efficiency, and improve the overall quality of the product. By automating repetitive and time-consuming test scenarios, product teams are able to focus their efforts on more complex and high-value testing activities, such as exploratory testing and risk-based testing.

Product Test Backup And Recovery

Product Test Backup and Recovery is a critical component of Product Management, which involves the process of testing and ensuring the effectiveness of backup and recovery systems for a product. This process ensures that in the event of a system failure or data loss, the product can be restored and continue to function properly without any major disruptions. During product development, it is crucial to have a reliable backup and recovery system in place to protect the valuable data and assets associated with the product. This includes backing up important files, configurations, databases, and other elements that are essential for the product's functionality. The backup process creates copies of these elements, which can be used to restore the product to a previous state in case of any failures or errors. The recovery aspect of the process involves the restoration of the product from the backup copies. This includes reinstalling the necessary files, configurations, and databases to bring the product back to its working state. The recovery process should be efficient and reliable, ensuring minimal downtime and loss of data. Product Test Backup and Recovery plays a crucial role in minimizing the impact of system failures and data loss. It helps to mitigate the risks associated with product development and ensures the continuity of the product's functionality. By regularly testing the backup and recovery systems, Product Managers can identify any potential weaknesses or issues and address them proactively to avoid any potential disruptions. In summary, Product Test Backup and Recovery is the process of testing and ensuring the effectiveness of backup and recovery systems for a product. It involves creating backup copies of essential elements and restoring the product from these backups in case of system failures or data loss. This process is vital for minimizing disruptions, protecting valuable data, and ensuring the continuity of a product's functionality.

Product Test Case Management

Product Test Case Management is the process of organizing, tracking, and managing the test cases that are used to verify the functionality and quality of a product during its development and release phases. It involves creating and documenting test cases, assigning them to specific test cycles or sprints, executing the tests, and tracking the results and defects. Test cases are detailed step-by-step instructions that define how to verify a specific feature or functionality of the product. They typically include preconditions, test inputs, expected outcomes, and any specific test data or configurations that need to be set up. By organizing test cases in a structured manner, product teams can ensure thorough test coverage and facilitate efficient testing processes.

Product Test Cases

Product Test Cases are a set of specific conditions or scenarios that are designed to test the functionality, usability, and performance of a product. They are an essential part of the product management process and are used to ensure that the product meets the intended requirements and functions as expected. Product Test Cases serve as a guide for the testing team, outlining the steps and expected outcomes for each test. They help identify any defects or issues with the product and provide a systematic approach to validating its quality and suitability for release.

Product Test Cloud Integration

A product test cloud integration refers to the process of connecting a cloud-based testing platform with a product management system in order to automate and streamline the testing and quality assurance processes for a product. This integration allows product managers to seamlessly manage the testing and quality assurance activities for their products within the same system they use to track and manage the development and release of the product. By integrating the product management system with the testing platform, product managers can have real-time visibility into the status and results of the testing activities, enabling them to make informed decisions about the product's release and quality.

Product Test Compliance

Product Test Compliance in the context of Product Management refers to the evaluation and verification process undertaken to ensure that a product meets all relevant legal, regulatory, and industry standards or requirements. It is an essential aspect of bringing a product to market and maintaining its ongoing compliance throughout its lifecycle. Product Test Compliance involves conducting various tests and assessments to assess the product's safety, performance, durability, and other relevant attributes. These tests are usually conducted by accredited third-party testing laboratories or internal quality assurance teams within the organization. The specific tests and standards required vary depending on the nature of the product and the market it is intended for.

Product Test Containerization

Containerization in the context of Product Management refers to the process of encapsulating an application and its dependencies into a single, isolated unit known as a container. A container provides a lightweight and portable environment that can be easily deployed and run consistently across different operating systems and infrastructures. In this approach, the application and all its required components, such as libraries, frameworks, and runtime environments, are packaged together within the container. This includes everything needed to run the application, ensuring that it operates reliably and consistently regardless of the underlying infrastructure.

Product Test Continuous Delivery (CD)

Continuous Delivery (CD) is a software development practice in the context of Product Management that focuses on delivering product updates and enhancements to end users in a rapid and frequent manner. It involves automating the entire software release process, from code development to deployment, in order to ensure a smooth and reliable delivery of new features and improvements. CD is built upon the principles of continuous integration and continuous deployment, but goes a step further by emphasizing the importance of delivering high-quality software increments to users at any given moment. Unlike traditional software release models, where updates are typically batched and deployed in larger intervals, CD enables product teams to release new features and bug fixes on a continuous basis.

Product Test Continuous Integration (CI)

Product Test Continuous Integration (CI) is a process in Product Management that involves automating the testing of a product's features and functionalities as part of the overall development and deployment strategy. It is a crucial aspect of the product development lifecycle as it allows for a seamless integration of new code changes and ensures the stability and quality of the product. In the context of Product Management, CI focuses on continuously verifying and validating the product's functionality, performance, and user experience. It involves implementing a systematic approach to test and review the product at various stages of the development cycle, from code commits to deployment.

Product Test Continuous Monitoring

Product test continuous monitoring is a practice in product management that involves consistently evaluating and analyzing the performance and quality of a product throughout its development lifecycle. It involves implementing a set of metrics and KPIs to measure how well the product is meeting its intended goals and objectives, and using this data to make informed decisions for future improvements and iterations. Continuous monitoring allows product managers to identify potential issues or areas of improvement early on in the product development process, ensuring that the product meets or exceeds customer expectations and remains competitive in the market. By regularly gathering data and feedback, product managers can detect any deviations from the desired outcomes and take appropriate actions to address them.

Product Test Coverage Analysis

Product Test Coverage Analysis is a systematic and comprehensive process in product management that evaluates the extent to which a product, feature, or component has been tested against the predetermined requirements, risks, and quality objectives. It assesses the sufficiency and effectiveness of test efforts in terms of covering the various aspects and functionalities of the product. The goal of Product Test Coverage Analysis is to ensure that all critical product requirements and scenarios are adequately tested, minimizing the likelihood of undetected defects and improving the overall quality and reliability of the product. It helps product managers identify potential gaps in test coverage and make informed decisions on prioritizing and allocating testing resources.

Product Test Dashboards

Product Test Dashboards, in the context of Product Management, refer to visual representations of data that provide insights into the performance and effectiveness of product tests. These dashboards are used to monitor, analyze, and communicate the results of various tests conducted on a product, helping product managers make informed decisions and improvements. The main purpose of Product Test Dashboards is to provide a centralized and easily understandable view of the test outcomes, allowing product managers to evaluate the success and impact of different product initiatives. The dashboards typically display key metrics, such as user engagement, conversion rates, retention rates, and customer satisfaction scores, among others.

Product Test Data Analytics

Product test data analytics is a process used in product management to analyze and interpret data collected from product testing activities. It involves the systematic examination of various data points and metrics to gain insights and make informed decisions about a product's performance, quality, and usability. The goal of product test data analytics is to extract meaningful information from test data to inform product development and improvement efforts. This data can include feedback from user testing, bug reports, customer surveys, and other sources of information related to the product's performance and user experience. By analyzing product test data, product managers can identify patterns, trends, and issues that may impact the product's success in the market. This analysis can provide valuable insights into the product's strengths and weaknesses, helping product managers make data-driven decisions about product features, enhancements, and future development efforts. Product test data analytics involves various techniques and tools to process and analyze the data. This can include statistical analysis, data visualization, and predictive modeling to uncover patterns, correlations, and potential areas for improvement. By leveraging these techniques, product managers can gain a deeper understanding of the product's performance, user satisfaction, and potential areas for optimization. Product test data analytics also plays a crucial role in assessing the impact of product changes or updates. By comparing test data before and after implementing changes, product managers can measure the effectiveness of the updates and evaluate whether they address the identified issues or improve the product's performance. In conclusion, product test data analytics is an essential component of product management that enables product managers to make informed decisions based on the analysis and interpretation of product testing data. By leveraging this process, product managers can gain insights into the product's performance, identify areas for improvement, and make data-driven decisions to enhance the overall product experience.

Product Test Data Anonymization

Product Test Data Anonymization refers to the process of removing any personal or sensitive information from the data collected during product testing, in order to protect the privacy and confidentiality of individuals involved. This is a crucial step in product management, as it ensures that any data shared or analyzed during the testing phase is stripped of any identifiable information, minimizing the risk of a data breach or misuse. During the product testing phase, various types of data are collected, including user feedback, usage patterns, and performance metrics. This data is invaluable for product managers, as it helps them understand how the product is being used, identify any issues or areas for improvement, and make informed decisions on future development. However, this data can also contain personal or sensitive information, such as personally identifiable information (PII), login credentials, or financial data. The process of anonymization involves several key steps. First, any personally identifiable information (PII) is removed or masked, such as names, contact details, or social security numbers. This ensures that individuals cannot be directly identified from the data. Additionally, any other information that could potentially be used to identify individuals, such as unique identifiers or IP addresses, is either removed or generalized to a broader level. Furthermore, product test data anonymization may also involve the removal of any sensitive information that is not directly linked to individuals but could still pose a risk if disclosed. This includes proprietary or confidential information, trade secrets, or any other data that could harm the company or

179

individuals if exposed. The goal is to ensure that the data being shared or analyzed is not only anonymous but also free from any potentially harmful information. By anonymizing product test data, product managers can strike a balance between utilizing valuable insights gained from testing and protecting the privacy and security of individuals. This allows for more accurate analysis and decision-making, as the focus remains on the product's performance and user experience rather than any specific individuals or their personal information. It also helps companies comply with data protection regulations and build trust with their users by demonstrating a commitment to data privacy and security.

Product Test Data Archiving

Product Test Data Archiving refers to the process of systematically storing and managing the data generated during the testing stage of a product's development. This data includes test results, defects, logs, and other related information that is collected during the testing phase. Archiving this data is essential for several reasons. Firstly, it allows product managers to have a historical record of the testing process for future reference. This can be useful when analyzing the product's performance, identifying patterns or trends, and improving the testing process in future iterations.

Product Test Data Classification

Product Test Data Classification refers to the categorization and organization of data collected from product testing activities in the field of product management. When managing a product, it is essential to conduct various tests to gather information about its performance, usability, reliability, and other important factors. These tests generate a significant amount of data, which needs to be classified to make it easily understandable and actionable.

Product Test Data Deletion

Product Test Data Deletion refers to the process of removing or erasing all the test data that has been generated and collected during the testing phase of a product development cycle. This data includes various artifacts such as test cases, test scripts, test plans, test results, and any other supplementary documents or files related to the testing process. The purpose of deleting test data is to ensure the confidentiality, integrity, and security of the product being tested. It is crucial to eliminate any traces of test data that might contain sensitive or proprietary information about the product, its functionality, or any potential vulnerabilities identified during the testing phase.

Product Test Data Encryption

Product test data encryption is a process in product management where sensitive test data is encoded or transformed using encryption algorithms in order to protect it from unauthorized access or use. This encryption ensures that the test data remains confidential and secure, reducing the risk of unauthorized usage, tampering, or theft. Test data encryption is an essential aspect of product management, particularly in industries where sensitive or confidential information is involved. It is necessary to ensure that the information collected during product testing, such as user data, financial information, or proprietary algorithms, is not exposed to hackers, competitors, or any unauthorized individuals. The process of test data encryption involves converting the original data into an unreadable format, using encryption algorithms and keys. This conversion process makes it extremely difficult for unauthorized individuals to decipher or access the original data. Only those with the appropriate encryption keys can decrypt and access the test data. This provides an added layer of security, even if the data is intercepted or breached. There are various encryption algorithms that can be used for test data encryption, such as Advanced Encryption Standard (AES), Triple Data Encryption Standard (3DES), or RSA. These algorithms employ mathematical functions to scramble the test data, making it nearly impossible to reverse-engineer without the encryption key. Product managers must ensure that proper encryption protocols and standards are implemented during the product testing phase. This includes securely storing encryption keys, regularly updating and rotating keys, and managing access controls to restrict unauthorized decryption. Additionally, product managers need to consider the performance impact of encryption on the testing process, as encryption can introduce additional processing overhead. In conclusion, product test data encryption is a critical aspect of product management to protect sensitive information during the testing phase. It involves converting the test data into an unreadable format using encryption algorithms and keys, making it difficult for unauthorized individuals to access or decipher the data. By implementing proper encryption protocols and standards, product managers can ensure the security and confidentiality of sensitive test data.

Product Test Data Generation

Product test data generation refers to the process of creating data sets or scenarios that are used to test the functionality, performance, and usability of a product or software application. It involves generating specific data inputs or test cases that simulate real-world scenarios to evaluate the product's behavior and performance under various conditions. Product managers use test data generation as a critical step in the product development lifecycle to ensure the quality, reliability, and effectiveness of the software or product being developed. By generating diverse and realistic test data, product managers can verify if the product meets the requirements, identifies potential defects or issues, and validates its overall functionality.

Product Test Data Governance

Product Test Data Governance refers to the process of managing and governing the data that is collected during product testing within a product management framework. It involves establishing policies, procedures, and guidelines to ensure the proper collection, storage, usage, and disposal of test data in a controlled and secure manner. The primary objective of Product Test Data Governance is to ensure the quality, reliability, and integrity of the data used for testing new products or features. It requires the implementation of robust data management processes, including data collection, storage, access control, and documentation, to support the product development lifecycle.

Product Test Data Loss Prevention (DLP)

Data Loss Prevention (DLP) is a product testing methodology used in the field of Product Management to ensure the security and protection of sensitive data within an organization. It involves the implementation of controls, policies, and technologies to prevent unauthorized access, disclosure, or loss of critical information. The primary goal of DLP is to identify, monitor, and protect sensitive data from being leaked, either intentionally or unintentionally, through various channels such as email, file transfers, printouts, removable media, and network communications. By analyzing data at rest, in motion, and in use, DLP solutions can detect and prevent data breaches, thereby avoiding financial loss, compliance violations, reputational damage, and legal implications for the organization. DLP product testing typically involves the following key activities: 1. Data classification and policy definition: This step involves identifying and categorizing sensitive data based on its importance and the level of protection required. Policies are then defined to govern the handling and transmission of this data to ensure compliance with regulations and internal security protocols. 2. Data discovery and monitoring: DLP solutions employ various techniques, such as content inspection, fingerprinting, and data loss risk analysis, to identify and locate sensitive data within the organization's infrastructure. Continuous monitoring helps in detecting any unauthorized attempts to access or transfer this data. 3. Incident response and remediation: When a potential data breach or policy violation is detected, DLP systems generate alerts and trigger appropriate actions, such as blocking or quarantining data, notifying stakeholders, or initiating investigation processes. Incident response plans are implemented to promptly address and mitigate any security incidents. 4. Reporting and compliance: DLP product testing includes the generation of comprehensive reports and audit trails to demonstrate compliance with regulatory requirements and internal policies. These reports provide insights into data usage patterns, policy effectiveness, and potential vulnerabilities, assisting in the formulation of future security strategies. In conclusion, Product Test Data Loss Prevention (DLP) is a vital component of Product Management that focuses on safeguarding sensitive data from unauthorized access, disclosure, or loss. By employing a combination of data classification, monitoring, incident response, and reporting, DLP solutions help organizations mitigate data security risks and ensure compliance with relevant regulations.

Product Test Data Management

Product Test Data Management refers to the process of collecting, organizing, and maintaining data related to the testing of products within a product management context. It involves the management of all relevant data that is generated throughout the product testing lifecycle, from planning and execution to analysis and reporting. At its core, Product Test Data Management aims to ensure that test data is accurate, accessible, and readily available for analysis and decision-making. It includes various activities such as data capture, storage, transformation, integration, and retrieval, with the ultimate goal of providing product managers with reliable and up-to-date information to make informed decisions regarding the development, quality, and market-readiness of a product.

Product Test Data Masking

Product Test Data Masking is a systematic process used in product management to obfuscate or anonymize sensitive data within a test environment. It involves replacing the actual data with synthetic or modified data that resembles the original information but does not reveal any confidential or personally identifiable details. The purpose of product test data masking is to ensure data privacy and security during testing and development, without compromising the overall functionality and authenticity of the product. During the product development lifecycle, various test environments are created to simulate real-world scenarios and evaluate the performance, functionality, and reliability of the product. These test environments usually consist of databases, servers, applications, or systems that contain sensitive data, such as customer information, financial records, or organizational resources. To maintain compliance with data protection regulations and safeguard customer privacy, it becomes crucial to mask or scramble this sensitive data in the test environment. The process of product test data masking involves several steps. Firstly, the data that needs to be masked is identified, which typically includes personally identifiable information (PII), financial details, social security numbers, or any other sensitive information that could be used to identify individuals or organizations. Once identified, data masking rules and techniques are applied to transform the original data into a masked version. This can involve techniques such as scrambling, encryption, tokenization, or substitution to alter the data while preserving its format or integrity. The masked test data is then used in the test environment, where it undergoes rigorous testing and analysis. By using masked data, product managers and developers can ensure that the application or system performs as expected, without exposing real customer data to potential vulnerabilities or breaches. Product test data masking provides a secure environment for testing, reducing the risk of data leaks, unauthorized access, or misuse of sensitive information. In conclusion, product test data masking is a vital aspect of product management that allows organizations to maintain data privacy and security while conducting thorough testing of their products. It ensures that sensitive information is protected during the testing process, reducing the potential risks associated with data exposure. By implementing effective data masking techniques, product managers can confidently test and enhance their products, ultimately providing a more secure and reliable experience for their customers.

Product Test Data Migration

Product test data migration refers to the process of transferring or moving test data from one system or environment to another. It involves the extraction of test data from the source system, its transformation and cleansing, and finally loading it into the target system or environment. This type of data migration is specifically focused on the test data used in product management. Test data is essential for verifying the functionality, performance, and quality of a product. It allows product managers and testers to simulate real-world scenarios and identify any issues or bugs before the product is released to the market.

Product Test Data Privacy

Data privacy refers to the protection of personal and sensitive information that is collected, processed, and stored by a product or service. In the context of product management, product test data privacy refers to the measures and practices in place to safeguard the data generated during the testing phase of a product's development lifecycle. Product test data includes various types of information, such as user interactions, system logs, error reports, and performance metrics. This data is crucial for identifying and resolving issues, improving the product's performance and user experience, and validating its functionality and stability. Ensuring product test data privacy involves several key aspects: 1. Data anonymization: Before sharing or analyzing test data, personally identifiable information (PII) should be masked or anonymized to prevent any potential identification of individuals. This includes removing or encrypting sensitive data such as names, contact details, and account information. 2. Secure storage: Test data should be stored securely, both during and after the testing phase. This means that adequate security measures should be in place to protect against unauthorized access, data breaches, or loss of data. These measures may include encryption, access controls, firewalls, and regular data backups. 3. Limited access: Only authorized personnel should have access to the test data, and this access should be strictly controlled and monitored. This helps to prevent data leaks or misuse by unauthorized individuals. 4. Clear data retention policies: Test data should not be stored indefinitely. Clear policies and procedures should be in place to determine how long test data should be retained and when it should be securely deleted or disposed of. 5. Compliance with regulations: Product test data privacy should comply with relevant laws and regulations, such as the General Data Protection Regulation (GDPR) in the European Union or the California Consumer Privacy Act (CCPA) in the United States. This includes obtaining consent for data collection and providing individuals with the necessary rights and control over their data. By ensuring robust product test data privacy practices, product managers can not only protect the privacy and confidentiality of user information but also build trust with their customers. This trust is vital for the success and adoption of the product, as it demonstrates a commitment to respecting user privacy and safeguarding their personal data.

Product Test Data Retention

Product Test Data Retention refers to the practice of storing and maintaining the data collected during product testing activities over a specific period of time for future reference and analysis. It involves archiving and preserving various types of data such as test plans, test scripts, test cases, test results, logs, and other related documents or artifacts that are generated during the testing process. The purpose of retaining product test data is to have a historical record of the testing activities and outcomes, which can be beneficial for multiple reasons: 1. Analysis and Improvement: Retaining test data allows product managers and development teams to assess the effectiveness of their testing strategies, identify patterns or trends, and gain insights into the product's performance and quality. It enables them to make data-driven decisions to improve the testing process and overall product quality. 2. Regulatory Compliance: Depending on the industry or domain, product testing may need to comply with certain regulatory requirements or standards. Keeping the test data on record assists in demonstrating compliance with these regulations, facilitating audits, and ensuring accountability. 3. Bug Tracking and Resolution: Test data retention aids in investigating and fixing software defects or issues found during testing. It provides a repository of information that can help developers pinpoint the root causes of bugs, reproduce them, and implement necessary fixes or enhancements. 4. Knowledge Transfer: Retained test data can serve as a valuable knowledge base for future product releases. It allows new team members or stakeholders to understand the product's testing history, test coverage, and previous issues encountered. This knowledge transfer ensures continuity in testing and prevents the repetition of past mistakes. Overall, the practice of product test data retention is crucial for effective product management, quality assurance, and continuous improvement. It helps maximize the value derived from testing efforts and provides a foundation for informed decision-making and problem-solving throughout the product lifecycle.

Product Test Data Security

Product test data security refers to the measures and protocols put in place to protect the confidentiality, integrity, and availability of data generated during the testing phase of a product within the context of product management. Test data security aims to ensure that sensitive information such as customer data, intellectual property, and proprietary information are safeguarded from unauthorized access, loss, or misuse during the testing process. It involves implementing appropriate controls and mechanisms to mitigate risks associated with data breaches, data leaks, or data corruption.

Product Test DevOps Integration

A product test DevOps integration refers to the practice of incorporating product testing into the overall DevOps process to ensure the quality and reliability of a software product. DevOps, short for development and operations, is a methodology that emphasizes collaboration, communication, and automation between software developers and IT operations teams. It aims to streamline and automate the software development and delivery process, enabling faster and more frequent releases. In the context of product management, a product test DevOps integration involves integrating product testing activities seamlessly into the DevOps workflow. This integration allows product managers to ensure that the software being developed meets the desired quality standards and provides a seamless user experience. It also helps identify and address any issues or defects early in the development cycle, reducing the cost and effort of fixing them later.

Product Test Disaster Recovery Planning

Product Test Disaster Recovery Planning refers to the process of developing a comprehensive plan to mitigate the impact of potential disasters on the testing activities carried out on a product. In the context of Product Management, disaster recovery planning for product testing is essential to ensure the continuity and effectiveness of the testing process, even in the face of unforeseen events or disruptions. The goal of disaster recovery planning is to minimize the impact of such events on the product testing lifecycle, ensuring that it can continue to progress smoothly with minimal downtime or loss of data. A disaster in this context could be any event that disrupts the normal functioning of the testing process, such as system failures, data corruption, natural disasters, or even human error. These events can have significant consequences, including the loss of critical testing data, delays in the testing timeline, and overall disruption to the product development cycle. Product Test Disaster Recovery Planning involves several key steps. Firstly, a thorough risk assessment is conducted to identify potential vulnerabilities and threats to the testing process. This includes evaluating the current infrastructure, systems, and tools used for testing, as well as identifying potential points of failure. Based on the findings of the risk assessment, a detailed plan is developed to address potential disasters. This plan outlines predefined actions and processes to be followed in the event of a disaster, such as backup and restoration procedures, alternative testing environments or tools, and communication protocols. The disaster recovery plan is regularly reviewed and updated to ensure its effectiveness and relevance over time. This may involve conducting regular audits of the testing infrastructure, identifying new risks or vulnerabilities, and incorporating emerging technologies or industry best practices into the plan. By having a well-defined disaster recovery plan in place, Product Management teams can minimize the impact of potential disasters on the testing process. This ensures that critical product testing activities can continue without major disruptions, reducing the risk of delays or compromise in product quality.

Product Test Disaster Recovery

Product Test Disaster Recovery is a crucial aspect of Product Management that involves implementing plans and strategies to recover and restore the functionality and integrity of a product in the event of a disaster or unforeseen issue during the testing phase. It focuses on ensuring that the product remains operational and minimizes downtime, ensuring that any potential setbacks or failures do not negatively impact the overall testing process. The primary objective of Product Test Disaster Recovery is to develop and implement a comprehensive plan that outlines the steps and processes to be followed in the event of a test disaster. This includes identifying potential risks and vulnerabilities that could lead to a disaster, such as infrastructure failures, data breaches, or system malfunctions. Once the risks are identified, the product manager works closely with the testing team to develop contingency plans, establish recovery procedures, and allocate resources to support the recovery efforts. To effectively execute Product Test Disaster Recovery, the product manager must have a deep understanding of the product's architecture, infrastructure, and dependencies. This includes knowledge of the testing environment, test data, and tools used in the product testing process. By analyzing and documenting these critical components, the product manager can create a recovery strategy tailored to the unique needs and requirements of the product. Product Test Disaster Recovery involves conducting regular risk assessments and evaluations to identify potential vulnerabilities and gaps in the recovery plan. This helps in proactively addressing any issues or shortcomings, reducing the chances of a disaster and enhancing the overall resilience of the product testing process. In the event of a disaster, the product manager coordinates with the relevant stakeholders, including the testing team, IT department, and other support teams, to execute the recovery plan. This may involve deploying backup systems, restoring data from backups,

184

addressing security breaches, or implementing alternative testing strategies. Overall, Product Test Disaster Recovery plays a critical role in ensuring the continuity and success of product testing efforts. By proactively preparing for potential disasters and implementing robust recovery procedures, product managers can minimize disruptions, mitigate risks, and maintain the integrity and functionality of the product during the testing phase.

Product Test Environment Provisioning

Product Test Environment Provisioning refers to the process of setting up and configuring the necessary infrastructure, resources, and tools required for testing a product within a controlled and isolated environment that closely resembles the production environment. This environment is specifically created to test the functionality, performance, and reliability of a product before it is released to customers. The provisioning of a product test environment involves several important steps. Firstly, the necessary hardware and software are acquired and installed. This includes servers, networking equipment, operating systems, databases, and any other software applications or tools that are required for testing. The environment should ideally reflect the production environment as closely as possible to ensure accurate testing results. Once the hardware and software components are set up, the next step is to configure and optimize the environment. This involves setting up network connectivity, configuring firewalls and security settings, and tuning the system to simulate real-world conditions. It may also involve setting up virtual machines or containers to mimic different user scenarios or test different configurations. After the environment is properly configured, the product testing team can start deploying the product and performing various types of tests. This may include functional testing to verify that the product meets the specified requirements, performance testing to assess how the product performs under different loads and conditions, and security testing to identify any vulnerabilities or weaknesses. The test environment should provide tools and resources to facilitate these tests, such as test scripts, test data, and monitoring tools. Throughout the testing phase, the provisioning of the test environment ensures that the environment remains stable and consistent. This includes managing and resolving any issues or defects that arise, monitoring the environment for any performance or security issues, and ensuring that the environment is always available and accessible to the testing team. Continuous maintenance and monitoring are crucial to ensuring accurate and reliable test results. In summary, product test environment provisioning is the process of setting up and configuring a controlled and isolated environment for testing a product. It involves acquiring and installing the necessary hardware and software, configuring and optimizing the environment to mimic the production environment, and providing resources and tools for testing. The provisioning of the test environment ensures accurate testing and helps in identifying and resolving any issues before the product is released to customers.

Product Test Environments

Product Test Environments, in the context of Product Management, refer to controlled, scalable, and isolated environments where products are tested to ensure their functionality, performance, and compatibility before they are deployed to production environments. These test environments simulate real-world conditions and enable product teams to identify and fix any issues, bugs, or shortcomings of the product, ensuring its reliability and effectiveness. Test environments are essential for product testing as they provide a separate and secure space to evaluate the product without impacting the live system or customer experience. They enable product teams to thoroughly test various features, scenarios, and interactions to ensure the product meets the desired requirements and serves its intended purpose efficiently.

Product Test Execution Tools

A product test execution tool, in the context of Product Management, refers to a software application or platform designed to facilitate the testing and evaluation of products throughout their development lifecycle. These tools assist product managers in efficiently coordinating and conducting various testing activities, including both functional and non-functional tests, to ensure the product meets the desired quality standards and customer requirements. Product test execution tools typically offer a range of features and capabilities that enable product teams to streamline their testing processes. These may include test case management, test execution tracking, defect tracking, test automation, and reporting functionalities. By leveraging these tools, product managers can effectively manage and monitor the testing activities, track the progress, and ensure the timely resolution of defects and issues that arise during the testing phase.

Product Test Execution

Product Test Execution refers to the process of conducting and monitoring the tests and experiments that are designed to evaluate the performance, functionality, and usability of a product. It involves the systematic execution of test cases and the collection of data and feedback to assess the product's quality and alignment with user requirements. The purpose of product test execution is to validate and verify the product's functionality, reliability, and performance against the expected standards and specifications. It aims to identify any defects, bugs, or usability issues that may arise during the product's usage by end-users. By conducting thorough and comprehensive tests, product managers can identify and rectify any issues before the product is launched in the market.

Product Test High Availability

High Availability (HA) testing is the process of evaluating the functionality and capabilities of a product under different scenarios to ensure it can deliver a consistently reliable and uninterrupted experience to its users. In the context of product management, HA testing is crucial to assess the product's ability to maintain its services and minimize downtime in the face of failures, disruptions, or other unforeseen events that may occur. During HA testing, various aspects of the product's availability are examined, including its ability to recover quickly and automatically from failures, its resilience to system or infrastructure issues, and its capacity to handle high volumes of traffic or transactions. The primary goal of this testing is to identify any weaknesses or vulnerabilities in the product's architecture, design, or implementation that may impact its availability or performance.

Product Test Incident Response

Product Test Incident Response in the context of Product Management refers to the planned and systematic approach taken by a product management team to identify, escalate, and resolve incidents that occur during product testing. When conducting product tests, incidents may occur that can have an impact on the overall functionality, reliability, or usability of the product. These incidents could range from minor issues to critical faults that can hinder the product's performance or pose risks to users. Therefore, having a structured incident response process is crucial to ensure that these incidents are effectively managed and resolved. Product Test Incident Response typically involves the following steps: 1. Identification: The first step is to identify and classify incidents based on their severity and impact on the product. This requires thorough monitoring and analysis of test results and feedback from testers or users. Incidents can be categorized as low, medium, or high severity based on their potential to cause harm or disrupt the product's functionality. 2. Escalation: Once incidents are identified, they need to be escalated to the relevant stakeholders, such as product managers, developers, or quality assurance teams. Clear communication channels and escalation procedures should be established to ensure that incidents are addressed promptly and by the appropriate individuals or teams. 3. Investigation: After escalation, a thorough investigation of the incident is conducted to determine its root cause. This may involve gathering additional information, replicating the issue, or conducting further tests. The purpose of the investigation is to understand the underlying factors contributing to the incident and assess its potential impact on the product. 4. Resolution: Based on the investigation findings, the product management team formulates a plan to resolve the incident. This may involve developing patches or fixes, updating product documentation, or implementing process changes to prevent similar incidents in the future. The resolution plan should be communicated to all relevant stakeholders, and the progress of the resolution should be tracked and monitored until the incident is fully resolved. 5. Documentation and Learning: Finally, it is essential to document all incidents, their resolutions, and the lessons learned from them. This information can serve as a valuable resource for future product testing and development efforts, helping to improve the overall quality and reliability of the product.

Product Test Infrastructure As Code (IaC)

Product Test Infrastructure as Code (IaC) is a methodology used in Product Management to automate the provisioning and management of test infrastructure resources, such as servers, databases, and network configurations, through the use of code. With IaC, Product Managers can define their test infrastructure requirements as code, using programming languages or configuration files, which can be version controlled, shared, and reused. This approach brings several benefits to product testing and development processes.

Product Test Load Balancing

Product Test Load Balancing is a critical aspect of Product Management that involves the systematic process of distributing testing tasks across multiple resources or testing environments to ensure optimal performance and efficiency of a product. Load balancing in this context refers to the distribution of testing workloads in a way that avoids overloading a single resource and maximizes the utilization of available resources. The primary goal of load balancing is to maintain an appropriate distribution of testing tasks to ensure that testing efforts are effectively managed and completed within the desired timeline.

Product Test Maintenance

Product Test Maintenance refers to the ongoing management and support of product testing activities throughout the product lifecycle. It involves the continuous monitoring, troubleshooting, and enhancement of product testing processes to ensure the accuracy, efficiency, and reliability of the testing results. In the context of Product Management, Product Test Maintenance encompasses several key tasks and responsibilities. Firstly, it involves the creation and maintenance of test plans and test cases, which outline the specific scenarios and criteria for testing the product's functionality, quality, and performance. These test plans and cases serve as a roadmap for the testing team, guiding them in systematically conducting tests and identifying any defects or deviations from the expected outcomes. Secondly, Product Test Maintenance involves the management and coordination of the testing resources, including test environments, tools, and equipment. This includes ensuring that the necessary testing environments are set up and configured correctly, that the testing tools are maintained and updated, and that the testing equipment is functioning properly. Regular maintenance and updates to these resources are essential to minimize disruptions to the testing process and to maximize the productivity and effectiveness of the testing team. An integral part of Product Test Maintenance is the analysis and reporting of testing results. This includes the collection and consolidation of test data, the identification and documentation of any issues or defects found during testing, and the generation of comprehensive reports for stakeholders. These reports help to provide visibility into the quality and performance of the product, enabling informed decision-making regarding product improvements or releases. Furthermore, Product Test Maintenance involves the continuous improvement and optimization of the testing processes. This includes the identification and implementation of best practices, the evaluation and adoption of new testing methodologies or technologies, and the regular review and refinement of the testing strategies and approaches. By continually enhancing the testing processes, Product Test Maintenance aims to increase efficiency, effectiveness, and scalability, ultimately leading to improved product quality and customer satisfaction.

Product Test Management Software

Product Test Management Software is a comprehensive tool used by product managers to plan, execute, and track the testing activities associated with product development. It allows product teams to efficiently manage the entire testing process, ensuring a smooth and successful launch of the product. At its core, Product Test Management Software helps product managers to streamline their testing efforts by providing a centralized platform to manage test cases, track test execution, and generate insightful reports. It allows product teams to effectively collaborate, prioritize tasks, and monitor progress throughout the testing cycle.

Product Test Metrics

Product test metrics refer to the specific measurements and data points used to evaluate the performance and success of a product during the testing phase of its development. These metrics provide valuable insights into the product's functionality, usability, and overall quality, helping product managers make informed decisions and improvements. There are several key metrics that are commonly used in product testing: 1. Defect density: This metric measures the number of defects or issues identified per unit of the product. It provides an indication of the product's overall quality and helps prioritize bug fixes and improvements. 2. Test coverage: Test coverage measures the extent to which the product's features and functionalities are being tested. It assesses the percentage of code or requirements that have been covered by tests, helping ensure adequate test coverage and identifying any gaps. 3. Test execution velocity: This metric measures the speed at which tests are executed. It helps measure the efficiency of the testing process and identifies any bottlenecks or areas for improvement. 4. Test cycle time: Test cycle time refers to the time it takes to complete a testing cycle, from the planning phase to the final reporting. This metric helps identify any delays or inefficiencies in the testing process and supports effective resource allocation. 5. Customer satisfaction: Customer satisfaction metrics capture end users' perceptions of the product's quality, usability, and overall experience. These metrics can be measured through surveys, feedback, or ratings, providing insights into user satisfaction and areas for improvement. 6. Test escape rate: The test escape rate measures the number of bugs or issues that are identified by end users after the product has been released. This metric helps evaluate the effectiveness of the testing process and identifies any gaps that need to be addressed. In summary, product test metrics provide valuable quantitative and qualitative data to assess the performance and quality of a product during the testing phase. By analyzing these metrics, product managers can make data-driven decisions to improve the product and enhance its overall success in the market.

Product Test Microservices

A product test microservice is a small, independent, and self-contained software component that is designed to test and validate specific features or functionalities of a product. It is an essential tool in the product management process as it enables teams to efficiently and effectively test the various aspects of a product, ensuring its quality, reliability, and functionality. Product test microservices are typically designed to perform specific tests or validations, such as unit testing, integration testing, end-to-end testing, performance testing, and security testing. Each microservice focuses on a specific aspect of the product and provides a dedicated environment for testing and validating that aspect. These microservices are modular and can be easily integrated into the overall product management ecosystem. One of the key advantages of using product test microservices is their ability to provide rapid feedback on the quality of the product. By automating the testing process and using microservices, product teams can quickly identify and address any defects or issues, enabling them to release a higher quality product to the market in a timely manner. Additionally, product test microservices enable product managers to gain valuable insights into the performance and usability of the product. The data collected from these microservices can be analyzed to identify patterns, trends, and potential areas for improvement. This information can then be used to make data-driven decisions and guide future product development efforts. In summary, a product test microservice is a small, self-contained software component that is used to test and validate specific features or functionalities of a product. It provides rapid feedback on product quality, enables data-driven decision making, and helps ensure the overall success of the product management process.

Product Test Performance Testing

The formal definition of Product Test Performance Testing in the context of Product Management is: Product Test Performance Testing is a process of evaluating and measuring the performance of a product under realistic conditions to ensure it meets the desired performance standards and specifications. It involves subjecting the product to various stress factors, such as high user loads, data volumes, and complex scenarios, to identify any performance bottlenecks, scalability issues, or system weaknesses.

Product Test Regression Testing

Product Test Regression Testing is a critical aspect of Product Management that involves evaluating the impact of changes to a product or software application on its existing functionality. It is a systematic and iterative process that aims to ensure the product continues to function as intended after any modifications or updates have been made. Regression testing is performed to identify and eliminate any unintended side effects or defects that may have been introduced during the development or modification process. It involves retesting previously tested functionality to confirm that it remains unaffected by the changes made. The goal is to prevent issues from arising due to unexpected interdependencies or interactions between components.

Product Test Reporting Compliance

Product Test Reporting Compliance in the context of Product Management refers to a formal process of ensuring that the testing of a product adheres to all relevant regulations, standards, and guidelines. This process involves documenting and reporting the results of various product tests, such as usability testing, performance testing, and safety testing, to demonstrate that the product meets the required compliance criteria. The purpose of this reporting is to provide evidence that the product has been thoroughly tested and is compliant with all applicable regulations and standards.

Product Test Reporting Tools

Product Test Reporting Tools are software applications or platforms that enable product managers to track and analyze data from product testing activities. These tools provide a comprehensive view of test results and enable product managers to make informed decisions based on the collected data. Product managers use these reporting tools to monitor the performance of their products during testing phases, such as alpha and beta testing. The tools allow them to gather and analyze data related to product functionality, usability, performance, and reliability. Product Test Reporting Tools enable product managers to generate detailed reports that provide insights into the success or failure of specific product features or functionalities. These reports often include metrics such as bug reports, test case execution status, pass/fail rates, and user feedback. Product managers can use this information to identify areas for improvement, prioritize bug fixes, and make data-driven decisions to optimize their product's performance. These reporting tools also facilitate collaboration among product teams. The tools often allow product managers to share test reports with other stakeholders, such as developers, designers, and marketers. By providing a centralized platform to access test results, these tools help ensure that all team members are well-informed about the product's performance and can align their efforts accordingly. Product Test Reporting Tools typically offer customizable dashboards and visualizations to help product managers interpret and present the collected data. These visual representations can include graphs, charts, and tables, making it easier for product managers to identify trends, patterns, and outliers in the test results. The visualizations also aid in communicating the test findings to other stakeholders, simplifying the understanding and decision-making process. In summary, Product Test Reporting Tools are essential for product managers to gather, analyze, and present data from product testing activities. These tools enable product managers to make data-driven decisions, improve product performance, and facilitate collaboration among different teams involved in the product development process.

Product Test Reporting

Product Test Reporting in the context of Product Management refers to the process of analyzing and documenting the results of testing a product to evaluate its performance, functionality, and usability. This reporting is essential for product teams to make informed decisions and improvements based on the findings from the testing phase. During product development, testing is conducted to uncover any issues, bugs, or areas of improvement within the product. This can involve various types of testing, such as functional testing, performance testing, usability testing, and user acceptance testing. The purpose is to ensure that the product meets the desired quality standards and fulfills the requirements of the target market. Once the testing phase is completed, the product team gathers and analyzes the test results to generate a comprehensive report. This report includes details about the tests performed, the specific metrics measured, and the outcomes of each test. The report may also contain recommendations for improving the product based on the identified issues or areas of concern. The Product Test Reporting serves several purposes within the product management process. Firstly, it provides valuable insights into the product's strengths and weaknesses from a user perspective. This information helps the product team identify areas where the product excels and areas where it needs improvement. Secondly, the report enables the product team to prioritize and address the identified issues or bugs. It serves as a reference point for developers

189

and designers to understand the problems and work towards finding effective solutions. Furthermore, the report plays a crucial role in communicating the product's performance to stakeholders and decision-makers. It helps them understand the current state of the product, the progress made, and the areas that require further attention or investment. In conclusion, Product Test Reporting in Product Management involves analyzing and documenting the results of product testing to evaluate its performance and functionality. This reporting serves as a guide for future improvements, helps prioritize bug fixes or enhancements, and facilitates effective communication with stakeholders.

Product Test Retesting

Product test retesting is a formal process within product management that involves conducting additional testing on a product that has already undergone initial testing. It is typically done to verify that any issues or bugs identified in the initial testing phase have been effectively resolved and that the product now meets the required quality standards. The purpose of retesting is to ensure that the product performs as expected and to validate that the fixes implemented during the bug-fixing phase have been effective in addressing the identified issues. It is an essential step before releasing the product to the market or deploying it to end-users, as it helps prevent potential negative user experiences and avoids costly recalls or customer dissatisfaction.

Product Test Risk Assessment

A product test risk assessment is a structured evaluation conducted by product management teams to identify and analyze potential risks associated with testing a new product or feature. This assessment helps identify potential issues that could hinder the successful launch or adoption of the product. The purpose of a product test risk assessment is to systematically evaluate the risks and their potential impact on the product, customers, and business. It allows product managers to create a risk mitigation plan and make informed decisions to address these risks before moving forward with the product testing phase.

Product Test Script Version Control

Product Test Script Version Control refers to the systematic management of different versions or iterations of product test scripts used in product management. A test script is a set of instructions or code that outlines the steps and expected results of a test scenario. Version control is the process of tracking and managing changes to these test scripts over time, allowing teams to review, compare, and access different versions. In the context of product management, version control for test scripts plays a crucial role in ensuring accuracy, traceability, and collaboration within the testing process. It allows teams to maintain a clear record of changes made to test scripts, including modifications, additions, and deletions. This facilitates effective communication and collaboration among team members, especially when multiple individuals are involved in creating or modifying test scripts. Version control also enables product managers to maintain an audit trail of changes made to test scripts. This is particularly valuable during regulatory compliance or quality assurance processes, as it helps demonstrate that proper testing procedures were followed and provides evidence of any modifications made for specific versions. Furthermore, product test script version control provides a mechanism for teams to easily revert to previous versions of test scripts if needed. This can be essential when encountering issues or unexpected results during testing, as it allows teams to quickly backtrack to an earlier known working version and investigate the root cause or compare results. It minimizes downtime and accelerates the troubleshooting process. By implementing version control for test scripts, product managers can also ensure consistency and standardization across different testing activities. It helps prevent inconsistencies or conflicts by providing a central repository where all test script versions are stored and accessible to team members. This centralized approach ensures that everyone is working with the latest and approved versions, reducing the risk of errors or misunderstandings. In conclusion, product test script version control is crucial for effective product management. It enables teams to manage changes to test scripts, maintain an audit trail, revert to previous versions, and ensure consistency across testing activities. By implementing version control practices, product managers can optimize the testing process and enhance collaboration within the team.

Product Test Scripting

Product Test Scripting refers to a structured process of creating a set of predefined steps and instructions for conducting tests and experiments on a product. In the context of Product Management, it is a critical component of the product development lifecycle that helps ensure product quality, user satisfaction, and overall success. The purpose of product test scripting is to systematically assess the performance, functionality, and usability of a product across different scenarios and use cases. By defining a clear testing plan and script, product managers can gather relevant data, identify potential issues, and make informed decisions to enhance the product's features, functionality, and user experience.

Product Test Security Scanning

Product Test Security Scanning is a process in product management that involves the identification, assessment, and mitigation of security vulnerabilities in a product through systematic scanning and testing. During the development and release of a product, it is crucial to ensure that it is secure and protected against potential attacks or breaches. Product Test Security Scanning helps identify and assess any security vulnerabilities, weaknesses, or loopholes present in the product. This process involves conducting comprehensive scans and tests on the product's code, configuration, and infrastructure to uncover any potential security risks. The objective of Product Test Security Scanning is to find and address vulnerabilities before the product is released to customers. By identifying and resolving security issues early on, the product team can minimize the risk of security breaches and ensure a more secure and reliable product. The process typically starts by performing a thorough assessment of the product's architecture and design. This involves analyzing its components, dependencies, and potential attack vectors. The next step is to conduct automated and manual security scanning and testing on the product. This can include techniques such as vulnerability scanning, penetration testing, and code reviews. Product Test Security Scanning enables the product team to uncover security weaknesses in areas such as authentication, access control, data encryption, and network security. Once vulnerabilities are identified, the team can prioritize and address them accordingly. This may involve fixing the vulnerabilities through code changes, configuration updates, or implementing additional security controls. The outcome of a Product Test Security Scanning process is a more secure product with reduced exposure to potential security threats. By proactively addressing security vulnerabilities, the product team can enhance its reputation, build trust with customers, and comply with industry regulations and standards.

Product Test Serverless Computing

Product Test Serverless Computing In the context of Product Management, serverless computing refers to a cloud computing model where the cloud provider dynamically manages and allocates resources to execute functions or logic without the need for infrastructure provisioning or management. This approach allows product teams to focus solely on developing and deploying their application code, rather than worrying about the underlying infrastructure. With serverless computing, the product team can write and deploy functions that perform specific tasks or implement specific features of the product. These functions are executed in response to events or triggers, such as HTTP requests, database changes, or scheduled tasks. The cloud provider takes care of automatically scaling the resources needed to execute these functions based on demand, ensuring high availability and efficient resource utilization. One key advantage of serverless computing is its cost effectiveness. Since resources are allocated and billed based on actual usage, product teams only pay for the execution time of their functions, rather than for idle server time. This makes serverless computing particularly suitable for applications with unpredictable or variable workloads, as it allows for automatic scaling up and down without incurring unnecessary costs. Another benefit of serverless computing is its scalability and elasticity. The cloud provider can automatically provision and deprovision resources as needed, based on the number of incoming events or triggers. This allows product teams to quickly and easily handle spikes in application usage without having to worry about infrastructure capacity planning and provisioning. Serverless computing also simplifies deployment and reduces operational overhead. Without the need to manage servers or infrastructure, product teams can focus on delivering new features and enhancements to their products, leading to faster time-to-market and increased innovation. Additionally, the cloud provider takes care of security, performance optimization, and maintenance tasks, freeing up the product team to focus on core product development.

Product Test Virtualization

Product test virtualization refers to the process of simulating or emulating the behavior and functionality of a product in a virtual or controlled environment to conduct testing and analysis. It involves creating a virtual representation of the product, its components, and their interactions to accurately mimic real-world scenarios and evaluate the performance, reliability, and compatibility of the product. In the context of product management, product test virtualization plays a crucial role in the development and release of high-quality products. It allows product managers to validate and verify the functionality and performance of a product before it is deployed or delivered to customers. By creating a virtualized environment that replicates the production environment, product teams can identify and address any issues or bugs that may arise during the product's lifecycle.

Product Test Vulnerability Assessment

A Product Test Vulnerability Assessment is a systematic evaluation of a product's potential vulnerabilities, weaknesses, and flaws that could be exploited by attackers or result in unintended consequences. This assessment is conducted to identify and assess the security and safety risks associated with a product, as well as to recommend mitigation measures to address these risks. The goal of a Product Test Vulnerability Assessment is to proactively identify and mitigate vulnerabilities before a product is released to the market. It helps product managers and development teams to understand the potential security and safety risks that their product may pose to users, systems, and organizations. By uncovering vulnerabilities early in the development lifecycle, product teams can make informed decisions and take necessary actions to bolster the product's security and safety posture.

Product Testimonials

A product testimonial, in the context of product management, refers to a statement or endorsement provided by a customer or user of a product that highlights their positive experience, satisfaction, and the benefits they received from using the product. It serves as a form of social proof and can be used as a marketing tool to build trust, credibility, and influence potential customers' purchasing decisions. Product testimonials play a crucial role in product management as they provide valuable insights and feedback from real customers. They serve as a direct source of information that can help product managers understand customers' needs, preferences, and pain points. By analyzing and leveraging these testimonials, product managers can make informed decisions to improve the product, identify new opportunities, and distinguish it from competitors.

Product Testing Procedures

Product testing procedures refer to the systematic processes and protocols followed by product management teams to evaluate and validate the performance, functionality, and quality of a product before it is launched in the market. This crucial stage is essential to ensure that the product meets the expectations and needs of the target audience and to identify and rectify any issues or defects. The goal of product testing procedures is to gather data and insights that help in making informed decisions regarding the product design, features, and overall viability. The testing phase involves various activities, such as: 1. Test Planning: This involves defining the scope, objectives, and test requirements for assessing the product. It includes identifying the target market, conducting competitor research, and establishing test criteria and metrics. 2. Test Design: This phase involves creating a detailed test plan and identifying the specific test cases and scenarios to be executed. It includes determining the types of tests to be conducted, such as functional, performance, usability, security, and compatibility testing. Test scripts and test data are also prepared in this phase. 3. Test Execution: This is the stage where the actual testing is carried out. The product is subjected to various tests based on the test cases and scenarios defined in the previous phase. The testing can be manual or automated, depending on the nature and complexity of the product. The focus is on verifying the product's functionality, performance, and reliability. 4. Defect Management: Any defects or issues identified during the testing phase are recorded, tracked, and managed. These defects are assigned priority and severity levels, and the product management team collaborates with the development team to rectify them. 5. Test Evaluation: Once the testing is completed, the results are analyzed, and the product's performance is evaluated against the predefined criteria and metrics. This helps in assessing whether the product meets the desired quality standards and user expectations. Overall, product testing procedures are vital for ensuring that the product meets the required standards of functionality, reliability, and performance before it is released to the market. By following a systematic approach to testing, product management teams can minimize risks, improve customer satisfaction, and maximize the chances of success for the product.

Product Testing

Product testing is a crucial aspect of product management that involves the evaluation and assessment of a product's performance, features, and usability to determine its quality and effectiveness. This process entails subjecting the product to various tests and experiments to identify any potential issues or areas for improvement. The primary objective of product testing is to ensure that the product meets the requirements and expectations of its intended users. It helps in identifying and resolving any defects or flaws in the product's design, functionality, or performance, thereby enhancing its overall quality. Additionally, product testing also serves as a means to validate the product's compliance with industry standards and regulations, ensuring that it is safe and reliable for use by consumers.

Product Total Quality Management (TQM)

Total Quality Management (TQM) is a strategic management approach aimed at continuously improving the quality of products throughout their lifecycle. It involves the participation of all employees in an organization, from top-level management to front-line workers, in order to achieve customer satisfaction and long-term success. TQM in the context of product management focuses on ensuring that products meet or exceed customer expectations and are free from defects or errors. It involves the integration of quality principles and practices into all stages of the product lifecycle, from design and development to manufacturing, distribution, and after-sales service.

Product Traceability

Product Traceability refers to the ability to track and trace a product throughout its entire lifecycle, from manufacturing to distribution and even after it has been sold to the end consumer. It involves capturing and recording critical information such as the origin of raw materials, production processes, quality control measures, and the movement of the product through the supply chain. The goal of product traceability is to provide full visibility and transparency into the journey of a product, ensuring that it meets regulatory requirements, quality standards, and customer expectations. It allows companies to efficiently manage their products, identify potential issues or defects, and efficiently recall or withdraw products if necessary.

Product Trademark

A product trademark is a type of intellectual property that provides legal protection for the unique name, logo, design, or symbol associated with a particular product. It is a distinct mark that helps consumers identify and distinguish the product from others in the market. In the context of product management, a trademark plays a crucial role in building brand recognition and brand loyalty. It serves as a visual representation of the product and the company behind it, communicating its quality, reliability, and overall identity to consumers.

Product Trademarks

A product trademark refers to a legally registered symbol, word, design, or combination thereof that distinguishes a product from other similar products in the market. It serves as a unique identifier for a particular product, representing its origin, quality, and reputation. Product trademarks play a crucial role in Product Management as they provide several benefits to both the company and the consumers. From a company's perspective, trademarks help protect their brand identity and create brand recognition in the market. Trademarks enable companies to differentiate their products from competitors and build customer loyalty. They also serve as a valuable marketing tool, conveying a message of quality, reliability, and consistency to consumers.

193

Product Training Materials

Product training materials refer to resources or resources designed to educate individuals or teams about a specific product. These materials aim to provide comprehensive information and instructions on how to effectively use, sell, or support the product. Product management entails the strategic planning, development, and promotion of products within an organization. The role of product managers is to ensure that products align with company objectives and meet the needs of target customers. As part of their responsibilities, product managers create and distribute product training materials to enable various stakeholders, such as sales teams, customer support representatives, and distributors, to acquire the necessary knowledge and skills to effectively engage with the product.

Product Training Resources

Product training resources refer to the resources that are used to educate and train product managers on the various aspects of a product. These resources can include training manuals, documentation, videos, online tutorials, and other materials that provide information and guidance on how to understand and effectively manage a product. The goal of product training resources is to provide product managers with the knowledge and skills they need to successfully manage and promote a product. These resources not only help product managers to understand the features and benefits of a product, but also provide them with the necessary tools to communicate these features and benefits to customers and stakeholders.

Product Training

Product training is a formal and structured process that aims to equip product management professionals with the knowledge and skills necessary to effectively manage and promote a specific product within an organization. It involves providing comprehensive information about the product, including its features, benefits, target audience, competitive landscape, and market positioning. The goal of product training is to enable product managers to make informed decisions, develop effective strategies, and support the successful launch and ongoing management of the product. During product training, individuals learn about various aspects of the product's lifecycle, such as its development, manufacturing, distribution, and support. They also gain insights into the market environment, including customer needs, industry trends, and competitor offerings. This knowledge helps product managers understand the unique value proposition of the product and align it with the overall business objectives.

Product Upgrades

A product upgrade is the process of enhancing or improving an existing product to meet the changing needs and preferences of customers, stay competitive in the market, and drive business growth. Product upgrades typically involve making modifications to the product's features, functionality, performance, design, or technology to deliver increased value to customers and maintain or expand the product's market share. These enhancements may be driven by various factors, including customer feedback, advances in technology, market trends, or the need to address competitive pressures.

Product Usability Testing

Product usability testing is a method used in the field of product management to evaluate the ease-of-use and effectiveness of a product by observing and gathering feedback from users who interact with it. This testing process provides valuable insights into how well the product meets the needs and expectations of its intended users. During product usability testing, a representative sample of users is chosen to perform specific tasks or scenarios using the product. These tasks can range from basic actions such as navigation or form completion to more complex interactions like using specific features or accomplishing specific goals. The users are observed and their actions, behavior, and feedback are documented and analyzed to identify any usability issues or areas for improvement. The objectives of product usability testing can vary depending on the stage of product development and the specific goals of the testing initiative. In early stages, the testing may focus on identifying major usability problems and gathering feedback for quick iterations and improvements. In later stages, the testing may aim to gather more detailed insights and validate the design decisions of the product. Product usability testing can help product managers in several ways. It provides actionable insights into user behavior and preferences, helping to uncover potential issues that could hinder product adoption and usage. It helps identify areas where the product can be simplified or enhanced to improve user satisfaction and overall user experience. Usability testing helps validate design decisions and can guide future product development efforts. In conclusion, product usability testing is an essential part of the product management process. It allows product managers to assess the usability of their product and collect valuable feedback from real users. By identifying usability issues and making necessary improvements, product managers can create products that are more intuitive, user-friendly, and aligned with user needs and expectations.

Product Usability

Product usability refers to the ease with which a product can be used by its intended users to achieve their goals effectively and efficiently in a given context of use. It involves evaluating and designing a product in such a way that it is intuitive, accessible, and functional for users, with a focus on enhancing user satisfaction and overall user experience.

Product Use Cases

A product use case is a formal definition that describes how a product is intended to be used by its users or customers, in the context of product management. It outlines the specific scenarios or situations in which the product is expected to provide value or solve a problem for the users. The primary purpose of defining use cases is to understand and document the various ways in which the product can be used, which helps product managers make informed decisions throughout the product development lifecycle. By understanding the different use cases, product managers can prioritize features, set clear product goals, and align the product roadmap with the needs and expectations of the target users. Use cases provide a comprehensive understanding of the product's functionality and the specific actions or tasks that users can perform with it. This includes both the core features and any additional features or functionalities that enhance the product's value proposition. Use cases also take into account the different user roles, such as administrators, end-users, or managers, and describe how each role interacts with the product. Furthermore, use cases help identify potential user pain points and areas for improvement. By analyzing the various use cases, product managers can identify user experience gaps, usability issues, or missing features that could hinder the product's adoption or satisfaction. This information can then be used to refine the product's design and prioritize future iterations or updates. In summary, a product use case is a formal definition that outlines how a product can be used by its users or customers. It helps product managers understand the different scenarios in which the product provides value, prioritize features, align the product roadmap, and identify areas for improvement. Defining use cases is an essential part of effective product management and ensures that the product meets the needs and expectations of its target users.

Product User Experience (UX)

User Experience (UX) in the context of Product Management refers to the overall experience that a user has when interacting with a product or service. It encompasses all aspects of the user's interaction, including their first impressions, the ease of use of the product, the satisfaction they derive from using it, and the overall value they perceive. UX is crucial in Product Management as it directly impacts customer satisfaction, loyalty, and ultimately the success or failure of a product. A positive UX can lead to increased customer adoption, higher retention rates, and positive word-of-mouth recommendations, while a negative UX can result in customer frustration, abandonment, and negative feedback. To ensure a good UX, Product Managers must take into account the needs and goals of their target users throughout the product development lifecycle. This involves conducting user research, understanding user behaviors and preferences, and incorporating these insights into the design, functionality, and usability of the product. Key factors that influence UX include the product's user interface (UI), its simplicity and intuitiveness, its responsiveness and speed, and its overall aesthetics. A well-designed UI should guide users through the product seamlessly, with clear and logical navigation, well-placed interactive elements, and intuitive interactions. Furthermore, UX also extends beyond the digital realm and includes any touchpoints a user has with a product, such as customer support, packaging, and post-purchase experiences. Each of these touchpoints

195

should be designed to enhance the overall user experience and create a positive emotional connection with the brand. In conclusion, User Experience is a critical aspect of Product Management, as it directly impacts customer satisfaction and product success. By understanding user needs, conducting research, and designing for simplicity, intuitiveness, and aesthetics, Product Managers can create a positive UX that differentiates their product from competitors and leads to increased customer adoption and loyalty.

Product User Feedback

Product User Feedback refers to the information or opinions provided by users of a product, with the purpose of improving or enhancing its design, features, functionality, and overall user experience. It plays a critical role in product management as it helps gather insights and perspectives from the end users, which can be used to make informed decisions and drive product development in the right direction. Product User Feedback can be obtained through various channels such as surveys, interviews, focus groups, online forums, social media platforms, customer support interactions, and user testing sessions. It allows product managers to gain a deeper understanding of how users perceive and interact with the product, identify pain points or areas for improvement, and uncover new opportunities for innovation. By actively seeking and analyzing user feedback, product managers can prioritize features or enhancements based on user needs and preferences, align product roadmaps with market demands, and ultimately create a product that delights customers and fulfills their requirements. It is a continuous and iterative process that involves ongoing communication and collaboration with users throughout the product lifecycle. Effective management of product user feedback involves establishing clear mechanisms for capturing and organizing the feedback, ensuring confidentiality and anonymity for users who provide feedback, and actively responding to and acknowledging the feedback received. It is important to aggregate and analyze the feedback in a systematic way, categorizing it into different themes or topics, and prioritizing the most impactful and feasible improvements. Furthermore, product managers should involve cross-functional teams such as engineering, design, marketing, and customer support in the feedback analysis to encourage a holistic approach to product development. This collaboration helps ensure that user feedback is considered in the context of technical feasibility, design constraints, market positioning, and overall business goals.

Product User Interface (UI)

A product user interface (UI) is the visual elements and controls that allow users to interact with a product. It encompasses everything that the user sees and interacts with on the screen, including buttons, forms, menus, and other graphical elements. The primary goal of a product UI is to provide a user-friendly and intuitive interface that allows users to easily accomplish their tasks and achieve their goals. It should be designed with the end user in mind, taking into consideration their needs, preferences, and capabilities. The UI should be visually appealing, consistent, and accessible to a wide range of users with different levels of technical expertise.

Product User Manual

A product user manual is a formal document that provides detailed instructions and information on how to use a product. It serves as a guide for users, helping them navigate the features, functions, and operations of a product effectively and safely. The primary purpose of a user manual is to educate and empower users to make the most out of their product, ensuring a positive user experience. The content of a product user manual typically includes a description of the product, an overview of its features, step-by-step instructions on how to assemble or set up the product, and a comprehensive explanation of its functionalities. It may also include troubleshooting tips, frequently asked questions, and safety precautions to prevent accidents or misuse.

Product User Manuals

A product user manual, also known as a user guide or instruction manual, is a document created by a company to provide detailed information on how to use and operate their product. It serves as a reference for users, helping them navigate through the product's features, functions, and settings. The purpose of a product user manual is to assist customers in understanding and effectively using the product. It typically includes step-by-step instructions, diagrams, and illustrations to provide clarity and guidance. The content of a user manual can vary depending on the complexity of the product and the target audience.

Product User Stories

A product user story is a concise, formal statement used in product management to describe a specific requirement or feature from the perspective of a user or customer. It is typically written in a user-centered format to capture the user's needs, goals, and desired outcomes. User stories serve as a valuable tool for effectively capturing, prioritizing, and communicating product requirements to the development team. User stories consist of two primary components: the "As a" statement and the "I want" statement. The "As a" statement identifies the type of user or customer that the story is focused on. This could be a specific role, such as a customer support agent or an end-user, or it could be a broader category of users, such as administrators or casual users. The "I want" statement describes the specific task, functionality, or improvement that the user desires. This statement should be clear, concise, and focused on a specific outcome or action. For example, a user story for a customer support software might be: "As a customer support agent, I want the ability to view and track customer interactions across multiple channels, so I can provide personalized and efficient support." This user story clearly identifies the type of user (customer support agent) and the desired functionality (viewing and tracking customer interactions) that will enable them to achieve their goal (providing personalized and efficient support). The formulation of user stories should follow a set of guidelines, known as the INVEST criteria, to ensure they are effective and actionable. User stories should be Independent, meaning they can be implemented and delivered without reliance on other stories. They should be Negotiable, allowing room for discussion and refinement during development. User stories should be Valuable, providing a meaningful benefit to the user or customer. They should be Estimable, allowing the development team to estimate the effort and resources required. User stories should be Small, ensuring they can be completed within a single development cycle. Finally, user stories should be Testable, enabling the development team to create tests to validate the functionality. Overall, user stories are a powerful tool for capturing and communicating user requirements in product management. By focusing on the needs and goals of users and customers, user stories enable product teams to deliver valuable and user-centered solutions.

Product Validation

Product validation, in the context of product management, refers to the process of gathering and analyzing relevant data and feedback to assess the viability and potential success of a product in the market. It involves systematically evaluating various aspects of the product, such as its features, pricing, target audience, and competition, to determine if it meets the needs and expectations of the target market. The purpose of product validation is to minimize the risks associated with bringing a new product to market by ensuring that it meets customer needs, aligns with market trends, and has a competitive advantage. It helps product managers make informed decisions about product development, marketing strategies, and potential opportunities for growth. During the product validation process, product managers use a range of techniques and methods to collect and analyze data. This may include conducting market research, surveys, interviews, and focus groups, as well as analyzing customer feedback, reviews, and sales data. By gathering and analyzing this information, product managers can gain valuable insights into customer preferences, market trends, and potential gaps or opportunities in the market. Once the data has been collected and analyzed, product managers can evaluate the product's fit within the market. This involves assessing whether the product meets customer needs, solves a problem, or fulfills a desire better than existing options. Product managers also consider the competitive landscape to determine if there are any direct or indirect competitors that may impact the success of the product. In conclusion, product validation is an essential step in the product management process that allows product managers to assess the viability and potential success of a product in the market. By gathering and analyzing data, product managers can make informed decisions about product development, marketing strategies, and potential opportunities for growth. Ultimately, product validation helps minimize risks and increase the chances of success for a new product.

Product Value Analysis

197

Product Value Analysis, in the context of Product Management, refers to the process of assessing the worth and benefits of a product or service in relation to its cost. It involves evaluating the various elements of a product, such as its features, quality, functionality, and brand reputation, against its price point and the perceived value it provides to customers. The aim of Product Value Analysis is to determine whether the product is meeting the needs and expectations of customers and whether it is priced appropriately to deliver value. This analysis helps product managers understand how customers perceive the product's value proposition and make informed decisions about pricing, positioning, and future improvements.

Product Value Proposition

A product value proposition is a concise statement that outlines the unique benefits and value that a product offers to its target customers. It communicates the key advantages and reasons why a customer should choose a particular product over its competitors. The value proposition is an essential component of product management, as it helps drive product development, marketing strategies, and overall business success. The product value proposition should clearly articulate the problems or needs that the product solves for customers and highlight its unique features or advantages. It should answer the fundamental question, "Why should customers choose our product?" A well-crafted value proposition demonstrates the product's differentiation from competitors and resonates with the target audience.

Product Vendor Management

Product Vendor Management refers to the process of identifying, evaluating, and managing relationships with vendors who provide products or services that are essential to the success of a product management team. It involves establishing and maintaining effective communication channels, negotiating terms and conditions, monitoring performance, and ensuring delivery of high-quality products within budget and on time. The primary goal of Product Vendor Management is to ensure that the product management team has access to the necessary resources, expertise, and support from external vendors to develop, launch, and maintain successful products. This involves aligning the vendor's capabilities with the product requirements and strategic objectives. It also requires establishing clear expectations and performance metrics to measure the vendor's effectiveness in meeting these requirements. Key activities involved in Product Vendor Management include vendor selection, contract negotiation, and ongoing vendor relationship management. During the vendor selection process, the product management team evaluates potential vendors based on their capabilities, experience, reputation, financial stability, and compatibility with the organization's values and culture. The team also considers factors such as cost, quality, scalability, and responsiveness in making the selection. Once a vendor is selected, contract negotiation takes place to define the terms and conditions of the vendor relationship. This includes specifying the scope of work, timelines, pricing, payment terms, intellectual property ownership, and dispute resolution mechanisms. The contract serves as a legally binding agreement between the product management team and the vendor, providing a framework for collaboration and accountability. Vendor relationship management involves ongoing communication, monitoring, and performance evaluation to ensure that the vendor meets the agreed-upon deliverables and quality standards. Regular meetings, performance reviews, and feedback sessions help to maintain a productive and mutually beneficial relationship with the vendor. This includes addressing any issues or conflicts that may arise during the course of the vendor engagement. In summary, Product Vendor Management is a vital aspect of product management that focuses on effectively sourcing, engaging, and managing relationships with external vendors to ensure the successful development and delivery of high-quality products. It involves selecting the right vendors, negotiating favorable contracts, and maintaining proactive communication and performance evaluation throughout the vendor relationship.

Product Versioning

Product versioning, in the context of product management, refers to the practice of assigning a unique identifier or number to a specific iteration or release of a product. This identifier helps to distinguish and differentiate different versions of the product, enabling the management of changes and updates over time. The process of versioning helps product managers and development teams keep track of the modifications and improvements made to a product as it evolves. By assigning a version number, such as 1.0, 2.0, or 3.1, each release can be easily identified and referenced. This is particularly useful when communicating with customers, partners, or stakeholders to ensure everyone is on the same page regarding the current state of the product.

Product Virtual Reality (VR) Modeling

Virtual Reality (VR) Modeling in the context of Product Management refers to the process of creating virtual representations of physical products using virtual reality technology. It involves creating three-dimensional (3D) models of products that can be interacted with in a virtual environment. VR modeling allows product managers to visualize and present their products in a more immersive and realistic manner. The primary goal of VR modeling in product management is to enhance the product development and marketing process. By leveraging VR technology, product managers can create virtual prototypes of their products, allowing them to visualize and test different design variations without the need for physical prototypes. This not only saves time and resources but also enables faster iterations and refinements during the product development stage. Furthermore, VR modeling enables product managers to showcase their products to stakeholders and customers in a more engaging and interactive way. By immersing users in a virtual environment, they can provide a realistic and immersive experience of using the product. This can help in improving product demonstrations, user testing, and gathering valuable feedback that can be used for product improvements. Additionally, VR modeling offers product managers the ability to simulate real-world scenarios and environments to evaluate the product's performance and usability. They can create virtual simulations of product usage in various contexts and analyze how the product behaves in different conditions. This allows for better understanding of potential limitations, identifying areas for improvement, and optimizing the product's design and functionality. In conclusion, VR modeling in product management is a powerful tool that enables product managers to create virtual representations of physical products, allowing for enhanced visualization, testing, and presentation. By leveraging this technology, product managers can streamline the product development process, improve product demonstrations, gather valuable feedback, and optimize the design and functionality of their products.

Product Vision

A product vision is a concise, high-level statement that describes the desired future state of a product or a product line. It serves as a guide for product management teams to align their efforts and make decisions that will lead to the successful development and launch of the product. The product vision outlines the overarching goals and objectives for the product, emphasizing its unique value proposition and the problem it aims to solve for customers. It provides a clear direction and focus, guiding the product development process from ideation to execution.

Product Warranty

A product warranty is a formal assurance provided by the manufacturer or seller of a product to the customer, guaranteeing to repair or replace the product if it fails to meet defined criteria within a specified period of time after its purchase. Product warranties serve as a promise to customers that the product they are purchasing is of good quality and will perform as expected for a certain duration. They provide a level of confidence to customers, reassuring them that the manufacturer or seller stands behind the product's reliability and performance.

Product Waterfall Development

Product Waterfall Development is a sequential and linear approach to product development that follows a structured timeline and predetermined set of phases. It is a widely used methodology in product management where the development process moves from one phase to the next, with minimal overlapping or iteration between phases. The key characteristic of the Waterfall Development is its sequential nature, where each phase depends on the completion of the previous one. The process typically starts with requirements gathering and analysis, followed by design, development, testing, and finally, deployment or release. Unlike agile methods, there is minimal room for changes or adaptations during the development process.

Project Tracking

Project tracking in the context of product management refers to the process of monitoring and managing the progress, tasks, and resources of a project throughout its lifecycle. Project tracking involves keeping a close eye on the various components of a project to ensure that it stays on track and meets its objectives. It includes tracking tasks, milestones, deadlines, budgets, and resources, and making adjustments as needed to keep the project on schedule and within budget. The key components of project tracking include: 1. Task Management: This involves breaking down the project into smaller tasks and assigning each task to the appropriate team members. Project tracking ensures that tasks are completed on time and that any delays or issues are identified and addressed promptly. 2. Milestone Tracking: Project tracking involves setting milestones, which are significant points in the project that represent the completion of a major phase or deliverable. Tracking milestones helps to gauge the progress of the project and ensures that it is moving forward as planned. 3. Resource Allocation: Project tracking involves monitoring and managing the resources required for the project, including people, materials, and equipment. It ensures that resources are allocated effectively and efficiently to meet project requirements. 4. Budget Control: Project tracking includes tracking and controlling the project budget to ensure that costs are kept within the approved budget. It involves monitoring expenses, comparing them to the budget, and taking corrective actions if necessary to avoid cost overruns. 5. Risk Management: Project tracking involves identifying and managing project risks and uncertainties. It includes assessing potential risks, developing mitigation strategies, and monitoring the project to identify and address any new risks that may arise. In summary, project tracking is a critical aspect of product management that involves monitoring and managing the progress, tasks, milestones, resources, and budget of a project to ensure its successful completion. By closely tracking these factors, product managers can effectively manage projects, make informed decisions, and ensure that the project is delivered on time, within budget, and to the satisfaction of stakeholders.

Prototyping Feedback

Prototyping in the context of Product Management refers to the process of creating a simplified version or mock-up of a product or feature before it is fully developed and launched. It involves creating a tangible representation or prototype that allows stakeholders to visualize and interact with the product, providing valuable feedback and insights before investing significant time and resources in the development phase. Prototyping plays a crucial role in product management as it helps to validate and refine ideas, test functionality and user experience, and identify potential issues or improvements early in the product development lifecycle. It allows product managers to gather important feedback from users, customers, and other stakeholders to ensure that the final product meets their needs and expectations.

Prototyping Platforms

A prototyping platform, in the context of product management, refers to a tool or software that enables product teams to create and test early versions of their product or features before full-scale development. It allows the team to quickly and efficiently validate ideas, gather feedback, and make necessary iterations to improve the user experience and functionality. Prototyping platforms typically offer a range of features and functionalities that facilitate the creation of interactive and realistic prototypes. These platforms often include drag-and-drop interfaces, pre-designed components, and a variety of tools for visual design, user flow, and interaction design.

Prototyping Tools

Prototyping tools are software applications that allow product managers to create interactive prototypes of their products. These tools are commonly used in the field of product management to gather customer feedback, test product concepts, and iterate on product designs before moving forward with development. With prototyping tools, product managers can visually represent the user interface and functionality of a product, simulating how it will look and behave in the hands of users. These tools often offer a variety of pre-designed components and templates that can be easily customized and arranged to create realistic mock-ups of the final product. The main purpose of using prototyping tools in product management is to validate product ideas and gather user feedback early in the development process. By creating interactive prototypes, product managers can simulate user interactions and get a sense of how well the product meets user needs and expectations. This allows product managers to make informed decisions and prioritize features based on user feedback, resulting in a better user experience. In addition to user feedback, prototyping tools also enable product managers to collaborate with other stakeholders, such as designers and developers. By sharing prototypes with team members and stakeholders, product managers can gather input and align everyone's understanding of the product vision. This helps to identify potential issues and refine the product design before committing to development. Overall, prototyping tools are essential for product managers as they provide a visual representation of product ideas and facilitate the validation and iteration process. By using these tools, product managers can reduce the risk of building products that don't meet user needs and increase the chances of creating successful and user-centric products.

Prototyping

Prototyping in the context of Product Management refers to the process of creating a preliminary version or model of a product that can be tested and evaluated before its final production. This allows product managers to gather feedback and make necessary adjustments to improve the product's design, functionality, and user experience. Prototyping is an essential step in the product development cycle as it helps product managers visualize and demonstrate the product's features, interactions, and overall concept to stakeholders, including developers, designers, and potential users. By creating a prototype, product managers can refine and validate their ideas, identify potential issues or challenges, and ensure that the final product aligns with the desired goals and requirements.

Quality Assurance Testing

Quality Assurance (QA) testing is a critical aspect of product management that focuses on verifying and validating the quality of a product or software application to ensure it meets the desired standards and requirements. It involves a systematic and comprehensive evaluation of the product's functionality, performance, usability, and reliability to identify any defects or issues that may exist. The primary objective of QA testing is to ensure that the product meets the expectations of the end-users and delivers an optimal user experience. It aims to uncover any bugs, glitches, or errors that may disrupt the product's functionality or hinder its usability. Through rigorous testing and analysis, QA testing helps identify and rectify any issues, ensuring that the product is reliable, stable, and performs as expected.

Quality Assurance Tools

Quality assurance tools refer to a set of processes, techniques, and software applications used in the field of product management to ensure that a product meets specified quality standards. These tools are an essential part of the product development lifecycle, enabling product managers to identify and rectify any defects or issues before the product is released to the market. One of the most commonly used quality assurance tools is the defect tracking system. This tool allows product managers to log and monitor any issues or defects encountered during the development process. It provides a centralized repository for recording and tracking the status of these issues, allowing product managers to prioritize and allocate resources for resolving them. By using a defect tracking system, product managers can ensure that no defects go unnoticed or unresolved, thereby enhancing the overall quality of the product.

Quality Assurance

Quality Assurance (QA) is a systematic process that ensures the product or service being developed meets the desired standards and specifications set by the organization. It is an essential component of Product Management and is responsible for evaluating and improving the quality of the product throughout its lifecycle. The primary objective of QA is to identify and prevent defects or errors in the product, ensuring that it meets the requirements and expectations of the end-users. This involves meticulous planning, monitoring, and controlling of various activities during the development process. QA starts right from the initial stages of product development, where it collaborates closely with the Product Manager to define the quality standards and establish the necessary processes and procedures. It involves conducting extensive research and analysis to understand the needs and preferences of the target market, which helps in setting realistic quality goals. Once the quality goals are established, QA plays a crucial role in defining and implementing the right metrics and indicators to measure the quality of the product. It sets up a framework for testing and inspection at different stages of development, allowing for timely identification and resolution of any quality issues or deviations from the standards. QA also ensures that the product is compliant with the relevant regulatory and legal requirements. It conducts thorough audits and reviews to verify the adherence to these requirements and takes necessary actions to rectify any non-compliance. Furthermore, QA continuously monitors and analyzes customer feedback and integrates it into the product development process. This feedback helps in identifying areas for improvement and refining the product quality over time. In conclusion, Quality Assurance is an integral part of Product Management that focuses on ensuring the quality and reliability of the product. It involves systematic processes, testing, and continuous improvement to meet the set standards and customer expectations. The success of a product heavily relies on the effective implementation of QA practices throughout its lifecycle.

ROI Calculation Models

ROI Calculation Models in the context of Product Management refer to the methodologies and approaches used to calculate the return on investment (ROI) of a product or product line. ROI is a financial metric that measures the profitability and efficiency of an investment by comparing the amount of return generated with the cost of the investment. Product Managers use ROI Calculation Models to assess the financial performance of their products and make data-driven decisions regarding resource allocation, pricing, and product strategy. These models enable Product Managers to evaluate the potential return and profitability of different product initiatives, as well as to compare the financial impact of various investment options.

Regression Testing Automation Tools

Regression Testing Automation

Regression testing automation is the process of automating the execution of a series of predefined test cases to validate the functionality of software after changes or enhancements are made. It involves retesting the existing features to ensure that they still work as expected and that new changes have not introduced any unintended side effects or defects. This type of testing is particularly important in the context of product management, where the focus is on delivering high-quality software products that meet the needs of the users. By automating regression testing, product managers can ensure that any modifications made to the software do not negatively impact its existing functionality. This helps to minimize the risk of introducing new bugs or regressions while improving the overall reliability and stability of the product.

Regulatory Compliance

Regulatory compliance in the context of Product Management refers to the adherence and adherence of a product to the regulations, laws, and standards set by regulatory bodies. These regulations are put in place to ensure that products are safe, reliable, and meet the requirements set for their specific industry or market. Compliance with regulatory requirements is crucial for product managers as it helps them navigate the complex landscape of regulations and ensure that their products meet the necessary standards. This involves understanding and interpreting the relevant regulations, identifying the requirements that apply to the product, and implementing processes and controls to ensure compliance. The first step in regulatory compliance is understanding the specific regulations that apply to the product. This may include local, national, or international regulations, depending on the target market and industry. Product managers need to familiarize themselves with the regulatory landscape and stay updated on any changes or updates to the regulations. Once the regulatory requirements are identified, product managers need to ensure that the product meets these requirements. This may involve conducting tests, inspections, and certifications to demonstrate compliance. Product managers may also need to work closely with cross-functional teams such as engineering, quality assurance, and legal to ensure that the necessary measures are implemented. In addition to meeting regulatory requirements during the product development phase, compliance also extends to the marketing, distribution, and use of the product. Product managers need to ensure that the product labeling, packaging, and marketing materials comply with relevant regulations. They may also be responsible for monitoring the product's performance and addressing any issues or complaints related to regulatory compliance. Failure to comply with regulatory requirements can have serious consequences for both the product and the company. Non-compliance can result in legal penalties, damage to the company's reputation, loss of customer trust, and even product recalls. Therefore, it is vital for product managers to prioritize regulatory compliance throughout the product lifecycle. Overall, regulatory compliance in product management is about ensuring that products meet the necessary regulations, laws, and standards to protect consumers and maintain the integrity of the market. It involves understanding, implementing, and monitoring compliance measures to ensure that products are safe, reliable, and meet the requirements set by regulatory bodies.

Release Notes Documentation

Release Notes Documentation refers to a formal document created by Product Managers to communicate updates, features, bug fixes, and improvements associated with a software product release. It is an essential component of the product management process, enabling effective communication between the product team, stakeholders, and customers. The purpose of Release Notes Documentation is to provide detailed information about the changes introduced in a particular software release. It serves as a reference guide for all stakeholders involved in the product, including developers, testers, customer support teams, marketing personnel, and end-users. The document outlines the key modifications made to the product, their impact, and any necessary instructions or prerequisites for utilizing the new features or resolving known issues.

Release Notes Management

Release Notes Management refers to the process of creating, organizing, and communicating the details of product releases to stakeholders, including customers, internal teams, and partners. It is an essential component of Product Management, as it enables effective communication and transparency throughout the product development lifecycle. The main purpose of Release Notes Management is to provide relevant and concise information about the changes, enhancements, and fixes included in a product release. These release notes serve as a comprehensive documentation of what has been added, modified, or removed from the product, allowing users and other stakeholders to understand the impact and benefits of the new release.

Release Notes Publishing

Release Notes Publishing refers to the process of creating and distributing documentation that informs customers and stakeholders about the changes, improvements, and bug fixes in a software release. It is an essential component of the Product Management function as it plays a crucial role in effectively communicating product updates and enhancements to users. The purpose of Release Notes Publishing is twofold. Firstly, it serves as a means of transparently sharing information with users, keeping them informed about the latest changes and updates in the software. This helps to manage user expectations, minimize confusion, and enhance user satisfaction. Secondly, it also caters to the needs of internal stakeholders such as customer support teams, training departments, sales teams, and marketing teams by providing them with detailed information on the changes in the software that they can use to support their activities.

Release Planning Tools

Release planning tools are software or online platforms used by product managers to effectively plan and manage the release of a product or feature. These tools typically provide a range of functionalities and features that assist product managers in creating and executing a well-structured and organized release plan. These tools offer various capabilities, such as: 1. Product Roadmap: Release planning tools typically include a product roadmap feature that allows product managers to visualize and communicate the high-level strategy and direction of the product. This helps in aligning stakeholders, setting priorities, and making informed decisions about the release timeline and content. 2. Release Calendar: A release calendar feature enables product managers to map out and schedule the releases, milestones, and key activities associated with each release. It provides a centralized view of all upcoming releases, helping the team to stay on track and meet deadlines. 3. Requirements Management: These tools often include functionality to capture, refine, and track requirements for each release. This helps product managers and their teams to prioritize and evaluate feature requests or enhancements, ensuring that the most valuable and feasible features are included in the release. 4. Resource Planning: Release planning tools often allow product managers to allocate and manage resources, such as development teams, designers, or testers, to support the release plan. This enables efficient utilization of available resources and helps in identifying any potential resource constraints or bottlenecks early on. 5. Progress Tracking: These tools provide visibility into the progress of the release plan, allowing product managers to track the completion of tasks, monitor milestones, and assess the overall progress of the release. This helps in identifying and addressing any delays or risks that could impact the release timeline. 6. Collaboration and Communication: Release planning tools often include collaboration features, such as the ability to assign tasks, leave comments, or share documents, facilitating effective communication and collaboration among team members. This promotes transparency, accountability, and efficient coordination throughout the release planning and execution process. Overall, release planning tools offer a comprehensive set of features and functionalities that enable product managers to streamline and optimize the release planning process. By leveraging these tools, product managers can ensure effective coordination, efficient resource allocation, and successful execution of releases, leading to customer satisfaction and business growth.

Release Planning

Release planning, in the context of product management, is the process of establishing a comprehensive and strategic approach to delivering a product or software to the market. It involves defining and prioritizing the features, functionalities, and requirements that will be included in each release, as well as mapping out the timeline and resources needed to successfully execute these releases. The goal of release planning is to create a well-structured roadmap that outlines the product's evolution and aligns it with the overall business objectives and customer needs. This process requires collaboration and coordination among various stakeholders, including product managers, development teams, marketing teams, and executives. During release planning, the product manager engages with stakeholders to gather feedback, insights, and requirements. They also analyze market research, competitor analysis, and customer feedback to identify the most valuable features and enhancements to include in each release. Once the features and functionalities are identified, the product manager works with the development team to estimate the effort, dependencies, and risks associated with each item. This helps in prioritizing and sequencing the deliverables to ensure maximum value is delivered to the customers in the shortest possible time frame. Release planning also involves considering external factors, such as user acceptance testing, regulatory requirements, or technology dependencies, that may impact the timing and scope of the releases. This requires close coordination between different teams and departments to ensure a smooth and successful product launch. Throughout the release planning process, the product manager continuously monitors and adjusts the plan based on changing market dynamics, customer feedback, and internal constraints. This iterative approach allows for flexibility and adaptability, ensuring that the product stays aligned with business goals and customer expectations. In summary, release planning is a critical activity in product management that entails defining and prioritizing features, mapping out timelines and resources, and aligning the product roadmap with business objectives. It involves collaboration among stakeholders, analysis of market research, and adaptation to changing dynamics to deliver a successful product to the market.

Requirements Gathering

Requirements gathering is the process of systematically collecting and documenting the needs and expectations of stakeholders for a given product or project. It involves conducting interviews, facilitating workshops, and performing other research activities to gather information and understand the requirements from various perspectives. The goal of requirements gathering is to ensure that the final product meets the needs and expectations of the stakeholders. This is accomplished by identifying, prioritizing, and documenting the functional and non-functional requirements of the product. Functional requirements define the specific features and functionalities that the product must have, while non-functional requirements focus on the performance, usability, and other quality aspects of the product.

Requirements Management

Requirements Management is a critical process within Product Management that involves systematically identifying, documenting, analyzing, organizing, prioritizing, and tracking the various requirements of a product throughout its lifecycle. The purpose of Requirements Management is to ensure that the product meets the needs and expectations of its users, stakeholders, and the market. It helps to define the scope of the product, its features, functionalities, and characteristics in a structured and well-documented manner. This process begins with the identification of requirements, which are the desired capabilities, characteristics, or functionalities of the product. These requirements can be gathered from various sources, including market research, customer feedback, stakeholder interviews, competitor analysis, and industry standards. Once identified, the requirements are documented in a clear and concise manner, using a standardized format and language. This documentation serves as a reference for all stakeholders involved in the product development process and provides a common understanding of what needs to be achieved. The next step in Requirements Management is the analysis of these requirements. This involves evaluating and prioritizing them based on their importance, feasibility, and impact on the product as a whole. The analysis helps to identify any conflicting or overlapping requirements and ensures that all requirements are aligned with the overall goals and objectives of the product. After the analysis, the requirements are organized and categorized based on their relationship and interdependencies. This helps in creating a clear and logical structure of the requirements, allowing for better understanding and management. Throughout the product development lifecycle, Requirements Management involves continuously tracking and monitoring the progress of the requirements. It ensures that the requirements are implemented correctly and that any changes or updates are properly documented and communicated to all stakeholders. Overall, Requirements Management is an essential practice in Product Management that ensures the successful development and delivery of a product that meets the needs and expectations of its users and stakeholders.

Requirements Traceability

Requirements Traceability is a critical practice in Product Management that involves linking and tracking requirements throughout the product development lifecycle. It is the process of documenting and maintaining the relationship between various product requirements and the artifacts, such as design documents, test cases, and source code, that implement or validate those requirements. The primary objective of Requirements Traceability is to ensure that all product requirements are met and to provide visibility into the impact of changes made during the product development process. By tracing requirements, product managers can effectively manage scope, prioritize development efforts, and ensure that the final product aligns with the initial requirements and customer needs. In practice, Requirements Traceability is typically implemented using a traceability matrix or a traceability graph. A traceability matrix is a tabular representation that maps product requirements to other relevant artifacts, such as design documents, test cases, and source code modules. This matrix allows product managers to quickly identify any missing or incomplete requirements and track their implementation throughout the development process. A traceability graph, on the other hand, is a visual representation that shows the relationships between different requirements and artifacts. It helps product managers visualize the dependencies and impact of changes on the overall product. This graphical representation enables better decision-making and facilitates communication between cross-functional teams. Requirements Traceability also plays a critical role in ensuring regulatory compliance and managing product risks. By maintaining a traceability link between product requirements and regulatory standards, product managers can demonstrate that the final product meets all the necessary compliance requirements. Additionally, traceability aids in identifying and mitigating risks associated with incomplete or ambiguous requirements, minimizing the likelihood of costly rework or customer dissatisfaction. In summary, Requirements Traceability is a fundamental practice in Product Management that involves documenting and maintaining the relationships between product requirements and the artifacts that implement or validate those requirements. It enables effective scope management, priority setting, and change impact analysis, ultimately ensuring the successful delivery of a product that meets customer needs and regulatory requirements.

Requirements Tracking

Requirements Tracking in the context of Product Management refers to the systematic process of capturing, documenting, and managing the various requirements and specifications needed for the successful development and delivery of a product. It involves keeping track of all the functional and non-functional requirements, as well as any additional constraints or dependencies, associated with a product. These requirements can include features, user stories, performance metrics, security considerations, and any other specifications that drive the development and implementation of the product.

Retail Distribution

Retail distribution in the context of product management refers to the process of getting products from the manufacturer or producer to the end consumer through various retail channels. It involves the management of the physical movement of products, as well as the coordination of activities and information among different entities involved in the supply chain. The retail distribution process starts with the manufacturer or producer producing the goods. These goods are then transported to distribution centers or warehouses, where they are stored until they are ready to be shipped to retail stores. From the distribution centers, the products are either directly delivered to the retail stores or to regional distribution centers, depending on the size and structure of the distribution network. Once the products reach the retail stores, they are placed on shelves or displayed in a way that is attractive to consumers. Retailers also handle activities such as pricing, promotions, and inventory management to ensure that the products are available to customers when they need them. Retail distribution involves the collaboration and coordination of various entities, including manufacturers or producers, distributors, wholesalers, and retailers. Communication and information sharing play a crucial role in this process, as all entities need to be aware of the product availability, delivery schedules, and any changes in demand or supply. The goal of retail distribution is to ensure that products are available to consumers in the right place, at the right time, and in the right quantity. Efficient distribution can help maximize sales, minimize inventory costs, and improve customer satisfaction. It also allows for faster delivery and reduces the risk of stockouts or overstocking. In summary, retail distribution in product management involves the movement of products from manufacturers to retail stores or directly to consumers. It encompasses activities such as transportation, warehousing, inventory management, and coordination among various entities in the supply chain. Effective retail distribution is vital for ensuring product availability, maximizing sales, and improving customer satisfaction.

Return On Investment (ROI)

Return on Investment (ROI) is a financial metric that is commonly used in product management to measure the profitability of a product or investment. It is a ratio that compares the net profit generated from a product or investment to the initial cost or investment. ROI is often used as a key performance indicator (KPI) to assess the success of a product or investment and to make informed decisions regarding resource allocation and future strategies. To calculate ROI, the net profit is divided by the initial cost or investment. Net profit is the total revenue generated from the product minus all expenses, including production costs, marketing expenses, and overhead costs. The initial cost or investment includes not only the direct costs associated with product development and production but also the indirect costs such as marketing and sales expenses. The ROI metric provides valuable insights into the effectiveness of product management strategies and investments. A positive ROI indicates that the product or investment is generating profits, which is a desirable outcome for any business. A higher ROI indicates a higher profitability and efficiency of the product or investment. Product managers can use the ROI metric to evaluate the performance of different products and make informed decisions regarding resource allocation. By comparing the ROI of different products, product managers can identify which products are generating the most profits and allocate resources accordingly. They can also use ROI to identify underperforming products that may require improvements or discontinuation. Furthermore, ROI can help product managers justify the allocation of resources towards product development and guide decision-making processes. It provides a measurable return on the investment and enables product managers to communicate the impact and value of their decisions to stakeholders.

Revenue Model

A revenue model is a framework that outlines how a company generates income from its products or services. It provides a structured approach to monetizing a product and helps guide strategic decisions related to pricing, sales, and distribution channels. Within the context of product management, the revenue model plays a crucial role in defining the financial viability of a product. It informs the overall product strategy by considering factors such as target market, value proposition, and cost structure in order to maximize revenue and profitability.

Roadmap Planning

A roadmap planning is a strategic tool used in product management to outline and communicate the vision, goals, and direction of a product or a product line over a certain period of time. It is a visual representation that provides a high-level overview of the product's strategy, key features, and timelines. The roadmap plan serves as a guide for product managers, development teams, stakeholders, and other key players involved in the product's lifecycle. It helps align everyone towards a common vision, facilitates communication, and ensures that all teams are working towards the same objectives.

Roadmap Visualization Software

A roadmap visualization software is a tool used in product management to create and communicate a strategic plan for a product or project. It allows product managers to visually represent the timeline, key milestones, and the overall direction of the product. The software provides a graphical representation of the roadmap, typically in the form of a timeline or Gantt chart. This visual representation helps product managers to easily understand and communicate the product strategy to stakeholders, team members, and executives.

Roadmap Visualization Templates

Roadmap Visualization Templates are visual representations used in Product Management to showcase the strategic direction and milestones of a product or project. These templates serve as a visual guide for the product team and stakeholders by providing a clear overview of the timeline, goals, and progress of the product roadmap. A roadmap is a strategic document that outlines the vision, objectives, and key initiatives of a product or project over a specific time period. It helps align the team and stakeholders around a common understanding of the goals and priorities. However, a textual roadmap can sometimes be difficult to interpret and comprehend, especially for individuals who are more inclined towards visual learning. This is where roadmap visualization templates come in handy. They transform the textual roadmap into a visually appealing and easy-to-understand format. These templates typically include timelines, milestones, objectives, and key initiatives represented through various visual elements such as charts, graphs, icons, or symbols. The primary purpose of roadmap visualization templates is to enhance communication and understanding among the product team and stakeholders. Visual representations are often more intuitive and can convey complex information in a simplified manner. By using these templates, product managers can effectively communicate the overall strategy, progress, and upcoming milestones to their team members and other stakeholders. Roadmap visualization templates also enable the product team to identify dependencies, prioritize tasks, and make informed decisions. The visual representation helps in spotting gaps, overlaps, or conflicts in the roadmap, giving the team an opportunity to adjust priorities or allocate resources accordingly. Additionally, these templates provide a holistic view of the entire product journey, allowing the team to understand how various initiatives and features are interconnected. Furthermore, roadmap visualization templates facilitate collaboration and alignment across different functions and teams involved in the product development process. They serve as a shared visual artifact that fosters discussions, encourages feedback, and enables everyone to contribute their perspectives towards a common vision. This collaborative approach enhances cross-functional understanding and ensures that everyone is on the same page regarding the product roadmap. In conclusion, roadmap visualization templates are essential tools in Product Management that help communicate the strategic direction and progress of a product or project. They provide a clear and intuitive visual representation of the roadmap, enabling effective communication, informed decision-making, and collaboration among the product team and stakeholders.

SWOT Analysis Frameworks

SWOT analysis is a strategic planning framework that helps Product Managers evaluate the internal and external factors affecting their product. SWOT stands for Strengths, Weaknesses, Opportunities, and Threats, and the analysis helps identify these aspects to develop effective product strategies. The first component of SWOT analysis is Strengths. Product Managers examine the internal strengths or positive attributes of their product. This includes features or functionalities that differentiate it from competitors, unique selling points, brand reputation, and customer loyalty. Understanding the strengths helps Product Managers capitalize on them to maintain a competitive edge. The second component is Weaknesses. Product Managers analyze the internal weaknesses or areas for improvement in their product. This includes aspects where the product is lacking, such as poor user experience, limited market reach, outdated technology, and pricing issues. Recognizing weaknesses allows Product Managers to take corrective actions to enhance the product and reduce vulnerabilities. The third component is Opportunities. Product Managers assess the external opportunities or potential areas for growth and advancement. This includes emerging market trends, new customer segments, technological advancements, regulatory changes, and partnerships. Identifying opportunities enables Product Managers to align their product strategies with market demands and create new avenues for revenue generation. The fourth and final component is Threats. Product Managers evaluate the external threats or challenges that may negatively impact their product's success. This includes intense competition, changing customer preferences, economic downturns, disruptive technologies, and legal or regulatory obstacles. Recognizing threats helps Product Managers anticipate and mitigate risks to protect their product's market position. In summary, SWOT analysis is a valuable framework in Product Management, enabling Product Managers to assess the internal strengths and weaknesses of their product and identify external opportunities and threats. This analysis forms the basis for developing effective strategies that leverage strengths, improve weaknesses, capitalize on opportunities, and mitigate threats. By using the SWOT framework, Product Managers can make informed decisions, enhance their product's performance in the market, and achieve sustainable growth.

SWOT Analysis

A SWOT analysis is a systematic evaluation of a product's strengths, weaknesses, opportunities, and threats. It is a strategic planning tool that helps product managers to understand their product's current position, identify potential areas for improvement, and evaluate external factors that could affect its success. The strengths of a product are its internal advantages or capabilities that give it a competitive edge in the market. These can include unique features, strong brand recognition, a loyal customer base, or a talented product development team. By identifying and leveraging these strengths, product managers can differentiate their product from competitors and attract more customers. On the other hand, weaknesses are internal limitations or shortcomings that hinder a product's performance or customer satisfaction. These can include outdated technology, poor user experience, lack of resources or expertise, or inefficient processes. By acknowledging and addressing these weaknesses, product managers can prioritize areas for improvement and enhance the overall quality of the product. Opportunities are external factors or market trends that product managers can capitalize on to drive growth and success. These can include new customer segments, emerging technologies, changing consumer demands, or untapped markets. By recognizing and seizing these opportunities, product managers can expand their product's reach, generate more revenue, and gain a competitive advantage. Finally, threats are external factors or challenges that could negatively impact a product's performance or market position. These can include intense competition, economic downturns, regulatory changes, or shifting customer preferences. By anticipating and mitigating these threats, product managers can develop contingency plans and minimize the potential risks to their product's success. In summary, a SWOT analysis is a valuable tool for product managers in assessing their product's strengths, weaknesses, opportunities, and threats. It allows them to make informed decisions, devise effective strategies, and ensure the long-term success and profitability of their product in the market.

Sales Closing Techniques

Sales closing techniques in the context of product management refer to the various strategies and tactics used by sales professionals to persuade potential customers to make a purchase. These techniques are employed during the final stages of the sales process, with the aim of sealing the deal and converting prospects into customers. One commonly used sales closing technique is the assumptive close. In this approach, the salesperson assumes that the prospect has already made the decision to purchase and proceeds to discuss details such as delivery options and payment terms. By assuming the sale has already been made, the salesperson creates a sense of inevitability and encourages the customer to confirm the decision. Another effective technique is the summary close. This involves summarizing the benefits and features of the product or service, highlighting how it meets the customer's specific needs and solves their pain points. By reaffirming the value proposition, the salesperson helps the prospect visualize the positive outcomes of the purchase, increasing the likelihood of a successful close. The direct close is a more straightforward approach, in which the salesperson simply asks the prospect for their decision. This technique requires confidence and assertiveness, as the salesperson must be comfortable directly asking for the sale without any additional persuasion or negotiation. Creating a sense of urgency is another effective sales closing technique. By indicating that the product or service is in high demand or that a limited-time offer is about to expire, the salesperson encourages the prospect to take immediate action. This technique leverages the fear of missing out (FOMO) and taps into the customer's desire for exclusivity or special deals. In conclusion, sales closing techniques in product management involve a range of strategies and tactics aimed at converting prospects into customers. By employing techniques such as assumptive closes, summary closes, direct closes, and creating a sense of urgency, sales professionals can increase their chances of successfully closing deals and generating revenue for their organization.

Sales Collateral Management

Sales Collateral Management refers to the process of organizing, creating, and distributing various types of sales collateral materials to support the sales team and improve overall sales performance. Sales collateral encompasses a wide range of resources such as brochures, product sheets, case studies, presentations, demos, and other supporting documents that are used during the sales process. The main objective of Sales Collateral Management is to ensure that the sales team has access to the most up-to-date, relevant, and accurate sales collateral materials that are necessary to effectively communicate with prospects and customers. It involves various activities such as creating new sales collateral, updating existing materials, organizing them in a centralized repository, and distributing them to the sales team in a timely manner.

Sales Collateral Organization

Sales Collateral Organization in the context of Product Management refers to the systematic and efficient management of sales and marketing materials that support the selling process of a product or service. It involves organizing, categorizing, and maintaining a library of various collateral pieces, such as brochures, presentations, case studies, product manuals, sales scripts, and other relevant materials. The primary goal of sales collateral organization is to ensure that sales teams have easy access to the right information and resources at the right time to effectively communicate the value proposition of the product and address the needs and concerns of potential customers. By having a well-organized and up-to-date collection of collateral, product managers can empower their sales teams to effectively engage with prospects throughout the sales cycle. Organizing sales collateral involves categorizing the materials based on their purpose, target audience, stage in the sales cycle, and product features. This categorization can be achieved through the use of folders or digital platforms that allow for easy navigation and searchability. Additionally, it is important to maintain version control to ensure that all collateral pieces are up-to-date and reflect the latest product information and messaging. Effective sales collateral organization also involves creating a system for tracking the usage and effectiveness of each collateral piece. This can be achieved by implementing analytics and feedback mechanisms to gather data on how often certain materials are accessed, how they are being used, and the impact they have on the sales process. These insights can guide product managers in continuously optimizing their collateral library and developing new materials that better align with the needs of the sales team and potential customers. In summary, sales collateral organization is a crucial aspect of Product Management that involves the systematic and efficient management of sales and marketing materials. By organizing and maintaining a library of relevant collateral, product managers can enable their sales teams to effectively communicate the value of the product and drive successful sales outcomes.

Sales Conversion Rate

The sales conversion rate is a metric in product management that measures the effectiveness of a sales campaign or funnel in converting potential customers into paying customers. It is expressed as a percentage and is a valuable indicator of a product's marketability and the success of sales and marketing efforts. The sales conversion rate is calculated by dividing the number of customers who make a purchase by the total number of leads or prospects in a given time period and multiplying by 100. The resulting percentage reflects the proportion of leads that successfully converted into customers. A higher sales conversion rate indicates that a product or sales campaign is performing well in converting leads into customers. It represents the efficiency of the product management team in nurturing and closing deals and can be used as a benchmark for future sales efforts. Product managers can use the sales conversion rate to identify areas for improvement in their sales and marketing strategies. By tracking the conversion rate over time, they can detect trends and patterns, allowing them to optimize their sales funnels and make data-driven decisions. There are several factors that can influence the sales conversion rate, including the quality of leads, the effectiveness of marketing materials, pricing, and competitive landscape. Understanding these factors and their impact on the conversion rate can help product managers refine their strategies and increase sales effectiveness. By continually monitoring and analyzing the sales conversion rate, product managers can identify opportunities to enhance product messaging, improve lead nurturing processes, or adjust pricing strategies. This metric provides valuable insights into the effectiveness of a product's sales and marketing efforts and can guide decision-making to drive revenue growth.

Sales Demo Techniques

Sales demo techniques refer to the strategies and tactics used by product managers to effectively demonstrate the features, benefits, and value of their products during sales presentations. These techniques are designed to capture the attention of potential customers, engage them in the demonstration, and ultimately persuade them to make a purchase. Product managers employ various methods to present their products in a compelling and persuasive manner, ensuring that key features and value propositions are highlighted and understood.

Sales Forecasting Models

Sales forecasting models are quantitative techniques used by Product Management to predict future sales performance based on historical data and other relevant factors. These models aim to provide insights and projections that can guide strategic decision-making, resource allocation, and sales planning. There are various sales forecasting models that Product Management teams can utilize, depending on the specific circumstances and needs of the organization. Some commonly used models include: 1. Time-Series Models: Time-series models analyze past sales data to identify patterns and trends, and then use this information to forecast future sales. These models can be simple, such as moving averages, or more complex, such as exponential smoothing or autoregressive integrated moving average (ARIMA) models. 2. Market-Driven Models: Market-driven models focus on external factors that can influence sales, such as market conditions, customer behavior, and competitor activities. These models often incorporate market research and data analysis to identify key drivers and predict sales based on changes in the market environment. 3. Econometric Models: Econometric models use statistical techniques to analyze the relationships between sales and various economic variables, such as GDP, inflation, or consumer spending. These models can help Product Management teams understand the impact of macroeconomic factors on sales performance and make forecasts accordingly. 4. Judgmental Models: Judgmental models rely on the expertise and experience of individuals or teams within the organization to make sales predictions. These models involve subjective assessments and qualitative analysis based on insights from sales representatives, managers, and industry experts. Ultimately, the choice of sales forecasting model(s) depends on the availability of data, the complexity of the market environment, and the level of accuracy required. By utilizing these models, Product Management can make informed decisions about pricing, production, inventory management, and marketing strategies, ultimately enhancing the organization's ability to meet customer demand, optimize resources, and drive profitability.

Sales Forecasting

Sales forecasting in the context of product management refers to the process of estimating and predicting the future sales performance of a specific product or product line. It involves analyzing historical sales data, market trends, customer behavior, and other relevant factors to make informed projections about future sales volumes and revenues. Product managers use sales forecasting as a crucial tool to make informed decisions related to production planning, inventory management, marketing strategies, and overall business growth. By accurately predicting sales volumes, they can optimize inventory levels, ensure sufficient production capacity, allocate resources effectively, and identify potential revenue opportunities.

Sales Funnel Visualization

A sales funnel visualization refers to a graphical representation or diagram used in product management to depict the various stages that potential customers go through before making a purchase. It illustrates the journey from the initial awareness of a product or service to the final conversion into a paying customer. The sales funnel visualization is typically divided into several stages, each representing a distinct step in the customer's decision-making process. These stages may vary depending on the nature of the product or service and the specific industry, but commonly include: Awareness: This is the first stage in the sales funnel, where potential customers become aware of the existence of a product or service. It is often achieved through marketing efforts such as advertising, content marketing, or social media campaigns. Interest: Once prospects are aware of the product or service, they enter the interest stage. Here, they actively seek more information and begin evaluating whether the offering meets their needs or solves their pain points. Product demonstrations, customer testimonials, and case studies can play a crucial role in nurturing their interest. Consideration: At this stage, potential customers have a strong interest in the product or service and are considering it as a viable solution. They may compare it with alternatives, perform a detailed evaluation, and seek recommendations from peers or industry experts. Decision: This is the critical stage where potential customers decide whether or not to make a purchase. It often involves factors like price, features, value proposition, and trust in the brand or company. Sales and marketing teams must address any remaining concerns or objections to increase the likelihood of conversion. Action: The final stage of the sales funnel is where the potential customer takes action and becomes a paying customer by making a purchase. This can involve completing an online transaction, signing a contract, or finalizing a deal. The purpose of visualizing the sales funnel is to gain a clear understanding of the customer's journey and identify potential bottlenecks or areas for improvement. By analyzing the movement of prospects through each stage, product managers can make data-driven decisions to optimize marketing strategies, streamline the sales process, and enhance overall conversion rates.

Sales Metrics

Sales metrics are quantitative measurements used in product management to track and analyze the performance of sales activities and strategies. These metrics provide valuable insights into the effectiveness of a product's sales efforts, helping product managers make data-driven decisions to improve sales performance. One key sales metric is the sales revenue, which measures the total amount of money generated from product sales within a specific period. Sales revenue is a fundamental metric in product management as it helps assess the financial success of a product and determine its profitability. By analyzing sales revenue, product managers can identify sales trends, evaluate the impact of different pricing strategies, and make informed decisions regarding product pricing and positioning. Another important sales metric is the customer acquisition cost (CAC), which measures the average cost incurred to acquire a new customer. CAC is calculated by dividing the total sales and marketing expenses by the number of new customers acquired. This metric helps product managers evaluate the effectiveness and efficiency of their sales and marketing efforts. By monitoring and optimizing CAC, product managers can identify potential areas for cost reduction and allocate resources more effectively to acquire new customers. Additionally, the sales conversion rate is a crucial sales metric that measures the percentage of leads or prospects that ultimately convert into paying customers. It indicates the effectiveness of the sales process and helps product managers understand the efficiency of their sales strategies. By monitoring the sales conversion rate, product managers can identify bottlenecks in the sales funnel, optimize sales tactics, and improve the overall conversion performance. Other important sales metrics in product management include average deal size, customer lifetime value (CLV), sales velocity, and sales

211

pipeline coverage. These metrics provide product managers with valuable insights into various aspects of the sales performance, enabling them to identify strengths, weaknesses, and opportunities for improvement. By regularly monitoring and analyzing these sales metrics, product managers can make data-driven decisions, optimize sales strategies, and drive revenue growth for their products.

Sales Qualified Leads (SQL)

Sales Qualified Leads (SQL) refer to potential customers who have already been vetted by the sales team and have shown a high likelihood of converting into paying customers. In the context of Product Management, SQLs play a crucial role in identifying and prioritizing leads that have the highest potential of driving revenue and growth for a product or service. Product Managers collaborate closely with the sales team to define the criteria for identifying SQLs, based on specific characteristics and actions that indicate a potential customer's readiness to make a purchase. These criteria typically include factors such as budget, authority, need, timeline, and fit with the product's target market. By working together with the sales team, Product Managers can ensure that the definition of SQLs aligns with the product's goals and target market, enabling the product team to focus on developing features and functionalities that meet the most important needs of potential customers. Once SQLs have been identified, the Product Manager plays a critical role in nurturing and guiding these leads through the sales funnel. This may involve providing sales reps with the necessary product knowledge and materials to effectively communicate the value proposition and benefits of the product to SQLs. In addition, Product Managers need to continuously analyze and evaluate the performance of SQLs to optimize the conversion rate and improve the overall sales process. This involves gathering and analyzing data on lead conversion rates, customer feedback, and market trends to identify areas of improvement and make informed decisions about product strategy and development. Ultimately, by effectively managing SQLs, Product Managers can ensure that the product is being marketed and sold to the right customers, resulting in increased sales, customer satisfaction, and long-term business growth.

Sales Strategy

A sales strategy in the context of product management is a structured approach designed to achieve sales objectives and drive revenue growth for a company's products or services. It involves analyzing market data, identifying target customers, and determining the most effective ways to reach and convert those customers into paying customers. The sales strategy typically starts with market research and analysis to identify key market trends, customer needs, and competitor offerings. This information is used to develop a deep understanding of the target customers, their pain points, and buying behavior. Based on this understanding, the sales strategy outlines specific goals and objectives. These goals may include increasing market share, expanding into new geographic markets, or targeting new customer segments. The strategy also includes a set of tactics and actions to achieve these goals, such as developing new marketing campaigns, hiring and training sales staff, or launching new product features. A key element of the sales strategy is the sales funnel, which outlines the customer journey from initial awareness to purchase. The strategy includes tactics to attract potential customers, engage them with the product or service, and ultimately convert them into paying customers. This may involve various marketing and sales channels, such as online advertising, social media, direct sales, or partnerships with resellers or distributors. The sales strategy is closely aligned with the overall product strategy and incorporates inputs from various stakeholders, including marketing, sales, and product development teams. It is a dynamic process that requires constant monitoring and adjustment based on market feedback and performance metrics. In summary, a sales strategy in the context of product management is a structured approach that guides a company's efforts to achieve sales objectives and drive revenue growth. It involves analyzing market data, identifying target customers, and developing tactics to reach and convert those customers into paying customers. The strategy is closely aligned with the overall product strategy and requires constant monitoring and adjustment to ensure its effectiveness.

Sales And Marketing Alignment

Sales and Marketing Alignment refers to the strategic coordination and collaboration between

212

the sales and marketing teams within the context of Product Management. It involves bridging the gap and fostering strong communication and integration between these two departments to maximize business outcomes and achieve shared objectives. The primary goal of Sales and Marketing Alignment is to ensure that both teams are working towards a common vision and are effectively supporting each other in the product lifecycle. This collaboration is crucial for Product Managers as it helps them gather valuable insights from marketing in terms of customer preferences, market trends, and competitive analysis, which can then be used to inform product development decisions. By aligning the efforts of sales and marketing, Product Managers can ensure that their products are effectively positioned in the market, gain a competitive advantage, and generate higher sales. The marketing team plays a vital role in creating awareness about the product, promoting its features and benefits, and building a strong brand image. The sales team, on the other hand, is responsible for closing deals and driving revenue. Through Sales and Marketing Alignment, Product Managers can leverage the expertise of both teams to develop targeted marketing strategies, identify and nurture high-quality leads, and improve conversion rates. The marketing team can share valuable customer insights and feedback with the sales team, enabling them to tailor their sales approaches and pitches to meet customer needs effectively. Collaboration between sales and marketing also facilitates the exchange of market intelligence and customer feedback, which helps Product Managers in refining and enhancing their product offerings. By aligning these two essential functions, Product Managers can ensure that customer feedback reaches the right channels, resulting in a faster feedback loop and more efficient product iterations.

Sales And Marketing Collaboration Tools

Sales and marketing collaboration tools are software platforms or applications that facilitate communication, collaboration, and coordination between the sales and marketing teams within an organization. These tools aim to align the efforts of both departments, ensuring a cohesive and integrated approach towards achieving the company's sales and marketing objectives. The purpose of sales and marketing collaboration tools is to improve efficiency, streamline processes, and enhance productivity within the sales and marketing teams. By providing a centralized platform for communication and collaboration, these tools enable teams to share information, exchange ideas, and work together seamlessly. One key feature of sales and marketing collaboration tools is the ability to centralize customer data and insights. These tools often integrate with customer relationship management (CRM) systems, allowing sales and marketing teams to access and update customer information in real-time. This not only eliminates the need for manual data entry but also ensures that both teams have a complete view of the customer, enabling them to tailor their sales and marketing efforts effectively. In addition to data integration, collaboration tools also offer functionalities such as task management, project tracking, and document sharing. These features promote transparency and accountability, as teams can assign tasks, monitor progress, and collaborate on projects within a single platform. By streamlining workflows and eliminating manual processes, these tools enable teams to work more efficiently, saving time and resources. Furthermore, sales and marketing collaboration tools often provide analytics and reporting capabilities. These features allow teams to track and measure the effectiveness of their sales and marketing initiatives, providing valuable insights for future planning and decision-making. By analyzing data on lead generation, customer engagement, and sales conversion, teams can identify areas for improvement and optimize their strategies accordingly. In conclusion, sales and marketing collaboration tools serve as a vital resource for product management. They facilitate effective communication, foster collaboration, and provide valuable insights for the sales and marketing teams. By leveraging these tools, organizations can enhance their sales and marketing efforts, drive revenue growth, and achieve their product management objectives.

Scrum Board Visualization

Scrum Board Visualization is a method used in Product Management to track the progress of tasks and projects in a visual and organized manner. It is an essential tool in the agile framework of development, particularly in Scrum methodology. The Scrum Board is a physical or digital board that visually represents the workflow of a project. It is divided into different sections such as "To Do," "In Progress," and "Done." Each section contains task cards or sticky notes that represent individual user stories or tasks. These task cards are moved across the board as progress is made, allowing the team to see at a glance the status of each task and the overall

213

progress of the project.

Scrum Board

A Scrum board is a visual representation of the tasks and progress of a project in Scrum methodology. It is an important tool for product management teams to track and monitor the work being done and ensure transparency and collaboration among team members. The Scrum board typically consists of three main columns: To Do, In Progress, and Done. Each task or user story is represented by a sticky note or index card that moves across the columns as it progresses through the project lifecycle. The board serves as a visual reminder of the tasks that need to be completed, the ones currently in progress, and those that have been completed. The To Do column represents the backlog or the list of tasks that have not yet been started. This column contains all the tasks that need to be done for the project. As team members start working on a task, it is moved to the In Progress column. This column shows all the tasks that are currently being worked on and ensures that team members are clear on the priorities and who is responsible for each task. Lastly, when a task is completed, it is moved to the Done column to indicate that it has been finished. The Scrum board is a visual representation of the team's progress and helps in several ways. Firstly, it allows the team to have a clear understanding of the project's status at any given time. By looking at the board, team members can easily see which tasks are pending, which are in progress, and which are done. This visibility helps ensure that everyone is on the same page and reduces the need for constant status update meetings. Secondly, the Scrum board promotes transparency and encourages collaboration. It allows all team members to see what tasks are assigned to whom and the progress being made. This transparency fosters better communication and coordination among team members, as they can easily identify potential bottlenecks or dependencies and work together to resolve them. Lastly, the Scrum board promotes accountability and ownership. As tasks are moved across the board, it is clear who is responsible for each task. This promotes a sense of ownership and enables team members to take responsibility for their assigned tasks. It also helps identify any potential delays or issues early on, allowing the team to take necessary actions to keep the project on track.

Scrum Framework

The Scrum Framework is a project management methodology that facilitates the efficient and iterative development of products by promoting collaboration, transparency, and adaptability. It is specifically designed for complex projects where requirements may change over time, and it emphasizes delivering incremental value to the customer early and often. In Scrum, product management involves a cross-functional team that includes the product owner, development team, and scrum master. The product owner is responsible for defining and prioritizing the product backlog, which is a list of features and enhancements that need to be developed. The development team, on the other hand, is responsible for self-organizing and determining how the work will be completed within the defined time frame called a sprint. The scrum master acts as a facilitator, enforcing Scrum principles and removing any obstacles that hinder the team's progress. The Scrum Framework operates under the principle of time-boxed iterations called sprints. Sprints typically last between one to four weeks and have a fixed duration. During each sprint, the development team works on a set of prioritized items from the product backlog in order to create a potentially shippable product increment. These increments are then reviewed and evaluated by the product owner and stakeholders during the sprint review, which helps gather valuable feedback to further refine and enhance the product. A key aspect of Scrum is its continuous feedback loop and iterative nature. After each sprint, the team holds a sprint retrospective to reflect on how they can improve their processes and increase efficiency. This feedback loop enables the team to adapt to changing requirements, customer needs, and market dynamics, ensuring that the product remains relevant and valuable. Overall, the Scrum Framework provides a flexible and collaborative approach to product management, enabling teams to deliver high-quality products in a predictable and efficient manner. Its focus on frequent communication, transparency, and adaptability makes it well-suited for developing innovative and complex products.

Scrum Master Role Description

A Scrum Master is a critical role in the context of Product Management. They are responsible for facilitating the adoption and implementation of Scrum practices within the product development team. The Scrum Master serves as a mentor and coach to the team, guiding them in effectively applying Scrum principles and methodologies. The primary role of a Scrum Master is to create a collaborative and self-organizing environment within the team. They help the team to understand and adhere to the Scrum framework, promoting transparency, commitment, and accountability. The Scrum Master acts as a servant-leader, supporting the team in overcoming any obstacles or challenges they may face in delivering a successful product. One of the key responsibilities of a Scrum Master is to ensure that the team follows the Scrum process and ceremonies. They facilitate the daily stand-up meetings, sprint planning sessions, sprint reviews, and retrospective meetings. During these meetings, the Scrum Master helps the team to identify and prioritize work, track progress, and make necessary adjustments to achieve the product goals. The Scrum Master also works closely with the Product Owner to ensure the product backlog is properly managed. They assist the Product Owner in grooming and prioritizing the backlog, ensuring that it is ready for the next sprint. The Scrum Master helps the team to understand and clarify the product requirements, ensuring that they have a clear understanding of the deliverables and customer expectations. In addition, the Scrum Master serves as a facilitator for the team, promoting effective communication and collaboration. They remove any barriers or impediments that may hinder the team's progress, fostering a culture of continuous improvement. The Scrum Master encourages the team to regularly reflect on their work and identify areas for improvement, facilitating a productive and iterative development process. In summary, the Scrum Master is a critical role in Product Management, responsible for guiding and mentoring the team in effectively applying Scrum practices. They create a collaborative and self-organizing environment, facilitate the Scrum process and ceremonies, and work closely with the Product Owner to ensure the successful delivery of the product.

Scrum Master Role Resources

A Scrum Master is a crucial role in the field of Product Management. They are responsible for ensuring that the Scrum framework is followed by the development team and that the product is delivered successfully. The Scrum Master serves as a facilitator, coach, and servant leader, helping the team to achieve high performance and delivering value to the stakeholders. As a facilitator, the Scrum Master helps the team by removing any obstacles or impediments that may hinder their progress. They ensure that the team has all the resources they need to complete their work, including the right tools, equipment, and support. The Scrum Master also helps to facilitate the communication and collaboration between the team members, ensuring that they are working together effectively and efficiently. As a coach, the Scrum Master helps the team by guiding them in adopting and adapting the Scrum framework. They provide guidance and support to the team members, helping them to understand and apply the principles, practices, and values of Scrum. The Scrum Master also helps to educate and raise awareness about Scrum within the organization, promoting its benefits and encouraging its adoption. As a servant leader, the Scrum Master serves the team by putting their needs first and helping them to be successful. They act as a servant leader, working for the benefit of the team and ensuring that they have the autonomy and authority to make decisions and take ownership of their work. The Scrum Master also acts as a servant leader to the stakeholders, working to understand their needs and priorities, and helping to ensure that the product is delivered to meet those needs. In summary, the Scrum Master role in Product Management is crucial for ensuring that the Scrum framework is followed and that the product is delivered successfully. They serve as a facilitator, coach, and servant leader, helping the team to achieve high performance and delivering value to the stakeholders.

Scrum Master Tools

A Scrum Master is a facilitative role in the Scrum framework that is responsible for ensuring the team follows Agile principles and practices to deliver high-quality products. The Scrum Master acts as a servant-leader, supporting the Product Owner and Development Team in their efforts to deliver value to the customer. Scrum Master Tools, in the context of Product Management, refer to the various techniques, approaches, and software that Scrum Masters utilize to enhance their effectiveness in guiding and managing the Scrum process. These tools help Scrum Masters track the progress of the project, promote collaboration and communication among team members, and encourage continuous improvement.

215

Scrum

Scrum is a framework used in Product Management to manage and control the development of complex products. It is an iterative and incremental approach that emphasizes collaboration, flexibility, and continuous improvement. In Scrum, the product development process is divided into small, self-contained work periods called sprints. Each sprint is typically two to four weeks long and focuses on delivering a working increment of the product. The team collaboratively plans the scope of work for each sprint, breaking it down into a prioritized list of tasks known as the product backlog. During the sprint planning, the team decides which items from the product backlog they will work on and creates a sprint backlog. The sprint backlog is a dynamic list that contains the tasks, estimated effort, and dependencies for each item selected for the sprint. The team commits to completing the tasks in the sprint backlog during the sprint. Throughout the sprint, the team holds daily stand-up meetings to provide updates on their progress, address any issues or impediments, and plan the activities for the next day. This short, time-boxed meeting fosters transparency, communication, and collaboration among team members. At the end of the sprint, the team conducts a sprint review to showcase the completed work to stakeholders and gather feedback. They also conduct a sprint retrospective, where they reflect on the sprint process and identify ways to improve their performance in future sprints. Scrum provides a framework for iterative development, allowing teams to respond to changing requirements and customer feedback. It promotes close collaboration between the product owner, development team, and stakeholders, ensuring that the product meets the needs of the customers and delivers value. Overall, Scrum enables Product Managers to effectively manage complex product development by breaking it down into manageable tasks, promoting collaboration, and providing a transparent and adaptable process.

Search Engine Marketing (SEM)

Search Engine Marketing (SEM) is a strategic digital marketing approach that focuses on promoting a product or service through search engines. It involves the process of increasing visibility and driving traffic to a website by using paid search advertising campaigns. SEM is a crucial component of product management, as it helps in reaching potential customers and generating leads. SEM primarily operates through paid search advertising, also called pay-per-click (PPC) advertising. It allows product managers to bid on specific keywords or search terms relevant to their products, ensuring that their ads appear prominently on search engine results pages (SERPs) when users search for those keywords. The ads are displayed above or alongside organic search results, attracting more visibility and increasing the chances of user clicks. The key benefit of SEM for product management is the ability to target specific customer segments. Product managers can create tailored ads based on demographics, locations, languages, and user preferences, maximizing the chances of converting leads into customers. SEM also allows for precise ad targeting by considering factors such as device type, time of the day, and search intent. This level of targeting helps product managers to optimize their ad campaigns and budget allocation. Another advantage of SEM is its measurable nature. It provides product managers with detailed metrics and insights on user behavior, ad performance, conversion rates, and return on investment (ROI). These insights enable product managers to analyze the effectiveness of their SEM campaigns, make data-driven decisions, and refine their strategies accordingly. In conclusion, Search Engine Marketing (SEM) plays a crucial role in product management by utilizing paid search advertising campaigns to increase visibility, drive traffic, and generate leads. It enables product managers to target specific customer segments, optimize ad campaigns, and gain valuable insights into user behavior. By leveraging SEM effectively, product managers can enhance brand awareness, increase conversions, and ultimately achieve business goals.

Search Engine Optimization (SEO)

Search Engine Optimization (SEO) is a strategic approach to improving the visibility and ranking of a product page or website in search engine results pages (SERPs). It involves optimizing various elements of the product page or website to make it more attractive to search engines, thus increasing organic (non-paid) traffic and ultimately driving conversions and sales. The goal of SEO in the context of Product Management is to increase the discoverability and visibility of a product page or website in search engine results, ensuring that it appears prominently to potential customers who are actively searching for related products or solutions. This helps in maximizing the reach and exposure of the product, and ultimately, its potential to generate revenue. SEO involves a combination of on-page and off-page optimization techniques. On-page optimization focuses on optimizing the content and structural elements of a product page or website to make it more search engine-friendly. This includes optimizing the product title, description, headings, URLs, and meta tags with relevant keywords and phrases that potential customers are likely to search for. It also involves ensuring the website's architecture, navigation, and internal linking structure are optimized for both search engines and users. Off-page optimization, on the other hand, involves improving the product page or website's visibility and authority in the online ecosystem. This is achieved through various inbound linking strategies, such as acquiring high-quality backlinks from reputable and relevant websites. Off-page SEO also involves managing and optimizing the product's online reputation through strategies like online reviews and ratings, social media presence, and influencer marketing. By implementing effective SEO strategies and continuously monitoring and optimizing the product page or website's performance, Product Managers can enhance the product's visibility, attract more qualified traffic, and improve its conversion rate. This not only contributes to the overall success of the product but also helps in outperforming competitors in search engine rankings and reaching a wider audience.

Social Media Advertising Platforms

Social media advertising platforms refer to online platforms or websites that allow businesses to advertise their products or services on various social media channels. These platforms provide tools and features that enable product managers to create, target, and optimize their advertising campaigns, ultimately reaching their target audience effectively. Product managers utilize social media advertising platforms to promote their products or services and increase brand visibility, engagement, and conversions. These platforms offer a range of advertising formats, such as display ads, video ads, sponsored content, and carousel ads, which product managers can choose from based on their campaign objectives and target audience preferences. Moreover, social media advertising platforms provide advanced targeting capabilities that allow product managers to reach specific demographics, interests, and behaviors. Through audience segmentation and targeting options, product managers can ensure that their ads are shown to the most relevant users, maximizing the chances of driving conversions and achieving desired outcomes. Additionally, these platforms provide analytics and reporting features, enabling product managers to track the performance of their advertising campaigns. They can measure metrics like impressions, clicks, conversions, and engagement to evaluate the success of their campaigns and optimize them for better results. By analyzing data and metrics, product managers can gain insights into audience behavior, ad performance, and overall campaign effectiveness, helping them make data-driven decisions and adjustments. In conclusion, social media advertising platforms play a crucial role in product management by providing tools and features to create, target, and optimize advertising campaigns on various social media channels. These platforms empower product managers to maximize brand visibility, engagement, and conversions by utilizing different ad formats and advanced targeting capabilities. Through analytics and reporting features, product managers can measure and analyze campaign performance, allowing them to make informed decisions and continually improve their social media advertising strategies.

Social Media Advertising

Social media advertising refers to the practice of promoting products or services through various social media platforms. It involves creating and distributing content in the form of ads or sponsored posts on platforms like Facebook, Instagram, Twitter, and LinkedIn, among others. Product management, within the context of social media advertising, is the strategic oversight and planning of the advertising campaigns for a particular product or set of products. It involves understanding the target audience, identifying the key messaging and positioning for the product, and selecting the most appropriate social media channels and ad formats to reach and engage the target market.

Social Media Marketing

Social Media Marketing, in the context of Product Management, refers to the strategic use of social media platforms and channels to promote and advertise products, with the purpose of increasing brand awareness, driving customer engagement, and ultimately, boosting sales. As part of the marketing mix, social media marketing leverages the power of various social networks, such as Facebook, Twitter, Instagram, LinkedIn, and YouTube, to effectively reach and communicate with a target audience. It involves creating and sharing relevant, engaging, and valuable content that aligns with the product's value proposition.

Sprint Management

Sprint Management is a crucial aspect of Product Management that focuses on planning, executing, and tracking the progress of time-bound product development cycles, known as sprints. Sprints are short, fixed-duration periods, typically ranging from one to four weeks, during which a Product Management team works on a specific set of features, enhancements, or bug fixes for a product. Sprint Management involves breaking down the product roadmap and prioritized backlog into smaller, manageable chunks of work that can be completed within each sprint.

Sprint Planning Tools

Sprint planning tools are software or digital platforms used by product managers to plan and organize the tasks and activities of a sprint in an agile development process. Agile development is a methodology that allows teams to collaborate and respond to changes and customer feedback in a flexible and iterative manner. A sprint is a short period, typically one to four weeks, during which a set of tasks or user stories are completed to deliver a workable increment or feature to the product. Sprint planning tools streamline the process of defining and assigning tasks, estimating effort, setting priorities, and tracking progress. These tools provide a centralized and visual platform where product managers and their teams can collaboratively plan, track, and review the tasks and activities of a sprint. With these tools, product managers can easily break down larger user stories or features into smaller, manageable tasks, assign them to team members, and track their progress in real time.

Sprint Planning

Sprint Planning is a crucial step in the Agile product development methodology, where the Product Management team collaboratively determines the set of features, tasks, and goals to be achieved in the upcoming sprint. During Sprint Planning, the Product Manager, Development team, and Scrum Master come together to discuss and define the sprint backlog - a prioritized list of user stories or product backlog items that will be implemented during the sprint. The purpose of this planning session is to determine what can realistically be achieved within the sprint timeframe and to establish a shared understanding of the work to be done.

Subscription Billing Platforms

A subscription billing platform is a software solution, typically used in product management, that enables businesses to automate and manage their recurring billing processes for subscription-based products or services. These platforms facilitate the creation and management of various subscription plans and pricing models, allowing businesses to easily set up and customize their offerings to meet the needs of their target customers. Subscription billing platforms often provide a range of features to support the entire subscription lifecycle, from sign-up and onboarding to billing and account management. With a subscription billing platform, product managers can efficiently handle subscription-related tasks and streamline their billing operations. These platforms offer flexible billing options, allowing businesses to choose between different billing cycles (e.g., monthly, quarterly, annually) and payment methods (e.g., credit card, online banking). They also provide automated invoicing and payment reminders, reducing manual effort and ensuring timely payments. Furthermore, subscription billing platforms offer various pricing and packaging capabilities, enabling product managers to easily experiment with different pricing models, such as tiered pricing, volume-based pricing, or usage-based pricing. This flexibility allows businesses to optimize their revenue streams and cater to different customer segments effectively. Moreover, subscription billing platforms often come with analytics and reporting features that provide product managers with valuable insights into their subscription business. These features allow them to track key subscription metrics, such as customer churn rate, average revenue per user, or subscription renewal rates. By analyzing this data, product managers can identify trends, make data-driven decisions, and refine their pricing and product strategies to maximize customer retention and revenue. In summary, subscription billing platforms are essential tools for product managers, providing them with the necessary capabilities to automate and manage the complex billing processes associated with subscription-based products or services. These platforms help optimize revenue generation and customer retention by offering flexible pricing options, automating billing tasks, and providing valuable subscription analytics.

Subscription Billing Systems

A subscription billing system, in the context of product management, is a software tool or platform that enables businesses to manage the billing and invoicing processes for their subscription-based products or services. In other words, it is a system that automates the collection, tracking, and management of recurring payments from customers who have subscribed to a particular product or service. These systems are designed to handle the complex billing requirements of subscription-based businesses, which typically involve recurring charges, different pricing tiers or plans, trials, discounts, and prorated billing. They offer a range of functionalities that streamline the subscription billing lifecycle, from customer signup and initial payment to ongoing invoicing, payment processing, and subscription management. Key features of subscription billing systems may include: 1. Automated billing and invoicing: The system automates the generation, delivery, and tracking of invoices or bills for subscription customers. This ensures accurate and timely billing, reducing manual errors and saving time for both businesses and customers. 2. Flexible pricing and plan management: These systems allow businesses to set up and manage various pricing tiers, plans, and options for their subscription products or services. They enable businesses to easily introduce new plans, update pricing, or offer discounts or promotions as needed. 3. Recurring payment management: The system facilitates the collection of recurring payments from customers, automating the payment processing and management. This ensures that payments are received on time and reduces the risk of non-payment or late payments. 4. Subscription lifecycle management: The system tracks and manages the entire subscription lifecycle, from customer onboarding and plan selection to renewal, upgrades, downgrades, or cancellations. It provides businesses with visibility into their customer base and enables them to effectively manage customer relationships. 5. Analytics and reporting: These systems generate reports and provide analytics on key subscription metrics, such as churn rate, customer lifetime value, revenue growth, and customer behavior. This helps businesses gain insights into their subscription business and make data-driven decisions. Overall, subscription billing systems play a crucial role in product management by simplifying and automating the billing processes associated with subscription-based products or services. They enable businesses to efficiently manage their subscription customers, improve cash flow, and enhance overall customer satisfaction.

Subscription Model Management

A subscription model management, in the context of product management, refers to the strategy and processes involved in developing and maintaining a subscription-based business model for a product or service. This model allows customers to pay a recurring fee in exchange for access to the product or service over a specified period. Subscription models are becoming increasingly popular across various industries as they provide a predictable and continuous revenue stream for businesses.

Testimonial Gathering

Testimonial gathering in the context of product management refers to the process of collecting and evaluating feedback and reviews from customers or users of a product. It is a crucial component of product management as it provides insights into the product's strengths, weaknesses, and overall performance. Testimonials can come in various forms, such as written reviews, ratings, or spoken endorsements, and can be collected through surveys, interviews, social media platforms, or dedicated review websites. By gathering testimonials, product managers can gain valuable information to assess customer satisfaction, identify areas for improvement, and make informed decisions about product development and marketing strategies. Testimonials serve as a source of qualitative feedback, providing insights into the user experience, customer preferences, and product features or functionalities that resonate the

219

most with the target audience.

UI Design Collaboration

UI design collaboration in the context of Product Management refers to the process of bringing together different individuals or teams to work collectively on designing user interfaces for a product. This collaboration involves the exchange of ideas, sharing of knowledge, and cooperation among the stakeholders to create a user-friendly and visually appealing interface that meets the needs of the users and aligns with the overall product strategy. Collaboration is a crucial aspect of UI design as it brings together the unique perspectives and expertise of various individuals, including product managers, designers, developers, and other relevant stakeholders. By working together, they can leverage their collective skills, experiences, and insights to ideate, iterate, and refine the UI design. Collaboration ensures that the UI design is not limited to the vision of a single individual but reflects a holistic approach that considers different viewpoints and addresses potential challenges.

UX Design Collaboration

UX design collaboration refers to the process of working together with various stakeholders, including UX designers, product managers, developers, and other team members, to create user-centered and well-designed products. It involves fostering effective communication, understanding user needs, and incorporating feedback from multiple perspectives throughout the product development lifecycle. In the context of product management, UX design collaboration plays a crucial role in ensuring that the product meets user expectations, is aesthetically pleasing, and provides a seamless user experience. Product managers are responsible for defining the overall product strategy and vision, while UX designers focus on understanding user behavior and designing intuitive interfaces. Successful collaboration between these roles is essential to deliver a product that not only solves user problems but also aligns with business goals. Throughout the product lifecycle, collaboration between product managers and UX designers involves various activities, such as: - Conducting user research to gather insights about user needs and preferences. - Defining user personas and scenarios to guide the design process. - Developing wireframes and prototypes to visualize and test design concepts. - Iteratively refining designs based on user feedback and usability testing. - Coordinating with developers to ensure the feasibility of implementing the design. - Conducting user acceptance testing to validate the final product before release. Effective UX design collaboration requires clear and open communication between product managers and UX designers. Both parties should actively share their expertise, insights, and concerns to create a shared understanding of the product requirements and constraints. Collaboration should be based on mutual respect and an appreciation for each other's roles and expertise. By collaborating closely, product managers and UX designers can leverage their combined skills and knowledge to create products that are not only functional but also user-friendly and visually appealing. This collaboration helps in reducing rework, improving the efficiency of product development, and ultimately delivering a product that meets user expectations and business objectives.

UX/UI Design Handoff

A UX/UI design handoff in the context of Product Management is the process of transferring the design and specifications of a user interface (UI) or user experience (UX) design from the design team to the development team. During the handoff, the design team communicates the intent and details of the design to the development team, ensuring a smooth transition and understanding of design decisions. This process is crucial for ensuring that the final product accurately reflects the design team's vision and meets user expectations.

UX/UI Testing

UX/UI testing, in the context of product management, refers to the evaluation process of a product's user experience (UX) and user interface (UI) design through various methods and techniques. It involves testing the usability, functionality, and overall user satisfaction with the product. UX testing focuses on evaluating how easy and enjoyable it is for users to interact with the product, ensuring that it meets their needs and expectations. This testing can involve tasks such as observing users as they navigate through the product, tracking their actions and feedback, and analyzing their overall experience. The goal is to identify any usability issues, pain points, or areas that need improvement to enhance user satisfaction. UI testing, on the other hand, assesses the visual design and layout of the product, ensuring that it is visually appealing, consistent, and easy to understand. This testing can involve evaluating the clarity of the interface elements, the placement of buttons and controls, the use of colors and typography, and the overall aesthetics of the design. The goal is to identify any inconsistencies, visual distractions, or design flaws that may negatively impact the user's perception and experience. Overall, UX/UI testing plays a crucial role in product management as it helps identify and address usability and design issues to ensure a positive user experience. It provides valuable insights and feedback that can inform the decision-making process of product managers, designers, and developers, helping them make informed changes and improvements to the product. By conducting UX/UI testing, product managers can deliver products that are user-friendly, visually appealing, and aligned with the needs and expectations of their target users.

Unique Selling Proposition (USP)

A Unique Selling Proposition (USP), in the context of Product Management, refers to a distinctive and compelling value proposition that sets a product apart from its competitors in the market. It is a clear and concise statement that highlights the unique benefits, features, and advantages that a product offers to its target customers. The USP plays a crucial role in product positioning and marketing strategy, as it helps create a strong brand identity and differentiation in a crowded marketplace. It enables the product to stand out and attract the attention of potential customers, leading to increased sales and market share.

Usability Testing Integration

Usability testing integration, in the context of product management, refers to the process of incorporating usability testing into the development and launch of a product. It involves the systematic evaluation of a product's usability and user experience, allowing product managers to identify and address any usability issues before the product is released to the market. Usability testing integration typically follows a structured approach, involving several key steps. First, the product management team defines the objectives and scope of the usability testing, determining which aspects of the product's usability will be assessed. This may include factors such as ease of use, efficiency, error prevention, and user satisfaction. Next, the team designs the usability testing plan, outlining the specific tasks and scenarios that users will be asked to perform during the testing phase. This plan may also include the selection of appropriate metrics and measurement techniques to evaluate the usability of the product. Once the testing plan is in place, the product management team recruits participants who represent the target user group of the product. These participants are given access to the product and are asked to perform the designated tasks while their interactions and experiences are observed and recorded. After the usability testing sessions are complete, the product management team analyzes the data collected, looking for patterns, trends, and issues that emerged during the testing phase. This analysis enables them to identify any areas of the product that may require improvements or modifications to enhance usability. Based on the findings from the usability testing, product managers can then make informed decisions about potential changes or adjustments to the product design, user interface, or feature set. This iterative process allows for continuous improvement and refinement of the product's usability and overall user experience. Overall, usability testing integration plays a crucial role in product management by providing valuable insights into the usability and user experience of a product. By incorporating this process into the product development lifecycle, product managers can ensure that their products meet the needs and expectations of their target users, resulting in enhanced customer satisfaction and increased product success in the market.

Usability Testing Labs

A usability testing lab is a dedicated facility or space used by product management teams to conduct research and evaluate the usability of a product or service. It provides a controlled environment where users can interact with the product or service while their actions, feedback, and overall experience are observed and recorded by a testing team. Usability testing labs typically consist of a testing room, equipped with necessary hardware and software, and an observation room where product managers, designers, and other stakeholders can watch the users' interactions in real-time. The facility is designed to mimic real-world conditions, allowing users to test the product in a natural and authentic way.

Usability Testing Moderation Platforms

A usability testing moderation platform is a software tool or platform used by product managers to conduct and facilitate usability testing sessions. It provides a centralized space for managing and moderating usability tests, allowing product managers to efficiently gather feedback and insights to improve user experience. Usability testing is a crucial part of the product development process, as it helps identify any usability issues or challenges that users may encounter when using a product or service. The goal of usability testing is to ensure that the product is intuitive, easy to use, and meets the needs and expectations of its target users.

Usability Testing Moderation

Usability testing moderation is a process in product management where a moderator facilitates and guides the usability testing sessions with users. The moderator's role is to ensure that the testing is conducted smoothly and efficiently, allowing for the collection of accurate and relevant data about the product's usability. The usability testing moderation process involves several key responsibilities for the moderator: Firstly, the moderator is responsible for recruiting and selecting suitable participants for the usability testing sessions. This requires the moderator to identify the target user group and find individuals who fit the criteria. The moderator ensures that the participants are representative of the intended user base, providing valuable insights into the product's usability from a diverse range of perspectives. Secondly, the moderator prepares the testing environment, including setting up the necessary equipment and ensuring that the testing environment is comfortable and conducive to the participants' concentration and feedback. The moderator also ensures that any required materials or prototypes are ready and available for the testing sessions. During the usability testing sessions, the moderator guides the participants through a series of tasks or scenarios, observing their interactions with the product and recording their feedback. The moderator encourages the participants to think aloud, articulating their thoughts and reactions as they navigate through the product. This allows the moderator to gain insights into the users' expectations, preferences, and pain points, helping to identify areas for improvement. The moderator ensures that the testing sessions stay focused and on track, keeping the participants engaged and motivated throughout the process. They may ask open-ended questions to elicit further feedback or clarification on specific issues. Additionally, the moderator takes notes and records any observations or issues that arise during the testing, capturing both qualitative and quantitative data for later analysis. After the usability testing sessions, the moderator reviews the collected data and consolidates the findings. They play a crucial role in analyzing the results, identifying usability issues and patterns, and making recommendations for product improvements. The moderator's insights and recommendations are essential in driving the iterative design and development process, ultimately enhancing the product's usability and user experience. In conclusion, usability testing moderation is a vital component of product management, ensuring that usability testing sessions are well-executed and yield meaningful insights. The moderator's role encompasses participant recruitment, preparation of the testing environment, guiding participants through tasks, recording feedback, and analyzing the results. By facilitating effective usability testing, the moderator helps inform product decisions and drives improvements to enhance user satisfaction.

Usability Testing Platforms

Usability testing platforms are tools or software used by product managers to evaluate the usability and user experience of a product or service. These platforms provide a structured approach to gathering feedback from users and assessing the effectiveness and efficiency of a product's design. Usability testing is a critical component of the product development process as it allows product managers to identify and address any usability issues or pain points that users may encounter. By observing and analyzing how users interact with a product, product managers can gain insights into user behavior, preferences, and needs, which can help inform product decision-making and improve overall user satisfaction.

Usability Testing Protocols

Usability testing protocols in the context of product management refer to the specific guidelines and steps followed to evaluate the usability of a product or service. Usability testing is a crucial part of the product development process, as it helps identify any usability issues or problems that may hinder the user experience. The protocols for conducting usability testing ensure that the testing process is systematic, objective, and focused on gathering meaningful insights about the usability of the product. These protocols typically include the following key elements: 1. Objective setting: Clearly define the goals and objectives of the usability testing, such as identifying specific usability issues or measuring user satisfaction. 2. Test plan development: Create a detailed plan outlining the testing methodology, tasks to be performed, and criteria for success or failure. 3. Participant recruitment: Select a representative group of participants based on the target audience for the product. Participants may include existing users, potential customers, or individuals with relevant expertise. 4. Pre-test briefing: Provide participants with an overview of the product, its purpose, and the tasks they will be required to perform during the testing session. 5. Test session execution: Conduct individual or group usability testing sessions, where participants are observed while performing specific tasks. The test facilitator should encourage participants to think aloud, providing insights into their thought process, difficulties, and preferences. 6. Data collection: Use a combination of qualitative and quantitative methods to collect data during the testing sessions. This may include video recordings, observation notes, surveys, or questionnaires. 7. Analysis and interpretation: Analyze the collected data to identify patterns, trends, and issues that may arise. Evaluate the effectiveness, efficiency, and user satisfaction of the product based on the test results. 8. Reporting and communication: Prepare a clear and concise report summarizing the findings from the usability testing. Communicate the results to the product team, stakeholders, and relevant decision-makers, highlighting key usability issues and possible recommendations for improvement. 9. Follow-up actions: Use the insights gained from the usability testing to prioritize and implement changes or updates to the product. This iterative process helps refine the product's usability and user experience over time.

Usability Testing Results

Usability testing is a crucial process in the field of product management that involves evaluating the ease of use and user satisfaction of a product or system. It is a methodical approach used to uncover usability issues and gather feedback from real users, with the goal of improving the overall user experience. The process of usability testing typically involves selecting a representative group of target users and observing their interactions with the product or system. This can be done through various means, such as conducting in-person sessions, remote sessions, or using specialized software tools. During the testing, users are given specific tasks to complete while their actions, reactions, and feedback are carefully monitored and recorded.

Usability Testing

Usability testing is a vital component of product management, serving as a method to evaluate a product's usability and overall user experience. It involves observing and measuring how easily and effectively users can interact with a product in order to identify any usability issues or areas for improvement. This testing typically involves a group of targeted users who are given specific tasks to perform with the product, while their interactions are closely observed by a researcher or product manager.The primary objective of usability testing is to uncover any usability problems within the product, such as confusing navigation, unclear instructions, or functional issues that may hinder the user's ability to accomplish their goals efficiently. By observing users as they interact with the product, product managers gain valuable insights into both the strengths and weaknesses of the user experience.

User Acceptance Testing (UAT)

User Acceptance Testing (UAT) is a crucial phase in the product management process that involves testing the product or software from the end user's perspective to ensure its readiness for deployment. It serves as the final validation before delivering the product to the market or the intended target audience. UAT aims to verify if the product meets the specified requirements, is user-friendly, performs as expected, and fulfills the intended business objectives. During UAT, the product is tested in a real-world environment, simulating real-life scenarios and conditions, with the purpose of discovering any potential flaws or shortcomings that may impact the user experience or hinder the product's functionality. This testing phase is typically conducted by actual end users, who are not involved in the development process, but represent the target audience or the end user persona identified during the product development cycle. The primary objectives of UAT are to assess the product's overall usability, functionality, and user satisfaction. It helps identify any gaps between the initial requirements and the final product, ensuring that the delivered product meets the expectations of the end users. UAT also provides insights into potential areas of improvement, allowing product managers to gather valuable feedback and make necessary adjustments or enhancements before the product launch. The UAT process involves creating a test plan, test scenarios, and test cases that cover different usage scenarios and user interactions. Testers execute these test cases and report any issues, bugs, or deviations from the expected behavior. The product manager and development team collaborate with the testers to address and resolve these issues, refine the product, and ensure its readiness for launch. UAT plays a crucial role in reducing the risk of delivering a flawed or subpar product to the market. It helps ensure the product's quality, functionality, and alignment with user expectations. By involving end users in the testing process, UAT helps validate the product's market fit and potential success, ultimately contributing to the overall success of the product management lifecycle.

User Behavior Analytics Platforms

User Behavior Analytics Platforms are software tools that collect, analyze, and interpret data on users' behavior within a digital product or service. These platforms use various techniques and algorithms to gather data from multiple sources, such as websites, mobile applications, and other online platforms. Product Managers utilize User Behavior Analytics Platforms to gain insights into user behavior and preferences. By collecting and analyzing data on how users interact with the product, these platforms help Product Managers understand user needs, preferences, and pain points. This information can then be used to inform product decisions, improve user experience, and drive product strategy. User Behavior Analytics Platforms offer a range of features and capabilities that enable Product Managers to effectively monitor and analyze user behavior. These platforms can track various metrics, such as user engagement, conversion rates, click-through rates, and time spent on different screens or pages. Product Managers can use these metrics to identify patterns, trends, and anomalies in user behavior. Additionally, User Behavior Analytics Platforms provide tools for segmenting users based on various attributes, such as demographics, behavior patterns, and user preferences. This segmentation allows Product Managers to better understand the different user groups and tailor the product experience to meet their specific needs. Furthermore, User Behavior Analytics Platforms enable Product Managers to conduct A/B testing and experiment with different features, designs, and user flows. By measuring and comparing user behavior in different test groups, Product Managers can make data-driven decisions about which features or designs are most effective in driving user engagement and achieving product goals. In conclusion, User Behavior Analytics Platforms play a crucial role in helping Product Managers gain insights into user behavior and preferences. By utilizing these platforms, Product Managers can make informed decisions about product strategy, design, and feature development, ultimately leading to improved user experience and business success.

User Behavior Analytics

User Behavior Analytics (UBA) in the context of Product Management refers to the analysis and interpretation of data related to the actions, behaviors, and preferences of users within a product or software application. UBA focuses on understanding how users interact with the product, their patterns of usage, and their overall experience. The goal of User Behavior Analytics in product management is to gain insights into user behavior and leverage these insights to drive product improvements, enhance user satisfaction, and increase overall product adoption. By analyzing user behavior, product managers can identify trends, patterns, and potential pain points, allowing them to make data-driven decisions and prioritize product enhancements based on user needs and preferences.

User Behavior Insights

User Behavior Insights, in the context of Product Management, refers to the study and analysis of how users interact with a product or service. It involves collecting and interpreting data on user behavior, preferences, and actions to gain a deeper understanding of user needs and expectations. This information is then used to inform product decisions and strategies, aiming to improve user satisfaction, engagement, and overall product success. Product Managers use User Behavior Insights to make data-driven decisions throughout the product development lifecycle. By closely tracking and analyzing user behaviors, they can identify patterns, trends, and areas for improvement. This includes understanding how users navigate through the product, what features they use most frequently, and which ones they find valuable. Additionally, User Behavior Insights provide insights into user pain points, frustrations, and areas of confusion, helping Product Managers to prioritize and address these issues.

User Behavior Tracking

User Behavior Tracking is a method of collecting data and insights on how users interact with a product or service. It involves monitoring and analyzing various user activities such as page views, clicks, downloads, and conversions to understand user preferences, behavior patterns, and pain points. This data helps product managers make informed decisions and improvements to enhance the overall user experience and achieve business goals. With user behavior tracking, product managers can gather quantitative and qualitative data about user engagement, navigation paths, and feature usage. This data is typically collected through various tools and technologies, such as analytics platforms, event tracking systems, and heatmaps. By systematically tracking and analyzing user behavior, product managers can identify trends, discover opportunities, and uncover problems that may inhibit user satisfaction or hinder product growth. One of the key benefits of user behavior tracking is the ability to gain insights into user needs and preferences. By understanding how users interact with a product, what features they use most frequently, or where they face difficulties, product managers can align their product roadmap and prioritize enhancements accordingly. This data-driven approach helps in developing user-centric products and features that address user pain points and delight the target audience. Additionally, user behavior tracking enables product managers to measure the effectiveness of product changes or feature releases. They can track metrics such as user retention rate, conversion rate, or average session duration to assess the impact of product updates. This information helps in identifying successful changes and determining whether product updates are meeting the intended goals or need further iteration. Furthermore, user behavior tracking plays a crucial role in optimizing the user experience. It helps identify bottlenecks, drop-off points, or confusing user flows within a product. By analyzing user behavior data, product managers can make data-informed decisions to improve user interfaces, simplify workflows, or enhance the overall usability of a product. In conclusion, user behavior tracking is a vital practice in product management that involves monitoring and analyzing user activities to gain insights into user preferences, behavior patterns, and pain points. This data-driven approach allows product managers to make informed decisions, optimize the user experience, and align their product roadmap with user needs and business goals.

User Churn Analysis

User churn analysis is a process in product management that involves examining and evaluating the rate at which customers stop using a product or service. It focuses on understanding why users are leaving and identifying measures that can be taken to reduce churn and retain more customers. The goal of user churn analysis is to gain insights into customer behavior, preferences, and satisfaction levels. By studying the reasons behind churn, product managers can make informed decisions and implement strategies to improve customer retention. This analysis helps identify patterns, trends, and potential areas of improvement, allowing for targeted interventions to be made. During user churn analysis, product managers collect and analyze various data points, such as customer usage patterns, feedback, and customer support interactions. They may also utilize data from surveys, user interviews, and social media sentiment analysis to gain a comprehensive understanding of why customers are leaving. Key metrics often examined during user churn analysis include churn rate, customer lifetime value, customer acquisition cost, and customer satisfaction scores. These metrics provide product managers with quantifiable data to measure the effectiveness of retention strategies and identify areas that need improvement. The insights gained from user churn analysis are then used to develop and refine strategies to mitigate churn. These strategies can range from product improvements and feature enhancements to targeted marketing campaigns focused on customer retention. Overall, user churn analysis plays a vital role in product management by enabling product managers to make data-driven decisions to improve customer retention. By understanding why users churn and implementing targeted interventions, product managers can enhance the overall user experience and drive long-term customer loyalty.

User Engagement Analytics

User Engagement Analytics refers to the collection, analysis, and interpretation of data related to user behavior and interaction with a product, with the aim of understanding and improving the overall user experience and driving user engagement. In the context of Product Management, User Engagement Analytics plays a crucial role in informing decision-making and strategy development. By closely monitoring and assessing user behavior, Product Managers can gain valuable insights into how users are interacting with their product, what features are being used most frequently, and where users may be experiencing difficulties or drop-offs in their journey. This data-driven approach enables Product Managers to make informed decisions regarding product enhancements, feature prioritization, and overall product roadmap planning. User Engagement Analytics encompasses a wide range of metrics and data points that can be collected and analyzed. These may include but are not limited to: 1. Active users: This metric tracks the number of users who are actively engaging with the product within a specific time frame. It helps Product Managers understand the size and growth of their user base and identify any trends or patterns in user activity. 2. Session duration: This metric measures the amount of time users spend using the product in a single session. It provides insights into user engagement levels and can help identify opportunities for increasing user stickiness. 3. Conversion rates: Conversion rates track the percentage of users who complete a desired action, such as making a purchase or signing up for a subscription. Analyzing conversion rates can help identify areas for improvement in the user journey and optimize conversion funnels. 4. Retention rates: Retention rates measure the percentage of users who continue to use the product over time. This metric is essential for understanding user loyalty and identifying strategies for increasing long-term engagement. 5. Feature usage: Tracking which features are being used most frequently and which are being ignored can help Product Managers prioritize feature enhancements and allocate development resources effectively. By leveraging User Engagement Analytics, Product Managers can make data-driven decisions that enhance the user experience and drive user engagement. It empowers Product Managers to constantly iterate and improve their product based on insights gained from user behavior, leading to higher user satisfaction, increased retention, and ultimately, greater business success.

User Engagement Tracking Tools

User Engagement Tracking Tools are software applications that enable Product Managers to measure and analyze the behavior and interaction of users with a product or service. These tools provide insights into how users are engaging with the product, allowing Product Managers to make data-driven decisions to enhance user experience and improve overall performance. By tracking various user actions and events, such as clicks, downloads, page views, and time spent on specific features, User Engagement Tracking Tools help Product Managers understand how users are using the product and where they may be encountering difficulties or obstacles. This information enables Product Managers to identify areas for improvement and make informed decisions on product enhancements and optimizations. These tools typically provide data visualizations and reports that allow Product Managers to easily interpret and analyze the collected user engagement data. Key metrics, such as user retention, conversion rates, and user satisfaction scores, can be monitored and tracked over time to gauge the product's success and effectiveness. User Engagement Tracking Tools also facilitate A/B testing, allowing Product Managers to compare the performance of different product variations or features. By measuring user engagement with each variation, Product Managers can identify which changes have the desired impact and deliver the best user experience. Furthermore, User Engagement Tracking Tools often integrate with other product management and analytics platforms, such as customer relationship management systems and marketing automation tools. These integrations provide a comprehensive view of user behavior across different touchpoints and help Product Managers connect user engagement data with other key business metrics. In summary, User Engagement Tracking Tools are essential for Product Managers to measure and analyze user interaction with a product or service. By leveraging these tools, Product Managers can gather valuable insights to optimize user experience, increase user satisfaction, and drive overall product success.

User Experience (UX)

User Experience (UX) in the context of Product Management refers to the overall experience that a user has while interacting with a product, system, or service. It encompasses all the aspects of the user's interaction, including their perceptions, emotions, and responses. UX is focused on ensuring that the product fulfills the needs and expectations of the user, while also being easy to use, visually appealing, and providing a seamless and enjoyable experience. It involves understanding the user's goals, preferences, and behaviors, and designing the product in a way that meets these needs.

User Feedback Collection

Product Management is a critical function within an organization that focuses on the strategic planning, development, and execution of products or services. It involves managing the entire lifecycle of a product, from its conception to its eventual retirement. The core responsibility of a Product Manager is to ensure that the right product is developed to meet the needs of the target market and to achieve the company's business goals. This involves conducting market research, analyzing customer needs and preferences, and collaborating with cross-functional teams such as engineering, design, and marketing to define the product vision and roadmap. Throughout the product lifecycle, Product Managers are responsible for gathering and prioritizing requirements, communicating product updates and progress to stakeholders, and making key decisions on product features, pricing, and positioning. They also play a crucial role in coordinating the development process, working closely with engineers and designers to ensure that the product is delivered on time and within budget. In addition to the development and launch phase, Product Managers also monitor the performance of the product in the market, collecting feedback from customers, analyzing market trends, and making data-driven decisions to improve the product and drive its success. They work closely with sales and marketing teams to develop effective go-to-market strategies and engage in ongoing product marketing and promotion activities. Product Management requires a combination of strategic thinking, business acumen, and strong communication and collaboration skills. Product Managers must be able to understand market dynamics, identify customer needs, and translate them into actionable plans. They need to balance the demands of different stakeholders and manage competing priorities to ensure the successful delivery of products that meet customer expectations and drive business growth. In summary, Product Management is a discipline that encompasses the end-to-end management of a product or service, from concept to retirement. It involves strategic planning, market research, cross-functional collaboration, decision-making, and ongoing performance analysis. Product Managers are responsible for ensuring the success of their products by aligning customer needs with business objectives and driving product development and marketing efforts accordingly.

User Feedback Integration

User Feedback Integration refers to the process of systematically integrating feedback from users into the product management workflow, in order to improve the product's features, functionality, and overall user experience. It involves gathering, analyzing, and incorporating user feedback into decision-making processes and product development cycles. User feedback can take various forms, such as surveys, interviews, usability testing, support tickets, and online reviews. This valuable input provides firsthand insights into users' needs, pain points, and preferences, helping product managers make informed decisions about feature prioritization, product roadmap, and design improvements. The integration of user feedback helps ensure that product development aligns with user expectations and requirements, ultimately driving product success and customer satisfaction. It allows product managers to iterate and evolve the product based on real user insights, rather than relying solely on assumptions or internal perspectives. To effectively integrate user feedback, product managers need to establish structured feedback collection processes. This includes methods for gathering feedback at different stages of the user journey, as well as mechanisms for categorizing and prioritizing the feedback based on its impact and relevance. Once feedback is collected, it needs to be analyzed and synthesized into actionable insights. This involves identifying common themes, patterns, and pain points among user feedback, as well as understanding the underlying motivations and goals of different user segments. Based on this analysis, product managers can then make data-driven decisions about what feedback to act upon, what improvements to prioritize, and how to incorporate user

227

insights into the product roadmap. This information can also be used to communicate product changes and updates to users, fostering transparency and building trust. By continuously integrating user feedback into the product management process, organizations can create products that better meet user needs, enhance customer satisfaction, and stay ahead of the competition in today's rapidly evolving market.

User Feedback

Product Management is a formal business function responsible for overseeing the development, launch, and ongoing management of a product or service. It involves the strategic planning, market analysis, and coordination of various activities to ensure the success of the product in the market. The primary goal of a Product Manager is to understand the needs and desires of the target market and translate them into a valuable product that meets or exceeds customer expectations. This involves conducting market research, gathering customer feedback, and evaluating competitors to identify opportunities and challenges in the market. Product Managers play a crucial role in defining the product vision and strategy. They work closely with cross-functional teams, such as engineering, design, and marketing, to determine the product requirements, features, and positioning. They act as the bridge between the company's stakeholders, customers, and the development team to ensure that the product aligns with the overall business objectives and the market demands. Throughout the product lifecycle, Product Managers are responsible for prioritizing and managing the product roadmap. They make informed decisions on new features, enhancements, or changes to existing products based on market trends, customer feedback, and business goals. They also collaborate closely with the engineering team to drive the product development process, ensuring that the product is delivered on time and within budget. Additionally, Product Management involves effective communication and coordination with various internal and external stakeholders. Product Managers work closely with sales and marketing teams to develop go-to-market strategies, pricing, and positioning plans. They also engage with customers to gather feedback, address issues, and gather insights to enhance the product's value proposition. In summary, Product Management encompasses the activities and responsibilities involved in managing the entire lifecycle of a product or service. It requires a deep understanding of customer needs, market dynamics, and business goals to develop and deliver successful products that meet the expectations of both customers and the company.

User Interface (UI)

User Interface (UI) refers to the design and presentation of the graphical elements and controls of a product that ensure a seamless and intuitive interaction between the user and the product. It encompasses the visual representation, layout, and functionality of the product's interface, aiming at providing a smooth and engaging user experience. In the context of product management, UI plays a crucial role in determining the success and adoption of a product. A well-designed and user-friendly interface enhances the product's usability, making it easier for users to navigate, understand, and interact with the various features and functionalities. It focuses on creating an intuitive and visually appealing interface that aligns with the target audience's expectations and needs.

User Onboarding Checklist

User onboarding checklist is a structured framework used in Product Management to guide the process of getting new users successfully acquainted with a product or service. It is a step-by-step approach aimed at optimizing user experience, reducing churn, and maximizing customer retention. The checklist serves as a roadmap for Product Managers to ensure that new users have a smooth and seamless onboarding experience. It encompasses various tasks and actions that need to be completed to create a positive first impression and help users understand the product's value proposition. The checklist typically includes essential elements such as: 1. User Registration: This step involves creating user accounts or profiles within the product or service. It may require collecting necessary information such as name, email address, and password. 2. Welcome Email: Sending a personalized welcome email to new users helps establish a connection and provides important information about the product, its features, and how to get started. 3. Product Tour: A guided tour or tutorial that introduces users to the core functionalities and key features of the product. This step helps users understand the product's value

228

proposition and its potential to solve their problems. 4. Interactive Onboarding: Providing interactive elements, such as tooltips, pop-ups, or interactive overlays, helps users understand specific steps or actions within the product. Interactive onboarding enhances user engagement and reduces confusion. 5. Onboarding Videos: Creating informative and concise videos that demonstrate how to use the product effectively can significantly enhance the onboarding process. Videos provide a visual and auditory medium to convey complex information in an easily digestible format. 6. Contextual Help: Offering contextual help options, like a knowledge base, FAQ section, or live chat support, helps users find answers to their questions or troubleshoot issues encountered during onboarding. This support system ensures that users have the resources they need to overcome any obstacles and continue using the product. 7. Progress Tracking: Providing users with a visual representation of their progress during onboarding can create a sense of achievement and motivation. Progress indicators or completion bars help users understand how much they have accomplished and how much is left to explore. By following a user onboarding checklist, Product Managers can foster a positive initial experience, establish trust, and set the stage for long-term customer satisfaction and retention. A well-executed onboarding process enhances user adoption, reduces the learning curve, and increases the likelihood of users becoming loyal advocates of the product.

User Onboarding Checklists

User Onboarding Checklists refer to a systematic approach used by Product Managers to guide new users through the initial experience of using a product or software application. These checklists are step-by-step guides that help users navigate and understand the various features and functionalities of the product, ensuring a smooth onboarding process. The purpose of User Onboarding Checklists is to orient and educate new users, enabling them to quickly grasp the core concepts and capabilities of the product. By breaking down the onboarding process into manageable tasks, these checklists set clear expectations and help users make the most of the product from the very beginning. In the context of Product Management, User Onboarding Checklists serve as a crucial tool to enhance user adoption, engagement, and satisfaction. By providing a structured framework, they help Product Managers ensure that users have a positive experience with the product, leading to higher retention rates and increased user loyalty. A well-designed User Onboarding Checklist typically includes essential steps, such as signing up, profile creation, product tours, feature introductions, and interactive tutorials. Each step or task in the checklist is carefully crafted to deliver a focused learning experience, presenting information in a concise and easily understandable manner. User Onboarding Checklists not only help new users navigate the product but also provide valuable insights to Product Managers. By tracking the completion of each task in the checklist, Product Managers can identify areas of improvement or potential bottlenecks in the onboarding process. This data-driven approach enables continuous optimization of the onboarding experience, leading to better user engagement and overall product success. In conclusion, User Onboarding Checklists are vital tools for Product Managers to ensure a smooth and effective onboarding process for new users. By providing clear guidance and breaking down complex tasks into manageable steps, these checklists enhance user understanding, engagement, and satisfaction. Additionally, they enable Product Managers to gather valuable data and insights for iterative improvements in the onboarding experience.

User Onboarding Flow Solutions

User onboarding flow solutions refer to the strategies, processes, and features implemented by a product management team to guide new users through the initial stages of using a product or service. The goal of user onboarding is to provide a seamless and intuitive experience that helps new users understand the value proposition of the product and encourages them to continue using it. A well-designed user onboarding flow solution typically includes a series of steps or screens that are presented to the user when they first sign up or log in to the product. These steps are designed to introduce the key features and capabilities of the product, and to help users understand how to navigate and use the product effectively. One common approach to user onboarding is to use a progressive disclosure technique, where only the most essential information and actions are presented initially, and additional features and capabilities are gradually introduced as the user becomes more familiar with the product. This helps to prevent overwhelming the user with too much information at once and allows them to learn and explore the product at their own pace. Another important aspect of user onboarding flow solutions is the use of interactive tutorials or walkthroughs. These tutorials provide a hands-on, experiential learning experience, guiding the user through the process of completing specific tasks or actions within the product. By actively engaging the user in the learning process, these tutorials help to improve comprehension and retention of the information being presented. In addition to tutorials, user onboarding flow solutions may also include contextual help and support features, such as tooltips, in-product messaging, and access to a knowledge base or help center. These resources are designed to provide users with easy access to information and assistance when they need it, helping to reduce frustration and support a positive user experience. Overall, user onboarding flow solutions are a critical component of product management, as they play a key role in driving user adoption, engagement, and satisfaction. By providing new users with a clear and guided path to experiencing the value of the product, user onboarding flow solutions help to set the stage for long-term success and retention.

User Onboarding Flows

User onboarding flows refer to the predefined set of steps that a user goes through when first interacting with a digital product or service. These flows are carefully designed and implemented by product managers to ensure that users have a smooth and successful initial experience with the product. The goal of user onboarding flows is to guide new users through the necessary actions and familiarize them with the key features and functionalities of the product. By providing clear instructions, informative tooltips, and interactive tutorials, the onboarding flows aim to educate users about the product's value proposition and help them become proficient in using its core functionalities.

User Onboarding Materials

User onboarding materials refer to a set of resources and tools that are created and provided to new users of a product in order to facilitate their initial understanding and adoption of the product. These materials are designed to guide users through the process of getting started with the product and familiarize them with its features, functionality, and benefits. The main objective of user onboarding materials is to ensure a smooth and successful onboarding experience for new users, enabling them to quickly grasp the value and potential of the product. By providing clear and concise instructions, tutorials, and documentation, these materials help users overcome any initial barriers and challenges they may face while using the product. User onboarding materials can take various forms, including written documents, videos, interactive tours, walkthroughs, and tooltips. They are typically delivered through multiple channels, such as email, in-app messaging, or a dedicated onboarding section on the product's website or dashboard. The materials are often tailored to different user segments or personas, considering their specific needs, preferences, and levels of familiarity with similar products. The content of user onboarding materials often covers a range of topics, such as product setup, basic navigation, key features and their benefits, data import/export, customization options, and frequently asked questions. The materials may also include best practices, tips, and tricks to help users maximize their productivity and achieve their desired outcomes with the product. Effective user onboarding materials are characterized by their clarity, simplicity, and user-centered approach. They should be easy to understand, follow, and reference, even for users with limited technical expertise. Additionally, they should be continuously updated and improved based on user feedback and evolving product needs. In summary, user onboarding materials play a crucial role in guiding new users through the initial stages of product adoption. By providing the necessary knowledge and resources, these materials contribute to a positive user experience, increased product engagement, and ultimately, user satisfaction and retention.

User Onboarding

User onboarding is the process of guiding new users as they successfully adopt and familiarize themselves with a product or service. It involves designing and implementing a series of actions and experiences that aim to facilitate users' initial interactions with the product, so as to ensure a smooth and effective onboarding experience. The primary goal of user onboarding is to remove any barriers or obstacles that may hinder users from getting started and achieving their desired outcomes with the product. It helps users understand the value proposition, features, and benefits of the product, thereby increasing their engagement and overall satisfaction. During the onboarding process, product managers focus on providing users with a structured and intuitive

230

introduction to the product. This may involve various components such as a welcome or tutorial guide, interactive tooltips, or contextual prompts that highlight key functionalities and explain how to navigate within the product. By highlighting the most important features and functionalities early on, product managers help users grasp the product's core value proposition and build confidence in its usage. User onboarding is not solely focused on teaching users how to use the product, but also on creating a positive and enjoyable experience. It is important for product managers to consider the user's perspective, motivations, and goals throughout the onboarding process. By understanding their target audience, product managers can tailor the onboarding experience to meet users' specific needs, preferences, and expectations. Additionally, user onboarding also serves as an opportunity for product managers to gather feedback and insights from new users. By actively seeking feedback during the onboarding process, product managers can identify areas of improvement and refine the product based on users' perspectives. In summary, user onboarding is a strategic process that aims to guide and familiarize new users with a product or service. It utilizes a range of actions and experiences to facilitate users' initial interactions, remove barriers, and enhance their overall experience. By focusing on the user's needs and goals, product managers can create a seamless onboarding experience that drives user engagement and satisfaction.

User Persona Creation Tools

A user persona is a tool used in product management to create a fictional representation of a target user or customer. It is created through the collection and analysis of qualitative and quantitative data, as well as market research. The purpose of creating user personas is to better understand the needs, goals, motivations, and behaviors of the target audience. It helps product managers and their teams to empathize with users and make informed decisions while designing and developing products or services. User personas typically include a combination of demographic information, such as age, gender, occupation, and location, as well as psychographic information, such as personal goals, preferences, and pain points. They often have a name and a photo to provide a visual representation of the persona.

User Persona Creation

A user persona is a fictional representation of a specific target user or customer group for a product or service. It is created by the product management team to better understand the needs, behaviors, and preferences of the intended users. The purpose of creating user personas is to bring clarity and empathy to the product development process. By accurately defining the characteristics, goals, and pain points of the target users, product managers can make informed decisions that align with user needs, ultimately leading to the creation of more successful and user-centered products.

User Persona Management

User persona management in the context of product management refers to the process of creating and maintaining detailed profiles or representations of the target users of a particular product or service. These user personas are fictional characters that embody the characteristics, needs, and goals of the actual users, and provide valuable insights to guide the development and design of the product. The first step in user persona management is conducting thorough research to gather data and information about the target user group. This research may involve surveys, interviews, observation, and analysis of user behavior and demographics. The objective is to collect relevant information that enables the creation of realistic and accurate user personas. Once the research is complete, the next step is to analyze and organize the gathered data to identify common patterns and characteristics that define the target user group. This information is then used to create fictional personas that represent the various types of users. Each user persona is given a name, background, job title, age, interests, and other relevant details that contribute to their realistic portrayal. These user personas are then used as a reference throughout the product development process. They help product managers and designers to keep the end user in mind when making decisions about the product's features, functionality, and design. By referring to the user personas, the team can prioritize the needs and goals of the target users and ensure that the product is tailored to meet their specific requirements. User persona management also enables effective communication and collaboration among the product team. By having a shared understanding of the target users,

231

team members can align their efforts and work towards a common goal. User personas serve as a tool to facilitate discussions and decision-making, as they provide a common reference point and help to avoid subjective opinions or personal biases. Overall, user persona management is a crucial aspect of product management as it helps to ensure that the product is developed with the end user in mind. It enables a user-centered approach, enhances the user experience, and increases the chances of success in the market by delivering a product that meets the needs and expectations of the target users.

User Persona Validation Methods

User persona validation methods in the context of Product Management refer to the techniques and approaches used to ensure the accuracy and effectiveness of user personas created for a product. User personas are fictional representations of the target users, which help product managers and teams understand user needs, motivations, and behaviors. One method for validating user personas is through qualitative research, such as in-depth interviews and observations. This involves engaging with real users, asking them specific questions, and observing their behaviors to gather valuable insights. By comparing these findings with the attributes and characteristics of the user personas, product managers can assess the accuracy and relevance of the personas.

User Persona Validation

A user persona validation in the context of product management refers to the process of verifying and refining the accuracy and effectiveness of user personas that have been created. User personas are fictional representations of the target users, which are based on research and analysis of user behavior, needs, and preferences. They help product teams understand and empathize with their users, enabling them to design and develop products that address their specific requirements. Validation is an essential step in the user persona development process as it helps ensure that the personas accurately reflect the characteristics and goals of the real users. It involves gathering quantitative and qualitative data to test the assumptions made during the persona creation process and identifying any gaps or inaccuracies that need to be addressed.

User Persona

A user persona, in the context of product management, refers to a fictional representation of a target user or customer group. It is a tool used by product managers to define and understand the various types of users who will interact with a product or service. By creating user personas, product managers can gain valuable insights into the needs, preferences, and behaviors of their target audience, which can then inform the design, development, and marketing strategies for the product. User personas are typically created based on research and data collected from real users or potential customers. This research may include interviews, surveys, market analysis, and user testing. The information obtained through this research is used to develop a detailed profile of a user persona, including demographic information, goals, motivations, pain points, and key attributes that influence their decision-making process. The purpose of creating user personas is to humanize the target audience and enable product managers to empathize with their needs and desires. By having a clear understanding of the different user personas, product managers can make more informed decisions throughout the product development process. They can prioritize features and functionalities that cater to the needs of specific user personas, tailor marketing messages to resonate with their motivations, and ensure that the user experience is intuitive and engaging for all target audiences. User personas serve as a common reference point for the entire product team, ensuring that everyone involved in the development process has a shared understanding of the target users. They also help facilitate communication and collaboration between different stakeholders, such as designers, developers, marketers, and customer support teams. By aligning their efforts around the needs of specific user personas, the product team can work together more efficiently and effectively to create a product that meets the expectations and demands of the target audience.

User Research Recruitment Platforms

User Research Recruitment Platforms are online platforms that connect product managers with potential participants for user research studies. These platforms offer a streamlined and efficient way for product managers to find and recruit individuals who match specific user profiles and demographics. Product managers use user research recruitment platforms to source participants for activities such as usability testing, interviews, surveys, and focus groups. These platforms typically have a large database of individuals who have expressed an interest in participating in user research studies. Product managers can search through the database and filter participants based on various criteria such as age, gender, location, and occupation. Once product managers have identified potential participants, they can send out invitations through the platform and schedule sessions for the research activities. These platforms often provide tools for managing participant recruitment, scheduling, and communications. Product managers can easily track the status of participant invitations and manage participant details all in one place. User research recruitment platforms offer several benefits to product managers. Firstly, they save time and effort by automating the participant recruitment process. Instead of manually searching for participants through various channels, product managers can quickly find and recruit individuals through a single platform. Secondly, these platforms help ensure that product managers find participants who closely match their target user profiles. This increases the validity and accuracy of the research findings, as the insights are gathered from individuals who are representative of the product's intended user base. Lastly, user research recruitment platforms provide a secure and convenient way for product managers to manage participant data and maintain privacy. These platforms typically have built-in data protection features and comply with relevant privacy regulations. In conclusion, user research recruitment platforms are valuable tools for product managers to efficiently find and recruit participants for user research studies. These platforms streamline the recruitment process, ensure the selection of relevant participants, and provide a secure environment for managing participant data.

User Research Recruitment

p { margin-bottom: 15px; } User Research Recruitment: User Research Recruitment in the context of Product Management refers to the process of identifying and selecting individuals who will participate in user research activities to provide valuable insights and feedback to inform the development and improvement of a product. The primary objective of User Research Recruitment is to gather data and feedback from real users in order to understand their needs, preferences, and behaviors. This information is crucial for Product Managers to make informed decisions throughout the product development lifecycle. By engaging with representative users, Product Managers can gain valuable insights into how users interact with the product, identify pain points, and uncover opportunities for improvement. During the User Research Recruitment process, Product Managers typically perform the following tasks: - Define the research objectives and target participant criteria: Product Managers first determine the specific goals and questions they want to address through user research. They then outline the desired characteristics of the participants, such as demographics, behavioral traits, or expertise, based on their research objectives. - Develop a recruitment plan: Product Managers create a strategy to attract and recruit participants who fit the defined criteria. This may involve leveraging online platforms, engaging with existing user communities, or reaching out to specific target groups. - Screen and select participants: Product Managers review applications or conduct screenings to assess the suitability of potential participants. They evaluate factors such as their relevance to the research objectives, availability, and ability to provide meaningful insights. - Coordinate logistics and scheduling: Product Managers manage the logistics of the research sessions, including arranging meeting times, locations, and communication channels. They ensure participants are adequately briefed and provided with any necessary materials. - Conduct user research activities: Product Managers facilitate various research methods, such as interviews, surveys, usability testing, focus groups, or field observations, to gather data directly from participants. They may ask participants to complete specific tasks or provide feedback on specific product features. - Analyze and synthesize findings: Product Managers analyze the data collected during the user research sessions, identify patterns, and extract valuable insights. They synthesize the findings into actionable recommendations that can guide product decisions and drive improvements. User Research Recruitment plays a critical role in enabling Product Managers to base their decisions on real user insights. By recruiting relevant and representative participants, Product Managers can gain a deeper understanding of user needs and preferences, leading to the development of products that better meet the expectations and requirements of the target audience.

233

User Research Repository

A user research repository is a centralized storage system that contains comprehensive information about user research activities conducted by a product management team. It serves as a reference tool for product managers, designers, and other stakeholders involved in the development process of a product or service. The purpose of a user research repository is to organize, document, and share the findings, insights, and learnings gathered from user research studies. It acts as a knowledge base that enables cross-functional collaboration and facilitates evidence-based decision-making throughout the product development lifecycle.

User Retention Strategies

User retention strategies in the context of product management refer to a set of techniques and actions designed to keep customers engaged and loyal to a particular product or service. These strategies focus on minimizing customer churn and maximizing their satisfaction and long-term value to the organization. One effective user retention strategy is to provide exceptional customer support. By promptly addressing user concerns and providing timely assistance, product managers can enhance the overall user experience and foster trust and loyalty. This can be achieved through various channels such as live chat, email, or phone support, ensuring that users feel supported throughout their journey with the product.

User Retention Strategy Platforms

User Retention Strategy Platforms in the context of Product Management can refer to digital tools or software solutions that assist product managers in designing and implementing strategies to retain users and encourage their continued engagement with a product or service. These platforms typically offer a range of features and functionalities, aiming to help product managers address the challenge of reducing user churn and increasing customer loyalty. One key aspect of user retention strategy platforms is the ability to analyze user behavior and gather relevant data. These platforms often include analytics tools that track user activity, such as the frequency and duration of product usage, as well as specific actions taken within the product. By gaining insights into user behavior, product managers can identify potential areas of improvement and develop targeted retention strategies. Another important feature of these platforms is the capability to segment users based on various criteria. This segmentation allows product managers to create personalized experiences and communications tailored to different user groups. For example, a platform may enable the creation of targeted email campaigns or in-app notifications, providing specific offers or incentives to different segments of users to encourage ongoing engagement. User retention strategy platforms can also facilitate A/B testing and experimentation. Through these platforms, product managers can create and test different variations of product features or user experiences to determine which approaches are most effective in driving retention. By iterating and optimizing based on user feedback and data analysis, product managers can continually enhance their strategies to maximize user retention. In addition, many of these platforms offer communication and engagement tools to facilitate ongoing interaction with users. This may include features such as in-app messaging, chatbots, or customer support integration. By maintaining a strong line of communication with users, product managers can address any issues or concerns promptly, increase user satisfaction, and ultimately, improve retention rates.

User Stories

User stories are short, concise descriptions of a specific feature or functionality that are written from the perspective of an end user. These stories are used in product management to capture and communicate the needs and requirements of the user, and to guide the development team in building the right product. Each user story consists of three essential elements: the role of the user, the action they want to perform, and the benefit they expect to gain from it. These elements are typically expressed in a simple sentence format, such as "As a [role], I want to [action] so that [benefit]." This format helps to clearly define the user's perspective and the value they seek from the product.

User Story Collaboration

User Story Collaboration refers to the process of gathering, discussing, and refining user stories as a collaborative effort within a Product Management team. User stories are concise, informal descriptions of desired features or functionalities of a product, typically framed from the perspective of an end user. They serve as a means to capture and communicate the needs of users and stakeholders in a structured and easily understandable format. During user story collaboration, the Product Management team engages in active discussions and exchanges of ideas to clarify and expand upon the initial user stories. This collaborative process involves various stakeholders, such as customers, developers, designers, and testers, who contribute their perspectives and insights to refine the user stories and align them with the overall product vision and goals. By collaborating on user stories, the Product Management team ensures that all relevant perspectives are taken into consideration and that the user stories accurately represent the needs and expectations of the users and stakeholders. This collaborative approach promotes a shared understanding and fosters a sense of ownership and accountability among team members. The user story collaboration process typically involves organizing collaborative sessions, such as brainstorming meetings or workshops, where team members can openly discuss and share their ideas. These sessions help in breaking down user stories into smaller and manageable tasks, identifying dependencies, and estimating effort and resources required for implementation. Effective user story collaboration leads to a more accurate and comprehensive set of user stories, which in turn enables the development team to prioritize and plan the implementation of features based on their value and impact on users. By involving all stakeholders, user story collaboration also helps in minimizing misunderstandings, reducing rework, and ensuring that the final product meets the desired requirements and expectations.

User Story Estimation Poker

User Story Estimation Poker is a collaborative technique used in Product Management to estimate the effort required to complete a user story or product feature. It involves a group of stakeholders, including the product manager, development team, and other relevant individuals, coming together to provide their input and reach a consensus on the estimated effort for each user story. The process of User Story Estimation Poker typically begins with the product manager presenting a user story or feature to the group. The user story is a brief description of a desired functionality or requirement from the perspective of the end user. It is important for the user story to be well-defined, understandable, and concise to ensure accurate estimation. Once the user story is presented, each participant in the estimation poker session is given a deck of estimation cards. These cards typically have numbers that represent relative sizes or effort levels, such as Fibonacci numbers (1, 2, 3, 5, 8, etc.) or T-shirt sizes (XS, S, M, L, XL, etc.). The use of relative sizing allows the team to focus on the relative complexity and effort required for each user story, rather than trying to estimate precise hours or days. Participants then take turns, one by one, selecting and revealing their estimation card for the given user story. The cards are displayed simultaneously to avoid any influence or bias in the estimations. If there is a significant difference in the estimations, the participants discuss the reasons behind their estimates and any potential factors affecting the effort required. This discussion ensures a shared understanding and alignment among the team members. The process continues until a consensus is reached, usually through further discussions and subsequent rounds of estimation. The aim is to converge towards a single estimation value that represents the collective agreement of the team. This consensus estimation is then recorded and used for further planning, prioritization, and resource allocation.

User Story Estimation Tools

User story estimation tools are techniques or methods used in the field of Product Management to assign relative effort or complexity to user stories during the process of Agile development. These tools are designed to help Product Managers, Scrum Masters, and development teams to prioritize and plan work, estimate project timelines, and allocate resources effectively.One commonly used user story estimation tool is the Planning Poker technique. In this method, a deck of planning poker cards with different numeric values or Fibonacci sequence numbers is used. The Product Manager or Scrum Master presents a user story to the team, and each team member selects a card that represents their estimate of the effort required to complete that user story. The estimates are then revealed simultaneously, and any significant discrepancies are discussed until a consensus is reached. Planning Poker allows for more accurate estimations by incorporating the insights and perspectives of the entire team.

User Story Estimation Workshops

A user story estimation workshop is a collaborative meeting that involves the product management team and other relevant stakeholders to estimate the effort required to complete a set of user stories in an agile development environment. The purpose of the workshop is to provide a more accurate understanding of the scope and complexity of the user stories, which in turn helps with planning, prioritization, and resource allocation. By involving multiple perspectives, the workshop fosters a shared understanding and alignment among the product team regarding the level of effort needed to deliver the desired features and functionality.

User Story Estimation

A user story estimation is a process in product management that involves assessing the effort and complexity of implementing a user story or feature. This estimation helps in planning and prioritizing the product roadmap, as well as managing the expectations of stakeholders. A user story is a concise description of a feature or requirement from the perspective of the end user. It is usually written in the form of a narrative and serves as a communication tool between the product team and stakeholders. User stories provide context and help the team understand the goals, needs, and expectations of the user. Estimating user stories involves breaking them down into smaller tasks or sub-stories, estimating the effort required for each task, and assigning story points or time estimates. Story points are a relative measure of complexity, workload, and risk associated with implementing a user story. They are often represented using a Fibonacci sequence (1, 2, 3, 5, 8, etc.) or other numerical scales. The estimation process typically involves the participation of the product manager, development team, and other relevant stakeholders. The team discusses the user story and identifies potential challenges, dependencies, and risks. They analyze the technical requirements, consider any constraints or limitations, and evaluate the impact on existing features or systems. The estimation process can be done using various techniques, such as Planning Poker or affinity estimation. Planning Poker involves the team members independently assigning story points to a user story and then discussing and reconciling the estimates. Affinity estimation involves grouping user stories based on their complexity and assigning a relative effort level, such as t-shirt sizes (XS, S, M, L, XL). Once the user stories are estimated, they can be prioritized based on their complexity, business value, and dependencies. This allows the product manager to plan and communicate the release schedule, manage stakeholder expectations, and make informed decisions about resource allocation and trade-offs.

User Story Grooming Solutions

User story grooming, also known as backlog refinement, is a critical activity in the field of product management. It involves analyzing and refining user stories to ensure they are well-defined, actionable, and ready to be included in upcoming sprints or development iterations. During user story grooming sessions, the product manager collaborates with the development team to review, clarify, and estimate the importance and complexity of each user story. The ultimate goal is to ensure that the development team has a clear understanding of what needs to be built, why, and how it should function. The process starts with the product manager presenting user stories from the product backlog. These user stories typically describe the desired functionality or feature from the perspective of the end user or customer. The team then engages in discussions, seeking clarification and additional information to fully comprehend the intent and requirements of each user story. Through these discussions, the product manager and development team address any ambiguity, remove redundancy, and identify any missing details or constraints. They work together to break down larger user stories into smaller, more manageable ones that can be completed within a single development iteration. During user story grooming, the team also assesses the complexity and effort required to implement each user story. This allows them to estimate the time and resources needed for development and prioritize the backlog accordingly. The team may use various techniques, such as story points or relative sizing, to assign a measure of effort to each user story. By refining user stories, the team creates a shared understanding of the product requirements and reduces the chances of misinterpretation or miscommunication during development. This process helps prevent delays, rework, and scope creep, ensuring that the development team focuses on delivering the highest value features to the end users. User story grooming is an iterative process that continues throughout the product development lifecycle. As new information becomes available or requirements change, the product manager and development team revisit and update the user stories to keep them relevant, accurate, and aligned with the overall product vision. In conclusion, user story grooming is a vital activity in product management that ensures user stories are well-defined, actionable, and ready for development. Through collaboration and refinement, the product manager and development team create a shared understanding of the product requirements, allowing for smooth and efficient development iterations.

User Story Grooming Workshops

A grooming workshop in the context of product management refers to a training session or program that aims to enhance the skills and knowledge of product managers in various aspects of their role. These workshops are designed to provide practical tools and techniques for managing products effectively and efficiently throughout their lifecycle. The main objective of grooming workshops is to help product managers develop a deeper understanding of the entire product development process, from ideation to launch and beyond. This includes gaining insights into customer needs, conducting market research, defining product requirements, creating product roadmaps, prioritizing features, and collaborating with cross-functional teams. During these workshops, participants learn about best practices and industry standards in product management. They acquire key skills such as problem-solving, decision-making, stakeholder management, and effective communication. The workshops also provide a platform for product managers to exchange ideas with their peers, share experiences, and learn from real-world case studies. Grooming workshops typically involve a combination of lectures, interactive discussions, hands-on exercises, and group activities. The facilitators, who are often experienced product managers or industry experts, guide the participants through practical exercises and provide personalized feedback to help them improve their skills. Overall, grooming workshops play a vital role in equipping product managers with the necessary knowledge and skills to excel in their roles. By attending these workshops, product managers can enhance their capabilities in areas such as product strategy, market analysis, user experience design, agile development methodologies, and product launch planning. Ultimately, the aim is to empower product managers to make informed decisions, drive successful product outcomes, and contribute to overall business growth.

User Story Grooming

User Story Grooming, also known as backlog refinement or backlog grooming, is a Product Management practice that involves reviewing and refining the user stories in a product backlog. It is a collaborative activity where the Product Manager, Scrum Master, and development team come together to ensure that each user story meets the required criteria and has a clear and actionable definition of done. The goal of User Story Grooming is to prioritize and prepare the product backlog for future sprints or releases. This process helps the team to better understand the customer needs, identify dependencies, estimate effort, and ensure that the user stories are ready for sprint planning.

User Story Management

User Story Management is a crucial aspect of Product Management that involves the process of capturing, organizing, and prioritizing user requirements in a structured manner. It enables product teams to effectively communicate and collaborate on the development of a product by capturing the needs and desires of the end-users. In the context of Product Management, user stories are concise descriptions of features or functionalities from the perspective of the user. They serve as a means to express what a user wants to accomplish with the product, why they want to do it, and what benefits they expect to achieve. User Story Management involves the following key elements: 1. Capturing User Stories: This involves working closely with users, stakeholders, and other relevant parties to identify and document their requirements. User stories are usually written in a simple, structured format as "As a [type of user], I want [an action] so that [a benefit]." They should be specific, measurable, achievable, relevant, and time-bound (SMART). 2. Organizing User Stories: Once user stories are captured, they need to be organized and grouped based on common themes or product features. This helps in understanding the overall scope of the product and identifying any overlaps or gaps in the requirements. Various techniques like user story mapping or affinity grouping can be used to effectively organize user stories.

237

User Story Mapping

User story mapping is a collaborative technique used in the product management process to visually organize and prioritize the features or functionalities of a product from the end user's perspective. It helps in understanding and detailing the user journey or workflow, and enables the product team to align their efforts effectively. A user story map is a two-dimensional representation of the product's user stories, which are concise descriptions of desired functionality from the perspective of the end user. The map consists of horizontal rows representing the different user activities or tasks, and vertical columns representing the priority or hierarchy of the features. The user stories are placed within the appropriate rows and columns, based on their relevance and importance to the user's overall experience. This technique provides a visual representation of the user's journey, allowing the product team to have a holistic view of the product's scope and prioritize the development efforts accordingly. It helps in breaking down complex features into smaller, manageable user stories, enabling iterative development and maximizing customer value. By mapping user stories, the product team can identify any gaps or missing functionality in the product, ensuring a comprehensive and user-centric design. It facilitates effective communication and collaboration among stakeholders, as it creates a shared understanding and vision of the product. Additionally, user story mapping enables the team to identify dependencies between different user stories or tasks, helping in managing project timelines and resources. Overall, user story mapping is a valuable technique for product managers to structure and prioritize the features of a product in a user-centric manner. It promotes collaboration, enhances communication, and ensures that the development efforts are aligned with the user's needs and goals.

User Story Templates

A user story template is a structured format used in product management to capture and describe a desired product feature or functionality from the perspective of the end user. It consists of a simple, concise statement that outlines the who, what, and why of a particular product requirement. The user story template typically follows the format: "As a [type of user], I want [some goal or objective] so that [some reason or benefit]." The "As a" section identifies the specific type of user or persona that the user story is addressing. This could be a customer, a specific role within an organization, or any other distinct user group. The "I want" section describes the specific goal or objective that the user is trying to accomplish. This should be framed in a way that is clear and actionable, focusing on the desired outcome rather than specifying the solution. The "so that" section provides the reasoning or benefit behind the user's goal or objective. It helps provide context and understanding for why the feature or functionality is important, which can be useful for prioritization and decision-making purposes. User story templates are widely used in agile development methodologies, such as Scrum, as a means of capturing and prioritizing product requirements. They allow product managers and development teams to clearly communicate and capture the intended functionality, while also providing flexibility for the development team to design and implement the most suitable solution. By using user story templates, product managers can ensure that product requirements are effectively communicated and understood by all stakeholders, including the development team, designers, and business owners. This helps foster collaboration and alignment throughout the product development process, ultimately leading to the creation of successful and user-centric products.

User Story Workflow

A user story is a concise description of a desired feature or functionality from the perspective of the end user. It is typically used in Agile software development methodologies, including Scrum, to capture requirements and prioritize work. User stories are written collaboratively by the product owner, development team, and stakeholders, and serve as a means of communication between these parties. A typical user story consists of three main components: the "As a" statement, the "I want" statement, and the "So that" statement. The "As a" statement identifies the type of user or persona who will benefit from the feature. The "I want" statement describes the specific functionality or capability that the user is seeking. The "So that" statement provides the rationale or goal behind the desired functionality. For example, a user story for an e-commerce website could be: "As a registered user, I want to be able to save items to my wishlist so that I can easily access them and make a purchase at a later time." User stories are often written on index cards or sticky notes and organized on a product backlog. They are typically

238

prioritized based on their business value and level of effort required for implementation. During sprint planning, user stories are broken down into smaller tasks and estimated by the development team. User stories are used throughout the development process to guide the team's work and ensure that the end product meets the needs of the users. They provide a shared understanding of the desired functionality and serve as a basis for discussion and collaboration among the stakeholders. User stories also help in defining acceptance criteria, which are the specific conditions that must be met to consider the feature or functionality complete.

User Testing Feedback

Product management is a strategic function within an organization that involves overseeing the development, planning, and execution of a product or service throughout its lifecycle. The primary goal of a product manager is to maximize the product's value and ensure its success in the market. They are responsible for understanding customer needs and market trends, defining the product vision, and creating a roadmap for its development. Product managers collaborate with cross-functional teams, including engineering, design, marketing, and sales, to bring the product to market.

User Testing Integration

User testing integration is a critical component of product management that involves the incorporation and assessment of user feedback during the development and iteration of a product or feature. It enables product managers to validate, refine, and optimize their product by gathering insights directly from the end users.During user testing integration, product managers incorporate various feedback loops, user research, and testing methodologies to gather data on the usability, functionality, and overall user experience. This can be done through several methods, such as usability testing, beta testing, A/B testing, surveys, and interviews.

User Testing

Product Management is a discipline within an organization that focuses on the strategizing, planning, development, and optimization of a company's products throughout their lifecycle. It encompasses activities related to product definition, market research, competitive analysis, prioritization, and product launch. The primary goal of Product Management is to align the product development and marketing efforts with the overall business objectives of the organization. This involves understanding the needs and preferences of the target market, identifying market trends, and assessing the competitive landscape to develop effective product strategies. Product Management involves gathering and analyzing market data to identify customer needs and trends that can inform product development decisions. This includes conducting market research, customer interviews, and surveys, as well as analyzing data from market research firms and other external sources. Based on the gathered insights, Product Managers define the features and specifications of the product, ensuring that it meets the target market's needs and aligns with the company's overall strategy. They work closely with cross-functional teams, including Engineering, Design, and Marketing, to ensure successful product development and launch. Throughout the product lifecycle, Product Managers are responsible for prioritizing features, managing the product roadmap, and making strategic decisions that optimize the product's performance and market success. They continuously evaluate market feedback and data to identify areas for improvement and make data-driven decisions to enhance the product's competitiveness. Product Managers also play a crucial role in product launch and go-to-market strategies. They collaborate with Marketing teams to develop effective positioning, messaging, and marketing plans that clearly communicate the value proposition of the product to the target audience. In summary, Product Management is a discipline that involves strategizing, developing, and optimizing products to meet the needs of the target market and align with the overall business goals of the organization. It encompasses activities related to market research, product definition, prioritization, and product launch, with the aim of ensuring the success and competitiveness of the product in the market.

User Training

User Training in the context of Product Management is a structured process that aims to equip users with the necessary knowledge and skills to effectively use a particular product or service. The goal of user training is to empower users to maximize the value they derive from the product, ensuring that they can utilize its features and functionalities to their fullest potential. User Training typically involves providing users with comprehensive information about the product, including its purpose, functionality, and usage instructions. This information is usually presented through various training materials, such as user manuals, tutorials, and online resources. Additionally, user training may also involve interactive sessions, workshops, or webinars, where users have the opportunity to ask questions, seek clarifications, and receive hands-on guidance on using the product. The benefits of user training in Product Management are numerous. Firstly, it enables users to become familiar with the product, reducing the learning curve and minimizing the risk of errors or misuse. This not only enhances the user experience but also increases user confidence and satisfaction. Secondly, user training allows users to discover and utilize advanced features and functionalities that they may not be aware of, thereby making the product more valuable and efficient. Thirdly, user training acts as a platform for gathering user feedback and suggestions, helping the product management team to understand user needs and preferences better and make informed decisions for product improvement. In conclusion, user training is a crucial aspect of Product Management that ensures users can effectively and efficiently utilize a product's features and functionalities. By equipping users with the necessary knowledge and skills, it enhances user experience, drives user satisfaction, and maximizes the value users derive from the product.

User-Centered Design (UCD)

User-Centered Design (UCD) is a product management methodology focused on creating products and experiences that meet the needs and preferences of users. It involves the active involvement of users throughout the design and development process, with the ultimate goal of delivering a product that is intuitive, enjoyable, and satisfying to use. In UCD, the needs and preferences of users are prioritized above all else. This means that the design and development team must have a deep understanding of the target users and their goals, tasks, and context of use. By conducting user research and gathering feedback, the team can uncover valuable insights that inform the design decisions. The UCD process typically involves several key stages. Firstly, the team conducts user research to gain a thorough understanding of the target users. This may include conducting interviews, surveys, and observations to uncover their needs, motivations, and pain points. This research forms the foundation for the rest of the design process. Next, the team uses this research to inform the creation of user personas, which are fictional representations of the target users. Personas help the team to empathize with the users and make design decisions that align with their needs and goals. With the personas in mind, the team then moves on to the ideation phase, where they generate potential solutions to the identified user needs. This may involve brainstorming, sketching, wireframing, and prototyping different design concepts. Once the initial designs are developed, the team conducts usability testing to gather feedback from users. This testing involves observing users as they interact with the product and collecting their feedback and insights. The team then iterates on the designs based on the user feedback, making adjustments and refinements as necessary. Throughout the UCD process, the team constantly seeks user input and feedback to ensure that the product meets the needs and preferences of the users. This iterative approach helps to minimize the risk of building a product that does not resonate with the target users, leading to a higher likelihood of success in the market. Overall, UCD is a user-centric approach to product management that prioritizes the needs of the users at every stage of the design and development process. By actively involving users and incorporating their feedback, UCD helps to create products that are more intuitive, enjoyable, and ultimately more successful in meeting user needs and expectations.

Value Proposition

A value proposition is a clear statement that explains the unique benefits and value that a product or service provides to its target customers. It outlines the reasons why customers should choose a particular product over competing alternatives in the market. A well-defined value proposition is essential for product management as it helps in effectively positioning and marketing the product. It helps the product manager understand the target customers' needs and priorities, and design the product features and messaging accordingly.

Voice Of The Customer (VoC)

Voice of the Customer (VoC) refers to the process of capturing and analyzing customer feedback and opinions to gain insights into their needs, expectations, and preferences regarding a specific product or service. In the context of Product Management, VoC plays a crucial role in ensuring that the product being developed aligns with customer expectations and delivers value. By actively seeking and listening to the Voice of the Customer, Product Managers can gather valuable insights to guide decision-making throughout the product lifecycle. This involves collecting feedback from various sources such as customer surveys, focus groups, customer support interactions, social media, and online reviews. The main objective of collecting the Voice of the Customer is to gain a deep understanding of what customers truly value and how they perceive the product. This information helps Product Managers to identify pain points, uncover unmet needs, and evaluate the overall customer experience. Once the Voice of the Customer has been captured, it can be translated into actionable requirements and product enhancements. The insights gained from customer feedback can guide product prioritization, feature definition, and product roadmap planning. Moreover, the Voice of the Customer empowers Product Managers to make data-driven decisions. By using qualitative and quantitative methods, they can analyze customer feedback to identify patterns, trends, and common themes. This allows them to validate assumptions, uncover hidden opportunities, and mitigate risks associated with product development. Ultimately, by incorporating the Voice of the Customer into the product development process, Product Managers can increase customer satisfaction, build customer loyalty, and differentiate their product from competitors. By continuously listening to customer feedback and iterating on the product based on those insights, companies can create products that truly address customer needs and deliver superior value.

Wholesale Distribution

Wholesale distribution in the context of product management refers to the process of selling products in large quantities to retailers, businesses, or other intermediaries who then sell them to end consumers. As a critical component of the supply chain, wholesale distribution involves sourcing products from manufacturers or suppliers and distributing them to various channels, such as wholesalers, retailers, or e-commerce platforms. The wholesale distributor acts as a middleman, bridging the gap between the manufacturer and the end consumer.

Wireframe Design Collaboration

A wireframe design collaboration refers to the process of multiple stakeholders, including product managers, designers, and developers, working together to create a visual representation of a product's layout and functionality. This collaborative effort allows for the exploration and refinement of ideas, features, and user interactions before the actual development process begins. Wireframes are simplified, low-fidelity drawings or mockups that outline the skeletal structure of a user interface. They serve as a blueprint or visual guide, capturing the basic layout, content organization, and navigation of a product or application. Wireframes are usually devoid of color, typography, and other graphical elements, focusing solely on the structure and hierarchy of the user interface. Product managers play a crucial role in wireframe design collaborations. They are responsible for understanding user needs, conducting market research, and defining the product vision. By participating in wireframe design collaborations, product managers can provide valuable feedback and insights regarding the product's features, workflows, and overall user experience. During the collaboration process, product managers work closely with designers and other stakeholders to ensure that wireframes align with the product's goals and requirements. They assess whether the wireframes effectively address user pain points, meet business objectives, and adhere to industry best practices. Additionally, wireframe design collaborations allow product managers to gather input from various perspectives and stakeholders. By involving a diverse group of individuals, such as designers, developers, and subject matter experts, product managers can tap into their collective expertise and ensure that the final wireframes account for technical feasibility and other practical considerations.

Wireframing Platforms

241

A wireframing platform is a software tool or application that allows product managers to create visual representations, or wireframes, of digital products or interfaces. These wireframes serve as a blueprint for the design and development of the final product, providing a visual guide for stakeholders and designers to collaborate and align their understanding of the product's structure and functionality. Wireframing platforms provide a range of features and functionalities to facilitate the wireframing process. These include pre-designed templates, drag-and-drop interfaces, and a library of pre-built UI components. Product managers can use these tools to quickly and easily create wireframes, adjusting and rearranging elements as needed to achieve the desired layout and flow of the product.

Wireframing Tools

A wireframing tool is a software or application used by product managers to create visual representations or mockups of a digital product's user interface (UI) design. These wireframe designs serve as a blueprint for the overall structure and layout of the product, capturing the basic elements and interactions without getting into specific visual details or aesthetics. Wireframing tools provide a simple and intuitive way for product managers to ideate, communicate, and collaborate with stakeholders, designers, and developers involved in the product development process. These tools typically offer a range of pre-designed UI elements, such as buttons, text boxes, menus, and icons, that can be easily dragged and dropped onto the canvas to create the wireframe design.

Wireframing

Wireframing in the context of Product Management refers to the process of creating a visual representation or blueprint of a digital product or website. It is a crucial step in the early stages of product development, where the focus is on the structure and layout of the user interface rather than the visual design or aesthetics. The primary goal of wireframing is to provide a clear and concise outline of the product's functionality, user flow, and content organization. It allows product managers, designers, and developers to collaborate and align their vision, ensuring that the final product meets the desired objectives and user needs.

Workflow Automation

Workflow automation in the context of product management refers to the use of technology and tools to streamline and optimize the processes involved in managing and developing a product. It involves the implementation of software applications and systems that automate repetitive tasks and standardize workflows, allowing product managers to focus on more strategic and value-adding activities. Workflow automation helps product managers to improve efficiency, reduce errors, and enhance collaboration across teams. By automating manual and time-consuming tasks, such as data entry, document management, and reporting, product managers can streamline their work and free up time for more important activities, such as analyzing market trends, gathering customer feedback, and making strategic product decisions.